Implementation of International Human Rights Commitments and the Impact on Ongoing Legal Reforms in Ethiopia

International Studies in Human Rights

VOLUME 131

The titles published in this series are listed at *brill.com/ishr*

Implementation of International Human Rights Commitments and the Impact on Ongoing Legal Reforms in Ethiopia

Edited by

Wolfgang Benedek
Tadesse Kassa Woldetsadik
Tesfaye Abate Abebe

BRILL
NIJHOFF

LEIDEN | BOSTON

Library of Congress Cataloging-in-Publication Data

Names: Benedek, Wolfgang, editor. | Tadesse Kassa Woldetsadik, editor. | Abebe, Tesfaye Abate, editor.
Title: Implementation of international human rights commitments and the impact on ongoing legal reforms in Ethiopia / [edited by] Wolfgang Benedek, Tadesse Kassa Woldetsadik, Tesfaye Abate Abebe.
Description: Leiden ; Boston : Brill | Nijhoff, 2020. | Series: International studies in human rights, 0924–4751 ; vol.131 | Includes index.
Identifiers: LCCN 2019054270 (print) | LCCN 2019054271 (ebook) | ISBN 9789004415942 (hardback) | ISBN 9789004415966 (ebook)
Subjects: LCSH: Human rights--Ethiopia. | Law reform--Ethiopia. | Human rights and international law.
Classification: LCC KRP2460 .I47 2020 (print) | LCC KRP2460 (ebook) | DDC 342.6308/5--dc23
LC record available at https://lccn.loc.gov/2019054270
LC ebook record available at https://lccn.loc.gov/2019054271

Typeface for the Latin, Greek, and Cyrillic scripts: "Brill". See and download: brill.com/brill-typeface.

ISSN 0924-4751
ISBN 978-90-04-41594-2 (hardback)
ISBN 978-90-04-41596-6 (e-book)

This book is printed on acid-free paper and produced in a sustainable manner.

Contents

PART 3
Vulnerable Groups

PART 4
Institutional and Remedial Issues

Preface

This publication emanates from a tripartite partnership project involving the Institute of International Law and International Relations at the University of Graz, Austria, the School of Law and Federalism at the Ethiopian Civil Service University (ECSU), and the Centre for Human Rights at Addis Ababa University (AAU). The partnership project was one component of the broader project 'Advanced Academic Partnership for Legal and Human Rights Education 2016-2019' (APPEAR Project-131 AAPLHRE) involving the three academic institutions. The project was initiated by the two Ethiopian universities and was implemented as a three-year partnership project from 2016 to 2019. It was funded by the Austrian Agency for International Development Cooperation (ADA) through the Austrian Academic Service (OeAD).

As part of the project, the joint problem-oriented research was coordinated by the School of Law and Federalism (ECSU). For that purpose a first research workshop was held in February 2017, where scholars from several Ethiopian universities presented the outlines of their contributions. The draft book chapters developed on that basis were presented at a second research workshop in January 2018. The contents were revised based on comments and suggestions received. This was followed by a collective review and editorial process by senior academic staff of the three partner institutions, which ultimately resulted in a third round of revisions and updates leading to the publication at hand.

The editors would like to thank the Austrian Academic Service (OeAD) and the Austrian Agency for International Development Cooperation (ADA) as well as all collaborators in the publication project for the excellent cooperation. Particular thanks go to Bernadette Knauders for managing the project so well and to Wanda Tiefenbacher for her profound language editing.

Finally, the editors want to thank Lindy Melman and Brill/Nijhoff publishers for the good cooperation in publishing this book.

Wolfgang Benedek, Tadesse Kassa Woldetsadik
and Tesfaye Abate Abebe
Addis Ababa – Graz, June 2019

Contributors

Tesfaye Abate Abebe
LL.D, Dean, College of Leadership and Governance, Ethiopian Civil Service University ECSU, Ethiopia.

Sisay Mengistie Addisu
Ph.D., Assistant Professor of Human Rights, Center for Federalism and Governance Studies, Addis Ababa University, Ethiopia.

Teguadda Alebachew
LL.B, LL.M in Constitutional and Public Law, Assistant Professor of Law, and former Head of the Constitutional Law Program, School of Law, Mekelle University. The author can be reached at tiguye@gmail.com.

Mekonnen Fiseha
LL.B, LL.M, Assistant Professor, Former Head of the School of Law, Mekelle University, Ethiopia.

Wondwossen Wakene Frew
Assistant Professor, School of Law, University of Gondar, Ethiopia.

Zerihun Yimer Geleta
Ph.D. Candidate, Institute of International Law and International Relations, University of Graz, Austria. He is also Assistant Professor at School of Law and Federalism, Ethiopian Civil Service University. The researcher can be reached at yimerzerihun@yahoo.com.

Mehreteab G. Ghebregergs
Assistant Professor, School of Law, Mekelle University, Ethiopia. The author can be reached at gefzam@gmail.com.

Gebrehiwot Hadush
LL.B, LL.M, Assistant Professor, Dean, College of Law and Governance, School of Law, Mekelle University, Ethiopia.

Yemane Kassa Hailu
Assistant Professor in Constitutional Law, Mekelle University School of Law, Ethiopia.

Mulu Beyene Kidanemariam
LL.B, LL.M, M.Phil, Lecturer, School of Law, Mekelle University, Ethiopia.

Sisay Kinfe
Assistant Professor, Center for Federalism and Governance Studies, Addis Ababa University, Ethiopia.

Tadesse Melaku
LL.B, LL.M, Assistant Professor, School of Law, Hawassa University Ethiopia. The author can be reached at tadessehello@gmail.com.

Biniam Mekonen
LL.B, LL.M, Lecturer, School of Law, Mekelle University, Ethiopia.

Asmelash Yohannes Teklu
Vice-Dean of the College of Law and Governance, Mekelle University, Ethiopia.

Abbreviations

ACHPR	African Charter on Human and People's Rights
ACHR	American Convention on Human Rights
ADA	American Disability Act
ANC	African National Congress
ANRS	Amhara National Regional State
art	article
arts	articles
ATP	Anti-Terrorism Proclamation
AU	African Union
CC	Constitutional Commission
CCI	Council of Constitutional Inquiry
CCRPD	United Nations Committee of the Convention on the Rights of Persons with Disabilities
CDC	Constitutional Drafting Commission
CEDAW	Convention on the Elimination of all forms of Discrimination Against Women
CIC	Constitutional Interpretation Council
CPC	Criminal Procedure Code
CPRW	Convention on the Political Rights of Women
CRC	Convention on the Rights of the Child
CRE	Commission for Racial Equality
CRPD	Convention on the Rights of Persons with Disabilities
CSA	Central Statistical Agency of Ethiopia
CSO	Civil Society Organisation
DSM	Diagnostic and Statistical Manual of Mental Disorders
ECHR	European Convention on Human Rights
ECtHR	European Court of Human Rights
EHRC	Equality and Human Rights Commission
EPRDF	Ethiopian People's Revolutionary Democratic Front
ESAT	Ethiopian Satellite Television and Radio
FDRE	Federal Democratic Republic of Ethiopia
FEAC	Federal Ethics and Anti-Corruption Commission
GPSDO	Guraghe People Self Help Development Organization
GTP	Growth and Transformation Plan
GTP II	Second Growth and Transformation Plan
HoF	House of Federation
HRA	Human Rights Act 1998

HRC	Human Rights Committee
IACrtHR	Inter-American Court of Human Rights
ICCPR	International Covenant on Civil and Political Rights
ICD	International Classification of Diseases
ICERD or CERD	International Convention on the Elimination of All Forms of Racial Discrimination
ICESCR	International Covenant on Economic, Social and Cultural Rights
ICRMW	International Convention on the Rights of Migrant Workers and their Families
IDEA	International Institute for Democracy and Electoral Assistance
ILO	International Labour Organization
MFA	Ministry of Foreign Affairs
MHA	Mental Health Act
MoLSA	Ministry of Labour and Social Affairs
MoWCYA	Ministry of Women, Children and Youth Affairs
NGO	Non-Governmental Organization
NMHS	National Mental Health Strategy
ODP	Oromo Democratic Party
OECD	Organization for Economic Cooperation and Development
OHCHR	Office of the United Nations High Commissioner for Human Rights
OLF	Oromo Liberation Front
OMN	Oromia Media Network
ONRS	Oromia National Regional State
OPDO	Oromo People Democratic Organisation
para	paragraph
paras	paragraphs
PWD	Person with Disability
PWDS	Persons with Disabilities
PWW	Proclamation on the Protection of Witnesses and Whistle-Blowers
SNNRS	Southern Nations, Nationalities and Peoples Regional State
TPLF	Tigray People's Liberation Front
TRNS	Tigray National Regional State
UDHR	Universal Declaration of Human Rights
UK	United Kingdom
UN	United Nations
UNCAT	United Nations Convention Against Torture and Other Cruel, Inhuman or Degrading Treatment or Punishment
UNESCO	United Nations Educational, Scientific and Cultural Organization
UNTS	United Nations Treaty Series
US(A)	United States (of America)

USD or US$	United States Dollar
VAT	Value Added Tax
VCLT	Vienna Convention on the Law of Treaties
WHO	World Health Organization
WOTC	Work Opportunity Tax Credit
WRD	World Report on Disability

Introduction

The relationship between international law and domestic legal systems is of crucial importance to the domestic constitutional order, both in theory and in practice. What matters most is the incorporation of international legal obligations into national laws and their subsequent implementation by domestic law-applying bodies such as courts, quasi-judicial bodies and other institutions. The 1995 Federal Constitution of Ethiopia entrenched many human rights norms and the language used is drawn from the core international human rights instruments, most of which have been ratified. The Constitution is 'receptive' of international human rights instruments in the domestic legal system, proclaiming them as an integral part of the law of the land. While not unequivocal in determining the status of international human rights instruments in the domestic legal system, it also enjoins international human rights principles as a rule of interpretation in determining the meaning of constitutional human rights norms.

However, the Constitution's 'friendly' approach to international law does not seem to have altered the general political and legal challenges affecting the implementation of international law at the domestic level. Despite the professed commitment by government authorities to the enforcement of international and domestic human rights standards in Ethiopia, the practice has yet to match the embodiment of the outlined principles. Factors negatively affecting the implementation of international human rights include, among others, legal, administrative, institutional, and attitudinal problems. It is thus not uncommon to hear criticisms that Ethiopia has failed to live up to its international human rights commitments.

Due to the fact the core international human rights treaties form the keystone of all efforts to promote and protect human rights at the national and international levels, there is a strong case to be made for increasing the coherence between domestic and international legal orders. It is positive that Ethiopia has a domestic legal system that encourages consistency with the international legal order, endeavors to discharge legal obligations in good faith, and overall shows an aspiration to play an increasing role in international and regional affairs. Furthermore, the implementation of international human rights norms indeed strengthens attempts to build a human rights culture in Ethiopia. The recent political reform processes are supported by in-depth analyses of the problems at stake and the development of recommendations, which inform about how to better utilise international human rights commitments as well as the human rights provisions of the Ethiopian Constitution.

 | DOI:10.1163/9789004415966_002

The contributions to this book have the objective of addressing key national problems in the field of human rights. They aim to deal with the gap between Ethiopia's human rights commitments and the practical problems associated with the realisation of human rights goals, mainly legal and institutional in nature. The methodological approach is focused on regional and universal practices and discourses. These indicate how to overcome major normative and institutional bottlenecks that impede the effective implementation of international and regional human rights standards in Ethiopia.

Keeping in mind international, regional and national perspectives, each contribution assesses how the realisation of an international human rights commitment in the domestic and regional contexts of Ethiopia plays out in practice. By drawing on thirteen case studies, the research at hand contributes to knowledge and policy-making and thus furthers the realisation of human rights in the specific research setting. It is expected that the analysis of the human rights commitments and implementation-related practices and challenges in the domestic and regional contexts of Ethiopia will contribute to enriching the discourse on the implementation of human rights commitments in a developing country.

The book is organised into thirteen chapters, divided into four parts: civil and political rights; economic social and cultural rights; vulnerable groups; institutional and remedial matters.

Part 1 focuses on domestic aspects related to the general topic of civil and political rights. The first chapter on 'Freedom of Expression and Incitement to Ethnic Hatred in Ethiopia' finds that Ethiopia has not enacted a unified law that regulates ethnic hatred, although different legislations governing various aspects of the subject are present. As key drawbacks, the chapter identifies a lack of definition of essential terms and the absence of a particular law that criminalises and punishes hate speech without unreasonably encroaching on freedom of expression – a theme that is currently the subject of legislative reform actions in Ethiopia. The chapter draws lessons from laws and institutions from the United Kingdom (UK) and the United States of America (USA) that deal with the issue.

The chapter on 'Extending Voting Rights to Citizens Abroad: Towards Institutionalising Diaspora Political Engagement in Ethiopia' investigates the need for extending voting rights to Ethiopians in the Diaspora based on economic and political rationales. It suggests that involving the Ethiopian Diaspora in voting will enable them to better contribute to the social, economic and political affairs of the country. Furthermore, it is argued that the principle of universal suffrage incorporated under international human rights instruments, to which Ethiopia is a party, will be meaningfully enforced if the Diaspora is granted voting rights.

The study on 'Cross-Examination and Witness Protection in Ethiopia: A Comparative Study' posits that witness safety is an important public interest, which warrants the restriction of cross-examination rights of the suspect. The analysis argues that while many states, including Ethiopia, have introduced measures restricting the confrontation requirement through the suppression of witness' identities, such an approach may constitute a drawback from the perspective of the defendants who find themselves unable to confront the accuser – if the judiciary decides not to disclose the identity of the state witness. Hence, the chapter suggests that in considering demands for anonymity, judges should exercise maximum caution to ensure that the human right of the suspect is not easily lost. In this light, the study concludes that the recent constitutional ruling in Ethiopia in favour of suppressing the identity of prosecution witnesses in a terrorism case fails to properly appreciate and balance the right of the accused. This causes serious doubt about the application of the right to cross-examination in Ethiopia.

Part 2 on economic, social and cultural rights opens with a chapter on 'The Need to Accommodate the Basic Rights of Ethno-National Minorities in the Oromia Regional State of Federal Ethiopia'. It investigates how legal frameworks in the Oromia Regional State address the rights of ethno-national minorities, focusing on the right to existence, equitable representation and self-government. The Zay community is taken as a case study. The research concludes that non-indigenous ethnic groups are excluded from effective and equitable representation in the legislative council of the Oromia National Regional State. Furthermore, it finds that in circumstances where such groups are accorded restricted representation rights in city councils, their decision-making powers remain ineffective. In consequence, ethno-national groups continue to face problems related to a lack of political recognition, representation and self-government, even in those territories where they are considered indigenous.

The chapter on 'Assessing the Right to Property, Eviction and Compensation in Ethiopia *vis-à-vis* International Human Rights Law' argues that urban development in Ethiopia is made at the expense of the property rights of farmers. The government interprets 'public interest' in a very broad manner in order to evict persons and this has caused serious detriment to the right to property. Furthermore, the study finds there is lack of a fair compensation regime and independent supervising body, which runs counter to the pertinent international human rights standards on the subject.

The chapter on 'Cultural Legitimisation of Human Rights: The Case of the Guraghe Ethno-Cultural Community in Ethiopia' investigates the internal discourse in the Guraghe communities for the transformation of customary laws and practices, in order to ensure the legitimisation of human rights – giving special attention to women's rights. The chapter finds that local practice is essentially dominated by urban-based male elites and traditional leaders, hence resulting in a selective prohibition of discriminatory and harmful practices against women in community-based customary laws. The study suggests that this could be improved if there was a robust policy on customary local institutions that guides the collaborative and integrated functioning with local government institutions.

Part 3 starts with a chapter on 'Legal Empowerment of Women through Property Rights in Ethiopia'. The chapter posits that women in developing countries, including Ethiopia, are adversely affected by the unequal distribution of assets and property rights, which results in women being forced to live on the edge of poverty. The study suggests that the legal empowerment of women through property rights can emancipate women by creating rights, opportunities and capacities. It also finds that while property rights of women are incorporated under international human rights instruments and commendable achievements have been recorded in Ethiopia in adopting laws that empower women, the practice remains beset by many challenges and has not been in accord with the legislative aspirations. Consequently, this requires that due attention is paid to strengthening the relevant institutions.

The chapter on 'Ensuring Compatibility of Ethiopian Law on Legal Capacity with Article 12 of the Convention on the Rights of Persons with Disabilities (CRPD)' suggests that the disability rights agenda has transformed from a medical model to a human rights model; disability rights have shown improvement in Ethiopia in terms of accessibility and employment. However, in terms of legal capacity for all, the study concludes that this has not yet moved to fulfil requirements of the CRPD. Ethiopia's framework on legal capacity retains a substituted decision-making model and provides for guardianship and tutorship systems, which give one person full powers over another. In this light, the analysis recommends that Ethiopia move towards a supported decision-making system in which everyone is accepted as a legally capable person while at the same time enjoying the support s/he needs in making decisions.

The chapter on 'The Right to Mental Health: A critical look at the State of Human Rights of the Mentally Ill in Ethiopia' analyses how international human rights instruments, to which Ethiopia is a party, provide various rights to persons affected by mental illness. It finds that national courts have been very passive in safeguarding the rights of mentally ill persons, particularly in the context of criminal proceedings. The study concludes that the Ethiopian legal system does not provide sufficient safeguards for accused persons. It recommends that the government should establish specialised hospitals on mental health and adopt a balanced and rights-friendly decision-making system and structure under the law.

The chapter on 'Exploring Tax Incentive Mechanisms to Strengthen the Inclusion of Persons with Disabilities in the Private Workforce in Ethiopia' analyses the availability and limitations of the tax incentive mechanisms in the promotion of the CRPD in Ethiopia. It concludes that tax incentive mechanisms could in fact increase employment rates of persons with disabilities and could furthermore be used as key instruments in strengthening the values of freedom and dignity of persons with disabilities on an equal footing to persons without disabilities.

Part 4 opens with a chapter entitled 'From 'Rights in Law' to 'Rights in Action': Towards an Effective Remedy for Human Rights Violations through Constitutional Complaint Procedures in Ethiopia'. The chapter appraises, in a comparative context, the decisions of the House of Federation on human rights issues submitted to it. The study argues that the House is far too remote to be considered a legitimate custodian of human rights, capable of transforming such ideals into actually consumable claims. The chapter furthermore holds that the House's legitimacy is seriously questioned, mainly due to a lack of political insulation, its institutional timidity and its human rights-restrictive jurisprudence. In the context of constitutional adjudication, this has seriously undermined the House's capacity as an institutional platform capable of ensuring access to an effective remedy for human rights violations.

The chapter on 'Enforcement of Constitutional Bills of Rights in the Regional States of Ethiopia' identifies that a cluster of fundamental rights and freedoms have indeed been enshrined in the federal and regional constitutions. Yet, the constitutions as such failed to explicitly provide remedies for violations and procedures for making claims before courts of law, other than in the broader framework of the right of access to justice. The chapter investigates the enforcement of constitutional human rights by courts in regional states in Ethiopia, taking the State of Tigray as a case study. It concludes that there is little space or institutional proclivity by the judiciary in the enforcement of the constitutional bill of rights. The study finds such rights are invoked very rarely and extremely selectively, a fact that gives way to concerning jurisprudential dearth in constitutional rights litigation in Tigray. In consolation, however, the study also finds there is an increasing trend of constitutional rights-based claims submitted before the Constitutional Commission.

The chapter on 'Assessing the Ethiopian House of Federation in Light of the Exhaustion of the Local Remedies Rule under the African Charter' presents an analysis of how the qualifications on exhaustion of local remedies are applied in the growing jurisprudence of the African Commission on Human and Peoples' Rights. The study does so by looking at a recent decision from the Commission where the Ethiopian House of Federation and its constitutional review mandate was scrutinised in the light of the local remedies rule. The chapter elaborates on the issue of whether the House of Federation qualifies as an organ offering remedies worthy of exhaustion for the purpose of admissibility before the Commission. It finds that the Commission has left out important considerations of the rule from its own jurisprudence, which, if duly considered, might have changed its final ruling that found the complaint inadmissible. The study concludes that if a proper and holistic assessment was made, the House of Federation and also the remedies it provides would both fall short of qualifying as effective.

In conclusion, the contributions to the present book seek to investigate the national experience in implementing international human rights commitments in practice and shed some light on the gaps and shortcomings that must be tackled to ensure compliance with international human rights standards in Ethiopia. The authors hope the contributions are used to inform policies, laws, strategies and practices relevant to realising human rights in Ethiopia, and can assist national initiatives to improve the democratisation process and strengthen human rights protection in practical settings. Moreover, it is expected that the studies and findings will contribute to the present reform process in Ethiopia and prompt further research and debates on the subject matters covered.

PART 1

Civil and Political Rights

Incitement to Ethnic Hatred in Ethiopia and Freedom of Expression

Asmelash Yohannes Teklu

Abstract

Ethiopia has yet to enact legislation that deals with incitement to ethnic hatred. Different laws do incorporate provisions designed to discourage hate speech.[1] However, these laws are defective in many aspects. Some of the problems include, inter alia, lack of definitions of essential terms such as 'incitement' and failure to outline the elements that could amount to ethnic hatred. The government also admitted that the absence of a law criminalising hate speech hinders efforts to implement article 29 of the Constitution of the Federal Democratic Republic of Ethiopia (FDRE).[2] Accordingly, this chapter provides a comparative analysis of laws[3] and institutions[4] from the United Kingdom (UK) with laws and practices from the United States (US) that deal with the subject area in question. This has the objective to provide more detailed information on how Ethiopia could pass legislation that would criminalise incitement to ethnic hatred. It also seeks to ascertain the approach Ethiopia takes to the balance between freedom of expression and ethnic hatred.

Keywords

freedom of expression – ethnic hatred – racism – tribalism – Ethiopia

1 See for example Federal Negarit Gazette Extraordinary Issue, 'Criminal Code of Ethiopia' Proclamation No. 414/2004, art 486(b); see also Federal Negarit Gazeta, 'Freedom of the Mass Media and Access to Information Proclamation' Proclamation No. 590/2008, art 40 which deals with Freedom of The Mass Media and Access to Information.

2 The Federal Democratic Republic of Ethiopia, 'National Human Rights Action Plan 2013–2015' (Addis Ababa, 2013) 59–60 <https://www.ohchr.org/Documents/Issues/Education/Training/actions-plans/Excerpts/NHRAP%20Ethiopia%20Draft%20213-2015.pdf.pdf> accessed 19 March 2018.

3 UK Race Relations Act 1976; UK Criminal Justice and Public Order Act 1994; UK Racial and Religious Hatred Act 2006; Council Directive 2000/43/EC on Implementing the Principle of Equal Treatment between Persons Irrespective of Racial or Ethnic Origin [2000] OJ L 180/22.

4 UK Commission for Racial Equality (CRE); UK Equality and Human Rights Commission (EHRC).

 | DOI:10.1163/9789004415966_003

1 Introduction

The thorny issue of ethnic hatred can fundamentally affect the matrix of other issues that may or may not necessarily be related to freedom of speech. Although it may sound 'romantic,'[5] the right to self-determination and secession, apart from its historical association with colonisation, is deemed one form of expression. On the one hand, both nationalism and tribalism in the context of self-determination serve as tools to express one's dissatisfaction with the status-quo. On the other hand, the essential principle of majority rules and minority rights is rightly squared with freedom of expression. The essential principle will fail to stand scrutiny if minority rights, such as rights to speech, opinion, write, etc. are not respected. Countries enact legislation essentially aimed at limiting expression to 'protect minority rights, in which issues such as pluralism, tolerance and "hate speech" feature centrally' or to expedite expression to 'promote minority rights, explore[s] cultural and linguistic rights and media access questions.'[6]

Besides, the rights of individuals are as sacred as their group rights. The identity of a person as manifested by his/her colour, cultural perspective, political orientation, religious preference, and other factors, cannot be fully realised if his/her freedom of expression and opinion is curtailed.[7] This implies that a person should neither be persecuted nor discriminated against for holding a viewpoint that is different from that of the mainstream.

The issue of ethnic hatred can be tied to many of the broad issues mentioned above. However, such issues are not considered suitable for this research. Rather, the scope of this article is limited to the problem of ethnic hatred in Ethiopia and it is fundamentally concerned with examining the adequacy of existing legal regimes. To this end, the chapter first begins with an examination of international and regional instruments on freedom of expression and ethnic hatred. This will help the reader to understand the limits of freedom of expression and the measures the international community has taken to address the problem at hand.

Second, the article discusses the boundaries of freedom of expression from a liberal and conservative approach. This is done by examining the approaches

5 Joshua Castellino and Jérémie Gilbert, 'Self-determination, Indigenous Peoples and Minorities' (2003) 3 Macquarie Law Journal 155.

6 Tarlach McGonagle, *Minority Rights, Freedom of Expression and of the Media: Dynamics and Dilemmas* (1st edn, Intersentia 2011).

7 United Nations Human Rights Committee, 'CCPR General Comment No. 34 – Article 19: Freedoms of opinion and expression' (11–29 July 2011) CCPR/C/GC/34 <www2.ohchr.org/english/bodies/hrc/docs/gc34.pdf> accessed 19 March 2018.

followed by the United Kingdom (UK) and the United States (US). As will be shown, these two countries do not afford the same protection and follow different approaches. They also provide varying meaning to essential terms such as 'incitement to ethnic hatred.' In addition, there are variations with regard to specific laws on ethnic hatred and the judicial interpretations of the scope of freedom of expression. This section will therefore assess and examine these differences.

Third, the article examines the scope of freedom of expression under the Constitution of the Federal Democratic Republic of Ethiopia (FDRE) and the approach, ie liberal or conservative, that Ethiopia has adopted to deal with the problem of ethnic hatred. The article concludes by taking into consideration the suitability of Ethiopia's current legal regimes and the methods in which ethnic hatred is currently dealt with. It proposes that the best way to deal with ethnic intolerance is to adopt a legal regime with new teeth that will help do away with the problem.

2 International Instruments on Freedom of Expression and Ethnic Hatred

Article 19 of the United Nations Declaration on Human Rights (UDHR) and the International Covenant on Civil and Political Rights (ICCPR) contain similar provisions on the right to freedom of expression. Article 19 of the UDHR states that 'Everyone has the right to freedom of opinion and expression; this right includes freedom to hold opinions without interference and to seek, receive and impart information and ideas through any media and regardless of frontiers.' Though the above provision seems absolute, the UDHR puts a general limitation on all fundamental rights by stating that 'any State, group or person' is prohibited from participating 'in any activity or to perform any act aimed at the destruction of any of the rights and freedoms set forth herein.'[8]

Article 19 of the ICCPR, on the other hand, espouses that limitations on freedom of expression must be 'provided by law.' Moreover, article 20(2) of the ICCPR states that 'any advocacy of national, racial or religious hatred that constitutes incitement to discrimination, hostility or violence shall be prohibited by law.' This requirement, ie limitation by law, '...would be interpreted as it has in the context of other ICCPR guarantees, i.e. that the limitation must be

8 See Universal Declaration of Human Rights (adopted 10 December 1948) UNGA Res 217 A(III) (UDHR), art 30.

sufficiently delineated in a State's law.'[9] A 'law' in this sense could refer to 'formal legislation or an equivalent unwritten norm or common law' but it excludes 'administrative provisions or vague statutory authorisation.'[10]

Moreover, article 19 of the ICCPR requires that a limitation on freedom of expression to be complied with if it is justified by one of the legitimate aims provided under sub-article 3 paragraphs (a) and (b), ie '…for respect of the rights or reputations of others; for the protection of national security or public order (*order public*), or public health or morals.'

The third test promoted by article 19 of the ICCPR is that the restriction must be 'necessary' to accomplish a lawful purpose. As the UN Human Rights Committee (HRC) held:

> This requirement of necessity implies an element of proportionality. The scope of the restriction imposed on freedom of expression must be proportional to the value, which the restriction serves to protect. It must not exceed that needed to protect that value. As the Committee stated in its General Comment 10, the restriction must not put the very right itself in jeopardy.[11]

However, article 19 of the ICCPR '…lacks a reference to necessity in a democratic society.'[12] For this reason, '…the relevant criterion for evaluating the necessity of interference is thus not the principle of democracy but rather whether it was proportional in the given case.'[13] Moreover, article 20(2) of the ICCPR bans 'any advocacy of national, *racial* or religious hatred that constitutes incitement to discrimination, hostility or violence.'

Apart from the instruments outlined above, there are also other specific instruments dealing with ethnic hatred. One of the primary areas in which

9 For further discussion, see Sarah Joseph, Jenny Schultz and Melissa Castan, *The International Covenant on Civil and Political Rights: Cases, Materials, and Commentary* (Oxford University Press 2005) 525; see also Manfred Nowak, *U.N. Covenant on Civil and Political Rights: CCPR Commentary* (2nd edn, N.P. Engel Publisher 2005) 447; see also *Gauthier v Canada,* (1999) UN Human Rights Committee, Communication No 633/1995, UN Doc. CCPR/C/65/D/633/1995, para 13.5.

10 Nowak (n 9) 460.

11 *Faurisson v France,* (1996) UN Human Rights Committee, Communication 550/1993, UN Doc. CCPR/C/58/D/550/1993, para 8. For further discussion see Joseph (n 9); see also Nowak (n 9) 447.

12 Nowak (n 9) 460.

13 Ibid.

incitement to ethnic hatred is discouraged is in the International Convention on the Elimination of All Forms of Racial Discrimination 1969 (ICERD or CERD).[14] Its preamble clearly stipulates that 'any doctrine of superiority based on racial differentiation is scientifically false, morally condemnable, socially unjust and dangerous.' Moreover, under article 4 it is stated that a state that gives its consent to be a party to CERD is required to take measures tackling incitement to 'discrimination, including ethnic hatred. This includes adopting laws that discourage incitement to any forms of hatred.' As stated under article 6, the adopted legislation must have teeth to discourage any form of ethnic hatred. A legislation that lacks compensation regimes for a violation of rights would fall short of meeting the requirement of providing 'effective protection and remedies.'[15]

Moreover, the international community has recognised the perils of underestimating ethnic hatred at the workplace[16] and in education.[17] For this reason, state parties to these instruments are obliged to ensure that workers and others enrolled at any level of education are not discriminated or ostracised because of their ethnicity. Furthermore, it is recognised that race-based discrimination of children's access to education would fall short of the obligations of a state under international law.[18]

14 See UN Educational, Scientific and Cultural Organization (UNESCO) Declaration on Race and Racial Prejudice (27 November 1978); see also UNESCO Recommendation concerning Education for International Understanding, Co-operation and Peace and Education relating to Human Rights and Fundamental Freedoms (19 November 1974); see also UNESCO Declaration on Fundamental Principles concerning the Contribution of the Mass Media to Strengthening Peace and International Understanding, to the Promotion of Human Rights and to Countering Racialism, Apartheid and Incitement to War (28 November 1978).

15 International Convention on the Eradication of Racial Discrimination (signed 21 December 1965, entry into force 4 January 1969) 660 UNTS 165 (CERD), art 6.

16 International Labour Organisation (ILO), Discrimination (Employment and Occupation) Convention No. 111 (signed 15 June 1958, entry into force 15 Jun 1960) <https://www.ilo.org/dyn/normlex/en/f?p=NORMLEXPUB:12100:0::NO::P12100_ILO_CODE:C111> accessed 14 March 2018.

17 UNESCO Convention Against Discrimination in Education (14–15 December 1960); see also UNESCO Recommendation concerning Education for International Understanding, Co-operation and Peace and Education relating to Human Rights and Fundamental Freedoms (19 November 1974).

18 UN Convention on the Rights of the Child (signed 2 November 1989, entry into force 2 September 1990) 1577 UNTS 3 (CRC).

3 The UK and the US Jurisprudence on Ethnic Hatred

The UK and the US follow different approaches to the prohibition of ethnic hatred. The US First Amendment, textually appearing as an absolute right, states that 'Congress shall make no law respecting an establishment of religion, or prohibiting the free exercise thereof; or abridging the freedom of speech, or of the press; or the right of the people peaceably to assemble, and to petition the Government for a redress of grievances.'[19]

However, the First Amendment is not absolute by virtue of judicial amendment. The US Supreme Court on several occasions has laid down the rules for limiting freedom of expression under the First Amendment. For example, in *Patterson v Colorado*,[20] the US Supreme Court applied the 'bad tendency test' by stating that the First Amendment was primarily occupied with preventing prior restraints, not subsequent punishment for 'speeches that may be deemed contrary to the public welfare.' Accordingly, a speech is gauged 'by the tendency of its effects. Speech tending to cause good effects enjoyed constitutional protection; but speech tending to cause bad effects – those that threatened the order or morality of a community or the security of society – did not.'[21]

However, in *Schenck v United States*,[22] the Supreme Court devised another test and held that speech can be abridged under certain circumstances, such as war. The court applied the 'clear and present danger' test in this case, which became controversial for years to come.[23] According to this test, 'the question in every case is whether the words used are used in such circumstances and are of such a nature as to create a clear and present danger that they will bring about the substantive evils that Congress has a right to prevent.'[24] However, this test was later abandoned and replaced by other tests.

19 The Bill of Rights Amendment I – Religion, Speech, Press, Assembly, Petition (adopted 4 March 1789, entry into force 15 December 1791) United States of America Constitution <https://www.law.cornell.edu/wex/first_amendment> accessed 12 March 2018.

20 *Patterson v Colorado*, 205 U.S. 454 (1907); the same test was applied in *Whitney v California*, 274 U.S. 357 (1927) and *Abrams v United States*, 250 U.S. 616 (1919).

21 Terry Eastland, *Freedom of Expression in the Supreme Court: The Defining Cases* (Rowman & Littlefield Publishers 2000) 1.

22 *Schenck v United States*, 249 U.S. 47 (1919).

23 For further commentaries, see David Cole, 'Agon at Agora: Creative Misreading in the First Amendment Tradition' (1986) 95 The Yale Law Journal 857; see also David A Strauss, 'Freedom of Speech and the Common-Law Constitution' in Geoffrey R Stone and Lee C Bollinger (eds), *Eternally Vigilant: Free Speech in the Modern Era* (University of Chicago Press 2001) 47–50; see also D G Barnum, 'The Clear and Present Danger Test in Anglo-American and European Law' (2006) 7 San Diego International Law Journal 263.

24 *Schenck v United States* (n 22) para 249.

The test that followed was defined by the 'incitement to imminent lawless action.'[25] In a retreat from earlier tests[26] that appeared to punish 'mere advocacy of violence,' the US Supreme Court held that '…a statute which, by its own words and as applied, purports to punish mere advocacy and to forbid, on pain of criminal punishment, assembly with others merely to advocate the described type of action…falls within the condemnation of the First and Fourteenth Amendments.'[27] The above test is composed of three parts: '(1) the speaker subjectively intended incitement; (2) in context, the words used were likely to produce imminent, lawless action; and (3) the words used by the speaker objectively encouraged and urged incitement.'[28]

In another twist to the scope of the First Amendment, the US Supreme Court in *Holder v Humanitarian Law Project* 'appeared to retreat dramatically'[29] from previous tests by holding that it is possible to restrict 'speech on the basis of its content.'[30] *Holder v Humanitarian Law Project* deviated from the incitement test of *Brandenburg v Ohio* by punishing purely political advocacy in relation to foreign terrorist groups.

Keeping this in mind, these are not the only tests applied by the US Supreme Court with regard to the scope of the First Amendment. Further tests include the 'balancing'[31] and 'redeeming social value'[32] tests. As discussed above, however, these different tests have been modified over the years and in some instances have been by-passed altogether without due consideration.[33]

In general, a speech will be prohibited only if it is believed that it contains advocacy of violence or child pornography; it threatens the order or morality of a community, or the security of the society. However, hate speech, including ethnic hatred, in general is not one of the protected speeches in the United

25 *Brandenburg v Ohio*, 395 U.S. 444 (1969).

26 *Whitney v California* (n 20).

27 *Brandenburg v Ohio* (n 25) para 449.

28 J Scott Harr, Kären M Hess and Christine H Orthmann, *Constitutional Law and the Criminal Justice System* (5th edn, Cengage Learning 2011) 142.

29 David Cole, 'The First Amendment's Borders: The Place of Holder v Humanitarian Law Project in First Amendment Doctrine' (2012) 6 Harvard Law and Policy Review 147.

30 *Holder v Humanitarian Law Project*, 130 S. Ct. 2705, U.S. Supreme Court 2010, para 22.

31 *Ward v Rock Against Racism*, 491 U.S. 781 (1989) (the Supreme Court balanced the interest of the complainants against the interest of the New York city holding that the government was within its legal boundaries to regulate 'the volume of amplified music at the bandshell so the performances are satisfactory to the audience without intruding upon those who use the Sheep Meadow or live on Central Park West and in its vicinity'); see also *Barenblatt v United States*, 306 US 109 (1959).

32 *Miller v California*, 413 U.S. 15 (1973) (primarily in obscenity cases).

33 For further discussion, see WJ Brenna, 'The Supreme Court and the Meiklejohn Interpretation of the First Amendment' (1961) 79 Harvard Law Review 11.

States. For this reason, the US approach is considered liberal. A Pulitzer Prize winner, Joan Vennochi, recently wrote 'hard as it is to accept, the right to express vile and repugnant thought is guarded by the Constitution.'[34] Several decisions of the US Supreme Court back up her argument. For instance, a message of hatred by a Ku Klux Klan leader was found to be protected under the US constitution.[35] In a similar fashion, the court came to the defence of a speech that 'arouses anger, alarm or resentment in others on the basis of race, color, creed, religion or gender.'[36] Moreover, it was held that 'notwithstanding the distasteful and repugnant nature of the words,'[37] the First Amendment is designed to shield people from liability.

On the other hand, the UK's approach is considered conservative due to the existence of stringent laws that regulate freedom of speech in general, and ethnically motivated hate in particular. The UK does not have a written constitution, and has only relatively recently adopted a written code of rights, the Human Rights Act 1998 (HRA). The European Convention on Human Rights (ECHR) becomes instrumental in domestic cases because of the 1998 HRA.

The construction of article 10 of the ECHR, which guarantees the right to freedom of expression, is not absolute. As one of the cornerstones of any democratic society,[38] a restriction on freedom of expression under article 10(2) of the ECHR could be justified if it is 'prescribed by law,' pursues legitimate aims, and is necessary in a democratic society. In accordance with *Handyside v UK*, any 'interferences entail a violation of Article 10 if they do not fall within one of the exceptions provided for in paragraph 2.'[39] Therefore, article 10 'is applicable not only to "information" or "ideas" that are favourably received or regarded as inoffensive or as a matter of indifference, but also to those that offend, shock or disturb the State or any sector of the population.'[40]

Though the European Court of Human Rights (ECtHR) acknowledged that member states have a 'margin of appreciation'[41] in laying down restrictions in

---

34 Joan Vennochi, 'There's no hate speech exception to the First Amendment' *The Boston Globe* (17 August 2017) <https://www.bostonglobe.com/opinion/2017/08/14/there-hate-speech-exception-first-amendment/q9m4IqfQvbo24nnlnPor1O/story.html> accessed 12 March 2018.

35 *Brandenburg v Ohio* (n 25).

36 *R.A.V. v City of St. Paul*, 505 U.S. 377 (1992) <https://www.oyez.org/cases/1991/90-7675> accessed 12 September 2017.

37 *Snyder v Phelps*, 562 U.S. 443 (2011) <https://www.oyez.org/cases/2010/09-751> accessed 12 September 2017.

38 *Handyside v UK* (1976) No 5493/72, ECHR 5, para 49.

39 Ibid para 43.

40 Ibid para 49.

41 *Autronic AG v Switzerland* (1990) No 12726/87, ECHR 12.

their domestic laws, it stressed that interferences 'prescribed by law' must be 'adequately accessible' and sufficiently clear.[42] However, 'the level of precision required of domestic legislation – which cannot in any case provide for every eventuality – depends to a considerable degree on the content of the instrument in question, the field it is designed to cover and the number and status of those to whom it is addressed.'[43]

In respect of the second requirement of article 10(2), ie pursuing legitimate aims, the ECtHR evaluates 'whether the reasons given by the national authorities to justify the actual measures of "interference" they take are relevant and sufficient.'[44] Article 10(2) contains an array of legitimate aims that could be taken into account by the member states. These are interferences:

> [...] in the interest of national security, territorial integrity or public safety, for the prevention of disorder or crime, for the protection of health or morals, for the protection of the reputation or the rights of others, for preventing the disclosure of information received in confidence, or for maintaining the authority and impartiality of the judiciary.

However, the jurisprudence of the ECtHR[45] and the construction of article 10(2) show that the fact that a certain restriction is 'prescribed by law' and has a legitimate aim does not mean national authorities are discharged of their obligation not to interfere with freedom of expression arbitrarily.

Therefore, the third requirement under article 10(2), ie 'necessary in a democratic society,' must be satisfied, which 'implies the existence of a pressing social need.'[46] This requirement is a limit on the 'domestic margin of appreciation'; it gives the ECtHR a power of 'supervision' over 'the aim of the measure challenged' and its 'necessity.' It covers not only the basic legislation but also the decision applying it, even one given by an independent court.[47]

The above discussion only focuses on the limitation of state power to restrict the right to freedom of expression. The interplay between article 10 and article 17 of the ECHR could also be approached from a different angle: the exercise of an expression by an individual *vis-à-vis* its scope. Article 17 bans any

---

42 See *Sunday Times v UK* (1979) No 6538/74, ECHR 1, para 49; see also *Herczegfalvy v Austria,* (1992) No 10533/83, ECHR 83; see also *Hashman and Harrup v UK,* No 25594/94, [1999] ECHR 1999-VIII.

43 *Rekvényi v Hungary,* No 25390/94, [1999] ECHR 1999-III, para 34.

44 See for example, *Handyside v UK* (n 38) para 50.

45 Ibid para 47.

46 *Vogt v Germany* (1995) No 17851/91, 21 EHRR 205, para 52.

47 *Handyside v UK* (n 38) para 49.

person or group from participating 'in any activity or perform[ing] any act aimed at the destruction of any of the rights and freedoms' provided in the ECHR. Thus, an expression that targets a certain race or ethnicity and discriminates or spreads hateful information would be appropriately treated an abuse of the right to freedom of expression as provided under article 10 of the same convention. For this reason, the ECtHR held that 'there is no doubt that any remark directed against the Convention's underlying values would be removed from the protection of Article 10 [freedom of expression] by Article 17 [prohibition of abuse of rights].'[48] In another case, the ECtHR held that a:

> [v]ehement attack on one ethnic group is directed against the Convention's underlying values, notably tolerance, social peace and non-discrimination. Consequently, by reason of Article 17 (prohibition of abuse of rights) of the Convention, the applicant could not benefit from the protection afforded by Article 10 (freedom of expression) of the Convention.[49]

The Court also stated that there is nothing funny about a comedy that degrades, disparages or encourages hate towards a certain race.[50] Overall, it can be concluded that the restrictive approach of the ECtHR is remarkably different from the liberal approach followed by the US Supreme Court.

In addition to article 10 of the ECHR, there are also specific laws in the UK that prohibit hate speech in general and ethnic hatred in particular. There are two types of crimes or offences related to ethnic hatred in the UK: racially aggravated offences and incitement to ethnic hatred.[51] Alternatively, they can also be categorised as 'aggravated offences' and 'public order offences of stirring up hatred.'[52] The fundamental difference between the two types of offences relates to the fact that the first one relates to inflicting racially motivated 'assault or wounding, harassment, damage and public order offences.'[53]

48 *Seurot v France,* No 57383/00, [2004] ECHR.

49 *Pavel Ivanov v Russia,* No 35222/04, [2007] ECHR.

50 *M'Bala M'Bala v France,* No 25239/13, [2015] ECHR.

51 Crown Prosecution Service (CPS), 'Racist and Religious Hate Crime – Prosecution Guidance' (2018) <https://www.cps.gov.uk/legal-guidance/racist-and-religious-hate-crime-prosecution-guidance> accessed 12 March 2018.

52 Law Commission, 'Hate Crime: The Case for Extending the Existing Offences' (Consultation Paper No 213, 2015) <http://www.lawcom.gov.uk/app/uploads/2015/03/cp213_hate_crime_appendix-b.pdf> accessed 3 April 2018.

53 Crown Prosecution Service (n 51); see also Public Order Act 1986, ss 4 and 5.

For instance, it is an offence in the UK to 'engage in an activity that infringes [on] a person's dignity,' or generate an environment that is 'intimidating, hostile, degrading, humiliating or offensive.'[54]

Incitement to ethnic hatred, on the other hand, is categorised under 'public order offences of stirring up hatred.' Therefore, incitement to racial hatred refers to a situation

> [w]hen the accused person says or does something, which is threatening, abusive or insulting and, by doing so, either intends to stir up racial hatred, or makes it likely that racial hatred will be stirred up. This can include such things as making a speech, displaying a racist poster, publishing written material, performing a play or broadcasting something in the media.[55]

Therefore, the offence of an incitement of racial hatred can be committed by any means (written, oral, conduct) publicly or privately with the intention of 'or having regard to all circumstances, racial hatred is likely to be stirred thereby.'[56] The cumulative reading of Sections 18(2) and 18(4) of the Public Order Act 1986 reveal that racially motivated remarks that fall short of communication (publically or privately) are not within the ambit of the law. Thus, a person will not be prosecuted for inciting racial hatred if s/he manages 'to prove that he was inside a dwelling and had no reason to believe that the words or behaviour used, or the written material displayed, would be heard or seen by a person outside that or any other dwelling.'[57] The 1986 Act has been further amended to include other offences. For instance, uttering words directed at a certain race at football matches is an offence in the UK.[58] Accordingly,

> (1) It is an offence to engage or take part in chanting of an indecent or racialist nature at a designated football match. (2) For this purpose – (a) 'chanting' means the repeated uttering of any words or sounds [(whether alone or in concert with one more others)]; and (b) 'of a racialist nature' means consisting of or including matter which is threatening, abusive or insulting to a person by reason of his colour, race, nationality (including citizenship) or ethnic or national origins.[59]

---

54 UK Equality Act 2010, ss 26.

55 Ibid.

56 Public Order Act 1986, ss 18.

57 Ibid, ss 18(4).

58 Football Offences Act 1991.

59 Ibid, ss 3.

Moreover, although it is beyond the scope of this chapter, the UK has also managed to pass legislation that criminalises incitement to religious hatred.[60]

To conclude, the term 'incitement to racial hatred' in the UK covers writings, speeches, posters, commentaries, and abuses in public or private places that can cause or are more likely to cause hatred towards a certain race. Moreover, it must be stressed that the UK's position with regard to freedom of expression and incitement to racial hatred is in line with the position of the ECtHR. This is in stark contrast to the position advocated by the US Supreme Court, which has been previously discussed.

4 Ethiopia's Domestic Law with Regard to the Issue at Hand

4.1 *The FDRE Constitution and the Right to Freedom of Expression*

Article 29 of the FDRE Constitution provides for the protection of freedom of expression. This article adopts a similar format in its protection of that right as is seen in article 10 ECHR, by declaring 'everyone has the right to freedom of expression without interference.'[61] Unlike 10 ECHR and the First Amendment, article 29 of FDRE Constitution further acknowledges that the medium of expression can be '...in writing, in print, in the form of an art, or through any medium ... of choice.'[62] This is a direct replica of article 19 (1) of the ICCPR.

Similar to article 10 but unlike the First Amendment, the FDRE Constitution specifically declares that the right to freedom of expression is not absolute. Article 29(6) proclaims that a limitation is only possible if the expressed view injures 'the well-being of the youth, and the honour and reputation of individuals' or contains 'propaganda for war as well as the public expression of opinion intended to injure human dignity.'

A major difference between article 29 of the FDRE Constitution and article 10 of the ECHR is the absence of some of the three-criteria-tests for limitations devised by the ECtHR, which complement the functioning of article 10.[63] The only criterion mentioned under article 29(6) is limitation 'through laws which are guided by the principle that freedom of expression and information cannot be limited on account of the content or effect of the point of view expressed.' Moreover, the FDRE Constitution fails to envisage the most obvious element of

60 Racial and Religious Hatred Act 2006.

61 Federal Negarit Gazeta, 'The Constitution of the Federal Democratic Republic of Ethiopia' Proclamation No. 1/1995, art 29(2).

62 Ibid art 29(5).

63 Prescribed by law, legitimate aim, and necessary in a democratic society; see *Handyside v UK* (n 38); see also *Sunday Times v UK* (n 42).

limiting the right: national security, protection of public order, health and/or morals. These are enshrined in both the ICCPR[64] and in article 10 ECHR.

However, although some of the criteria of limitation tests are absent in the FDRE Constitution, it could be argued that their implementation in the Ethiopian legal system is possible by virtue of article 13 (2) of the FDRE Constitution, which states that:

> The fundamental rights and freedoms specified in this Chapter shall be interpreted in a manner conforming to the principles of the Universal Declaration of Human Rights, International Covenants on Human Rights and International instruments adopted by Ethiopia.

Consequently, the protection and promotion of human rights as guaranteed in the FDRE Constitution have to be considered in light of the international standards set by the UDHR and other conventions ratified by Ethiopia. Otherwise stated, any human rights instrument ratified by Ethiopia thus becomes not only part and parcel of the domestic laws of Ethiopia, but also provides guiding principles for the interpretation of the rights guaranteed by the FDRE Constitution. Thus, once adopted, they are applicable in the same manner as any law enacted by the Ethiopian Parliament.

Consequently, article 19 of the ICCPR becomes crucial in the interpretation of article 29 of the FDRE Constitution. Article 19 of the ICCPR espouses that limitations on freedom of expression must be 'provided by law.' This requirement '…would be interpreted as it has in the context of other ICCPR guarantees, i.e. that the limitation must be sufficiently delineated in a State's law.'[65] A 'law' in this sense could refer to 'formal legislation or an equivalent unwritten norm or common law,' but it excludes 'administrative provisions or vague statutory authorisation.'[66]

Moreover, article 19 of the ICCPR requires that a limitation on freedom of expression would have to be complied with if it is justified by one of the legitimate aims provided under sub-paragraphs (a) and (b) of sub-article 3, ie '…for respect of the rights or reputations of others; for the protection of national security or public order (*ordre public*), or public health or morals.' One of the legitimate aims relevant to this article is the protection of the rights of both

64 International Covenant on Civil and Political Rights (adopted 16 December 1966, entry into force 23 March 1976) 999 UNTS 171 (ICCPR), art 19(3).

65 For further discussion, see Joseph (n 9) 525; see also Nowak (n 9) 447; see also *Gauthier v Canada* (no 9) para 13.5.

66 Nowak (n 9) 460.

major and minor ethnic groups and the prohibition of incitement to ethnic hatred.

Despite some difference in the construction of article 19 of the ICCPR, the three criteria discussed above are more or less similar to those applied by the ECtHR with regard to article 10 ECHR. For that reason, interference with the right to freedom of expression in Ethiopia could be evaluated based on the above-mentioned tests.

One issue that requires emphasis here is whether article 29 of the FDRE Constitution is sufficiently designed to give effect to the prohibition of incitement to ethnic hatred. One argument that can be justifiably raised is concerning the broad phrases such as 'honour and reputation of individuals' or 'public expression of opinion intended to injure human dignity' that simply refer to defamation cases. Similar phrases are broadly written under article 24 of the FDRE constitution. Thus, the FDRE Constitution in this regard is similar in its approach to the United States' liberal interpretation of the First Amendment. As a result, a person in Ethiopia will not face legal consequences for inciting hatred against a certain ethnicity or individuals belonging to it. The validity of this argument can be established from the fact that defamation cases are quite different from issues of incitement to ethnic hatred.

It is also possible to produce an equally relevant argument. It is true that 'there is little common understanding of what dignity requires substantively within or across jurisdictions.'[67] However, the phrase 'human dignity' is broad enough to refer to the prohibition of incitement to ethnic hatred. Accordingly, 'human rights are intimately related to the notion of human dignity.'[68] As a result, 'the concept of 'human dignity' plays an important role in the development of human rights adjudication, not in providing an agreed content to human rights but in contributing to particular methods of human rights interpretation and adjudication.'[69]

Consequently, limitations of the right to freedom of expression to protect the rights and freedoms of others are justified under articles 24 and 29 of the FDRE Constitution. Though article 29 does not specifically address the notion of incitement to ethnic hatred, it would not be far from the truth if argued that any expression that intends to undermine the human dignity of a person does not have a legal protection in Ethiopia. This argument is supported by the fact

67 Christopher McCrudden, 'Human Dignity and Judicial Interpretation of Human Rights' (2008) 19(4) European Journal of International Law 655.

68 Willy Moka-Mubelo, *Human Rights and Human Dignity. In: Reconciling Law and Morality in Human Rights Discourse. Philosophy and Politics – Critical Explorations* (Springer 2017).

69 McCrudden (n 67).

that Ethiopia has either ratified or adopted international instruments that prohibit incitement to ethnic hatred.[70] Accordingly, article 13 of the FDRE Constitution requires that the rights and freedoms enshrined within need to be interpreted in the spirit of international instruments adopted by Ethiopia. As a conclusion with regard to the FDRE Constitution, we can safely say that racially aggravated offence is unlawful in Ethiopia. However, the constitution is not clear when it comes to incitement to ethnic hatred. In the following sections, it will be seen if the legislature has devised a distinction between a criminal offence that is actually committed as a result of ethnic hatred, and an incitement to ethnic hatred that causes any actual injury.

4.2 *Specific Legislative Acts of Parliament and Incitement to Ethnic Hatred*

There are piecemeal acts of parliament that indirectly address the issue at hand. Their details are provided below.

The Criminal Code of Ethiopia[71] contains some articles that criminalise hate speech. For example, article 486(b) of the code states:

> Whosoever by whatever accusation or any other means foments dissension, *arouses hatred*, or stirs up acts of violence or political, racial or religious disturbances, is punishable with simple imprisonment or fine, or, in serious cases, with rigorous imprisonment not exceeding three years.

This is a very broad provision that encompasses offences deemed to be punishable for the reason that either they 'arouse hatred' or actually 'stir up acts of violence.' In a similar manner to Section 18 of the Public Order Act 1986 of the UK, Ethiopian law is not concerned with the manner in which the act is communicated. Thus, Ethiopian law criminalises speeches, publications, or oral communications that 'arouse hatred' or actually 'stir up acts of violence.' Ethiopian law also punishes acts of 'spreading of human diseases'[72] and 'refusal to provide medical assistance' out of hatred.[73]

However, the above articles have different connotations from the 'public order offences of stirring up hatred' as discussed above with regard to the UK law. Unlike the UK law, the Ethiopian law only punishes those acts that *actually*

70 See for example ICCPR (no 64) art 20(2); see also CERD (no 15), accession by Ethiopia in 1976.

71 FDRE Criminal Code (no 1), adopted in 2004. (emphasis added)

72 FDRE Criminal Code (no 1) art 514.

73 Ibid art 537.

provoke conflict or arouse hatred, and punishes those people who perform or refuse to do some acts out of hatred. However, it does not cover those acts that are more *likely* to provoke or arouse hatred. Thus, incitement to ethnic hatred is not covered specifically under the above-mentioned articles of the code. For instance, a person who refuses to give medical aid out of ethnic hatred will be dealt with by the law. Nevertheless, the same person will be spared from criminal liability if s/he incites his/her colleagues to do the same act, as the act of incitement would not be considered. In the UK, on the other hand, s/he will be punished not only for actually refusing to provide medical aid out of hatred, but also for inciting others to do the same. This is where the fundamental difference between the UK law and Ethiopian law lies.

Ethiopia's advertisement law[74] also contains some provisions that are significantly relevant to ethnic hatred. The Proclamation does not explicitly deal with ethnic hatred. However, as discussed in the sections above, the mere existence of the word 'human dignity' in the Proclamation is enough to broadly argue that ethnic hatred is an offence in Ethiopia. Accordingly, article 7(2) criminalises an 'advertisement that violates … human dignity of individuals, nation, nationalities or peoples, and defames the reputation of an organization.' However, the prohibitions come with a caveat.

The strict interpretation of the above Proclamation can convey the meaning that something advertised as violating human dignity must not be legally prohibited or deemed immoral. Such a legal prohibition will be enforceable if it is an act of parliament. Therefore, for a person to be held liable, it is necessary to prohibit what s/he has advertised in the first place. As it is not stated explicitly in the Proclamation, a person will not be held liable for advertising materials that incite ethnic hatred. This is the same problem observable with regard to the Constitution and the Criminal Code of Ethiopia. On a more positive note, however, the Advertisement Proclamation broadly defines the 'means' of advertisement, as it includes the 'mass media, outdoor advertisement, telecom, postal, internet web site and fax services, cinema, film, video and any other related means of advertisement dissemination.'[75] As discussed above, this is a similar approach as the one followed by the UK.[76]

At the same time, the Freedom of the Mass Media and Access to Information Proclamation states that 'where any factual information or matter injurious to the honor or reputation of any person is reported in a mass media, such person shall have the right to have his reply inserted, free of charge in the

74 Federal Negarit Gazeta, 'Advertisement Proclamation' Proclamation No. 759/2012.
75 Ibid art 2(2).
76 See the discussion above with regard to the Public Order Act 1986, ss 18.

publication in which the report appeared.'[77] This Proclamation has many limitations. For one thing, the prohibition deals with defamation cases, as it is merely concerned with 'information or matter injurious to the honor or reputation of' individuals. Second, the Proclamation cannot be interpreted broadly to be applied to ethnic hatred cases as it does not even contain phrases like 'human dignity,' which could have been helpful in extending its reach. More importantly, the remedy available for defamation under the Freedom of the Mass Media and Access to Information Proclamation is 'the right to have his reply inserted, free of charge in the publication….' However, it is not possible to right wrong 'aggravated offences' or an incitement to ethnic hatred by simply providing the right to insert a 'reply' in a publication. These are serious offences, which need to be dealt with severely. All in all, the above Proclamation does not have the right tools to help root out either 'aggravated offences' or an incitement to ethnic hatred.

The last Proclamation to be considered in this article is the Broadcasting Service Proclamation.[78] Article 30(4) of this legislation prohibits the broadcasting of expressions that '(a) violate the dignity (c) maliciously accuse or defame individuals, nation/nationalities, peoples or organizations; (d) cause dissension among nationalities or instigate dissension among peoples; or (e) incite war.' In this case, the first sub-section and the last sub-section are worth considering. As stated above, the concept of 'human dignity' plays an important role in the interpretation and adjudication of human rights.[79] Thus, although the legislation does not specifically deal with ethnic hatred, any broadcasting that violates 'dignity' will face the full force of the law. Accordingly, we can conclude that the offence of ethnic hatred and the ensuing effect of an expression that injuries human dignity will have severe consequences. The above argument may be good on its own merit. However, as the legislature has made it clear with regard to inciting a war, it should also have included an unambiguous provision that criminalises inciting ethnic hatred.

In conclusion, the legislations discussed above do not directly address inciting to ethnic hatred.

The coming to power of Prime Minster Abiy Ahmed seems to bring new changes to some of the controversial laws. For example, Ethiopia's Anti-Terrorism Proclamation is under revision. Moreover, the country has amended the

77 Federal Negarit Gazeta, 'Freedom of the Mass Media and Access to Information Proclamation' Proclamation No. 590/2008, art 40.

78 Federal Negarit Gazeta, 'Broadcasting Service Proclamation' Proclamation No. 533/2007.

79 McCrudden (n 67).

Charities and Societies Proclamation.[80] It was also reported that the country would enact a new legislation on hate speech.[81] However, it is not yet known to what extent the drafters have managed to prepare a bill. In addition to that, a civil society organisation successfully conducted 'a workshop with a view to enhancing awareness on hate speech for social media activists.'[82] The writer believes that similar workshops would pave the way for enacting a law that could address the problem at hand.

4.3 *The Gravity of Ethnic Hatred in Ethiopia*

The problems of ethnic hatred in the West and in countries like Ethiopia have different causes. In the West, the tension is between white people and people of colour. The laws and judge-made rules discussed above are geared up to address this tension. On the other hand, in a country as diverse as Ethiopia, the tension is amongst people of the same colour, but who are constitutionally and legally recognised as different nations and nationalities.

There is no need to go back as far as the founding fathers of modern Ethiopia to understand the tension amongst different ethnic groups. Nevertheless, it is enough to look back into the now infamous quote of the former Ethiopian dictator, Mengistu H/Mariam, who once publicly encouraged/incited the public to cleanse a certain ethnic group in order to put down the rebellion in Tigray. To quote him directly, he said that 'ዓሳውን ለመያዝ ውሃውን ማድረቅ.'[83] This is different from directly telling people to kill Tigriyans. To put it differently, the above quotation does not fall under the UK's 'racially aggravated offence.' By any standard, however, it is the clearest example of an incitement to commit a certain criminal act motivated by racial hatred. History recently repeated itself when a journalist in exile was accused of using the exact same phrase.[84]

80 Federal Negarit Gazeta, Charities and Societies Proclamation' Proclamation No. 1113/2019.

81 'News: Ethiopia preparing new bill to curb hate speech' *Addis Standard* (23 November 2018) <https://addisstandard.com/news-ethiopia-preparing-new-bill-to-curb-hate-speech/> accessed 11 March 2019.

82 'Human Rights Project conducts awareness creation workshop on hate speech' *MSN News* (23 February 2019) <https://www.msn.com/en-za/news/other/human-rights-project-conducts-awareness-creation-workshop-on-hate-speech/ar-BBU3eG8> accessed 11 March 2019.

83 A direct translation would be 'you have to dry the well to catch the fish.' Mengistu was unable to shut down the rebellion in Tigray. He believed that the Tigryan tribe supported the rebellion. As a means of terrorising the population, he advised his soldiers to kill the mothers and fathers who were sending their sons and daughters into the battle zones.

84 Mesay Mekonne, a journalist for the Ethiopian Satellite Television and Radio (ESAT) TV, caused public outrage when he was quoted using the same phrase.

During Ethiopia's controversial 1997 general election, a certain member of the House of Representatives and a very small number of supporters of Kinjit[85] were heard chanting 'ትግሬ ወደ መቀሌ ንብረት ወደ ቀበሌ.'[86] A person chanting similar songs in the UK would be held criminally responsible under the Public Order Act 1986. However, the writer doubts the effectiveness of the existing legislation in Ethiopia to cover similar chants.

The real causes behind the displacement of thousands of Amharas from Southern Nations and Nationalities of Ethiopia are uncertain.[87] In any case, the displacement has been politicised. As a result, it has reached a level where verifying facts from fiction has become difficult. Yet, one thing is certain: due to the displacement, many people have lost not only their livelihood, but also their lives.[88] According to one high-ranking government official, people were subjected to different forms of abuse and were targeted because ethnically they were Amhara.[89]

The displacement of the ethnic Amhara is not the only instance of abuse. A large number of ethnic Tigrayans were displaced from Gondar and other places of the Amhara region.[90] Their properties were burned down and they were forced to abandon their properties to save their lives. To add an insult to injury, thousands of ethnic Oromos were forced to flee the Ethio-Somalia region in 2017.[91]

Other horrible instances of attacks motivated by ethnic hatred are worth mentioning here. In 2018, a person was lynched by a mob in a broad daylight in front of hundreds of people.[92] This is not an isolated incident. Some reputable

---

85 The now defunct Coalition for Unity and Democracy (CUD).

86 Assets must be returned to Kebele and Tigrayans must go to Mekelle. Mekelle is the capital city of Tigray region. 'Kebele' is an Amharic word for the smallest administrative unit in Ethiopia.

87 'Southern Nations and Nationalities' is the name of one of the regions in Ethiopia.

88 borkena – Ethiopian News, 'Ethiopian government official admitted persecution of Amhara in Ethiopia' *Youtube* (25 August 2015) <https://www.youtube.com/watch?v=jgu9r4F_QB4> accessed 20 March 2018.

89 Ibid.

90 Habtom Videos, 'Ethiopia: Ethnic Tigrayans flee to avoid anti-government protesters' (21 August 2016) *Youtube*, <https://www.youtube.com/watch?v=iWtt9tLdSko> accessed 20 March 2018.

91 'What is behind clashes in Ethiopia's Oromia and Somali regions?' *BBC News* (18 September 2017) http://www.bbc.com/news/world-africa-41278618 accessed 19 March 2018.

92 Engidu Woldie, 'Ethiopia: Arrest in mob killing of innocent man in Shashemene' *ETHSAT* (13 August 2018) <https://ethsat.com/2018/08/ethiopia-arrest-in-mob-killing-of-innocent-man-in-shashemene/> accessed 9 March 2019.

reports show that 'a surge in ethnic violence, sometimes in the form of mob attacks, has displaced nearly 1 million people ....'[93]

Despite the above-mentioned internal displacements and horrible crimes, the government does not seem to have a clear strategy to prevent similar instances. Arresting violators of the law does not seem to deter people from engaging in these sort of offences. This is especially troubling considering the fact that Ethiopia is home to an ethnically diverse population.

The displacements themselves could be categorised under Section 4 and 5 of the UK's Public Order Act for the reason that there were racially motivated attacks. In the Ethiopian context, the attacks can also be considered under the Criminal Code of Ethiopia and the specific legislation previously discussed. However, it is difficult to even remotely conceive that the instances outlined above were spontaneous attacks. It would not be far-fetched to argue that these racially motivated attacks were the results of tensions and conflicts that were brewing for years. To be more specific, incitements to hatred against other ethnic groups have been covertly and overtly promoted not only by ordinary residents but also by low-ranking government officials. The deputy Prime Minister, Demeke Mekonnen, has partially confirmed this in an interview.[94]

In general, it would be unfair to criticise either the regional governments or the federal government for not acting before things got out of control. The finger should rather be pointed at the federal legislature for not passing a clear legislation on incitement to ethnic hatred. A re-evaluation of Ethiopian law, as discussed above, shows that the current legal regimes are not sufficient to tackle incitements to ethnic hatred.

5 Conclusion

The construction of the FDRE Constitution, specifically article 29, does not seem to support a liberal interpretation like that of the First Amendment in the US. There is no ambiguity with regard to article 29 on this point, as it clearly states that any 'expression of opinion intended to injure human dignity' does not have a legal protection in Ethiopia. For this reason, it has been shown above that Ethiopia does not follow the liberal approach of the US. The FDRE Constitution's approach on the limit of freedom of expression rather closely

93 Aaron Maasho, 'Ethnic unrest tarnishes new Ethiopian leader's reforms' Reuters (24 August 2018) <https://www.reuters.com/article/us-ethiopia-violence/ethnic-unrest-tarnishes-new-ethiopian-leaders-reforms-idUSKCN1L914V> accessed 7 March 2019.

94 borkena – Ethiopian News (n 88).

resembles the approach taken by the ECtHR. However, as of now, the general prohibition under the FDRE Constitution has not been supported by a specific legislation.

It is questionable why the government has so far failed to devise legislation that addresses an incitement to ethnic hatred. If the legislature is of the opinion that the existing legislation is broad enough to address the issue at hand, we have shown above why this mentality is entirely mistaken. The real questions that remain are how long it will take for legislation to be devised, and what sort of calamity is necessary to force the legislature to change its way of thinking.

It is always tempting to point fingers at past or current political arrangements in Ethiopia. It could also simply be argued that resource scarcity is one of the main causes for the rise of ethnic hatred in Ethiopia. It is beyond the scope of this article to discuss the root cause of these problems. Our interest is rather limited to the sufficiency of the existing legal arrangements to tackle existing problems revolving around ethnic hatred. After a thorough discussion, we can safely argue that Ethiopia does not have a law that clearly addresses incitement to ethnic hatred. For this reason, the government acknowledged that the absence of a law criminalising 'hate speech' (specifically ethnic hatred) hinders efforts to implement article 29 of the FDRE Constitution.[95]

With the advent of social media, it has become rather simple to spread hateful messages targeting a certain ethnicity. A recent study attempted to show that compared to the Facebook messages posted overall, there are very few messages that provoke/incite ethnic hatred.[96] However, this research has limitations: For one thing, it was only conducted between February and June 2015. Thus, it does not cover a long and recent period of time to show the extent of the problem. Second, the messages studied only encompassed 13,000 posts during the above-specified timeframe. Accordingly, it is difficult to take these samples as representative of the hateful messages that are being recycled all year round. Due to these limitations, it is not possible to simply write-off the effect of social media and its own role in spreading messages that incite ethnic hatred.

Accordingly, as has been evident in the past, it is very much guaranteed that more racially motivated attacks or provocations and incitements are to be

95 FDRE National Human Rights Action Plan (no 2) 58–59.

96 I Gagliardone et al., 'Mechachal: Online Debates and Elections in Ethiopia – From Hate Speech to Engagement in Social Media. Report Two: Discussing Politics and History in Social Media' (University of Oxford and Addis Ababa University, 2015) <http://pcmlp.socleg.ox.ac.uk/wp-content/uploads/2015/12/Report-2.pdf> accessed 19 March 2018.

expected unless the legislature is willing to act on the issue. This could be done either by amending the specific legislation discussed above or by enacting a specific legislation on incitement to ethnic hatred. The proposed legislation must contain provisions that define essential terms such as 'incitement,' and it must outline the elements that could amount to an incitement to ethnic hatred.

Extending Voting Rights to the Ethiopian Diaspora: Towards Institutionalising Diaspora Political Participation in Ethiopia

Teguadda Alebachew

Abstract

This chapter seeks to establish the need for extending voting rights to Ethiopians in the Diaspora by invoking a right to vote and its political and economic justifications. For this purpose, a qualitative research method is employed. Ethiopian citizens residing abroad are generally reported to be highly politicised, huge in number, and educated; they keep connected and concerned about home affairs. Thus, depending on how they are treated and engaged, the Ethiopian diasporic citizens possess the potential either to present a challenge or to forgo their tremendous potential to the country. Although voting is not the only practice attached to the political participation of citizens abroad, voting in home-country elections is one of the most formally practiced enactments thereof and reflects membership to a political community. As such, allowing Diaspora citizens to participate in elections in Ethiopia would result in their constructive engagement in the social, economic and political affairs of the country. Their participation in elections would also have the effect of legitimising governance in general and democratic institutions, particularly so in Ethiopia. Furthermore, it has the importance of institutionalising Diaspora political participation in Ethiopia, which is currently incoherent and obscure. The writer argues that efforts made towards Ethiopian Diaspora engagement, which are more focused on securing Diaspora citizens' economic and social engagement, will not be successful without granting them the right to vote. On the other hand, the principle of universal suffrage, which is duly recognised under the International Covenant on Civil and Political Rights (ICCPR) and the Universal Declaration on Human Rights (UDHR), cannot be fully achieved unless citizens living abroad are entitled to vote in elections of their home country. As such, the relevant international laws should be clear enough to oblige member states to enforce this citizens' right despite their geographical distance. The relevant international laws should also make the respective responsibilities and obligation of the host states clear. When it comes to the International Convention on the Rights of Migrant Workers and their Families (ICRMW), despite the clear recognition of political rights of migrant workers and their families in their country of origin, it is important that those states which are potentially regarded as host states also become members to the Convention.

 | DOI:10.1163/9789004415966_004

Given the considerable number of Ethiopian migrant workers and their families overseas, it is hence also vital that Ethiopia becomes a member to the ICRMW.

Keywords

Diaspora – Ethiopia – Political Rights – Voting Rights – Migration

1 Introduction

Ethiopian citizens in the Diaspora may participate in the politics of their country of origin in various different capacities, such as by participating in voting, financing political parties, shaping political ideologies, offering civic education, standing as candidates for office, and holding the government accountable. However, and most importantly, voting signifies solid ties to a certain political community. The extension of voting rights to Diaspora citizens would thus also give citizens abroad a broad window of opportunity to participate in the politics of their country of origin.

Political engagement of emigrants in their home country has been on the rise globally in the past few decades.[1] A 2007 report by International IDEA indicates that 115 countries across the world have recognised and institutionalised political participation of their Diaspora citizens in the politics of their home country.[2] Although the Federal Democratic Republic of Ethiopia's (FDRE) Constitution extends the right to vote to all citizens alike, it has never been enabled for citizens in the Diaspora to exercise this right formally.

This research aims at building the need for Diaspora citizens' participation in elections in Ethiopia based on a right to vote and its political and economic justifications. In doing so, the writer has investigated current international law and international trends on Diaspora voting and the justifications extending citizens this right. She has also studied a breadth of literature addressing the Ethiopian Diaspora in general, including their specific features, numbers, educational status, as well as their commitment to and interest in local matters. Relevant Ethiopian laws and policies regarding Diaspora political participation

1 Nadja Braun and Maria Gratschew, 'Introduction' in International Institute for Democracy and Electoral Assistance (IDEA) (ed), *Voting from Abroad* (IDEA, 2007) 1 <https://www.idea.int/sites/default/files/publications/voting-from-abroad-the-international-idea-handbook.pdf> accessed 12 June 2018.

2 Ibid 3.

in general and voting rights in particular were also studied, in order to identify both the available legal and policy challenges and also the opportunities on Diaspora political participation. Interviews with members of the Diaspora Engagement Directorate of the Ministry of Foreign Affairs and the Ethiopian Diaspora Association in Addis Ababa were also conducted.

2 Voting Rights for Diaspora Citizens in the Country of Origin: The International Experience and Laws

2.1 *Defining Diaspora*

Various terminologies are used to describe individuals who reside in countries other than their country of origin, including 'emigrants', 'immigrants', and 'refugees', 'Diasporas', 'exiles', 'transnational or overseas communities', and 'expatriates'.[3] Specifically, the term 'Diaspora',[4] contrary to its previous usage, has gradually been used to describe all transnational individuals and communities who reside in another country both temporarily or permanently, who emigrated with reason, and who do have an interest in keeping ties with their country of origin either emotionally or materially.[5] The African Union (AU) Commission defines the 'African Diaspora' as peoples of African origin living outside

3 While the term 'emigrants' represents an act of leaving one's country, 'immigration' refers to the act of entering a destination country. 'Migration', on the other hand, represents a mass movement of people, whether it is internally or across borders.

4 The concept of Diaspora comes mostly from the history of the Jewish people and the saga of the African slave trade. It is therefore associated with the notion of forced displacement as a result of conflict, persecution, or discrimination. Over time, the use of the term has become more flexible and has grown to include individuals in search of a better life and opportunities they believe `do not exist in their country of origin, but who continue to sustain a relationship with that country'. According to Gabriel Sheffer, 'Modern Diasporas are ethnic minority groups of migrant origins and acting in host countries but maintaining strong sentimental and material links with their countries of origin – their homelands'. Gabriel Sheffer, *A New Field of Study: Modern Diasporas in International Politics* (Croom Helm 1986) 3. See also Fiona B Adamson, 'The Growing Importance of Diaspora Politics' (2016) 115(784) Current History, 292.

5 See Council of Europe Parliamentary Assembly, 'Democratic Participation for Migrant Diasporas' (Report by the Committee on Migration, Refugee and Displaced Persons, 2013) 5 <http://website-pace.net/documents/19863/168397/20141127-RigoniDiaspora-EN.pdf/e089137f-444a-4ed8-9bf9-bb393a2c4ab6> accessed 27 April 2018. Robin Cohen, an author on the subject, has for instance proposed a variety of examples of Diasporas based on the categories 'victim' (such as the Jews and Armenians), 'trade' (Chinese and Lebanese), 'imperial' (British), and 'labour' (indentured Indians). Others have identified 'conflict-generated' or 'refugee' diasporas (Tamils and Syrians, for example). The term 'Diaspora' also represents those individuals who, while being legal migrants, don't hold citizenship of the host state, as

the continent irrespective of their citizenship and nationality, who are willing to contribute to the development of the continent and the building of the African Union.[6] The term 'migrant' also relates to 'Diaspora' and encompasses various circumstances for emigrating and settling outside the home country. According to Van Hear, the term 'migrant' covers diverse groups of people including settlers, temporary contract workers, professionals, refugees, and asylum seekers.[7] As such, the two terms are increasingly used interchangeably. In Ethiopia too, the term 'Diaspora' is widely used interchangeably with the term 'migrant' to address all emigrants who emigrated due to varying circumstances, irrespective of the duration of their stay outside the country. The Ethiopian Diaspora Policy has also defined 'the Ethiopian Diaspora' as those Ethiopians and foreign nationals of Ethiopian origin residing outside Ethiopia.[8] Accordingly, the policy regards all individuals residing outside Ethiopia as 'Ethiopian Diasporas' regardless of their current citizenship status, reason for emigration, or duration of residence in another country.

The 'Diaspora citizen' specifically refers to those individuals residing in another country while retaining their Ethiopian citizenship. This group of citizens may also include those who reside in another country with a different status, including as students, migrant workers and their families (as per the definition of ICRMW), refugees, asylum seekers (who have not yet received refugee status), persons servicing their home country in another state as military or diplomatic personnel, self-employed citizens, or those employed in international organisations and non-governmental organisations (NGOs). Even though Ethiopian Diasporas who have already gained citizenship of the host state equally possess significant potential to their country of origin and are hence worth being conferred political rights, the scope of this study is limited to the political participation of Diaspora citizens irrespective of their reason for emigration and duration of their residency in the foreign country. The terms

---

well as those who do. See Robin Cohen, *Global Diasporas: An Introduction* (2nd edn, Routledge Publishing 2008).

6 *'Diaspora Division'* African Union <https://au.int/en/diaspora-division#main-content> accessed 27 April 2018. See also the report of the full discussion on the definition of the term 'African Diaspora' made by the panel of experts as referred to them by the African Commission. See African Union, 'Report of the meeting of experts from members of States on the Definition of African Diaspora' (Executive Council's Sixth Ordinary Session in Abuja, Nigeria, January 2005) <http://www.dirco.gov.za/diaspora/definition.html> accessed 27 April 2018.

7 See generally Nicholas Van Hear, *New Diaspora: Mass Exodus, Dispersal and Regrouping of Migrant Communities* (University of Washington Press 1998).

8 Ethiopian Ministry of Foreign Affairs, 'Federal Republic of Ethiopia Diaspora Policy' (Addis Ababa, 2013) 8 <http://www.ethiopianembassy.org/PDF/diaspora%20policy.pdf> accessed 9 May 2018.

'migrant/emigrants' and 'Diaspora' will be used interchangeably throughout this contribution to the extent that they both describe citizens not resident in Ethiopia, regardless of their reason for emigration and duration of their residency outside Ethiopia.

2.2 *Voting Rights for Diaspora Citizens in the Country of Origin: The International Experience*

For a long time, emigrants who reside in another country and abandoned their homeland were regarded as destitute[9] and traitors, who deserted their country and no longer had an interest in their country of origin.[10] As a result, they were far from the attention of both the international community and of the sending and receiving states. Later on, globalisation, catastrophes and the emergence of new technologies, which resulted in mass movement of citizens across borders, created both a strong interest in and commitment to home affairs for the Diaspora.[11] In turn, the increased interest in and commitment to home affairs forced states and non-state actors to acknowledge the Diaspora as influential global actors. To this end, state and non-state actors across the world have made polices and strategies addressing the Diaspora.[12] In view of exploiting the potential of their respective Diasporas, state actors in particular have come up with different engagement polices. One of these policies is engaging Diaspora citizens in national politics through extending to them the right to vote. External voting has since become an international practice.

Since the start of the 20th century, countries like New Zealand, Australia, Canada, the United States of America (USA) and India have introduced external

---

9 Barbara Schmitter Heisler, 'Sending States and Immigrant Minorities – the Case of Western Europe' (1986) 485(1) The ANNALS of the American Academy of Political and Social Science, 76.

10 Alan Gamlen, 'Creating and Destroying Diaspora Strategies: New Zealand's Emigration Policies Re-Examined' (2011) Working Paper 31 International Migration Institute, 4 <https://www.imi-n.org/publications/wp-31-11> accessed 2 May 2018.

11 The number of international migrants worldwide has continued to grow rapidly in recent years, reaching 258 million in 2017, up from 220 million in 2010 and 173 million in 2000, respectively. United Nations, 'International Migration Report' (Economic & Social Affairs, 2017) 4 <http://www.un.org/en/development/desa/population/migration/publications/migrationreport/docs/MigrationReport2017_Highlights.pdf> accessed 28 April 2018. See also Nadja Braun and Maria Gratschew (n 1) 1.

12 The Diaspora serves as an important source of trade, capital, technology, and knowledge for countries of origin and destination. See The World Bank, 'Migration and Development' (World Bank Group, 2016) 16–20 <http://pubdocs.worldbank.org/en/468881473870347506/Migration-and-Development-Report-Sept2016.pdf> accessed 1 January 2018.

voting by allowing their citizens abroad to vote in national elections.[13] Yet, such a right was only conferred to citizens abroad serving their nation's interest either as military or diplomatic personnel or in any other capacity in the interest of the nation.[14] Since the 1970s, a large number of states have also extended voting rights to citizens abroad without official duties. More than 115 countries worldwide have now recognised and institutionalised Diaspora political participation in homeland politics.[15] Voting rights of citizens abroad are variously referred to as 'non-resident voting', 'out of country voting', 'absentee voting', 'external voting' and 'voting of emigrants'. These terms are often used interchangeably and will also be used interchangeably in this chapter.

Despite the increase of countries who have adopted external voting, the degree and conditions on which external voting has been allowed and practiced vary across countries. There is a variation in the groups of people allowed to vote from abroad, as well as the specific circumstances under which this right is extended. For example, some countries only allow external voting within a limited number of years after voting for certain groups abroad, either based on the number of years spent abroad or based on the commitment to their country of origin. Others allow external voting only in certain elections or only in very few foreign countries.

Beyond the traditional restrictions for voters nationally, states make additional eligibility requirements for external voters.[16] In Germany, the United Kingdom, and Canada, emigrants are eligible to vote as long as they have not left their country for more than 25, 15, and five years, respectively. Permanent legal residents cannot vote in the Philippines unless they confirm that they will

13 Even before the 20th century, the state of Wisconsin in the United States of America (USA) had allowed its soldiers fighting for the Union during the Civil War to vote in 1862. Others also cite the Roman Empire as first having extended voting rights to Senators of the Empire residing in the newly founded colonies. Jean-Michel Lafleur, 'The Enfranchisement of Citizens Abroad in a Comparative Perspective' (Conference on 'Political Rights in the Age of Globalization', University of St. Gallen, 2013) 2 <https://www.coursehero.com/file/24961552/Lafleur-120913doc/> accessed 1 January 2018. See also Andy Sundberg, 'The History and Politics of Diaspora Voting in Home Country Elections' (Paper prepared based on information from Andrew Ellis and other sources in *'Voting from Abroad': The International IDEA Handbook,* 2007) 1 <https://www.overseasvotefoundation.org/files/The_History_and_Politics_of_Diaspora_Voting.pdf> accessed on 27 April 2018.

14 Ibid.

15 28 African countries and 16 countries in the Americas have external voting. A fairly high number of European countries (41) allow it, as well as ten in Oceania and 20 in Asia. See Nadja Braun and Maria Gratschew (n 1) 3.

16 Sundberg (n 13) 6–7. See also Council of Europe Parliamentary Assembly (n 5) 7.

reside back in the Philippines within three years of voter registration.[17] A few countries, such as Israel, Taiwan, El Salvador, and Slovakia have extended voting rights to all their non-resident citizens abroad, provided that they come home to vote.[18]

A variety of methods is employed to administer external voting, such as mail voting, Internet voting, proxy voting, and in-person voting at polling places in embassies and consulates abroad.[19] There are also countries that require non-residents to return home to cast ballots in-person on the election days. In most states, external voters cast their vote in a constituency in their last place of residence before they left the country. However, in a few countries in Europe, Latin America, and Africa, Diaspora voters have been provided with separate representation in national legislatures.[20] Emigrants in constituencies abroad elect emigrant representatives. Emigrant parliamentarians, beyond advocating for the interest of the emigrant population, supposedly enjoy powers equal to the rest of the elected parliamentarians in national constituencies, when it comes to having a voice in drafting legislation and influencing the control of government.

Furthermore, many African governments have been reaching out to Diasporas abroad seeking their economic and political participation at home. More than half of all African countries (30 out of the 53) are reported to have extended to their nationals overseas an opportunity to acquire foreign citizenship whilst retaining their home country rights.[21] While some states are considering dual citizenship measures, others want to engage expatriates without granting them full citizenship rights.[22]

17 Peter J Spiro, 'Perfecting Political Diaspora' (2006) 18 New York University Law Review, 212.

18 Ibid. See also Hajnalka Juhász, 'External Voting in the International Practice: A Comparative Analysis and Overview' (2014) 16 Minority Studies 47, 53–54.

19 Sundberg (n 13) 4.

20 These countries include Algeria, Angola, Cape Verde, Colombia, Croatia, Ecuador, France, Italy, Mozambique, Panama, Portugal, Romania and Tunisia. See Lafleur (n 13) 8. See also Noreen Bowden, 'Should Citizens Living Overseas be allowed to Vote?' (International Diaspora Engagement Alliance, 2012) <http://www.diasporaalliance.org/should-citizens-living-overseas-be-allowed-to-vote/> accessed 30 April 2018.

21 Beth E Whitaker, 'The Politics of Home: Dual Citizenship and the African Diaspora' (2011) (45) 4 The International Migration Review 755, 1.

22 Ibid. Countries such as Benin, Mali, and Senegal have established ministerial-level offices to handle expatriate affairs. In Ethiopia too, foreign nationals of Ethiopian origin are made to enjoy certain rights in Ethiopia. See the Federal Negarit Gazeta, 'Proclamation to provide Foreign Nationals of Ethiopian Origin with Certain Rights to be Exercised in their "Country of Origin"' Proclamation No. 270/2002.

2.3 *International Law and Political Participation of the Diaspora in the Country of Origin*

2.3.1 Political participation under the International Covenant on Civil and Political Rights (ICCPR)

The International Covenant on Civil and Political Rights (ICCPR) is the first international convention to recognise the right to elect and be elected as a matter of international obligation.[23] The Covenant under article 25 extends these rights to all citizens alike without any distinction on the grounds mentioned under article 2 of same Covenant and without unreasonable restrictions.[24] Prohibited grounds of restriction mentioned under article 2 include race, colour, sex, language, religion, political or other opinion, national or social origin, property, birth or other status.[25] Restrictions on the grounds other than those mentioned under article 2, yet which are reasonable, are possible under article 25. Hence, states can make legitimate restrictions on the right to elect and be elected within the bounds of articles 25 and 2 of the Covenant. The case in point is whether a state's restriction on the right to vote of citizens abroad on the grounds of residency is reasonable and legitimate. As is stated under article 2, residency is not among the list of the prohibited restrictions of the right to vote. As a result, several states have stipulated residency as an eligibility requirement, thereby restricting voters who reside outside their country. Whether 'residency' can be captured by the last expression under article 2, ie 'other status', is also arguable. The Human Rights Committee (HRC) in another but related case has once commented that the requirement of residency for

23 One may say that right to elect and be elected had been proclaimed by, even before the ICCPR, under arts 1, 2, 3 of the 1953 UN Convention on the Political Rights of Women, which was signed on 31 March 1953 by 123 member parties. However, since the Convention confers the right to elect and be elected only to women, it cannot be said that the Convention is the pioneer in acknowledging the former as a universal right for all. Convention on the Political Rights of Women (adopted on 31 March 1953, entered into force on 7 July 1954) 193 UNTS 135 (CPRW) <http://www.un.org.ua/images/Convention_on_the_Political_Rights_of_Women_eng1.pdf> accessed 2 May 2018.

24 International Covenant on Civil and Political Rights (adopted 16 December 1966, entered into force 23 March 1976) 999 UNTS 171 (ICCPR) art 25. As opposed to the ICCPR, the European Convention on Human Rights (ECHR) does not define the right to vote by citizenship. The convention simply states that 'The High Contracting Parties undertake to hold free elections at reasonable intervals by secret ballot, under conditions which will ensure the free expression of the opinion of the people in the choice of the legislature'. See generally the European Convention on Human Rights (signed 4 November 1950, entered into force on 3 September 1953) ETS 5 (ECHR) <https://www.echr.coe.int/Documents/Convention_ENG.pdf> accessed 2 May 2018.

25 Ibid art 2.

the purpose of registration of voters is reasonable.[26] As opposed to the ICCPR, the American Convention on Human Rights (Pact of San José, Costa Rica) under article 23 has expressly stated that residency can be invoked as a legitimate restriction on the right to vote.[27]

To sum up, the lack of a clear provision under the ICCPR addressing the right to vote of citizens abroad, as well as the HRC's interpretation of article 25, indicating that residency can be used as legitimate ground for restriction, has reinforced the state's prerogative when it comes to external voting. The prerogative of the state on external voting has sometimes been used by states to advance the political goals of governments in member states in which the trend in the extension of external voting is witnessed. Historically, as discussed in this chapter, most governments have extended external voting because they anticipate some level of electoral support from citizens overseas.

2.3.2 Political Participation under the International Convention on the Protection of the Rights of All Migrant Workers and Members of their Families (ICRMW)

The International Convention on the Protection of the Rights of All Migrant Workers and Members of Their Families (ICRMW) is the only international convention that specifically addresses the right to vote of citizens abroad. Yet, the applicability of the law is limited only to those citizens that fall under the definition of 'migrant workers and their families', as provided under articles 2 and 4 of the Convention. The Convention under article 41 states that migrant workers and their families have the right to elect, to be elected, and to participate in the public affairs of their country of origin.[28] The Convention defined 'migrant workers' as those persons who are to be engaged, are engaged, or have been engaged in a remunerated activity in the state of which they are not

26 Office of the High Commissioner for Human Rights, 'ICCPR: General Comment No. 25: art 25 (Participation in Public Affairs and the Right to Vote), The Right to Participate in Public Affairs, Voting Rights and the Right of Equal Access to Public Service' (12 July 1996) CCPR/C/21/Rev.1/Add. 7, General Comment No. 25, paras 4–11.

27 Member states may through a law regulate the exercise of the rights of citizens to vote *only on* the basis of age, nationality, *residence*, language, education, civil and mental capacity, or sentencing by a competent court in criminal proceedings. See American Convention on Human Rights 'Pact of San José, Costa Rica' (signed 22 November 1969, adopted 18 July 1978) 1144 UNTS 123, art 23 <http://www.oas.org/juridico/English/treaties/b-32.html> accessed 27 April 2018.

28 International Convention on the Protection of the Rights of All Migrant Workers and Members of Their Families' (signed on 18 December 1990, entered into force on 1 July 2003) 2220 UNTS 3 (ICRMW) art 41 <https://www.ohchr.org/Documents/ProfessionalInterest/cmw.pdf> accessed 1 January 2018.

nationals.[29] Contrastingly, the 'families of migrant workers' refer to persons married to migrant workers or having a relationship, which according to applicable law produces effects equivalent to marriage, as well as their dependent children and other dependent persons who are recognised as members of the family by applicable legislation or applicable bilateral or multilateral agreements between the states concerned.[30] The Convention applies at all times in the emigration process of the emigrant workers and their families, including in the departure, transit and destination states. The Convention is not applicable to persons with other forms of emigration status, such as refugees, students, trainees, seafarers, state diplomatic personnel, persons sent or employed by international organisations and agencies, and persons residing in another state as investors.[31] The Convention must be applied to all migrant workers and members of their families without distinction on the basis of sex, race, colour, language, religion or conviction, political or other opinion, national, ethnic or social origin, nationality, age, economic position, property, marital status, birth or other status.[32]

By addressing the issue of the right to vote of migrant workers and their families, the Convention has avoided the possible restriction the country of origin would make on the grounds of residency. Beyond this, the Convention imposes obligations on member states that are sending states, to take practical measures to enforce the right to vote of migrant workers and their families residing in a foreign state. However, the fact that the Convention is applicable only to limited groups of emigrants and the Covenant only has 51 member states,[33] thereby constituting only the sending states, has made the Covenant practically less relevant towards realising the voting rights of citizens abroad. None of the current 51 signatories to the Covenant are countries in North America, Western Europe, New Zealand or Australia, which are regarded as main receiving states and regions.[34]

29 Ibid art 2(1).

30 Ibid art 4.

31 Ibid art 3.

32 Ibid art 1(1).

33 See the list of member states and signatories to the ICRMW. United Nations Office of the High Commissioner of Human Rights, 'Ratification Status for CMW – International Convention on the Protection of the Rights of All Migrant Workers and Members of Their Families' <http://tbinternet.ohchr.org/_layouts/TreatyBodyExternal/Treaty.aspx?Treaty=CMW&Lang=en> accessed 2 May 2018.

34 Ibid.

2.3.3 Political Participation in the 1951 Convention Relating to the Status of Refugees

The Convention, despite dealing with persons who are forced to leave their country due to reasons related to political prosecution, lacks an explicit provision addressing the political rights of this group of peoples both in the sending and receiving states. It also does not prohibit state parties to restrict overseas citizens' right to vote on the basis of residency. Despite this fact, there is however a growing international experience in according refugees a right to take part in elections in their country of origin. There is an argument that unlike other types of expatriate citizens, refugees have not left their country of origin voluntarily or in search of better life, but rather due to compelling circumstances mainly resulting from the undemocratic behaviour of the departure state. As such, the participation of refugees in national elections has gained special treatment in the issue of external voting. Refugees' participation in national elections, especially in post-conflict societies, had been found to be healing and has had the effect of legitimising institutions and politics at home.[35]

Except for the ICRMW, the relevant international laws such as the ICCPR and the Convention Relating to the Status of Refugees are silent on the political participation of overseas citizens in their country of origin. To this end, it is difficult to say that there is an international obligation to extend voting rights to citizens living abroad. Despite the multifaceted importance of the participation of non-resident citizens in national elections, the non-regulation of the right as a matter of international obligation has left the issue to fully fall under the discretion of the government of the country of origin.

The provision of external voting does not only require the willingness and commitment of the sending state, but also that of the receiving states. Receiving states need to be willing, consent, and provide facilities for another country's elections to be held within their territory.[36] Firstly, the receiving state must allow another state to undertake an election within its territory, as this would otherwise encroach on the sovereignty of the former. Secondly, the receiving state must be willing to maintain peace and order before and during the election days. Holding an electoral campaign in the streets of the receiving state for another country's election would also require the willingness of the receiving state. This is particularly demanding in cases where the campaign

35 Ruma Mandal, 'Political Rights of Refugees, Legal And Protection Policy Research Series' (United Nations High Commissioner For Refugees, 2003) 4–5 <http://www.refworld.org/pdfid/3fe820794.pdf> accessed 2 August 2017.

36 The host state can play different role. See Lacy Brett, 'Host Country Issues' in IDEA (ed), *Voting from Abroad* (IDEA, 2007) 141.

involves ethnic tensions among the Diaspora community, which would obviously disrupt the peaceful coexistence of the society in the receiving state.

The non-regulation of the matter under international laws also left unaddressed the respective role and obligation of the receiving state in realising the participation of emigrant citizens in national elections. This fact has thus forced those states, which have currently allowed for external voting, to depend largely on the principle of reciprocity, goodwill and diplomatic cooperation with receiving states. In some cases, diplomatic cooperation may not be possible. For instance, because the Swiss concept of sovereignty did not allow foreigners to vote in Switzerland, it has prevented Switzerland from making an agreement with receiving states for external voting.[37] In addition, Canada and Belgium do not want their territories to be considered part of another country's constituency.[38] The Australian government has also been against Australian citizens running for a seat in the legislature of another country while they live in Australia.[39]

Yet, it is possible for a sending state to organise the election in its embassies and consulate offices without any prior consent of the receiving state. Under international law, such offices are considered part of the territory of the sending state. However, this is not always cost-effective as embassies and consulate offices are usually located in one place, usually in capital cities; however, emigrants are found spread in all parts of the country. As a result, emigrants would have to incur travel costs to reach the places where they can cast their vote.

Given the relevance of the participation of emigrants in national elections and considering the principle of universal suffrage, it would have been desirable for mainstream international law to have rules addressing the matter explicitly, stipulating the specific respective roles and obligations of the sending and receiving states on the implementation of external voting.

2.4 *Justifying Political Participation of Diaspora Citizens in Their Country of Origin*

The right to vote is defined based on citizenship both under national and international laws. To this end, Diaspora enfranchisement should logically emanate from their citizenship status. However, practice rather shows that citizenship has not been enough to qualify nationals overseas to enfranchise in their

37 Ibid 138.

38 Ibid 139.

39 Mascitelli Bruno and Simone Battiston, 'Challenging the Australian Government Approach towards Expatriate Voting: The Case of Italy' (2009) 44(3) Australian Journal of Political Science 513.

country of origin. Owing to a lack of agreement in addressing the issue specifically in relevant international law, voting rights of citizens abroad in their country of origin has remained within the mandate of states. Government policies on extending voting rights to their citizens abroad are largely motivated by the reciprocal benefits they would receive from their Diaspora community, which goes beyond their mere citizenship. As the expansion of political rights to others naturally weakens their power, it is highly unlikely that governments extend external voting rights based on genuine consideration of the rights of their citizens abroad.[40]

Extending to non-resident citizens a right to decide on who shall govern the country of origin has been debated. Opponents of external voting argue that extending voting rights to non-resident citizens is dangerous, as there is an opportunity that these citizens may develop loyalty to their country of residence.[41] It is also argued that granting voting rights to overseas citizens is wrong, since they are not directly affected by the governance at home or are not making a contribution in/to the country.[42] According to counter-arguments, citizens abroad send remittances and make investments back home and hence, this should make them seen as contributing to their country like citizens residing at home.[43] Arguments supporting external voting portray the disenfranchisement of non-resident citizens in national elections while they are making investments at home as absurd, as investing would make them affected by the governance inside their country of origin.[44] In countries where citizens abroad are required to pay income tax to their home countries, external voting is justified as appropriate.[45]

The change of perception towards emigrants being destitute or defectors has significantly influenced governments' determination in engaging their Diaspora citizens in home politics. Migrants are now viewed as being successful by those in the homeland[46] and are often considered national heroes. Diaspora citizens are increasingly seen as economically useful, especially in

40 Jack William and Roger Lagunoff, 'Dynamic Enfranchisement' (2006) 90 Journal of Public Economics 551, 552.

41 Lafleur (n 13) 2.

42 Bowden (n 20). See also Caroline Carter, 'The Right to Vote for Non-resident Citizens: Considered through the Example of East Timor' (2011) 46 Texas International Law Journal 655, 661–664.

43 Ibid.

44 Ibid.

45 Ibid.

46 Philippe Fargues, 'International Migration and the Demographic Transition: A Two-Way Interaction' (2011) 45(3) International Migration Review 588, 595.

sending states, which tend to be developing countries. Sending remittance, transfer knowledge and technology, and making direct investments at home are areas in which Diaspora citizens are economically beneficial to their country of origin.[47] Countries in Latin America and the Caribbean, but also Africa, for instance, are highly dependent on financial assistance from those that have emigrated. Reports show that as of the mid-2000s, remittance in some states in these regions exceeded foreign aid and complemented export revenue.[48] The financial power of emigrants of the Dominican Republic has resulted in pressuring the government to extend to them external voting rights.[49]

Diaspora citizens from developing countries who reside in democratic states are also considered to have potential to transfer social and political capital to their countries of origin. The Diaspora communities can promote in their countries of origin the values they consider positive in their country of residence. In the last two decades, the Diaspora has become one of the driving forces in bringing democratic experiences to their countries of origin.[50] Their experience of democratic values, transparency, accountability, equality, non-discrimination, and justice will make them play a critical role both in holding accountable the government in power, and in helping to raise peoples' civil and political consciousness.

The inclusion of citizens abroad is also increasingly regarded as important in the process of nation building, for example in Namibia in 1989 and South Africa in 1994.[51] Particularly in post-conflict countries, the participation of refugees in national elections has been considered significant for reconciliation, to restore peace, and to legitimatise institutions and politics in the new state.[52]

For countries with a considerable number of citizens living abroad, non-participation of non-resident citizens was found to call into question the legitimacy of the election itself. In 2000, there were 70 countries in which migrants accounted for ten percent of the population, and there were six countries in

47 Joseph Mayton, 'Voting Abroad is Every Citizen's Right' *The Guardian* (21 July 2010) <https://www.theguardian.com/commentisfree/2010/jul/21/voting-abroad-citizen-right> accessed 30 April 2018.

48 Alejandro Portes and Cristina Escobar and Alexandria Walton Radford, 'Immigrant Transnational Organizations and Development: A Comparative Study' (2007) 41(1) International Migration Review 242, 243–244.

49 Barry Kim, 'Home and Away: The Construction of Citizenship in an Emigration Context' (2006) 81(1) New York University Law Review 11, 57. Also see Sundberg (n 13) 3.

50 See Council of Europe Parliamentary Assembly (n 5) 6.

51 Sundberg (n 13) 3.

52 Grace Jeremy, 'External and Absentee Voting' in *Challenging the Norms and Standards of Election Administration* (International Foundation for Electoral Systems 2007) 35–38.

which migrants made up more than 60 percent of the population.[53] In Lebanon and Armenia, for instance, non-resident citizens constitute twelve and six million, compared to four and three million who live inside the country, respectively.[54] The participation of the Diaspora citizens in such cases could significantly affect election results. Their participation could also hugely impact the overall political competition and the multi-party system. Diaspora citizens from less democratic states who reside in democratic states are widely believed to be opponents to governments at home. Moreover, external voting is highly relevant to the many people whose job involves frequent travel to foreign states.

Giving citizens abroad the opportunity to vote can have positive results that go beyond mere participation in choosing leaders, such as keeping peace and security of the country. In some cases, the Diaspora using its money and knowledge can cause civil unrest in the country of origin, depending on how they are treated and how they perceive politics in their home countries. Thus, politically engaging the Diaspora is important to address political differences, ethnic polarisation and ethnic conflicts at home.

Historically, voting rights have been extended to citizens overseas for one or more of the following reasons in different countries: for the recognition of their economic potential to the country; as an acknowledgement of their active participation in World War I and II in Spain; in response to the demand of the Diaspora, as was the case in the United States (USA); due to the demand of the Diaspora using their financial influence, as it was the case in Dominican Republic.[55] In 1980, the United Kingdom (UK) government granted UK citizens overseas the right to vote, anticipating electoral support from them.[56] This was also true in Argentina, Mexico, and Turkey very recently.[57] In Austria, the introduction of external voting in 1990 followed a resolution of the Constitutional Court.[58] External voting was also employed as a reconciliatory mechanism to reinforce institutions in post-conflict countries such as in Kosovo and

53 Nadja Braun and Maria Gratschew (n 1) 2.

54 Hafthor Brynjar Erlingsson, 'Adoption of External Voting in Latin America and The Caribbean' (Master Thesis, University of Nevada 2014) 8 <https://digitalscholarship.unlv.edu/thesesdissertations/2177/> accessed 1 May 2018.

55 Sundberg (n 13) 3.

56 Ibid 2.

57 Friedemann Voge, 'Why Erdoğan is chasing Turkey's overseas voters so hard' *The Conversation* (16 March 2017) <http://theconversation.com/why-erdogan-is-chasing-turkeys-overseas-voters-so-hard-74469> accessed 3 May 2018.

58 Ibid.

in Bosnia and Herzegovina.[59] To sum up, countries' experiences dictate that the adoption of external voting is legitimised by one or more reasons, including the right to vote and its economic and political justifications.

3 Ethiopians Overseas and Their Role and Influence in Home Affairs

3.1 *The Ethiopian Diaspora Overseas: The History of Migration, Numbers and Its Overall Condition*

In earlier times, it was rare that Ethiopians left their country and established domicile in another country. Later on in the 19th century, incidents such as oppositions to the imperial rule by regionally-based groups, the Italian invasion in 1930, and religious pilgrims to Jerusalem and Mecca supposedly caused Ethiopians to migrate to foreign states.[60] In the 1940s through to the 1960s, emigration to pursue Western education is also noted to be part of the Ethiopian population emigration drives.[61] In the 1980s, following the coming into power of the military regime (*Derg*), large number of Ethiopians from all segments of society emigrated to foreign states.[62] Emigrants during this time were largely refugees who were escaping political persecution by the regime. In this period, Ethiopians were reported to be the largest group to immigrate to the USA, contributing considerably to the current Ethiopian Diaspora population in North America, which is the second largest African Diaspora next to Nigeria.[63] The Ethiopian Diaspora is currently also the fifteenth-largest emigrant group in Europe.[64] Substantial numbers of Ethiopians also live concentrated in Arab countries, South Africa, Botswana, Equatorial Guinea, Sudan, Kenya and other parts of the world.[65]

---

59 Mandal (n 35) 13–20.

60 Bahru Zewdie and Gebre Yintiso and Kassahun Berhnau, 'Contribution of the Ethiopian Diaspora to Peace-Building: A Case Study of the Tigray Development Association (TDA)' (University of Jyväskylä, Diaspora Peace Project, 2010) 7–11 <https://jyx.jyu.fi/dspace/bitstream/handle/123456789/36888/DIASPEACE_WP8[1].pdf?sequence=1> accessed 30 April 2018.

61 Ibid.

62 Katie Kuschminder and Melissa Siegel, 'Understanding the Ethiopian Diaspora Engagement Policy' (2010) United Nations University UNU-MERIT Working Paper Series #2011-040, 2 <https://www.merit.unu.edu/publications/working-papers/abstract/?id=4469> accessed 30 April 2018.

63 Ibid. See also Katie Kuschminder, 'Diaspora Engagement in Ethiopia: Finding its footing' (2010) Migration Policy Brief Series 4 <mgsog.merit.unu.edu/ISacademie/docs/PB4.pdf> accessed 30 April 2018.

64 Ibid.

65 Ethiopian Ministry of Foreign Affairs (n 8) 5–6.

While the exact size of the Ethiopian Diaspora population is unknown, it is estimated that over 2.5 million people of Ethiopian origin live temporarily and permanently in different parts of the world.[66] On the one hand, the Ethiopian Ministry of Foreign Affairs estimates the total number of the Ethiopian Diaspora to be between two and three million.[67] The Ethiopian Diaspora Association in Addis Ababa, on the other hand, raises the number to four million.[68] Like the problem on the exact number of the Ethiopian Diaspora population abroad, it is also difficult to find data showing how many of them have still retained their Ethiopian citizenship or have gained citizenship of their country of residence. It is also difficult to identify how many of them fall into the categories of migrant workers and their families, refugees, military personnel, self-employed citizens, students, or government delegates. Yet, some authors report that the Ethiopian Diaspora largely consists of refugees that have been dispersed due to politics in the homeland.[69] More so, Ethiopia currently has over 55 embassies and consulate offices overseas.[70] This indicates that a considerable number of Ethiopians also live abroad whilst assuming different kinds of government responsibilities. On top of all, migration from Ethiopia still continued with large number involving both skilled and unskilled labourers.[71]

The Ethiopian Diaspora is known as largely educated.[72] For instance, the Diaspora in USA, which covers the largest percent of the total Ethiopian Diaspora population abroad, is reported to have similar educational attainment

66 International Organization on Migration (IOM) Special Liaison Office in Addis Ababa, Ethiopia, '50 years of Continental Continuity' (2007) 4(2) The Migrant Newsletter <https://ethiopia.iom.int/volume-4-issue-2> accessed on 1 January 2018.

67 Interview with Ephrem Beshah, Director General and Senior Expert, Diaspora Engagement Directorate (Addis Ababa, 18 August 2017). There has never been an attempt by the Ethiopian government to officially count its Diaspora community.

68 Interview with Daniel Abebe, Public Relations Officer, Ethiopian Diaspora Association (Addis Ababa, 20 August 2017).

69 Sarah Gebretsadik, 'Politics, Practices, And Potentials: Analyzing The Role of Diaspora-Owned Businesses in Ethiopia's Development' (Master Thesis, York University 2015) 62 <https://yorkspace.library.yorku.ca/xmlui/handle/10315/30714> accessed 1 January 2018.

70 Beshah (n 67).

71 See generally Maastricht University and Deutsche Gesellschaft für Internationale Zusammenarbeit (GIZ), 'Study on Migration Routes in the East and Horn of Africa' (2017) <https://www.merit.unu.edu/publications/uploads/1517475164.pdf> accessed 1 January 2018.

72 Yohannes Gebresellasie, 'Ethiopian Diasporas Vote for Your Country' *Aigaforum* (17 January 2018) <http://aigaforum.com/article2018/ethiopian-diasporas-vote-for-your-country.htm> accessed 3 May 2018.

as the population of the USA.[73] In the USA, Ethiopians work as advisors to the White House, legislative assistants, executives, professors, lawyers, entrepreneurs, as well as in the service sector, in research institutes, in the media, in the army, in the Air Force, etc.[74] The Ethiopian Diaspora in Europe, Australia, Botswana, Equatorial Guinea and partly South Africa is also largely believed to be well-educated. A large percent of the Ethiopian Diaspora population in the Netherlands, for instance, is reported to range from middle to highly educated; the few remaining ones have a lower level of education.[75] Yet, significant numbers of unskilled Ethiopian immigrant labourers are found in South Africa and Middle Eastern countries.

Apart from the formal education the Diaspora is likely to have received in the foreign state, the culture of democracy, good governance, and non-discrimination that such citizens have observed in their stay abroad is also considered to be important for their contribution to their country of origin. This specifically refers to those Diaspora communities who reside in countries with established democracies.

The Ethiopian Diaspora is very connected and keeps concerned about home matters.[76] With globalisation bringing affordable and prompt telecommunication technologies, social media and lower-cost travel, it also enabled Diaspora citizens to keep up to date and concerned about conditions at home. The Ethiopian Diaspora population owns several social, professional, cultural and religious associations where they meet regularly, exchange information about matters related to home and practice the Ethiopian culture.[77] The Diaspora also owns various media outlets through which it can keep informed and can debate about home issues in a familiar language. The limited access to information and publicly-controlled media back home, on the other hand, made

73 Migration Policy Institute (MPI), 'The Ethiopian Diaspora in the United States' (Rockefeller Foundation-Aspen Institute Diaspora Program, 2014) <https://www.migrationpolicy.org/sites/default/files/publications/RAD-Ethiopia.pdf> accessed 30 April 2018.

74 Yilma Adamu, 'Prime Minster Abiy's Diaspora Visit' (Ethiopian Media Forum, 2018) <http://ethioforum.org/prime-minster-abiys-diaspora-visit/> accessed 2 May 2018.

75 While 17 percent of them are defined as having a high level of education, 61 percent received middle level and the rest 22 percent received lower level education. See Anthony Otieno Ong'ayo, 'Diaspora Engagement in a Constricted Political Space, the Case of Ethiopian Diaspora Organization in the Netherlands' (2014) European Centre for Development and Policy Management, Discussion Paper 168, 11. <https://ecdpm.org/publications/diaspora-engagement-constricted-political-space/> accessed on 1 May 2018.

76 Jennifer M Brinkerhoff, *Institutional Reform and Diaspora Entrepreneurs: The In-Between Advantage* (Oxford University Press 2016) 139.

77 Terrence Lyons, 'Conflict-generated Diasporas and Transnational Politics in Ethiopia' (2007) 7(4) Conflict, Security & Development 529, 536.

the Diaspora media accepted by the majority of the Diaspora population and citizens in Ethiopia.

The Ethiopian Diaspora located particularly in North America and Europe is noted to be highly politicised.[78] However, the Diaspora is highly divided on the basis of ethnicity and political outlooks and is only unified when it comes to its solidarity in the struggle against the government back home. The division among Diaspora citizens goes so far that it manifests itself in social and cultural events, as well as in places of worship. However, in the struggle to bring change in home politics, a growing sense of camaraderie developed over the past few years among the Oromo and Amhara Diaspora nationalists,[79] who are the most vocal about home politics. The solidarity between these two Diaspora groups was also reflected in the unrest in the Amhara and Oromiya regions in the past few years. The demonstrators in Gondar in 2016, for instance, supported the questions raised by protestors in the Oromiya Region.[80]

3.2 *The Ethiopian Diaspora and Its Economic, Social and Political Involvement in Ethiopia*

3.2.1 Economic and Social Contribution

Undoubtedly, the Ethiopian Diaspora is one of the major contributors to Ethiopia's economy. It contributes to it in many ways, such as through sending remittances, transferring knowledge and technology, sending social capital, making physical investments, and creating job opportunities at home. In fact, remittance is one of the greatest contributions the Diaspora community makes to the Ethiopian economy. In the last decade, the rise in the number of migrations from Ethiopia and the measures taken by the government to increase remittance inflow, albeit limited, indeed resulted in a boost in remittance inflow to Ethiopia. In those years, Ethiopia was marked among the top ten Sub-Saharan African countries to have received high amounts of remittances.[81]

78 Haftu Gebrezgabiher, 'The Ethiopian Diaspora among the most Polarized' *Horn Affairs* (10 November 2016) <https://hornaffairs.com/2016/11/10/ethiopia-diaspora-polarization/> accessed on 3 May 2018. See also Tedla D Tekle, 'The Ethiopian Diaspora, Liberation Movements, Conflict and my Zelalem' *Ethio-Explorer* (22 July 2015) <https://debirhan.com/2015/07/the-ethiopian-diaspora-liberation-movements> accessed 30 April 2018.

79 Jill Craig, 'Ethiopia Protests Highlight Growing Solidarity between Oromia, Amhara Regions' *Voice of America* (9 August 2016) <http://www.voanews.com/a/ethiopia-protests-oromia-amhara-regions/3457240.html> accessed 1 May 2018.

80 Daniel Berhane, 'Ethiopia: Massive Protest Held in Gondar City' *Horn Affairs* (31 July 2016) <http://hornaffairs.com/2016/07/31/ethiopia-massive-protest-gondar/> accessed on 3 May 2018.

81 Christopher Gaukler, 'Improving Quality and Quantity of Formal Remittance Flows in Ethiopia' (ACP-EU Migration Action, Baseline Assessment Study, 2016) 9 <https://

Remittances to Ethiopia have risen to US$ 4 billion in 2016 from US$ 3.7 billion in 2015 and from a mere US$ 1.5 billion in 2014.[82] The remittance from the Diaspora in North America always constitutes the largest share of the total remittance sent to Ethiopia. For instance, in 2015, 44 percent of the US$ 3.7 billion remittance sent to Ethiopia was received from the Diaspora communities living in North America.[83] Diaspora remittance contributes a large share to the country's gross domestic product (GDP) and surpasses both Ethiopian export earnings and money from development aid.[84] For instance, in 2016, the US$ 4 billion remittance amounted to 5.3 percent of the country's GDP.

Despite an increase in the inflow of remittances, there is consensus that Ethiopia has not yet been able to tap into the full remittance potential of the Diaspora. The remittance inflow to Ethiopia is reported to have only been one-sixth of the full potential.[85] In Ethiopia, formal remittance channels are reportedly under-utilised. Evidence also shows that an enormous amount of remittance is transferred through informal channels.[86] The limited influx of remittance can be put down to several different reasons. While according to the Ethiopian Ministry of Foreign Affairs this occurrence is due to illiteracy and lack of access to banks primarily, others also mention the political discontent of the Diaspora towards the government. Obviously, this relates to the situation in Ethiopia before the current reform.[87] For instance, during the recent unrest, an international movement among the Diaspora was called for a boycott of remittance to Ethiopia with the goal of weakening the government

acpeumigrationaction.iom.int/sites/default/files/docs/BAReports/eth_ba_report_20_april.pdf> accessed on 1 January 2018.

82 Tesfa-Alem Tekle, 'Ethiopia's Earnings from Remittances on the Rise' *Sudan Tribune* (25 July 2016) <http://www.sudantribune.com/spip.php?article59720> accessed 3 December 2018. See also Kevin Mwanza, 'Ethiopia's Diaspora Remittance Rise, Illegal Immigrants Holding it Back' *Moguldom* (25 July 2016) <https://moguldom.com/130201/130201/> accessed 3 December 2018.

83 'Remittances to Ethiopia in 2015 top $3b' *Mereja* (26 July 2015) <https://mereja.com/news/1045767> accessed on 3 May 2018.

84 Ethiopian Broadcasting Corporation (EBC) (2016).

85 B Nega and others 'Using Resources from Migrants for Development in Ethiopia' (Ethiopian Economic Association – Ethiopian Economic Policy Research Institute, Report prepared for the International Organization for Migration, 2004).

86 Alemayhu Geda and Jacqueline Irving, 'Ethiopia' in Sanket Mohapatra and Dilip Ratha (eds), *Remittance Markets in Africa* (The World Bank 2011) 118.

87 Ethiopian Ministry of Foreign Affairs, 'Baseline Assessment Summary – Improving Quality and Quantity of Formal Remittance Flows in Ethiopia' (Addis Ababa, 2016) 3 <https://acpeumigrationaction.iom.int/sites/default/files/docs/BAReports/eth_ba_report_20_april.pdf> accessed 3 May 2018.

politically.[88] Consequently, the formal remittance inflow has shown a significant reduction. In the past few years (during the unrest), Ethiopia consecutively lost remittance inflows amounting to US$ 765 million, US$ 1402 million and US$ 1681 million in 2015, 2016 and 2017, respectively.[89] Ethiopia has also been in critical shortage of foreign currency.[90]

In terms of making direct investments at home, it is reported that approximately 10 percent of domestic investment in the last decade has been from the Diaspora members and 90 percent of this investment is located in Addis Ababa.[91] Yet, if seen in terms of numbers, only 3000 to 4000 Diaspora members are actually involved in investments at home.[92] The number is significantly low given the estimated total number of the Ethiopian Diaspora population overseas.

3.2.2 Role and Influence on Ethiopian Politics Back Home

Diaspora actors have been involved in Ethiopian politics for the past 50 years, from those that helped the toppling of the *Derg* to current ones who have undertaken all possible efforts to bring about the current political reform within the ruling party. The Diaspora actively supported the rebel groups back home in the demise of the military junta (*Derg*).[93] Their involvement has had a significant impact on the nation, and it will continue to do so in the future. Following the toppling of the *Derg*, the Diaspora was also involved in the formation of the new state in every possible way, although they were not successful

88 The Seventeen Civic and Political Organizations, in a press release, have urged Ethiopians to halt sending money for three months. They have also called for a reduction by one third for six months after the end of the three-month halt. See ESAT News, 'Ethiopia: Groups call halt on remittance to punish regime' *ESAT News* (27 December 2016) <https://ethsat.com/2016/12/ethiopia-groups-call-halt-remittance-punish-regime> accessed 30 April 2018. Also ESAT News, Ethiopia: Worldwide task force calls for remittance embargo' *ESAT News* (2 January 2018) <https://ethsat.com/2018/01/ethiopia-worldwide-task-force-calls-remittance-embargo/> accessed 1 May 2018.

89 Ayele Gelan, 'Ethiopia: How Can the Country Boost Remittance Inflows?' *All Africa* (24 July 2018) <https://allafrica.com/stories/201807250451.html> accessed 14 December 2018.

90 Ibid.

91 E Chacko and P Gebre, 'Diaspora Investments, Motivations, and Challenges: The Case of Ethiopia' (International Conference on Diaspora and Development, The World Bank, 2009).

92 Gebretsadik (n 69) 59.

93 The Tigray People's Liberation front (TPLF) in particular had a strong backing from the Diaspora in the armed struggle with *Derg*. Dereje Feyissa, 'The Peace Building Dimension of the Rights of Movements of the Ethiopian Muslim Diaspora' (2011) DISPACEA Working Paper 4, 9 <http://www.diaspeace.org/> accessed on 1 May 2018.

in creating the new state they imagined.[94] The Diaspora has shown optimism that the new state would be the beginning of a new democratic and prosperous Ethiopia. However, for many and particularly for those who were active in Ethiopian politics, the creation of the new state was far from their hopes and imagination. While some were against the creation of the new state on the basis of ethnicity, others raise questions on the genuine implementation of ethnic rights.[95] As a result, the Diaspora has continued its involvement and remained concerned about politics in Ethiopia, also it comes to the new state.

The Diaspora participates in Ethiopian politics in a variety of ways. It sponsors political parties in Ethiopia both financially and ideologically. Ethiopian political leaders, including those in the government as well as those in the opposition, regularly send delegations to brief their respective communities in North America to solicit political and financial support. The Diaspora in return mobilises support, raises money, publishes newspapers and internet sites, and lobbies on behalf of their organisations.[96] The Diaspora's support to the opposition political parties during the 2005 election was particularly significant.[97] Following the 2005 election, the Diaspora came up with multiple different strategies that went beyond supporting opposition political parties back home. The strategies were focused on creating pressure and on weakening the political base of the government in office. The Diaspora used various techniques, such as lobbying politicians and policy makers in the West to put international pressure on the government, lobbying foreign governments and international organisations to squeeze loans and aid to the government, as well as organising demonstrations condemning the government's alleged violation of human rights while at the same time calling for democracy, rule of law and regime change in Ethiopia. They even tore, burnt and disrespected the current flag, and instead used the tricolour flag without the emblem as a way of opposing politics back home.[98] The Oromo Diaspora, on the other hand, often used what is known as the Oromo Liberation Front (OLF) flag.[99] Humiliating high-ranking government officials, including the late Prime Minister Meles Zenawi as he went out for a government mission in a foreign state, as well disrespecting

94 The creation of the new state based on ethnicity was one of the points the Ethiopian Diaspora seriously opposed to and which made them remain concerned about the politics at home.

95 Feyissa (n 93).

96 Lyons (n 77).

97 Ibid 597.

98 See generally Goshu Wolde Tefera and A Peter Castro, 'Flag Politics in Ethiopia and the Ethio-American Diaspora' (2016) 8(1) Journal of International and Global Studies.

99 Ibid.

Ethiopian embassies overseas were also among the techniques used by the Diaspora community to create pressure on the government.[100]

In the past few years, the Diaspora also influenced politics at home through channelling political information and shaping the political debate using social media and satellite television. This was particularly evident in the recent social unrest. The Diaspora played a critical role in raising awareness about atrocities taking place in Ethiopia, provoking local residents to protest against the government. The limited freedom of speech, limited access to public information, and low level of credibility of the local media outlets in turn made information channelled and debated by the Diaspora easily entrenched in the general public political discourse in Ethiopia. As a result, the government was pressured to give counter-responses to and take measures against the information channelled and debates framed by the Diaspora. The role and influence of the Diaspora in framing the political debates following the *Irreecha* incidents can be cited as a case in point. During the event, a helicopter was flying above the crowd dropping leaflets wishing them a happy festival. Soon after the accident, the Diaspora media started to frame the accident as a deliberate action of the police firing over the panicking crowd.[101] The Diaspora then called for a five-day protest aiming to take destructive measures on investments made in the Oromiya region, which were allegedly owned by government-affiliated persons and foreign nationals' investments partnered with government persons. Accordingly, a significant number of investments across the Oromiya region was destroyed within the week following the protest. In the aftermath of the destruction, the government declared a six-month state of emergency blocking social media, among others, intending to limit the Diaspora influence.[102]

100 For example, the BBC reported on 8 September 2016 that Diaspora activists entered Ethiopia's British Embassy in London to demonstrate on behalf of their fellow citizens in the Oromia and Amhara regions of Ethiopia, and they replaced the current national flag with the tri-colour flag. The same also happened on the Ethiopian Embassy in Sweden. The Ethiopian Embassy in Washington DC also faced similar attacks several times from the diaspora community living in the USA. Dickens Olewe and Damian Zane, 'Anti-government protesters get into Ethiopian embassies' *BBC News* (8 September 2016) <https://www.bbc.com/news/live/world-africa-37294661?ns_mchannel=social&ns_source=twitter&ns_campaign=bbc_live&ns_linkname=57d177fbe4b0270fef35207c%26Ethiopia%20protesters%20get%20into%20London%20embassy%26&ns_fee=0#post_57d177fbe4b0270fef35207c> accessed 3 May 2018.

101 James Jeffrey, 'Ethiopia: From Washington, Influencing Ethiopia's Politics' *All African* (10 December 2016) <http://allafrica.com/stories/201612120257.html> accessed 1 May 2018.

102 Al Jazeera News, 'Ethiopia declares state of emergency over protests' *Al Jazeera News* (10 October 2016) <http://www.aljazeera.com/news/2016/10/ethiopia-declares-state-emergency-protests-161009110506730.html> accessed on 1 May 2018.

The Diaspora also played a similar role in the Addis Ababa Master Plan Expansion Project of the city government, framing the issue as land-grabbing and thereby aiming to make the Oromo people landless. The same was also true for the unrest that occurred in parts of the Amhara Region in the past few years. The Amhara Diaspora nationalists created a wave of Amhara consciousness among Amhara peoples residing in and outside the country. The influence of social media was abounding with a number of Diaspora bloggers channelling political information, focusing particularly on atrocities faced by the Amharas.

Terrence Lyons argues that conflict-generated Diasporas are often key actors in homeland conflicts by financing parties involved in civil war and framing conflict issues. Involvement by conflict-generated Diasporas on home matters, she argues, may contribute either to increased polarisation or to new opportunities for peace. Lyons categorises segments of the Ethiopian Diaspora as conflict-generated Diasporas, which play a key role in homeland conflicts both by providing financial support and by framing the conflicts through their control over media outlets and other institutions.[103] As the Diaspora is very connected with its homeland, it has an opportunity to frame conflicts and to sponsor the most militant, uncompromising leaders back home.[104] Lyons concludes that the Ethiopian Diaspora has the capacity to make conflict resolution more difficult and the conflicts more protracted.[105] This assertion seems credible when looking at the role the Diaspora had taken in the recent unrest in Oromiya and parts of the Amhara Region. This unrest was allegedly framed, catalysed and actualised by the Diaspora communities in Europe, North America, Australia and other parts of the world. In this particular case, the government had also seen and felt the influence of the Diaspora on home politics.[106] Previously, the Ethiopian government did not generally consider the political involvement of the Diaspora as genuine.[107] The government was often heard calling the Diaspora 'remnants of the old regime', who are enunciating to bring the old regime back to Ethiopia. It also allegedly called these groups 'instruments of foreign groups', who enforce foreign agendas in Ethiopia.[108]

Besides, the Ethiopian People's Revolutionary Democratic Front (EPRDF) led government used to consider the political polarisation in the diaspora as

103 Lyons (n 77).
104 Ibid.
105 Ibid.
106 Jeffrey (n 101).
107 Feyissa (n 93) 6.
108 They use terms such as 'Puppets of Imperialism', *'ye-qedmo-serAt nafaqiwoch'*, 'Hamburger dudes', 'cabby boys' etc. to refer to the Diaspora abroad. See Adamu (n 74).

anchored by the 'Vocal Diaspora', consisting of extreme minorities.[109] It also labelled the rest a 'silent majority' and the 'devoted-few' (government supporters), who both participate actively in the development of the country.[110] Such perception of the government, however, seems to have significantly changed with the appointment of the new Prime Minster. The newly-appointed Prime Minster – Abiy Ahmed – has come up with a different and sensible understanding and position regarding the role, interest and potential of the Diaspora socially, economically and politically. In his address to the Parliament during his appointment, the Prime Mister boldly described the Diaspora as part of the Ethiopian political community despite their residence overseas. He has also confirmed the Diaspora's potential to the economy, to democracy and to good governance in Ethiopia. A few months after his appointment, he travelled to the USA and Europe to meet and discuss with the Diaspora. While this is a leap forward, such goodwill on the part of the government needs to be institutionalised so that it can show continuity.

3.2.3 Diaspora Engagement Efforts in Ethiopia

Ethiopia generally has a young history of Diaspora engagement efforts. The EPRDF government was initially suspicious and, in some cases, also exclusionary when it comes to the participation of the Diaspora on home matters. The government's exclusion of some of the Diaspora-based political parties in the formation of the new state during the transitional period was a case in point.[111] This resulted in a rough relationship between the government and the Diaspora for quite some time. Consequently, the positive contribution of the Diaspora to their country during the war with Eritrea is believed to have motivated the EPRDF-led government to make some Diaspora engagement efforts.[112] In 2002, immediately after the end of the war, the government established an Expatriate Office within the Ministry of Foreign Affairs (MFA) to liaison with the Diaspora.[113] Since then, the government has taken some consecutive measures including scaling up the former Expatriate Office to the Diaspora Engagement General Directorate Office. Diaspora affairs were also mainstreamed in the relevant federal and regional government offices. Laws and directives aiming at easing home bureaucracies in order to encourage the Diaspora to increase its remittance and to invest back home were also issued. As a way of encouraging the

109 Beshah (n 67).
110 Ibid.
111 Feyissa (n 93) 5.
112 Beshah (n 67).
113 Feyissa (n 93) 6.

contribution of foreign nationals of Ethiopian origin in the development and economic growth of Ethiopia, the government also issued a proclamation granting them certain rights and privileges in Ethiopia.[114] In 2013, for the first time in the Ethiopian history, a Diaspora Policy was adopted to ensure that the knowledge, skills, and financial resources of Ethiopians in the Diaspora contribute to development, economic growth, poverty reduction, good governance and democracy in Ethiopia. However, in terms of engaging the Diaspora politically, except for the mere expression of interest under the Diaspora Policy,[115] practical measures to formally engage them in the home politics have not been taken until now.

Those Ethiopian Diaspora engagement initiatives that were taken in the last two decades are generally criticised for only addressing a small number of Diasporas, thereby excluding large segments of the Diaspora population.[116] The government has not been successful in mobilising all groups of the Diaspora to contribute to their country to the fullest of their potential. This is partly because the government engagement effort has been focused more on ensuring Diaspora economic participation, while neglecting their concerns over local politics and governance. The Charities and Societies Law issued in the aftermath of the 2005 election, as well as the Anti-Terrorism Law have also been barriers to Diaspora engagement in Ethiopia.[117] Resulting from the current political reform within the EPRDF, these two laws are being revised. It is generally hoped that the revision of the two laws will allow the Diaspora community to participate in home politics in a variety of ways.

Following the recent political reform within the governing party, there is generally a good reception of the Diaspora as being part of the Ethiopian political community, whose voice and opinion matters. Different vocal Diaspora political activities have been welcomed to the country. The Parliament has also removed the names of different Diaspora individuals and organisations from the country's list of 'terrorists'.[118] Prominent Diaspora media outlets such as

114 See Federal Negarit Gazeta, 'Proclamation to provide Foreign Nationals of Ethiopian Origin with Certain Rights to be Exercised in their "Country of Origin"' Proclamation No. 270/2002.

115 Ethiopian Ministry of Foreign Affairs (n 8) 15.

116 European Centre for Development and Policy Management, 'Diaspora Engagement in a Constricted Political Space, the Case of Ethiopian Diaspora Organization in the Netherlands' (2014) Discussion Paper 168, 31–32.

117 Feyissa (n 93) 7.

118 AFP, 'Ethiopia lifts "terrorist" designation on three groups' *News 24* (5 July 2018) <https://www.news24.com/Africa/News/ethiopia-lifts-terrorist-designation-on-three-groups-20180705> accessed 31 December 2018.

the Ethiopian Satellite Television and Radio (ESAT) and Oromia Media Network (OMN), which were very active in mobilising the current change, are now allowed to run from Ethiopia. For the first time ever, the Diaspora itself is seen as being optimistic and supportive of the government and politics at home. It is however crucial that this smooth relationship is institutionalised through law so that it will have continuity and bear fruit.

3.3 *Voting Rights of Diaspora Citizens in Ethiopia: Investigation of Laws and Policies*

The Ethiopian Constitution grants political rights in general and voting rights in particular based on citizenship. Article 38(1) of the FDRE Constitution reads:

> Every Ethiopian national, without any discrimination based on colour, race, nation, nationality, sex, language, religion, political or other opinion or other status, has the following rights: (a) To take part in the conduct of public affairs, directly and through freely chosen representatives; (b) On the attainment of 18 years of age, to vote in accordance with law; (c) To vote and to be elected at periodic elections to any office at any level of government; elections shall be by universal and equal suffrage and shall be held by secret ballot, guaranteeing the free expression of the will of the electors.[119]

The new Law proc No. 1162/2019, like its predecessors, stipulates the requirements to vote, which includes: '(A) any person who is an Ethiopian; (b) 18 years old and above at the time of the registration; (c) *has been residing within the constituency for at least 6 months may be registered as an elector*'.[120]

Thus, the requirement of residency automatically excludes Ethiopian citizens abroad from participating in elections in Ethiopia. In this regard, the ability of the Diaspora citizens to vote in elections in Ethiopia is thus dependent on the political will and commitment of the government to take the lead. The government needs to be willing to initiate the lift of the requirement of residency, to ensure that Ethiopians abroad will be able to vote in Ethiopia. To this end, the Ethiopian government under the Diaspora Policy in Section 5.6. promised to engage the Diasporas in good governance and democracy. The Policy specifically stipulated that citizens who are resident abroad will be enabled to

119 Federal Negarit Gazeta, 'The Constitution of the Federal Democratic Republic of Ethiopia' Proclamation No. 1/1995, art 38(1).

120 Federal Negarit Gazeta, 'The Ethiopian Electroal, Political Parties Registration and Election's Code of Conduct Proclamation No. 1162/2019, art. 18(1).

participate in national elections.[121] The Policy also stipulated that Ethiopian nationals living in Ethiopia while simultaneously having a permanent resident permit in another country will be able to vote in elections in Ethiopia.[122] Despite expressing its willingness in the Policy, the government did not take further measures to let the Diaspora participate in elections in Ethiopia until now. The Policy is a document of aspirations and hence neither grants a right nor imposes an obligation. The enforcement of the aspiration outlined in the Policy requires a law that translates the aspiration in to a legally binding right. More so, the requirement of residency has not been adjusted to include an exception, which allows non-resident citizens to vote. Yet, the government still claims to have an interest in implementing external voting.[123]

The Diaspora, on the other hand, apart from its interest and active involvement in home politics, has never asked for a right to vote.[124] External voting has never been an agenda in the political demands of the Diaspora. However, the Ethiopian Diaspora Association in Addis Ababa confirmed to the author that the Diaspora would be happy if the government allowed it to vote.[125] The Association described to the author that the Diaspora community needs representation in Ethiopia.[126] According to the Association, the Diaspora needs to be represented both in the Executive and in the House of Peoples' Representatives.[127]

Ethiopia is not a member to the international Convention on the Rights of Migrant Workers and their Families (ICRMW),[128] where political rights of emigrant workers and their families in their country are duly recognised. Ethiopia's non-ratification of this convention is a paradox, given Ethiopia is one of the major sending states. The ratification of the Convention would give these groups of Ethiopian emigrants a right to claim for voting rights. The ratification of the Convention would also put the government under international pressure to provide the rights contained to its emigrant citizens.

121 Ethiopian Ministry of Foreign Affairs (n 8).
122 Ibid.
123 Beshah (n 67).
124 Ibid.
125 Abebe (n 68).
126 Ibid.
127 Ibid.
128 International Labour Organisation (ILO), 'Trafficking in Persons overseas for Labour Purpose: the Case of Ethiopian Domestic Workers' (Addis Ababa, 2011) 75.

4 Conclusion

As discussed above, the Ethiopian Diaspora population possesses a huge economic and social potential to make a meaningful contribution to the social and economic development of the country. The Diaspora can contribute to the economic development of the country through sending remittances, making investments back home, lobbying to promote state interests abroad, or facilitating bilateral trading relationships. Acknowledging the potential of the Diaspora, the Ethiopian government has gradually taken steps towards various engagement measures. However, these engagement measures have not been able to fully tap into the potential of the Diaspora. This may be due to many reasons. First, the government's engagement endeavours have not been as comprehensive as they should be to ensure the participation of all types of citizens residing abroad. Second, the government's engagement measures have been focused on the economic contribution of the Diaspora, while neglecting their political interest and concerns about home politics. A Diaspora that has concerns about the politics at home cannot be fully engaged economically unless it is also engaged politically. Extending voting rights to citizens in the Diaspora is one way of engaging the Diaspora politically. This form of engagement is also crucial for Ethiopia in terms of promoting democracy, peace and stability. Depending on how well it is engaged, the Ethiopian Diaspora has the potential to promote democracy, good governance, national consensus, peace and stability in Ethiopia. A Diaspora that is properly engaged can contribute to unearthing atrocities committed by the government, human rights violations, and malpractices. It also contributes to raising civic and political consciousness of resident citizens to stand up for their rights and fight the undemocratic behaviour of the government. A disregarded Diaspora, however, has a potential to cause civil unrest and instability in the home country. The Diaspora's potential in causing unrest and ethnic conflicts can be critical in countries like Ethiopia, where ethnicity and ethnic narratives are abundant. The Diaspora is a powerful entity that has information, knowledge, money and media with a formidable potential to influence politics at home. The extension of voting right to the Diaspora citizens must also be considered as a matter of state obligation to enforce the constitutional rights of citizens.

Allowing citizens abroad to participate in national elections would create a feeling in the Diaspora that they are valuable parts of the political community and that they can make constant positive contributions to their country. On top of that, Diaspora participation in national elections would allow the Diaspora to express its concern and interest on governance at home in an organised and institutional manner. Their formal participation as voters would minimise their tendency to engage in activities that disrupt peace and security and that are against the national interest and good image of Ethiopia. Engaging the Diaspora politically is important to address political differences, ethnic polarisation and ethnic conflicts at home. The granting of voting rights to citizens abroad is also crucial in strengthening the legitimacy of the state and its democratic institutions.

To conclude, when states reach out to their Diasporas it can be seen as a unifying measure, which shows that those who live abroad are still valued and that the state would welcome an eventual return to the homeland. Voting has been proven to be effective in keeping the Diaspora communities' ties solid with their country of origin. The current unprecedented cooperation between the Diaspora and the government, which has taken place following the political reform in the ruling party, should be taken as an opportunity to establish a framework for institutionalised Diaspora engagement in Ethiopia.

If Ethiopia makes the decision to extend voting rights to its citizens overseas, it must then look at the specifics of how this practice will be managed. A decision about which citizens will receive voting rights in which elections and by what means must be made first. It is also important to hold public consultation processes and, most importantly, to engage with the Diaspora communities on the matter. Public expectations should be carefully managed, and the costs and consequences of external voting should be given full consideration. Given the large number of Ethiopian emigrant workers overseas, it is also important that Ethiopia becomes a party to the ICRMW.

The Right to Cross-Examination and Witness Protection in Ethiopia: A Comparative Study

Tadesse Melaku

Abstract

Cross-examination, particularly in the context of criminal proceedings, is guaranteed under international human rights law and the Ethiopian constitution. The opportunity to confront and examine one's accusers is key to ensuring the fairness of a court trial and, possibly, also the final decision by enabling the accused to challenge the authenticity and trustworthiness of the testimony against them. However, states are increasingly confronted with another pressing consideration – the safety of state witnesses – who could be subject to intimidation or even risk their lives for testifying in court. Now, witness safety is seen as an important public interest which warrants the restriction of the right to cross-examination of the suspect. Without such measures, witnesses could be unwilling to testify for fear of reprisal. As a result, many states, including Ethiopia, have introduced measures restricting the confrontation requirement through, among others, the suppression of witness identity. However, this has its own drawback from the perspective of the defendants, who find themselves unable to confront their accusers – should judicial bodies decide not to disclose the identity of state witnesses. A review of the academic literature and foreign case law reveals that when considering demands for anonymity, judges should exercise maximum caution to ensure that the human right of the suspect is not lightly lost. However, a recent constitutional ruling in Ethiopia in favour of suppressing the identity of a prosecution witness in a terrorism case failed to properly appreciate and balance the right of the accused person, causing serious doubt about the implementation of the fundamental human right to cross-examination in the country.

Keywords

Anti-Terrorism Proclamation – Right to Cross-Examination – Ethiopian Constitution – Fair Trial – Protection of Witnesses and Whistle-blowers

 | DOI:10.1163/9789004415966_005

1 Introduction

Cross-examination is viewed as key to a fair court trial and, possibly, also a just outcome. It provides an opportunity to challenge the trustworthiness of a witness and to expose lies and contradictions in witness' oral accounts. The demeanour of the witness, the manner of their testifying, the behaviour they manifest while testifying, and their physical and emotional reaction to cross-examination questions may hold the key to determining the authenticity of the testimony. Therefore, the significance of confrontation with the witness for the defence is beyond any doubt. In view of this, the International Covenant on Civil and Political Rights (ICCPR) and the Constitution of the Federal Democratic Republic of Ethiopia (FDRE) embody the cross-examination requirement.

However, guaranteeing the well-being of those who give evidence is essential to establishing that a criminal act is (and should be) an equally important public policy. If the witness refuses to come forward and give evidence for fear of revenge by the accused and their associates, that would have a chilling effect on the criminal justice system. Today, many states, including Ethiopia, have enacted laws providing for the protection of witnesses. Ethiopia's proclamations on witness protection and terrorism authorise the suppression of information about witness identity and the admissibility of hearsay and intelligence reports as evidence in court, thereby restricting the right to confront and examine one's accusers.

Organised into three sections, the article seeks to explore the tension and conflict between the right of the accused to challenge the testimony of state witnesses and the need to ensure the safety of witnesses. The first section provides a historical account of cross-examination and its restriction, focusing on its history in Europe and Ethiopia. The next section dwells on foreign laws and court decisions with a view to better understanding the concept and limitations necessitated by the well-being of witnesses. The final section examines relevant laws in Ethiopia on the subject. Apart from legal analysis and exposition, the article also seeks to examine the merits of a constitutional opinion by the Council of Constitutional Inquiry (CCI) in favour of withholding witness identity. This momentous decision offers an opportunity to explore an otherwise neglected area in Ethiopia. The ruling was made following a petition contesting the validity of the anti-terrorism and witness protection proclamations by *Mehadi Aley and others,* who had been put on trial for terrorism-related charges. At the heart of the case is the tension between the right of suspects to confront their accusers on the one hand, and the safety of crime witnesses on the other.

2 Why Cross-Examination?

Cross-examination is said to be 'basic to any civilized notion of a fair trial', 'of paramount importance to the rights of the defence and the fairness of the trial'[1] and 'the greatest legal engine ever invented for the discovery of truth'.[2] Cross-examination is one aspect of the right to fair and public trial guaranteed under international human rights law[3] as well as the Ethiopian Constitution.[4] Article 14(5) of the ICCPR, a part of Ethiopia's legal regime,[5] guarantees the right 'to examine, or have examined, the witnesses against him'.

In the case of *Mattox v United States*,[6] the Supreme Court of the United States outlined the reasons for face-to-face examination: to ensure that witnesses would testify under oath and understand the serious nature of the trial processes; to allow the accused to cross-examine witnesses who testify against them; and to assess the credibility of a witness by observing that witness' behaviour.[7] The appearance of the witness in the courtroom enables the judge and the accused to observe their reactions while being questioned and this may be crucial to assessing the credibility and trustworthiness of the evidence.[8]

Many of the fundamental human rights are limited to safeguarding other important interests, although the confrontation right has no restrictions under the Ethiopian Constitution. An absolute right is problematic, not least, in relation to the right to cross-examination in a criminal trial. In the words of Brems,

1 David Lusty, 'Anonymous Accusers: An Historical and Comparative Analysis of Secret Witnesses in Criminal Trial' (2002) 24 Sydney Law Review 361 <http://www.austlii.edu.au/au/journals/SydLawRw/2002/17.pdf > accessed 23 September 2017.

2 Ibid.

3 Universal Declaration of Human Rights (adopted 10 December 1948) UNGA Res 217 A(III) (UDHR), art 10; see also International Covenant on Civil and Political Rights (adopted 16 December 1966, entry into force 23 March 1976) 999 UNTS 171 (ICCPR), art 14(5).

4 Federal Negarit Gazeta, 'The Constitution of the Federal Democratic Republic of Ethiopia' Proclamation No. 1/1995, art 20(4).

5 Ibid art 9(4).

6 *Mattox v United States*, 156 U.S. 237 (1895) <https://supreme.justia.com/cases/federal/us/156/237/> accessed 23 September 2017.

7 Australian Government – Australian Law Reform Commission, 'Traditional Rights and Freedoms – Encroachments by Commonwealth Laws – 10. Right to Confront Witnesses and Test Evidence' (ALRC Interim Report 127) <https://www.alrc.gov.au/publications/right-confront-witnesses-and-test-evidence> accessed 12 September 2017.

8 Ibid.

'The priority of human rights that holds in principle does not hold in every concrete case'.[9]

Daniel Betancourt observes:

> To resolve whether anonymity should be allowed or not, first, we have to consider that law is not an exact science. In law, there are general rules, but always there are some exceptions. It is not possible to have only one formula and give the same interpretation to every case. For that reason, justice needs to adapt and courts should interpret the legal bodies according to the specific case. Every rule has exceptions [sic], and without doubt anonymity as well.[10]

As the review of foreign case law indicates, witness safety is considered a reason that warrants a restriction on the confrontation clause, without which obtaining testimonial evidence would be a daunting task. Lack of protection to the safety of the witness, their family or property could render the criminal justice system impotent.[11] That is why states are taking steps, particularly so in the face of rising organised crimes and terror. In Britain, for example, many witnesses experienced one of 'the gravest'[12] intimidations in relation to the conflict in Northern Ireland in the early 1970s. Thus, Lusty observes:

> The main obstacle to dealing effectively with terrorist crime in the regular courts of justice is intimidation by terrorist organizations of those persons who would be able to give evidence for the prosecution if they dared… The fear of revenge upon 'informers' is omnipresent… It extends to all classes of society. It is not an idle or irrational fear. It is justified in fact by many well-authenticated instances of intimidation, and not least, by the example, familiar to all other potential witnesses, of a witness who

9 Eva Brems, 'Conflicting Human Rights: An Exploration in the Context of the Right to a Fair Trial in the European Convention for the Protection of Human Rights and Fundamental Freedoms' (2005) 27(1) Human Rights Quarterly 294.

10 Daniel Soto Betancourt, 'Anonymity as Protective Measure for Victims and Witnesses vs The Rights of Accused' (Master Thesis, Tilburg University, 2010) 47–48 <http://arno.uvt.nl/show.cgi?fid=120647> accessed 23 September 2017.

11 See Harris as quoted in Nicholas Fyfe and Heather McKay, 'Desperately Seeking Safety: Witnesses' Experiences of Intimidation, Protection and Relocation' (2000) 40(4) The British Journal of Criminology 675.

12 Lusty (n 1) 385.

was shot dead in his home in front of his infant child the day before he was due to give evidence on the prosecution of terrorists.[13]

3 Cross-Examination and Witness Anonymity in the Past

This section examines the development and evolution of cross-examination, as well as its consequences and anonymity in the European and Ethiopian traditions. Although anonymity has existed in both Europe and Ethiopia, there are differences in the way it was enforced. In the former, suppression of witness' identity was practiced in exceptional circumstances, while Ethiopia's tradition is characterised by an open and confrontational litigation between the accuser and the accused. Testimonial statements were given in secret, at least with regard to *afersata*, as will be shown below.

3.1 *The European Historical Account*

The practice of face-to-face confrontation in a court trial goes back to ancient times. An early illustration of this right is provided in the biblical account of the trial of Paul (c.60 AD), who was accused of sedition as 'a ringleader of the sect of the Nazarenes'. Roman Governor of Judea, Festus, refused requests for the summary execution of Paul, declaring 'It is not the manner of the Romans to deliver any man up to die before the accused has met his accusers face to face, and has been given a chance to defend himself against the charges'.[14]

However, the cross-examination faced a set-back during the Middle Ages after the administration of justice was criticised for being too lenient towards the accused. Then, the Catholic Church and European states introduced stringent procedures in the name of protecting public interest.[15] A system of inquisitional investigation and prosecution was introduced as a result of which any person could be charged based on vague and unfounded allegations.[16] Governments legalised torture as a lawful crime investigation technique. The Church, on its part, employed inquisition to investigate offenses involving heresy and, with respect to this offense, it too used torture and capital punishment.

Restrictions on defence witnesses were strictly applied, but such restrictions did not apply to state witnesses, hence the double standard nature of the trial. As Lusty notes, 'all statements adverse to the accused [were] freely

13 Ibid.
14 Ibid 363.
15 Ibid.
16 Ibid.

received, whether based on knowledge or prejudice, hearsay evidence, vague rumors, general impressions, or idle gossip'. This approach was justified as proper in dealing with the then-pressing issue of heresy in view of 'the high risk of reprisals against those who testified against their neighbors'.[17] The English philosopher Bentham criticised the inquisition as a system whereby evidence was taken under a 'veil of secrecy' and the door was left 'wide open to mendacity, falsehood, and partiality'.[18]

Even then, witness anonymity was considered an exception that applied only when a demonstrated risk to a witness existed and the matter was to be determined on a case-by-case basis.[19] In other words, withholding names and identities of witnesses was not a matter of principle but of exception. Ultimately, the inquisition was abolished in 1834 and the period of its application is described 'as among the darkest blots on the record of mankind'.[20] It is also viewed as an instrument of revenge for political and personal reasons that paved the way for 'perjury and malicious testimony'.[21]

By the beginning of the 20th century, face-to-face examination was considered a valuable means to check the truthfulness of testimonies. In the end, the adversarial system emerged as a mechanism to counter-balance the weight of the testimony of the accuser and to ensure the equality of arms in the legal battle.[22] At any rate, the recent revival of witness protection measures in many countries is not without a historical precedent. Europe used it and so did Ethiopia, as will be outlined below.

3.2 *The Ethiopian Historical Account*

Ethiopia is a big country with over eighty ethno-linguistic communities and an extensive history. Any attempt to cover the entire country and its long tradition would be a formidable exercise in the face of time and space constraints, not to mention the lack of written materials about the experience in many parts of Ethiopia. In view of this, this chapter considers the highland, mainly Christian part of the country for purpose of analysis.

Although customary law holds a marginal place in the modern state law of Ethiopia, it is still the predominant mode of conflict resolution outside the

17 Ibid 366.

18 Australian Government (n 7).

19 Lusty (n 1) 368.

20 Ibid.

21 Ibid 369.

22 Fern Nesson and Charles Nesson, 'Confrontation: Getting It Right' *The Harvard Law Record* (9 September 2015) <http://hlrecord.org/2015/09/confrontation-getting-it-right/> accessed 23 September 2017.

state apparatus, including in criminal matters. Stanley Fisher notes that the multitude of ethnic communities have their own dispute settlement procedures operating parallel to the state structure.[23] The FDRE Constitution confines the power of customary courts to deciding personal and family matters and only with the consent of the disputing parties.[24] Nonetheless, customary courts are very active, especially in the countryside. Endalew Lijalem states:

> In many regions of Ethiopia, customary norms are more [sic] strong, relevant, and accessible than imposed and top-down legal norms. Moreover, experiences in different regions of Ethiopia show that people, even after passing through the procedures and penalties in the formal criminal court, tend to use customary dispute resolution mechanisms for reconciliation and in order to control acts of revenge.[25]

Here, two of the most widely used traditional modes of crime investigation and prosecution are considered: *afersata* and *leba shay*.

3.2.1 Afersata

Afersata (Afan Oromo) was likely the most common mode of crime investigation and prosecution used in the past. It is also known as *awuchachign* in (the former provinces of) Shewa and Wollo; and as *ewuse* in Gojam.[26] Concerning its operation, after community inquiry is initiated by the injured party and in the case of serious offences by local officials, the village leader or elder would call a meeting of the community for inquiry. At the gathering, every individual would, turn by turn, communicate the name of the person whom they suspected of committing the crime to the elder.[27] Fisher describes the procedure in detail:

---

23 Stanley Z Fisher, 'Traditional Criminal Procedure in Ethiopia' (1971) 19(4) The American Journal of Comparative Law 709, 716.

24 FDRE Constitution (n 4) art 34 (5).

25 Endalew Lijalem, 'Ethiopian Customary Dispute Resolution Mechanisms: Forms of Restorative Justice?' (ACCORD African Centre for the Constructive Resolution of Conflicts, 2014) <http://www.accord.org.za/ajcr-issues/%EF%BF%BCethiopian-customary-dispute-resolution-mechanisms/> accessed 20 September 2017.

26 Some Amharic words used by Fisher (himself not a native speaker of Amharic) with English vernacular are modified to make them consistent with the commonly-used approach. Thus, 'affersata' is written as *afersata*, 'auchachin', as *awuchachign* and 'iwus', as *ewus*. See Fisher (n 23) 716.

27 Aberra Jembere, *An Introduction to the Legal History of Ethiopia: 1434–1974* (Shama Books 2012) 239.

> The technique used was to summon all inhabitants of the neighborhood where the crime was committed, and to sequester them until they named the criminal. Failure to attend the *afersata* was sanctioned by an 'absence fine' and the assembly's failure to name the criminal resulted in communal liability to repair damage caused by the offense. The wish to avoid this liability, together with the serious hardship caused by sequestration of the whole community (it was reportedly decreed 'not a cow be milked nor a baby suckled' until the investigation was over), provided ample incentive to name the offender if that was possible.[28] The crowd of those shut-in will select seven or eight or nine 'mirtoch', or chosen ones, who will sit apart with the clerk. First, each of the chosen will take oath... Then ... each will swear saying 'what I saw and heard I will not hide'; 'even if he is my father I will tell ... if I spoke a lie, may God likewise extinguish me!' and sweeping the ground with the stalk of maize and its cob he swears, 'May God thus sweep away our seed if I lie'. Also, there may be closed eggs, a closed gourd, and a sickle, on which each will swear, saying, 'If I conceal what I have seen and heard, may He close me as this gourd and cut my stomach thus!' So, all present will take the oath. Also, there will be two or three 'birds' who swear that they will tell what they hear to none but the clerk. Or perhaps the chosen ones will pass from group to group questioning each person and will find someone who saw or heard. Then they will return to the clerk and say, 'we have heard the mouth of the bird tell that so-and-so was the thief'. It may be fifteen days before the thief is found and, when the birds have spoken, the priest will come bearing the Cross and Picture of Mary and will sit beside the chosen ones. Then one by one, they will all pass and strike the Cross and Picture and swear, 'May He perforate me as the Cross! May he obliterate me as the Gospel! I saw not!' But the 'bird' will swear, 'Having seen I spoke not with lies', having related all in secret to the chosen ones.

This was a collective community endeavour to find out a crime suspect and establish their guilt. During this cumbersome process, participants could not return to their homes or tend to their livestock and crops. Swearing in the name of God and Virgin Mary can be considered as having been a very powerful psychological force to persuade people to speak the truth. One should also

28 Fisher (n 23) 717.

note Ethiopians, at least in the past, had always been God-fearing people and had deep reverence to spiritual life.[29]

Based on the reliability of the sources, testimonies were divided into three groups: first, testimonies by eye-witnesses – those who saw the commission of the crime first-hand; second, testimonies by those who witnessed relevant facts and circumstances about the occurrence of a crime soon before or after its commission, and; third, testimonies by those who would testify based on hearsay.[30] The latter were called *wof* (literally, a bird). An appeal was possible against conviction passed based on the testimony of *birds* only. It is interesting that the identity of witnesses was not known to the accused or the public; the elder responsible to hear testimony was confined to keeping their names confidential. As a result, the suspect had no opportunity to confront their accusers.[31] In other words, the accused had no opportunity to question the witnesses against them. In this vein, traditionally, Ethiopia had allowed for anonymous testimony.

Afersata became unpopular because of the concurrent inconvenience it caused to people who had to endure being separated from family, cattle and farms for days, sometimes for weeks. The villagers had to also shoulder the burden of feeding local officials during the event. This had likely encouraged people to make false accusations or false confessions.[32] Witness anonymity sometimes led to false accusations. Thus, Fisher observes, 'some criminals and others reportedly took advantage of the anonymity of the "birds" to accuse innocent persons, perhaps personal enemies, who could never learn the identity of their accusers'.[33] Having regard to such incidents, Emperor Haile Selassie passed the Afersata Proclamation in 1933 to curb the unintended consequences of the institution.

3.2.2 Leba Shay

The *leba shay* institution was another widely used crime investigation technique among inhabitants of the highland areas (including present-day Eritrea) and among the Oromo.[34] The method was particularly applied to apprehend thieves and the fruit of their crimes. *Leba shay* operated as follows: A young

29 As Blaten Geta Mahteme-Selassie Wolde Meskel pointed out, Ethiopians attached great value to the virtues of justice, religion, patriotism and respect for social status. See Blaten Geta Mahteme-Selassie as quoted in Jembere (n 27) 238.

30 Fisher (n 23) 719.

31 Jembere (n 27) 239.

32 Fisher (n 23).

33 Ibid.

34 Ibid.

boy, before the age of puberty, was made to drink a beverage made of an intoxicating herb, presumably made of hashish 'mixed with other substances such as opium or stramonium'.[35] Then, the intoxicated boy was tied with a strip of cloth on his waist and the chief thief-seeker followed him, holding the other tip of the strip, until the boy was said to have identified the criminal. Both Fisher and Aberra Jembere give similar accounts on functioning of the *leba shay* institution. The following excerpt is from Aberra's book:

> ...in the house where he [the boy] collapsed he would again be made to drink the beverage so that he could identify the particular individual from among inhabitants of the house. The boy would push aside anyone he meets entering the house of the suspected culprit. Any person on whom he laid his hand would be taken as a suspect and brought before a court of law.[36]

According to some accounts, Emperor Minilik II intended to abolish the practice and, in an attempt to discredit it, he once falsely stated his ring had stolen, even though he was hiding it under his clothes. Nonetheless, the *leba shay* boy immediately discovered the hidden item without any difficulty. Consequently, the Emperor decided to maintain the institution. Supporters of the institution claimed that the mere threat of using it would convey a message to culprits to return the fruit of their crime and would also deter potential wrong-doers.

However, this practice was not without controversy. First, the boy's 'sniffing out' of the accused was considered conclusive evidence to prove guilt. Second, the role of thief-seeker involved a conflict of interest, in that payment for his service came from the fine imposed on the convicted person, thus acting as an incentive to secure false accusation.[37] Fisher elaborates: 'there are numerous reports of such abuses, extending even to accusations that the thief-seeker acted in cahoots with thieves, corruptly agreeing to provide 'protection' by seeing to it that innocent parties were always 'tagged' by the boy'. Having regard to this, the governments of the day took some reform measures to minimise abuses, such as capping the fee and punishing those who falsely accused innocent people.[38] Similarly to *afersata*, *leba shay* attracted many criticisms. Nonetheless, in the absence of trained professional detectives and prosecutors, it is likely to have served as a deterrence for potential offenders. Far from being

35 Ibid.
36 Jembere (n 27) 238.
37 Fisher (n 23).
38 Ibid.

scientific, both *afersata* and *leba shay* involved a great deal of superstitious and irrational approaches.

4 Cross-Examination and Anonymity at Present

This section discusses the practice of some jurisdictions, focusing on case laws in order to learn how foreign courts handle the conflict between witness protection measures and the face-to-face examination principle.

4.1 *Experiences from Other Jurisdictions*

To start with the United States (US), witness protection is not in principle available there, 'even in situations where the defendant or her associates threaten the physical safety of the witness.[39] The US Constitution's confrontation clause does not have any limitations.[40] The Constitution guarantees the right of the accused to be confronted with witnesses against them.[41] However, despite the absence of constitutionally defined restrictions on the right, judges have qualified it particularly in the aftermath of the women's rights movement, which led to the enactment of rape shielding laws. These laws give immunity to rape victims from being questioned about their prior sexual life during cross-examination, and courts have been consistent in upholding the validity of those laws.[42] Other protection devices include pre-trial detention of the accused and other safety programmes. In recent times, federal and state judges have increasingly granted requests for anonymity.[43] Anonymous informants are also allowed insofar as there is *other* evidence sufficient to prove the charge. For example, in *Romero v State,*[44] a US court held that confrontation can be restricted only to uphold 'an important public interest and when the reliability

39 Nora Demleitner, 'Witness Protection in Criminal Cases: Anonymity, Disguise or Other Options' (1998) 46 American Journal of Comparative Law Supplement 641.

40 The United States (US) and Ethiopia also share the notion of constitutional supremacy, which puts the instruments at the top of the legal hierarchy within the respective jurisdictions.

41 The Bill of Rights Amendment VI – Rights of Accused in Criminal Prosecutions (adopted 4 March 1789, entry into force 15 December 1791) United States of America Constitution <https://www.law.cornell.edu/wex/first_amendment> accessed 12 September 2017.

42 Demleitner (n 39) 641–645.

43 Ibid.

44 *Romero v State,* 493 S.W.2d 206 (1973) <https://www.courtlistener.com/opinion/2456036/romero-v-state/> accessed 14 September 2017.

of the testimony is otherwise assured'.[45] Here, the *important public interest* is the safety of a witness.[46]

In another case, the court of appeal came up with certain criteria to determine the admissibility of evidence given in a disguise, wearing artificial moustache and wig. The court reasoned:

> Applying that rule here, the CI's [confidential informant] disguise in the form of a wig and mustache was necessary to further an important state interest, namely a witness's safety. The government offered reasons for protecting the CI's identity, given his continuing involvement in Sinaloa Cartel drug investigations as an undercover agent. Second, the reliability of the CI's testimony was otherwise assured, because (1) he was physically present in the courtroom, (2) he testified under oath, thus impressing him with the seriousness of the matter and the possibility of penalty for perjury, (3) he was subject to cross-examination while Appellant could see him, (4) despite his disguise, the jury was able to hear his voice, see his entire face including his eyes and facial reactions to questions, and observe his body language. These are all key elements of one's demeanour that shed light on credibility. Thus, we hold that in this case, the disguise in the form of a wig and mustache did not violate the Confrontation Clause.[47]

In *Smith* v *Illinois*,[48] a key prosecution witness testified under a false name. The witness was cross-examined in his testimony, but the trial judge prevented the defence from ascertaining his true name and address. The Supreme Court reversed the conviction by a majority, stating:

---

45 *Romero v State* (ibid) as discussed in 'Open Issue: The Constitutionality of Permitting Testimony by A Disguised Witness' *Federal Evidence Review* (6 February 2013) <http://federalevidence.com/blog/2013/february/disguised-witness-and-confrontation-clause> accessed 21 September 2017.

46 Emphasis added. Another exception is the case of child witnesses in view of their low-level personal emotion. In Maryland v Craig, the Supreme Court decided to allow an alleged child victim 'to testify by one-way closed circuit television'; the court added: face-to-face confrontation may cause 'serious emotional distress for the child'; See *Maryland v Craig*, 497 U.S. 836 (1990) <https://supreme.justia.com/cases/federal/us/497/836/> accessed 20 September 2017. See also 'Right to Confront Witness' *Legal Information Institute* <https://www.law.cornell.edu/wex/right_to_confront_witness> accessed 20 September 2017.

47 *United States v Jesus-Castaneda*, 712 F.3d 1283 (2013) <http://federalevidence.com/pdf/2013/01Jan/US.v.Jesus-Casteneda.pdf> accessed 7 October 2017.

48 Lusty (n 1) 379.

> In the present case, there was not, to be sure, a complete denial of all right of cross-examination. But the petitioner was denied the right to ask the principal prosecution witness either his name or where he lived... Yet when the credibility of a witness is in issue, the very starting point in 'exposing falsehood and bringing out the truth' through cross-examination must necessarily be to ask the witness who he is and where he lives. The witness' name and address open countless avenues of in-court examination and out-of-court investigation. To forbid this most rudimentary inquiry at the threshold is to effectively emasculate the right of cross-examination itself.

In *R v Taylor*, the British High Court held that 'the right of the accused to see and know the identity of his accusers should only be denied in rare and exceptional circumstances. Whether the exception was made was pre-eminently a matter for the discretion of the court'.[49] The court proceeded to set out the following standards in exercising the discretion:

a) There must be real grounds for fear of the consequences in cases where the evidence was given and the identity of the witness was revealed;
b) The evidence must be sufficiently relevant and important to render it unfair to make the Crown proceed without it;
c) The Crown must satisfy to the court that the creditworthiness of the witness has been fully investigated and disclosed;
d) The court must be satisfied that there is no undue prejudice to the accused;
e) The court can balance the need for protection of the witness, including the extent of that protection, against unfairness or the appearance of unfairness.[50]

Moving on to the European example, the European Court of Human Rights (ECtHR) held that before a suspect is convicted, they must, in principle, have an opportunity to challenge the truthfulness and reliability of a testimony.[51] The ECtHR, however, acknowledged exceptions to the right of the defendant 'to be confronted with witnesses against him'.[52] In *Ludi v Switzerland*,[53] the court overturned a criminal verdict 'based on a written statement by an

49 *R v Taylor*, as cited in ibid 393.
50 Ibid.
51 Lorena Bachmaier Winter, 'Transnational Criminal Proceedings, Witness Evidence and Confrontation: Lessons from the ECtHR's Case Law' (2013) 9(4) Utrecht Law Review 127.
52 European Convention on Human Rights (signed 4 November 1950, entered into force on 3 September 1953) ETS 5 (ECHR), art 6(3)(d).
53 Bachmaier Winter (n 51).

undercover agent and a written transcription of telephone conversations with the defendant'. In this case, the accused had no opportunity to examine the state witness before or during the trial. However, in *Asch v Austria,*[54] the ECtHR did not find a violation of the European Convention on Human Rights, even though the first instance court relied on evidence given by a police officer and by a physician who examined the victim-witness – a case in which the victim refused to testify at the trial. Thus, the conviction handed down based on the pre-trial record was affirmed. Here, the evidence from the investigating police officer and the physician corroborated the witness's pre-trial statement. In other words, the domestic court did not depend solely on the testimony of the victim-witness. On the contrary, in *P.S. v Germany,*[55] the domestic court, in finding the accused guilty, relied entirely on a statement of an eight-year-old girl who was allegedly sexually abused by her music teacher. The German court did not require the victim to testify at the trial so as to protect her personal development. The ECtHR deemed the conviction a breach of the suspect's right under the ECHR, since a pre-trial statement of the witness became the sole and decisive evidence in finding the accused guilty of the crime he was charged with.

When it comes to the African continent, South Africa is said to have 'experienced one of the worst intimidations anywhere in the world'[56] during the apartheid era; the threat was directed against former African National Congress (ANC) members who appeared in court to testify against their former freedom fighter colleagues. In 1985, the high court decided the case of *S v Leepile,* in which the state demanded the withholding of the identity of its witnesses. In rejecting the request, the judge noted:

> No investigation could be conducted by the accused's legal representatives into the witness' background to ascertain whether he has a general reputation for untruthfulness, whether he has made previous inconsistent statements, nor to investigate other matters which might be relevant to his credibility in general; it would make it more difficult to make inquiries to establish that the witness was not at places on the occasions mentioned by him; it would further heighten the witness' sense of impregnability and increase temptation to falsify or exaggerate.[57]

54 Ibid.

55 Ibid.

56 Lusty (n 1) 401.

57 Ibid 402.

It is also worth noting that intimidation often results from underlying social grievances. As South Africa's experience shows, prosecution witnesses under apartheid were frequently targeted because their participation as witness against former colleagues was considered a betrayal of a just cause and as collaboration with an unjust regime. Thus, it comes as no surprise that the ANC 'openly called for the assassination of known informers and detailed brutal killings of former members who served as state witnesses', describing them as 'just reprisals'.[58] Similar accounts also took place in Europe in the Middle Ages. Individuals who testified before the inquisition, as was considered earlier, became targets of violence because their action was deemed to have exposed fellow citizens to unjustified punishment.[59] In short, the motive for revenge is much deeper than just hate for individual witnesses.

In other jurisdictions, witnesses have encountered serious, and in some cases, life-threatening intimidation.[60] The degree of risk also varies greatly.

> [The defence] who will often attempt 'to make witnesses appear so inconsistent, forgetful, muddled, spiteful, or greedy that their word cannot be safely believed is of little surprise ... witnesses frequently leave the witness box 'angrily and in tears'. In addition, simply being in the witness box makes individuals vulnerable to verbal abuse and threats shouted from the public gallery or being stared at by the accused. Moreover, when trials end or adjourn, suspects, victims, and witnesses may all move out of the room into public waiting areas of the court building where further intimidations occur'.

However, putting aside organised and other serious offenses, most witnesses do not face a serious risk to their lives. Rather they tend to experience 'verbal threats, intimidation, harassment, assault, property damage, or simply, fear of reprisal as a result of their cooperation with'[61] law enforcement personnel.

The long absence of legal regulation in this area is no longer a problem. Progress has been made in recent times, thanks mainly to 'the increased impact of organised criminal and terrorist groups'.[62] On the global level, the

---

58 Ibid 401.

59 Ibid 368.

60 Karen Kramer, 'Witness Protection as a Key Tool in Addressing Serious and Organized Crime' (United Nations Asia and Far East Institute, Fourth Regional Seminar on Good Governance for Southeast Asian Countries, 2011) 5 <https://www.unafei.or.jp/publications/pdf/GG4/Fourth_GGSeminar_P3-19.pdf> accessed 5 October 2017.

61 Ibid.

62 Ibid 11.

American courts permit the testimony of an absent witness,[67] but there is clear divergence between US and Ethiopian laws. In Ethiopia, the accused cannot cross-examine the witness at the preliminary inquiry; the witness is a passive observer, the prosecutor together with the judge being the main actors.[68] Thus, this provision violates article 20 (4) of the FDRE Constitution. Second, the same argument can be made against article 145, which reads, 'The deposition of an expert taken at a preliminary inquiry may be read and put in evidence … although he is not called as a witness'.[69] Both provisions deny the suspect the chance to put questions to state witnesses. They also evade the requirement and purpose of a court oath, which witnesses must invariably undertake before testifying. The administration of oath sends a message to witnesses about the consequences of their word in a court of law and the sanction for perjury.[70] So, articles 144 and 145 of the CPC override the confrontation and oath requirements, both of which are key reliability-ensuring mechanisms.

Third, as per article 137 of the CPC, testimony based on one's 'direct or indirect knowledge' is permissible as evidence in court. Again, this defeats the rationale for the confrontation right, although foreign courts consider do hearsay under strict conditions.[71] Such evidence is given by someone who has no first-hand knowledge of the alleged act, but rather bases a statement on what they have heard others say. Such evidence is problematic, as the witness is incapable of properly answering cross-examination questions.

The constitutionality of the hearsay rule has not been tested in Ethiopia to date; now, it is also incorporated into the anti-terrorism law of 2009. In regard to the position of foreign judges, in the US it has been ruled that hearsay restricts or violates the confrontation rule,[72] but it can be lawful if two conditions are present: when the witness is unavailable and, if during previous court proceedings such as preliminary inquiry, they had testified against the same defendant and *were subject to cross-examination by that defendant*.[73] To sum

67 *Barber v Page*, 390 U.S. 719 (1968) <https://supreme.justia.com/cases/federal/us/390/719/> accessed 13 September 2018.

68 Negarit Gazeta, 'Criminal Procedure Code of the Empire of Ethiopia' Proclamation No. 185/1961 (CPC), art 80 and the following set forth the procedure for preliminary inquiry.

69 Ibid art 144(2).

70 Ibid. Under art 136 (2), the CPC requires the administration of oath or affirmation before taking witness testimony.

71 *Barber v Page* (n 67).

72 *Delaney v United States*, 263 U.S. 586 (1924) <https://supreme.justia.com/cases/federal/us/263/586/> accessed 12 September 2017.

73 *Barber v Page* (n 67).

up, there are legal rules in Ethiopia that raise eyebrows when assessed against the constitutional and the human right to confrontation.

4.2.2 Protection of Witnesses and Whistle-blowers

Testimony is perhaps the most widely used prosecution evidence, and without it, the criminal justice system would be ineffective, particularly when it comes to serious crimes. Without witness protection, the government's ability to prosecute and ultimately safeguard the public from crime would significantly diminish. Those who witnessed the commission of a crime would be discouraged from reporting and testifying for fear of reprisal.

The position of the witness raises both a legal and a moral question. The witness is a person trapped by the duty to testify; it is not a matter of personal choice but of legal duty. Failing to do so amounts to 'refusal to aid justice',[74] and is punishable criminally.

While the right of the accused is unambiguously stated in the FDRE Constitution and the ICCPR, no parallel safeguard exists for witnesses. Ethiopia is no exception in this regard. The right of the accused is front and centre in international and national law. Contrastingly, little attention is paid to the well-being of the witness, who could be subject to harassment and even risk their lives for cooperating with the prosecution. In terms of the law, the witness has been 'the forgotten soul of the criminal justice system'.

Lawmakers have put off responding to this pressing social problem. Of course, legal provisions occasionally do emerge on the subject, but they are far from sufficient. To start with the FDRE Constitution, article 20 (1) refers to *in camera* proceedings with a view to ensuring the privacy of parties, public moral, and national security. Here, the word *parties*, if interpreted literally, does not encompass the witness. Thus, the personal safety of the witness has no constitutional basis for protection in Ethiopia.[75] Other piecemeal rules include one that requires judges to deny bail if the suspect 'is likely to interfere with witnesses or tamper with evidence'.[76] Once again, the concern here is not the

74 Art 448 of the CPC (n 68) states: '(1) Any person who had been lawfully summoned to appear in judicial or quasi-judicial proceedings as an accused person, witness, expert, interpreter, assessor or juror, or ordered to produce or send an accused person or evidence: (a) fails or refuses to appear without sufficient cause; or (b) fails to produce or send the accused person or evidence; or (c) having appeared, refuses, contrary to law, to answer questions or to obey orders, is punishable…'.

75 This is also the case in other systems such as the US, but courts elsewhere have read some overarching interests (such as public policy and necessities of the case) to limit face-to -face examination. See Lusty (n 1) 377.

76 CPC (n 68) art 67(c).

witness's security, but rather the preservation and integrity of their testimonial evidence. If the safety of the witness is protected as a result of the denial of bail, it is incidental. If there is any specific rule on the subject, it is only article 444 of the Criminal Code, which makes it a crime to assault, suppress or harm: *'any person who gives information or evidence to justice authorities or is a witness in criminal cases'.*[77] Only the PWW provides comprehensive coverage on witness safety measures and programmes.

Proclamation No. 699/2010 has been enacted 'to protect witnesses and whistle-blowers of a criminal offense from direct or indirect danger and attack they may face as a consequence thereof and thereby to ensure their safety'.[78] This legislation applies to all crimes punishable with rigorous imprisonment for ten years or more (regardless of the minimum prison term threshold) or with capital punishment.[79] This Proclamation sets out preconditions before anonymity is granted. The conditions are: first, the offence must be such that it cannot be proved by means other than the testimony of the witness or information from the whistle-blower requiring protection; and, second, there is reason to believe that a threat of serious danger exists to the life, physical security, freedom or property of the witness or their family.

Article 4(1) of the Proclamation details the measures and programmes applicable, individually or jointly, including the following: physical protection of person, residence and property of the witness, relocation at the expense of the state, change of identity, provision of self-defence weapons, immunity from prosecution for an offence for which the witness provides information, free medical service in public health institutions, counselling and opportunity for employment and education, and covering the cost of living in case of loss of capacity to work as a result of reprisal. Most of these programmes may not affect the right of the defence to fair trial. As pointed out by Kramer, the purpose of protection 'should never provide a motivation to testify but merely remove or counter the witness' view that he or she is in danger if he/she cooperates'.[80] It is not meant to be an incentive to testify, for that would lead to a potential conflict of interests.

However, other provisions of the Proclamation restrict or deny fair trial. The list of such rules affecting the accused person's right includes: changing identity of witness, prohibition against the accused to contact the witness, taking

77 Federal Negarit Gazette Extraordinary Issue, 'Criminal Code of Ethiopia' Proclamation No. 414/2004, art 444.

78 Federal Negarit Gazeta, 'Protection of Witnesses and Whistleblowers of Criminal Offences Proclamation' Proclamation No. 699/2010, preamble para 3.

79 Ibid art 3(1).

80 Kramer (n 60) 5.

testimony *in camera* and behind a screen, and providing evidence via electronic devices.[81] In such cases, it would be difficult or even impossible to expose contradictions, lies and prejudices, thereby reducing the chances of the defendant to refute the charges against them. What if the witness is not telling the truth? What if the witness has a motive to falsely incriminate the suspect? How can the defence challenge the untrustworthiness of a witness by exposing, for example, their prior criminal record for perjury, misrepresentation or forgery? Should someone spend the rest of their life behind bars or lose their life because of false accusations? Cross-examination contributes to the fairness of the trial and to the prevention of unwarranted convictions.

As the US Supreme Court once stated, confrontation is meant to prevent conviction 'based on the charges of unseen and unknown – and hence unchallengeable individuals'.[82] The way the witness reacts to questions has evidentiary value; it is also part of the broader notion of fair trial. The demeanour of the witness, the manner of their testifying, the behaviour they manifest while in the witness box, whether the witness is cooperative, evasive or nervous when answering questions, the character and personal impression they create, their physical and emotional reactions, can all give clue to determining the authenticity of the oral evidence.

In addition to the proclamation on witness protection, one should add that the ATP authorises the removal of witness information from court records (including the publication and dissemination of such information),[83] the admissibility of intelligence report involving terror (even if such report does not mention the source or method of information-gathering),[84] hearsay evidence,[85] digital or electronic evidences,[86] evidence gathered through surveillance, information obtained through interception by foreign law enforcement bodies,[87] and written confession and voice and video recording.[88] The law does not provide guidance on how to weigh the probative value of these evidences or whether they are sufficient to make a case against the suspect. For example, the law says nothing about the status of a 'written confession' secured under

81 Proclamation No. 699/2010 (n 78) art 4.

82 *Lee v Illinois*, 476 US 530 (1986) <https://www.oyez.org/cases/1985/84-6807> accessed 14 September 2017.

83 Federal Negarit Gazeta, 'Anti-Terrorism Proclamation' Proclamation No. 652/2009, art 32(1)(b).

84 Ibid art 23(1).

85 Ibid art 23(2).

86 Ibid art 23(3).

87 Ibid art 23(4)

88 Ibid art 23(5).

coercion. As for intelligence report, the High Court of New Zealand once rejected a request by the prosecutor to withhold names of undercover agents, stating that the officers were of the highest integrity and, if their identity were to be revealed, they would not testify. The judge reasoned that:

> I cannot agree with the submission. The real risk of prejudice to the defense and of' conviction of the innocent would remain. A private assessment by the prosecution of the credibility of a police officer is no substitute in the interests of' justice for a proper check of his background by the accused whose liberty is at stake and who stands condemned on the undercover officer's evidence if his credibility is unchallenged…; unless and until the defense ascertains the officer's name, his background cannot be adequately checked in order to see whether there is justification for attacking his credibility.[89]

Both Proclamation No. 652/2009 and Proclamation No. 699/2010 give no indication as to whether hearsay and intelligence reports are to be used as corroborative or conclusive evidence. In US case law, the non-disclosure of parts or of all information about a witness is permitted but it has to be corroborated by other evidence.[90] For both American courts and the ECtHR, witness anonymity is tolerated only in exceptional conditions; when allowed, the testimony is insufficient for conviction. Only time will tell how Ethiopia's judges will interpret the law but Parliament has failed to stress the role of cross-examination as a fundamental right in deciding demands for anonymous testimony.

The two Proclamations differ from each other with regard to who decides on the issue of witness protection measures. Article 32 states that 'where the court, on its own motion or on application made by the public prosecutor or by the witness, is satisfied that the life of such witness is in danger…'.[91] Accordingly, the power to allow or disallow an application rests with the court, but Proclamation No. 699/2010 gives the power to the Ministry of Justice (now replaced by the Federal Attorney General) and the Federal Ethics and Anti-Corruption Commission (FEAC), to make the decision of which is not appealable.[92] It follows that Proclamation No. 699/2010 has impliedly repealed the power of courts under Proclamation No. 652/2009. This line of interpretation

89 See *R v Hughes* as discussed in Lusty (n 1) 399.

90 Kramer (n 60) 6.

91 Proclamation No. 652/2009 (n 83) art 32.

92 The Republic of India, 'The Witness Protection Bill', Bill No. 341 (2015), art 3(3) <http://164.100.47.4/billstexts/lsbilltexts/AsIntroduced/3109LS.pdf> accessed 14 September 2017; Also, in South Africa, the director, an appointee of the justice minister, is in

is further strengthened by the explicit reference to the federal high court, which is empowered to approve protection agreements the Ministry makes with child witnesses. So far as adults are concerned, the responsibility is entrusted to the Attorney General and the Commission.[93] This is nothing short of appropriation of judicial power by the legislature in favour of the executive. In contrast to Ethiopian law, a US judge held that 'the State or the witness should at the very least come forward with some showing of why the witness must be excused from answering the question. The *trial judge* can then ascertain the interest of the defendant in the answer and exercise an informed discretion in making his ruling'.[94] It is a matter of conventional wisdom that judges, if allowed to operate independently, would become custodians of human rights. The transfer of court power to the executive should therefore be seen as a matter of grave concern.

4.2.3 The Case of Mehadi Aley and Others

The case involves a constitutional complaint by three people accused of terror charges.[95] Among others, the accused objected to the withholding of names and addresses of witnesses invoking article 32 of Proclamation No. 652/2009, which has bestowed power upon judges to rule on anonymity applications. The defence argued that the failure to disclose witnesses' identity by the prosecutor violated the law and pleaded for disclosure. The defence also mentioned the absence of any limitation to the confrontation right in the FDRE Constitution. The accused demanded to know the state witnesses in advance so that they could prepare for defence before the commencement of the trial. They argued that their advance preparation and cross-examination of the state witnesses were crucial for the fairness of the trial and the search for the truth. Consequently, the court granted the request for a constitutional ruling on the validity of article 32(b) and article 4(1)(h)(j) of Proclamations No. 652/2009 and No. 699/2010, respectively.

After considering the petition, the Council of Constitutional Inquiry (CCI) reasoned that what can be understood from this provision (i.e. from article 20 (4)) is that it is an affirmation of the right of witnesses to cross-examination; however, the defence has no right to demand the disclosure of names and addresses of witnesses. At the same time, the FDRE Constitution also does not

charge to decide on witness protection applications. See Republic of South Africa, 'Witness Protection Act 112 of 1998', art 10(3)(a)(b)(c).

93 Proclamation No. 699/2010 (n 78) art 9(1)(2).

94 J White as quoted in Lusty (n 1) 380 (emphasis added).

95 *Mehadi Aley and others*, File No. 2356/2009, Council of Constitutional Inquiry (29 Hamle 2009).

impose a duty on the prosecution to disclose such information. This is clearly and categorically expressed in the FDRE Constitution. The CCI, in an apparent attempt to establish the intent of framers of the Constitution, noted that 'the reason for not including a requirement for disclosure of witness identity in the constitution is that it would pose danger to the safety of witnesses rather than ensure the fairness of the trial'.

This conclusion by the CCI is unwarranted and a stretch in view of the fact that constitutions do not deal with details like the one at hand. In the end, the CCI did not find any inconsistency between the FDRE Constitution and the Proclamations.[96] Contrary to this, Lusty, commenting on the US case law, remarks that 'the right of an accused to know the true identity of his or her accusers lies at the heart of the right of confrontation'.[97] Again, in *Barnard* v *Williams,* a New Zealand judge held: 'the name could well lead to a line of inquiry that will throw doubt on or even destroy the value of testimony ... to suppress identity is to change the character of the proceedings and ignore what I believe is a basic principle'[98] in a court trial.

The CCI should have clearly spelled out the absence of any constitutional limit to face-to-face examination of one's accusers. It would have made sense if the CCI had tried to justify the contested laws on pragmatic considerations using teleological reasoning. The CCI rather offered a remote and unwarranted opinion to conclude that the fathers of the FDRE Constitution anticipated the withholding of the identity of witnesses. What is more, the CCI failed to properly articulate the importance of fundamental rights, in this case the right to cross-examination, and the reasoning offered is mechanical and devoid of appreciation for fundamental human rights.

5 Conclusion

International human rights law has taken an important step by guaranteeing the fairness of a court trial, especially in criminal cases.[99] One such step is the right of the accused to cross-examination, which presupposes prior knowledge by the accused of names and addresses of witnesses and their physical presence

96 The same conclusion was reached by the House of Federation (HoF) in the case of *Merera Gudina,* who also challenged the constitutionality of withholding names of prosecution witnesses. Tamiru Tsige: 'Dr. Meera Gudina gave his plea; proclamation on witness protection does not contradict the constitution' (Reporter, Vol.23, No.1823, p.32).

97 Lusty (n 1) 380.

98 Ibid 397.

99 ICCPR (n 3) art 14.

during the trial. On the other hand, witnesses could be subject to harassment and life-threatening situations because of their role. Unless the safety of witnesses is assured, the effectiveness of the criminal justice system would be in great jeopardy.

Ethiopia's legislature has passed laws that provide for protection measures and programmes, including the concealment or change of witness' identity. While these overdue legislative measures should be welcome, care should be taken during implementation not to stretch their application too far – for this may negatively affect the success of the defence and the fairness of trials. The withholding of witness information will significantly diminish the ability of the defence to show the unreliability of the testimony by a state witness.

Therefore, while the need for exercising maximum caution in applying witness protection laws is very understandable, the recent constitutional holding of the CCI does not warrant an optimistic outlook about the implementation of cross-examination rights in Ethiopia. The decision for the suppression of identities of state witnesses was taken without properly balancing this constitutionally guaranteed human right of persons put on trial. The CCI also failed to give sufficient reasoning that could have supported its ruling – despite the unique opportunity offered in the proceedings for developing a constitutional jurisprudence on the subject.

PART 2

Economic, Social and Cultural Rights

The Need to Accommodate the Basic Rights of Ethno-National Minorities in the Oromia Regional State of Federal Ethiopia

Sisay Mengistie Addisu

Abstract

International human rights law recognises various rights of minorities. Following the adoption of a federal constitutional framework that politically recognises and legally guarantees the rights and freedoms of all ethno-national groups in Ethiopia, all regional states adopted their own state constitutions, except for Oromia and the Ethiopian Somali national regional states. These constitutions formally recognise the existence and the protection of the rights of minorities in their respective administrative territories. This chapter investigates how the legal framework of the regional state of Oromia addresses issues related to the fundamental rights of ethno-national minorities and how the regional government has endeavoured to implement any such rights. In this light, the study attempts to address three interrelated issues on the rights of ethno-national minorities concerning the right to existence, equitable representation, and self-government. It does so by taking certain non-indigenous communities as a case study. Various laws (international, continental, national, and regional), as well as related documents are utilised in this analysis as important data sources in addition to the semi-structured interviews conducted with key stakeholders and institutions. The findings of this research reveal that non-indigenous ethnic groups living in the Oromia National Regional State (ONRS) are in fact excluded from effective and equitable representation in the legislative and administrative councils of the region. Even in circumstances where they have been given restricted representation rights in some city councils, their decision-making powers remain ineffective. As a result, this chapter argues that despite the promises made by the federal government to empower all ethno-national groups of the country, the latter continue to face problems related to a lack of political recognition, equitable representation, and the right to self-government – even in territories where they are considered indigenous.

Keywords

Accommodation – non-indigenous community – self-government – ethnic minorities – Ethiopia

 | DOI:10.1163/9789004415966_006

1 Introduction

This chapter mainly deals with the current legal, political and practical means of accommodation of non-Oromo ethno-national minorities in the Oromia National Regional State (ONRS) in Ethiopia in relation to their fundamental rights of self-determination. It examines the Revised Constitution of the ONRS so as to explain the question of how the legal framework and political practices of the regional state address the rights of existence, representation and self-government of ethno-national minorities living in the region. This investigation serves as an initial point to grasp the nature of legal frameworks, political policies and practices of the region in relation to the treatment and accommodation of non-Oromo ethno-national minorities.

The chapter is structured into five sections – including introductory remarks which briefly discuss the political and legal background of the Oromia regional state. Sections 2 and 3 examine the legal and political frameworks, as well as the practical measures adopted by the regional government. Section 4 critically investigates sub-constitutional laws of the regional state in relation to the status of the rights of non-Oromo ethno-national groups residing in the region. While the Revised Constitution of Oromia does not explicitly recognise non-Oromo ethno-national minority groups, there are certain sub-constitutional laws and administrative measures taken by the regional government that have tried to accommodate certain interests of non-Oromo ethno-national minorities in urban areas of the region; this is particularly true in relation to language use in primary education and the representation of non-Oromo minority groups in some city administrative councils that are identified as first and second grade cities. The last section draws conclusions focusing particularly on the key legal and political problems of the region and the limited nature of the measures adopted by the regional state in relation to the issues at hand.

2 General Background Information Relating to the ONRS

In Ethiopia, the Oromos are estimated to constitute about 35 million of the 105 million inhabitants of the country.[1] In fact, the Oromo ethnicity is one of the most numerous ethno-national groups in Eastern Africa in general, and the most populous ethnic group in Ethiopia. It shares a common language and

1 'Ethiopia People 2018' *The Odora* <https://theodora.com/wfbcurrent/ethiopia/ethiopia_people.html> accessed on 17 June 2018.

once also displayed a widely shared religious and traditional system of governance. In this regard, Martial De Salviac rightly pointed out that:

> The Oromo constitutes a homogenous race, from the same blood and the same ethnic group, slightly varied due to nuances resulting from the differences in climate and from rare cross-breeding. The multitude of the tribe speak only one language, made supremely remarkable in Africa and above all in the Nile basin where a Pleiade of nations, several of which are no more than 20,000 subjects, are juxtaposed and intermingled in the checker pattern, presenting an equal diversity of language.[2]

John Markakis on his part stated that the Oromo comprise a nation of many tribes, each of whom operate quite independently of the rest and could strike out entirely on its own. This segmented structure of Oromo organisation hence divides the Oromo ethnic group into numerous independent tribes, owing to inter-tribal warfare.[3] Although the majority of the people of Oromo have been situated in the fertile central, south-western and south-eastern parts of Ethiopia, they have also been historically marginalised in the cultural, political and economic structures within the highland empire, a situation that worsened from the mid-nineteenth century onwards.

According to some writers, a plethora of recent important social, cultural and political factors contributed to the development of a greater sense of harmony among the Oromo people. This is particularly evident in the context of 'Oromummaa,' an element of culture, nationalism and political vision of the people of the Oromo at large, which has the power to serve as a manifestation of the collective identity of the Ethiopian Oromo national movement.[4]

To Assafa Jalata, the foundation of 'Oromummaa' is built on overarching principles embedded within Oromo traditions and culture – at the same time, it has universal relevance for all oppressed peoples of the country and its neighbouring nations. He strongly argues that prejudices and stereotypes towards the Oromo people have, consciously or unconsciously, influenced Ethiopians and Ethiopian studies. He notes that Ethiopians, particularly Ethiopian scholars and Ethiopianists influenced by racist assumptions and stereotypes, have never respected the Oromo people's tradition, culture or social

2 Martial De Salviac, *An Ancient People in the State of Menelik: The Oromo, Great African Nation* (Ayalew Kanno tr, Ayalew Kanno 2005) 12–13.

3 John Markakis, *Ethiopia: Anatomy of a Traditional Polity* (Shama Books 2006) 31.

4 Assafa Jalata, 'Being in and out of Africa: The Impact of Duality of Ethiopianism' (2009) 40(2) Journal of Black Studies 189, 205–209.

norms and thereby have undermined the Oromos' political struggle for social justice, democracy and human rights under a variety of pretexts.[5] Such and other social, economic and political factors led the Oromo resistance to become visible over time, including for example in the context of the Oromo Independence Movement of 1936; in the same year, a confederation of Oromos from Hararge, Shoa, Jimma and Ilubabor came together under the umbrella of the Western Oromo Confederation.[6]

By the mid-1960s, Oromo nationalism was also dominated by the Mecha-Tulema socio-economic organisation, a self-help development association with a strong political motive and cultural attributes led by the dominant figure, General Tadesse Biru. Biru's influence and nationalist movements culminated in his arrest by the order of Emperor Haile Selassie's regime in 1966.[7] Moreover, in the Bale Province, local leader Wako Gutu emerged as the most important foe of what was considered a battle for Oromo's liberation from the Amhara-dominated Ethiopian state. His armed resistance began in the 1940s and since, the Oromo people of the area have become more militant. This has culminated in vanguard Oromo elites establishing a political organisation called the Oromo Liberation Front (OLF) in 1973, mostly calling for the 'total liberation of the entire Oromo nation from Ethiopian colonialism.'[8]

It took decades of various forms of struggle for broader justice and democracy, involving both the Oromo and other peoples in Ethiopia, before the adoption of a highly progressive constitutional framework in 1995 that recognised the right to self-determination and secession of nations, nationalities and peoples. The regional state of Oromia was established during the transitional period in Ethiopia following the adoption of Proclamation No. 7/1992. While general recognition was granted to all ethno-national groups under the Transitional Period Charter, there was no unified or strongly consolidated national regional state administering all areas inhabited by the Oromo people until Proclamation No. 7/1992 become fully effective. However, in 1992 the Oromos established their own regional state consisting mainly of places and adjacent geographic areas where the people of the Oromo nation predominantly live, and in tandem with similar measures as adopted in other regional states of Ethiopia. Under article 2(1) of the 2001 ONRS Revised Constitution, the regional state shares internal borders with almost all regional states of Ethiopia except Tigray,

5 Ibid 205–206.

6 Ibid.

7 Saheed A Adejumobi, *The History of Ethiopia* (Greenwood Press 2007) 111 < https://epdf.tips/the-history-of-ethiopia4230b683efd0eb6139fc5e2badc20e1a86388.html> accessed 18 June 2018.

8 Ibid 126.

and also shares international borders with Kenya to the South and Sudan to the West.[9]

3 International Law and the Rights of Minorities to Political Participation

The right to political participation is a universal human right, which entitles citizens to take part in government decision-making directly or through freely-chosen representatives. Political participation is also a condition for realising the needs and aspirations particularly of minority community members in various realms of public life. The right to recognition and political participation is guaranteed under various international human rights instruments. The foundational legal articulation of these rights can be found in the 1948 Universal Declaration of Human Rights (UDHR), and is further formalised and elaborated on in later treaties, most notably in the International Covenant on Civil and Political Rights (ICCPR).

Article 21 of the UDHR provides, '[1] everyone has the right to take part in the government of his country, directly or through freely chosen representatives.'[10] Besides, article 25 of the ICCPR declares every citizen shall have the right and opportunity 'to take part in the conduct of public affairs…; to vote and be elected in genuine periodic elections…; and to have access, on general terms, to public service…'[11] Of particular importance to the issue at hand is the General Comment by the United Nations (UN) Human Rights Committee concerning article 25 of the ICCPR, which clearly states that political participation covers not only the central/federal government but also extends to regional state and local government levels.[12]

Additionally, the African Charter on Human and Peoples' Rights (ACHPR) under article 13 provides that '[e]very citizen shall have the right to freely

9 Although article 2(1) of the 2001 ONRS Revised Constitution (n 16) in its last paragraph clearly states that the Oromia region is bordered with Sudan, this matter remains unsettled and contentious between the Benishangul Gumuz and Oromia regional states.

10 Universal Declaration of Human Rights (adopted 10 December 1948) UNGA Res 217 A(III) (UDHR), art 21.

11 International Covenant on Civil and Political Rights (adopted 16 December 1966, entry into force 23 March 1976) 999 UNTS 171 (ICCPR), art 25.

12 United Nations Office of the High Commissioner of Human Rights, 'CCPR General Comment No. 25: Article 25 (Participation in Public Affairs and the Right to Vote) The Right to Participate in Public Affairs, Voting Rights and the Right of Equal Access to Public Service' (12 July 1996) CCPR/C/21/Rev.1/Add.7 <https://www.refworld.org/docid/453883fc22.html> accessed 17 June 2018.

participate in the government of his country, either directly or through freely chosen representatives, in accordance with provisions of the law.'[13] By virtue of article 9(4) of the 1995 Constitution of the Federal Democratic Republic of Ethiopia (FDRE), the aforementioned international and continental treaty documents become an integral part of the law of the land.[14] From this, it follows that governments, both at the federal and regional tiers, have the duty to ensure that the right to recognition and political participation is respected and ensured across the board.

Besides, article 39 of the FDRE Constitution is an important provision to recognise and protect the rights of ethno-national minorities and to secure their equitable representation at all levels of government institutions. In this regard, sub-article 3 of the same provision provides for a mechanism of recognising and protecting ethno-national minority groups that are not indigenous to a particular regional state and are stripped of their right to self-governance and equitable representation.[15] In other words, this constitutional provision is particularly useful to ethnic groups found in regional states outside of their own home regions, or to ethnic minority groups who might not have a region of their own.

In this light, it could be submitted that the wordings of article 39(3) offer non-Oromo ethno-national minority groups living in the ONRS the right to full measures of self-government and equitable representation in whichever part of the region they reside and work in. In this regard, the fact that a certain ethno-national group already has an established regional state is by no means a justification to deny the right to existence as a distinct ethno-national group, self-governance, or equitable representation.

4 Legal Frameworks and Political Practices of the ONRS

Following the adoption of Proclamation No. 7/1992, the Oromia regional state promulgated its own constitution in January 1993, which was subsequently amended in 1995 in accordance with the FDRE Constitution. Again, the Revised Constitution was reworked in October 2001 in order to determine the separation of powers among the regional state organs, strengthen the regional

13 The African (Banjul) Charter on Human and Peoples' Rights (signed 27 June 1981, entry into force 12 October 1986) OAU Doc. CAB/LEG/67/3 rev. 5, 21 I.L.M. 58, art 13.

14 Federal Negarit Gazeta, 'The Constitution of the Federal Democratic Republic of Ethiopia' Proclamation No. 1/1995, art 9(4).

15 Ibid art 39(3).

state's political power, and re-organise the administrative structure of the regional state, thereby enhancing good governance in the region.[16] Unlike the previous versions, the 2001 Revised Constitution institutionally organises three major government organs of the region: the legislative council (*Chafee*), the executive body (administrative council), and the judiciary.[17] Article 2 (1) of the Revised Constitution strongly stipulates that the Oromia National Regional State is the uninterrupted territory inhabited by the people of the Oromo nation and other peoples who made a choice to live in the region; however, the first paragraph of the preamble and article 39 of the same Constitution 'exclusively' recognise the existence of the Oromo nation.

In consequence, the Revised Constitution gives all political and administrative powers solely to this specific ethnic group without considering the very existence, important roles, and fundamental rights and freedoms of the millions of non-Oromo ethnic groups of Ethiopia who are settled in the same region. Besides, from the very beginning, the Revised Constitution did not seem to provide serious consideration to non-Oromo ethno-linguistic groups living in the region, in some cases irrespective of their claims of indigenous status.[18] In other words, unlike the aforementioned seemingly inclusive provisions, article 8 of the Revised Constitution exclusively grants sovereign power to the 'People of the Oromo Nation' by stipulating that the supreme power of the Oromia region resides with the People of Oromo.

Under article 39, the Revised Constitution preserves the right to self-determination including secession to the people of the Oromo nation. This strong constitutional stipulation suggests that the right to exercise self-determination, including the right to self-government as provided by the regional state constitution, is reserved only to the people of the Oromo nation. Because of this, the constitution of the Oromia region not only ignores the rights of non-indigenous ethno-national minorities but also those of indigenous ethno-linguistic minority groups, such as the Zay community.[19] This approach in constitutional design has only reinforced the sovereignty of Oromo people.

---

16 Magalata Oromoyaa, 'Enforcement Proclamation of the Revised Constitution of 2001 of the Oromia Region' Proclamation No. 46/2001 (ONRS Revised Constitution), para 3.

17 Ibid art 46.

18 Interviews with members of the community strongly showed that although the Zay and Garo communities have identified themselves as indigenous nation-nationalities of the region, the 2001 ONRS Revised Constitution and the practical application thereof do not recognise and thereby do not give any political space to these and other non-indigenous communities of the region.

19 Christophe Van Der Beken and Yonatan Tesfaye, 'Empowerment and Exclusion: The Legal Protection of Internal Minorities in Ethiopia' in Asnake Kefale and Assefa Fiseha (eds),

According to Daba, the fundamental reason for the non-recognition of the existence of non-Oromo ethno-national minority groups in the Oromia region is attributed to the narrow definition of the concept of 'nations, nationalities and peoples' of Ethiopia under the FDRE Constitution; the wrong assumption comes not only from the law-makers of the Oromia region, but also from those who framed the FDRE Constitution in 1995.[20]

As mentioned above, the Oromia regional state constitution unequivocally declares that the ONRS is owned and governed exclusively by the Oromo nation.[21] Moreover, the Revised Constitution strongly stipulates that 'the people of [the] Oromo nation shall have the right to maintain their distinct identity, preserve and promote their history and heritage, to speak, develop and make use, in any other manner, of their own language and enjoy their culture.'[22] However, nothing is provided in this regard on the rights of non-Oromo nations, nationalities and peoples of the country living in the region, including indigenous groups who wish to preserve, exercise and develop their cultural and language rights. Such an approach in constitutional design, accompanied by political and administrative measures, violates not only the fundamental rights of such groups as guaranteed under the FDRE Constitution, but also the principles of accommodating diversities as laid down under the same Constitution, which is meant to apply across the Federation. Concerning this issue, Woldemariam writes:

> In Oromia, all types of minorities are not recognized. Non-territorial minorities (and all other types of new minorities) beyond the preview of the law, are exposed to violations of both their basic human and minority-specific group rights. The total *de jure* neglect of their existence in the region has paved way for the violations of rights and made it extremely difficult, if not impossible, for victims to seek redress for rights violations.[23]

With regard to the violations of minority rights in the Oromia regional state, Fiseha also writes that 'in 2002, as a result of mobilization orchestrated by local

Federalism and Local Government in Ethiopia (Addis Ababa University 2015) 62.

20 Tokuma Daba, 'Legal and Practical Responses to the Rights of Minorities in Oromia Region' (LL.M Thesis, Addis Ababa University, 2010) 86 <https://chilot.me/wp-content/uploads/2013/01/the-legal-and-practical-protection-of-the-rights-of-minorities-in-self-administering-nations-of-ethiopia-the-case-of-oromia.pdf> accessed 18 June 2018.

21 ONRS Revised Constitution (n 16) art 2.

22 Ibid art 39 (1).

23 Getachew Assefa Woldemariam, 'Constitutional Protection of Human and Minority Rights in Ethiopia: Myth v. Reality' (PhD Dissertation, Melbourne Law School, 2014) 111.

political elites, a large number of the Amhara were evicted from the southwest Oromia to the Amhara region, and their quest to return remains an unsettled issue.'[24] Woldemariam, on his part, further explains the important reason why the regional officials and politicians made this decision consciously and clearly:

> The root cause of these violations of rights of non-Oromo ethno-national minority groups is the sentiment strongly held by the Oromo political elite – who were part and parcel of the national political elite that framed the federal constitution – that Oromia belongs only to the Oromo people and other ethno-national groups, especially Amhara, do not belong there.[25]

Since article 8 of the Revised Constitution of Oromia does not vest sovereign power to non-Oromo ethnic groups in the region as such, the latter cannot exercise their right to fair and equitable representation and active political participation in the regional state – let alone claim the right of self-government for territorially-concentrated ethnic groups of the region. This sharply contrasts the fact that many regional constitutions provide special representation arrangements for non-indigenous ethno-national minorities in the form of quota systems in regional legislative councils.[26] The following table provides the names and size of non-indigenous communities living in the Oromia region whose population comprises more than 50,000 people.[27]

24 Assefa Fiseha, 'Intra-Unit Minorities in the Context of Ethno-National Federalism in Ethiopia' (2016) 3 Ethiopian Journal of Federal Studies 53.

25 Woldemariam (n 23) 112.

26 Zikre Hig Gazeta, 'The Revised Constitution of the Amhara National Regional State Approval Proclamation' Proclamation No. 59/2001, art 45(3); Lisane Hig Gazeta 'Benishangul Gumuz National Regional State Constitution' Proclamation No. 31/2002, art 48(2); Negarit Gazeta 'The Revised Constitution of the Gambella Peoples' National Regional State Constitution' Proclamation No. 27/2002, art 50(2); and Debub Negarit Gazeta, 'The Revised Constitution of the Southern Nations, Nationalities and Peoples National Regional State' Proclamation No. 35/2001, art 50(2) allow for such kind of arrangement.

27 The 2007 Population and Housing Census Report shows that in the Oromia region, there are several nations, nationalities and peoples of Ethiopia whose total number is accounted as more than 3 million. See Central Statistical Authority, '2007 Population and Housing Census Report' (Addis Ababa, April 2012) <http://unstats.un.org/unsd/censuskb20/Attachment489.aspx?AttachmentType=1> accessed 18 June 2018.

Table 1 Names and Size of Non-indigenous Communities in Oromia Region

	Nation/Nationality	Population	Coverage by percent
1	Amhara	1,961,277	7.22
2	Guragie	251,453	0.93
3	Gedeo	245,160	0.90
4	Somali	89,793	0.33
5	Yem	84,607	0.31
6	Welaita	64,552	0.24
7	Tigray	61,805	0.23
8	Hadia	52,813	0.19
9	Sidama	52,604	0.19
10	Siltie	50,216	0.18
	Total	2,914,280	10.72

SOURCE: CENTRAL STATISTICAL AUTHORITY, '2007 POPULATION AND HOUSING CENSUS REPORT' (ADDIS ABABA, APRIL 2012)

It is important to note that this exclusionary policy is also systematically pursued and supported by the definitional part of the Revised Constitution, which clearly stipulates that:

> …the people of the Oromo nation shall be construed as meaning those people who speak the Oromo language, who believe in their common Oromo identity, who share a large measure of common culture as Oromos and who predominantly inhabit in a contiguous territory of the regional state.[28]

This entails, among others, a denial of the claims of the indigenous Zay community to assert their distinct identity and to thereby exercise their right to self-government. Until very recently, the community's formal quest for distinct status was accorded little attention. Similarly, while residents of seven *kebele* administrative units in Grar Jarso *Wereda*, who are ethnic Amhara, are formally represented in the legislative council of the *Wereda*, they have not been able to play a meaningful role in the socio-political realms of the locality in decision-making processes. This is simply due to the fact they do not understand or

28 ONRS Revised Constitution (n 16) art 2.

speak Afan Oromo, the working language of the region.[29] As a result, they are not only impeded in their active participation in the *Wereda* legislative and administrative councils, but also unable to get equitable representation in the regional council. Based on these facts, it could therefore be contended that such discriminatory approaches towards non-Oromo nations, nationalities and peoples largely assimilates their status to that of internal migrants or peoples on the move, who come from other regional states for the purpose of temporary economic gains (or other objectives).[30]

In the past, such practice was dominated by initiatives of the regional government to further cement discriminatory approaches. In this regard, Woldemariam argues that even though major cities in the Oromia region are completely controlled and run by the Oromos, regardless of their number, in 2003 the regional government introduced a legal scheme to pro-actively establish the political dominance of ethnic Oromos by setting what is called 'false thresholds.'[31] For instance, Proclamation No. 65/2003 reserved 30 percent of the seats of urban councils for ethnic Oromos, as well as 5 percent of the seats in rural *kebele* administrative units surrounding urban centres.[32] This legislation was amended in 2006 following the 2005 national election, which shook the regional state government; it introduced further thresholds by favouring members of the Oromo ethno-national group living in urban centres.

Under the amended Proclamation, the seats in designated cities and rural *kebeles* that surround urban centres were not only raised, but also a 50 percent reservation for Oromos city dwellers became applicable in the same manner as in the rural *kebele* councils.[33] In this regard, Daba in his research finds a strong tension between the Oromo nation and other nation-nationalities and peoples of Ethiopia, particularly between the Oromo nation and the people of Amhara living in the regional state of Oromia. In the same vein, according to Daba:

> ...while the latter strongly claims that they are demographically legitimate to control and establish city administration in the region, the former

29 Kasaye Shimelis, 'The Accommodation of Minority Rights in Oromia National Regional State: A Case Study of Grar Jarso Wereda' (MA Thesis, Addis Ababa University, 2016) 59–60.

30 Christophe Van der Beken, 'Ethiopia: Constitutional Protection of Ethnic Minorities at the Regional Level' (2007) 20(1–2) Africa Focus 105, 125.

31 Woldemariam (n 23) 115.

32 Magalata Oromiyaa, 'The Urban Local Government of the Oromia National Regional State' Proclamation No. 65/2003, arts 13(3) and (4).

33 Magalata Oromiyaa, The Amended Urban Local Government of the Oromia National Regional State Proclamation No. 116/2006, arts 2(4) and (5).

> strictly claims that they are politically legitimate owners of the region as significant number of Amhara ethno-national group came to towns of Oromia region by evicting native/indigenous people of the Oromo nation. Particularly, the Oromos forward historical justification and raise affirmative action as a defense.[34]

Concerning this, Van Der Beken and Tesfaye also strongly suggest that 'the Oromia revised constitution considers only one ethno-national group, the Oromo, as indigenous people to the region, so that the indigenous group at city level can be no other than the Oromo nation.' This explains why article 13(3) of Proclamation No. 65/2003 on the Oromia city administration establishment states that 'where the Oromos are minority in a given city, the regional executive council may reserve up to 30 percent of the seats for Oromos.'[35] Moreover, Proclamation No. 113/2006 repealed this provision and increased the percentage of seats in city councils that could be reserved for the Oromo to 50 percent. This legal guarantee served not only as instrument to encroach on the equitable representation rights of ethno-national minorities living in the region, but also falsely empowered the executive branch of the regional government to decide on the amount of threshold whenever it found necessary. In this regard, Daba strongly argues in favour of the presence of this legal arrangement and control by the Oromo nation; he explains:

> …the Oromo will not have any claim in cities within their region since due to the cultural dominance and opportunities in the past, the number of Amhara people in the region is by far greater than the number of the Oromo people in cities. During the expansion of towns and cities, Oromo farmers have been evicted. Hence, unless the right of the indigenous group is given better attention, they are going to be deprived of the right to have full control over those cities in their region.[36]

Furthermore, Daba submits that article 33 of the Revised Constitution is an essential safeguard that guarantees the right to equality and non-discrimination, as it entitles every Ethiopian citizen to assume political authority and to be employed in every sector, provided s/he speaks the working language of the region.[37] However, this provision requires the ability to speak and write Afan

34 Daba (n 20) 7.

35 Van Der Beken and Tesfaye (n 19) 74.

36 Daba (n 20) 92.

37 Ibid 87–88.

Oromo, the working language of the region, to be treated equally whenever an employment opportunity becomes available in the region.

In practice, the same constitutional provision orients the regional government's political thinking and legal position; hence, any Ethiopian citizen who lives in the region and understands the working language of the national regional state has the right to work in any of the region's public or governmental employment positions, which can either be obtained through election or placement procedures.[38]

However, the language requirement imposes both a considerable barrier as well as grounds for discrimination of equals on the basis of a highly questionable factor. On the other hand, it is important to highlight that the regional constitution does not state anything specific related to the guaranteed representation of ethno-national minorities. Therefore, non-Oromo ethno-national minorities as a group have only a rare chance to be elected and represented at *Chaffee Oromia,* as they stand little chances of winning an election when competing with Oromos from the specific local electoral constituency – a problem which is further exacerbated by their inability to speak the working language of the region.[39] The root causes of such non-inclusive approaches can be traced back to the strong nationalist and political sentiment and influence of the Oromo Liberation Front (OLF), as well as the cultural bias of the regional state government.[40]

It should be stated at this point that the goal is not to only portray negative images of the legal and political developments registered in the region; in fact, despite the challenges, the regional state has embarked on taking some positive political and administrative measures towards language use and representation rights in order to accommodate the concerns of non-Oromo ethnic groups who mostly live in the urban areas of the region. In the last ten years, regional officials have taken a more positive orientation towards issues of representation of non-Oromo ethno-national groups and have endeavoured to revisit the policy of the region that has discriminated against non-indigenous communities. In other words, while it may not be sufficient, the regional state

---

38 ONRS Revised Constitution (n 16) art 33.

39 Guta Balcha, 'Minority Rights Protection in Oromia National Regional State: A Case Study of the Zay People' (MA Thesis, Addis Ababa University, 2016) 55 <http://etd.aau.edu.et/bitstream/handle/123456789/17509/Guta%20Balcha.pdf?sequence=1&isAllowed=y> accessed 18 June 2018.

40 Interview with Milkesa Midega, Lecturer, Dire Dawa University and PhD candidate in Federalism and Governance Studies, Addis Ababa University (Addis Ababa, 5 November 2016) and Melese Abayneh, former Head, Legal and Administrative Affairs Standing Committee of *Chaffee Oromia* (Addis Ababa, 17 November 2016).

has tried to recognise and allow for representation rights of residents in urban areas identified as first and second grade cities.

5 Sub-constitutional Regional Laws and the Rights of Ethno-National Minorities

Despite the readings of the preamble, under articles 8 and 39 of the 2001 Revised Constitution, the rights to be elected and to elect are equally guaranteed to all residents of the regional state.[41] According to Daba, this will to some extent enable the representation of non-Oromo nation-nationalities and peoples indirectly; all regional officials are elected by all residents of the region including non-Oromos, while sovereign power which is exercisable by delegating power to the *Chaffee* resides only in the hands of the Oromo people.[42] However, experience shows that until now, *Chaffee Oromia* has not had any representatives from non-Oromo ethnic groups living in the region. To a measure, this is due to the policy of the governing party, the Oromo People Democratic Organization (OPDO, now changed to Oromo Democratic Party – ODP), who proposes that only members of the Oromo nation can be elected as representatives of both the House of Federation (HoF) and House of Peoples' Representatives at the federal level – even though there are few non-ethnic persons fluent in Afan Oromo and who have become members of the governing party. In this regard, Daba submits that if one plainly follows the Revised Constitution, no other ethno-national group would have had a seat even in city councils of first and second grade urban centres of the region; this relatively accommodative approach clearly indicates that the Proclamation, at least legally, to a certain extent not only recognises the very existence of non-Oromos, it also guarantees the rights of political participation and representation in almost all city councils of first and second grades in the region.[43]

Furthermore, Issa Boru Tola, a member of *Chaffee Oromia*, strongly argues that Amharic as a federal language is broadcast on Oromia Radio and Television platforms and is also particularly used as a medium of instruction in primary education in certain urban areas and rural localities – particularly in those where the number of Amharic-speaking people has become important.[44]

41 ONRS Revised Constitution (n 16) art 38 (1).

42 Daba (n 20) 82.

43 Ibid 83.

44 Interview with Issa Boru Tola, Chairperson of Legal and Administrative Affairs Standing Committee of *Chaffee Oromia* (Addis Ababa, 1 November 2016).

Because of this, in 2016/2017, there were 376,798 students attending primary education in Amharic language across 1027 elementary schools; however, this figure represents only 5 percent of the total student population of the region – most of them located in urban areas.[45]

Such practical and positive political and administrative measures taken by the regional government indicates that in the Oromia region, practice in fact extends far better recognition and protection to Amharic-speaking ethno-national minority groups than the constitutional framework of the region. This explains why only few Oromo scholars and political elites strongly argue against the fact that the language and cultural rights of ethno-national minority groups living in the Oromia region in general, as well as the Amhara in particular are, to a certain extent, politically recognised, legally protected, and socially accepted. This is because about 7.8 percent of the primary schools in the region are using the Amharic language as a medium of instruction.[46] In this regard, Balcha also submits that the Amhara people living in the region have practically enjoyed minority-status related rights, which are not outlined in the Revised Constitution and other basic laws. He further acknowledges that not all ethno-national minority groups in Oromia are treated and represented alike; relatively speaking, the Amhara are more privileged in using their own language than the other ethnic groups.[47] According to Balcha, the Amhara can at least send their children to government-financed elementary schools where education is offered in Amharic language. On the other hand, Legesse strongly argues that in Oromia, a large portion of people belonging to other 'nations, nationalities or peoples' are shut-off from the political process simply because of their ethnic make-up. Non-Oromo people living in the region, he noted, are therefore denied the right to get primary education in own language even through their sheer number would justify it.[48]

When considering sectoral analyses a means of demonstrating minority rights and accommodation, it should be noted that before 1999, the regional government's education policy as such was not accommodative of different languages; however, from this it cannot follow that all ethnic groups living in the region were entirely denied such a right.[49] Patten and Kymlicka submit

45 Interview with Teferi Habtamu, Oromia Region Education Bureau Data Administration Officer (Addis Ababa, 1 November 2016).

46 See for instance Midega (n 40).

47 Balcha (n 39) 68.

48 Yared Legesse Mengistu, 'Protection of National Minorities in Multinational Federations: A Comparative Analysis' (PhD Dissertation, Central European University, 2010) 31.

49 Currently, in almost all rural and also in many urban areas of the Oromia region, non-Oromo parents are forced to send their children to schools whose language of instruction

that naturally, mother-tongue instruction is surely relevant for the effectiveness of the right to education, as receiving an education enables a person to master (one of) the official language(s) of the state concerned.[50] Moreover, in the instructional processes, when a mother tongue is used as a medium of instruction for children at least 6–8 years old, the results are impressively positive – in this vein, minority children register enhanced self-confidence, self-esteem, classroom participation, lower dropout rates, higher levels of academic achievements, longer stay periods in school, better performance in tests, and greater fluency and literacy abilities.[51] Balcha, quoting the Head of the Education Bureau of the ONRS, holds that in the majority of towns and cities in the region,[52] there are Amharic-speaking schools financed by the regional government.

Yet, ethno-national groups other than the Oromo and Amhara in fact have no chance of educating their children using own mother tongue. Due to the insufficient numerical size of many ethno-national minority groups and also due to economic constraints on the part of the region, it is submitted that it would be very challenging to establish schools providing primary education in their own mother tongues to every ethno-national group.[53]

Nevertheless, when examining the history of the people of Oromo, neglect and exclusion of non-Oromo ethnic groups are not the main features of the Oromo's social, political as well as administrative culture; in fact, unlike many others, the Oromo are known for smooth assimilation and socialisation processes using the *Mogasa* system of accommodation.[54] On this, Levine writes that the community:

---

is 'Afan Oromo'; others prefer to keep their children at home or are forced to send them to cities far from their residential area, hence facing unnecessary costs. However, this cumbersome condition has to a certain extent been rectified since 1999 mainly in first and second grade cities of the region, as well as in certain rural areas where a substantial number of Amharic-speaking people live together.

50 Alan Patten and Will Kymlicka 'Introduction: Language Rights and Political Theory: Context, Issues and Approaches' in Alan Patten and Will Kymlicka (eds), *Language Rights and Political Theory* (Oxford University Press 2003) 20.

51 For further readings, see the following study reports: UNESCO, *Improving the Quality of Mother Tongue-Based Literacy and Learning: Case Studies from Asia, Africa and South America* (UNESCO Publishing 2008) <https://unesdoc.unesco.org/ark:/48223/pf0000177738> accessed 18 June 2018; see also UNESCO, *Global Monitoring, Teaching and Learning* (UNESCO Publishing 2014) <https://unesdoc.unesco.org/ark:/48223/pf0000225660_eng> accessed 18 June 2018.

52 Balcha (n 39) 68.

53 Ibid 52.

54 According to Alemayehu Haile, researcher at the Oromo Cultural Center, *Mogasa* is a social response to make a non-Oromo individual who is ready to be part of the Oromo

> ...experienced comparable accommodation and acculturation in relation to their enemies in the southwest. I have already mentioned the convention whereby hostilities were renounced when [Oromo] tribesmen attended markets in the Guraghe region, and the existence of trade and ritual relationships which different [Oromo] tribes established with both the Konso and the Derasa.[55]

Of course, it is evident that for dispersed ethno-national minorities, it would be appropriate to secure their legal and political recognition and the practical protection of fundamental rights and freedoms through considering all avenues. These would include, for example, introducing the proportional electoral system or guaranteed seats at all levels of legislative and executive branches of regional government. In addition, there should be an opportunity to learn the language of the majority. On the one hand, this would be in order to compete for employment; on the other hand, it would aid the assumption of political and administrative authority without denying them of their own cultural rights.[56] Therefore, in large measure, the effective protection of ethno-national minorities and their fundamental rights depends on the actions taken by the federal and regional governments. Such is also the case regarding their political inclusion.

From this it follows that the law-enforcing agencies of the regional state, ranging from the Office of the Chief Administrator (ie the resident of the regional state) all the way through to local administrative officials should be required to follow and to comply with the higher normative order established by the FDRE Constitution. This would ensure respect and protection of the fundamental rights of all people in Ethiopia, including those of non-Oromo ethno-national minorities living in the region – whether they are indigenous or not.

Again, to the extent that this predicament of minorities is caused by the absence of minority-specific electoral laws or a minority-rights oriented legislative framework, which could have ensured fair and equitable representation along the lines of the FDRE Constitution (which reserves 20 seats for

people as being seen as equal to members of the Oromo nation.

55 Donald N Levine, *Greater Ethiopia: The Evolution of a Multiethnic Society*, (University of Chicago Press 1999) 81.

56 For example, in South Tyrol, an autonomous province of Italy, Italian-speaking people and the indigenous Ladin ethnic group should learn German and Italian in schools and vice versa, without denying the cultural rights of the Ladin ethnic community, https://www.micura.it/de/begegnung/ladinische-kultur/die-schule-in-den-ladinischen-taelern, accessed 18 May2019.

United Nations (UN) General Assembly has adopted a resolution which calls for the implementation of 'measures to minimize inconvenience to victims, protect their privacy, when necessary, and ensure their safety, as well as that of their family and witnesses on their behalf, from intimidation and retaliation'.[63] As part of this global movement, Ethiopia enacted a legislation governing the protection of witnesses and whistle-blowers.

4.2 *Ethiopia's Legal Framework and the Decision of the Council of Constitutional Inquiry (CCI)*

4.2.1 The Right to Cross-Examination

Under article 20 (4) of the FDRE Constitution, accused persons are entitled to have 'full access to any evidence presented against them, to examine witnesses testifying against them'.[64] A literal interpretation of this provision does not warrant any restriction on the confrontation requirement.[65] Yet, the Anti-Terrorism Proclamation (ATP) and the Proclamation on Protection of Witnesses and Whistle-blowers (PWW) both provide for restrictions on the exercise of cross-examination. This move by the federal legislature appears justifiable on pragmatic considerations, in the interest of the public and individual witnesses.

The confrontation right under the Ethiopian Constitution admits no limits. However, the above-mentioned legislative acts stipulate substantial modifications to the right. Before it is possible to delve further into the validity of the statutes, it makes sense to briefly turn to other legal rules that conflict with article 20(4) of the FDRE Constitution.

First, article 144 and 145 of the Criminal Procedure Code (CPC) make out-of-court testimony and expert opinion admissible as evidence in court.[66] Article 144(1) reads, 'The deposition of a witness taken at a preliminary inquiry may be read and put in evidence ... where the witness is dead or insane, cannot be found, is so ill as not to be able to attend the trial or is absent' from the country.

63 United Nations (UN) General Assembly, 'Declaration of Basic Principles of Justice for Victims of Crime and Abuse of Power' (29 November 1985) A/RES/40/34, annex para 6 (d) <https://www.un.org/documents/ga/res/40/a40r034.htm> accessed 12 October 2017.

64 The 1931 and 1987 Constitutions of Ethiopia did not specifically guarantee the right to cross-examination. Art 52 of the 1955 Constitution of Ethiopia, likely modeled after the Sixth Amendment to the US Constitution (n 41), recognised the right of the accused 'to be confronted with the witnesses against him'.

65 Whether such limits call for a constitutional amendment is, however, another matter. As the experience of some states in the US reveals, such limits must only be applied after constitutional change.

66 The constitutionality of these provisions has not been challenged in Ethiopia to date.

ethno-national minorities), similar approaches could be devised heeding to the regional contexts as well.

Of course, caution needs to be taken as many of the legal and political measures that hinder minority representation and participation do not necessarily take the form of legislative or constitutional bans or restrictions. On the contrary, they may manifest through a number of political and practical obstacles, sometimes inadvertently and at other times intentionally. Regardless, the effects are the same, namely the exclusion or reduction of minority representation in regional politics.[57] In this regard, in addition to potential remedies entailed as a result of constitutional uncertainty or indifference in relation to the promotion of the rights of ethno-national minorities, tools commonly applied in the region should be re-thought and re-worked thoroughly in order to heed to higher protective standards on minorities. Such tools for example include ethnic gerrymandering, ie creating electoral units in certain urban areas which reduce the representation of ethno-national minorities in city councils. It is submitted that leaving the fate of ethno-national minorities wholly to the constitutional and political workings of regions would naturally entail negative effects on their fundamental rights to the recognition of their existence, equitable representation, and self-government. If the regional state's measures, both in law or in fact, fall short of the standards set under the FDRE Constitution and international human rights regimes, the federal government should take pro-active steps to ensure their treatment in regions is in accordance with the FDRE Constitution. In this regard, it is very important to note that the FDRE Constitution has specific provisions directing the Federation that it:

> shall, on its own initiative, request a joint session of the House of the Federation and of the House of Peoples' Representatives to take appropriate measures when state authorities are unable to arrest violations of human rights within their jurisdiction. It shall, on the basis of joint decision of the House, give directives to the concerned state authorities.[58]

From this reading it follows that the federal government should maintain vigilance to prevent any direct or indirect actions taken by any regional state that violate minority rights and freedoms in general, and ethno-national minority

57 For further understanding, see Proclamation No. 65/2003 (n 32) as amended by Proclamation No. 113/2006 (n 33), which established first and second grade city councils of the Oromia National Regional State.

58 FDRE Constitution (n 14), art 55(16).

groups in particular. Since the near 'total domination' of one ethno-national group over the resources and institutions of government agencies results in the effective exclusion of non-Oromo ethno-national communities, measures should be taken to comprehensively approach the matter on all fronts – legal, institutional, and political. The continued passivity, if not remedied in time, could have detrimental effects on the grander vision of building a functioning federal political system in Ethiopia. It is only through balanced political participation and the all-inclusive accommodation of ethno-national minorities in political as well as administrative power structures, that positive and sustainable compliance can be brought about with the federal constitutional order and the internationally recognised rights of minority groups.

6 Conclusion

The discussions above shows that in the Oromia National Regional State (ONRS), only the Oromo nation is legally empowered and politically recognised to control the regional polity – this entails multi-faceted ramifications on various aspects of the protection of minority rights. Afan Oromo is the only prescribed language of governance and of the legal system at all levels of the ONRS. It is also the medium of instruction of formal education in all elementary schools – except in some urban areas of the region identified as first and second grade cities. Likewise, media and other public affairs of the regional state are mainly conducted using Afan Oromo.

This language policy has discriminatory effects and in some measures also compromises the cultural distinctness of other non-Oromo ethno-national minorities living in the region – including the indigenous people of the Zay community. Such policy inclination to systematically force the 'integration' of non-Oromo ethno-national groups inhibits their access to schooling in most rural areas of the region, as well as opportunities to develop their own social capital. It also fosters socio-political challenges including non-representation in their own affairs, which further marginalises many ethno-national minority groups who live in the region.

This development is the product of several intertwined political and administrative measures and inactions, some pursued intentionally and others inadvertently. To start with, various policy measures adopted by the regional state promote legitimate causes of the Oromo nation without giving due consideration to rights of minorities, which are equally protected under the FDRE Constitution. Besides, the regional constitutional and other legal frameworks are structured in such a way as not to afford full guarantees to the cultural distinctness, autonomy and representation of ethno-national minorities. Moreover, although the regional government has promised and has politically committed to recognising, respecting and protecting the rights of such minorities under the Revised Constitution,[59] in practice it has not yet complied with its constitutional promises and political commitments.

Under articles 39(2) and (3) of the FDRE Constitution, cultural autonomy and the right to self-government are not only duly acknowledged, but also constitutionally entrenched. However, contrary to such stipulation, discriminatory practices against non-Oromo ethno-national minorities have persisted in the region from the very beginning of the establishment of the regional state by denying the mere existence of minorities in the region – including the indigenous people of the Zay. This is not only unsustainable on the long term, but the violations will also lead to tensions, mistrust, inequalities and episodes of inter-communal violence that exhibit ethno-national features.

In this light, maintaining an accommodative political culture and enforcing a system of democratic governance that fully recognises all ethno-national minorities in the regional state becomes absolutely imperative. Such recognition entails a radical re-orientation of the constitutional order at the national and regional levels; at the same time, legal and political reforms in the region could focus on taking actions that balance the cultural and political interests of the Oromo and non-Oromo peoples in the region in equal measures, thereby fostering grander visions of the federal polity in which the rights, welfare and voices of every citizen count.

---

59 ONRS Revised Constitution (n 16) art 103(2) clearly provides that the state shall respect the identity of nations, nationalities and peoples living in the region and shall accordingly have the duty to strengthen unity, equality and fraternity among them.

Assessing the Right to Property, Eviction and Compensation in Ethiopia *vis-à-vis* International Human Rights Law

Zerihun Yimer Geleta

Abstract

For over two decades, Ethiopia has been witnessing rapid changes in its urban landscape. This is, among other reasons, due to a shift in policy from a command-economy to a market-oriented economy, which has paved the way for enormous private and public investments. Accordingly, the size of cities and towns in the country has undergone dramatic expansions, often at the expense of poor farmers. The land has been taken away from poor farmers through expropriation/eviction for the purpose of new road construction, low-cost housing projects, real estate development, and other infrastructure expansions. The government seems to have adopted a broad interpretation of 'public interests' to justify the expropriation/eviction, which is detrimental to the protection of property rights of citizens, including lack of fair compensation and independent oversight mechanisms, which gave rise to widespread grievances. This chapter deals with the protection of the right to property in general, and the protection against evictions in particular. It analyses the practice in Ethiopia in light of the relevant international human rights standards. In addition to policy and legal reforms, the researcher recommends administrative measures to be designed to protect land tenure as part of the right to property, in order to reduce undue expropriations/evictions and to provide fair compensation to victims.

Keywords

property rights – eviction – compensation – international human rights – Ethiopia

1 Historical Development of the Right to Property

Prior to the coming into existence of various international human rights instruments, domestic laws had recognised the right to property as one of the fundamental human rights. For instance, the 1776 Virginia Declaration of

 DOI:10.1163/9789004415966_007

Rights declared property an inherent right of all men.[1] The Fifth Amendment to the United States (US) Constitution protects the right to property.[2] Similarly, Madison considered the right to property a precondition for individual rights in his essay in the following way:

> Government is instituted to protect the property of every sort; as well that, which lies in the various rights of individuals, as that which the term particularly expresses. This being the end of government, that alone is a just government, which impartially secures to every man, whatever is his own.[3]

The 1789 French Declaration of the Rights of Man and the Citizen states, 'property is an inviolable and sacred right'.[4] The Declaration further prohibits the deprivation of property rights except for public necessity, legally determined and only on the condition that the owner has been previously and equitably indemnified.[5] Similarly, most constitutions of European liberal democracies and other countries include bills of rights, often inspired by the American and French counterparts that protect the right to private property.

The American Founders and the early European proponents of liberal democracy understood that the legal protection of private property against arbitrary interference creates a sphere of inviolability that is crucial for the enjoyment of other freedoms. The promotion of the protection of private property is important because if all housing, media outlets, organisations, and religious institutions were publicly owned, the government would be able to exert undue control over a large portion of its own citizens' lives, direct their productive

1 *Virginia Declaration of Rights of 1776'* Britannica Encyclopaedia <https://www.britannica.com/topic/Virginia-Declaration-of-Rights> accessed 12 April 2018.

2 The Fifth Amendment to the United States (US) Constitution was that 'no person shall be deprived of life, liberty or property without due process of law; nor shall private property be taken for public use without just compensation'. See for further details the Fifth Amendment (Amendment V) to the United States Constitution (1791) < https://constitution.findlaw.com/amendment5.html> accessed 27 May 2017.

3 James Madison, 'Chapter 16: Property' in *The Founders' Constitution* (1792) (Volume 1 Document 23) <http://press-pubs.uchicago.edu/founders/documents/v1ch16s23.html> accessed 23 May 2017.

4 'The French Declaration of the Rights of Man and the Citizen from 1789' The History Guide (9 April 2014), art 17 <http://www.historyguide.org/intellect/declaration.html> accessed 23 May 2017.

5 Ibid.

capacities, and suppress dissent.[6] The classical understanding of the right to property primarily entails a negative obligation that protects against arbitrary expropriation and regulation of private property. It also entails a positive obligation, which is limited to adopting the appropriate legal framework and protecting against the transgressions of the right by third parties.[7] Generally, the historical development of the right to property indicates that it was first recognised under municipal law before getting international recognition.

2 The Right to Property, Eviction and Compensation under International Human Rights Law

2.1 *The Right to Property under International Human Rights Law*

Various international human rights instruments have recognised the right to protection of property. For instance, the Universal Declaration of Human Rights (UDHR) guarantees everyone the right to own property alone, as well as in association with others.[8] Similarly, regional human rights instruments have recognised property rights. For instance, the First Protocol to the European Convention for the Protection of Human Rights and Fundamental Freedoms recognises the peaceful enjoyment of possessions to every natural or legal person.[9] Likewise, the American Convention on Human Rights recognises that everyone has the right to the use and the enjoyment of property.[10]

As a constitutive part of a property, the right to housing is the most important component of this right. Accordingly, the right to housing has been recognised as a distinct human right since the adoption of the UDHR in 1948. Accordingly, the UDHR recognises housing for everyone as one of the important components to exercise the right to a standard of living adequate for the

6 Jacob Mchangama, 'The Right to Property in Global Human Rights Law' (2011) Cato Policy Report <https://www.cato.org/policy-report/mayjune-2011/right-property-global-human-rights-law> accessed 21 May 2017.

7 Ibid.

8 Universal Declaration of Human Rights (adopted 10 December 1948) UNGA Res 217 A(III) (UDHR), art 17 <http://www.un.org/en/universal-declaration-human-rights> accessed 21 May 2018.

9 Protocol 1 to the European Convention for the Protection of Human Rights and Fundamental Freedoms (signed 20 March 1952, entry into force 18 May 1954) ETS 9, art 1 <https://www.refworld.org/docid/3ae6b38317.html> accessed 18 May 2018.

10 American Convention on Human Rights 'Pact of San José, Costa Rica' (signed 22 November 1969, adopted 18 July 1978) 1144 UNTS 123 (ACHR) <http://www.refworld.org/docid/3ae6b36510.html> accessed 22 April 2017.

health and well-being of a person and their family.[11] Similarly, the International Covenant on Economic, Social and Cultural Rights (ICESCR) guarantees the right of everyone to an adequate standard of living for themselves and their family, including adequate housing.[12] Similarly, the United Nations Committee on Economic, Social and Cultural Rights (the Committee), specifically under its General Comment 4, elucidates contents of the right to adequate housing and indicates that the adequacy of housing has various components, including legal security of tenure, affordability, and accessibility for disadvantaged groups.[13] Furthermore, the International Covenant on Civil and Political Rights (ICCPR) implicitly contains a provision relevant to the protection of the right to housing.[14]

As a basic component of the right to property, different international human rights instruments further provide for the protection of the right to adequate housing.[15] Similarly, at the regional level, the African Charter on Human and Peoples' Rights (the Banjul Charter) in article 14 explicitly recognises the right to property. Accordingly, the right to property is guaranteed and can only be limited to pursue the interest of the public or in the general interest of the community, and in accordance with the provisions of appropriate laws. While

11 In addition to housing right, art 25 of the UDHR recognises to everyone the right to a standard of living adequate for the health and well-being of himself and his family, including food, clothing, medical care and necessary social services, and the right to security in the event of unemployment, sickness, disability, widowhood, old age or other lack of livelihood in circumstances beyond his control.

12 International Covenant on Economic, Social and Cultural Rights (adopted 16 December 1966, entered into force 3 January 1976) 993 UNTS 3 (ICESCR), art 11(1). See also International Covenant on Civil and Political Rights (adopted 16 December 1966, entered into force 23 March 1976) 999 UNTS 171 (ICCPR), art 17 which provides that 'no one shall be subject to arbitrary or unlawful interference with inter alia, his privacy and that everyone has the right to the protection of the law against such interference or attacks'.

13 United Nations Committee on Social, Economic and Cultural Rights, 'CESCR General Comment 4 – The right to adequate housing (Art. 11(1) of the Covenant)' (1991) E/1992/23, para 8.

14 See ICCPR (no 12) art 17 prohibiting arbitrary or unlawful interference with property right and protection of the law against such interference.

15 See International Convention on the Elimination of All Forms of Racial Discrimination (signed 20 November 1963, entry into force 4 January 1969) 660 UNTS 195, art 5(e)(iii) which prohibits any discrimination with regard to the right to housing. See also the Convention on the Rights of the Child (signed 20 November 1989, entry into force 2 September 1990) 1577 UNTS 3 (CRC), art 27(3) which makes the right to adequate housing an integral part of the realisation of other basic rights of children. Also the Convention on the Elimination of All Forms of Violence Against Women (signed 18 December 1979, entry into force 3 September 1981) 1249 UNTS 13 (CEDAW) art 14(2)(h) ensures the right to housing specifically for rural women.

interpreting article 14 of the Banjul Charter, the African Commission on Human and Peoples' Rights (the African Commission) has treated land as a property. Hence, there is recognition of the right to property based on different cases submitted to the African Commission. For instance, in the *Endorois case*, the African Commission underscored that the initial step in the protection of traditional African communities is the acknowledgment that the rights, interests, and benefits of such communities in their traditional lands constitute 'property' under the Banjul Charter.[16] The African Commission stated that the right to property is a 'justiciable' right to the use of land by an indigenous community without a real title.[17] In a similar case concerning the forced eviction of people from their village in Darfur, it argued that it did not matter if the victims had title to the land which they possessed (and derived a livelihood from) for generations and found the deprivation of the use of their property in violation of article 14.[18]

It can be inferred from article 14 of the Banjul Charter that it sticks to the conventional approach on the protection of the right to property, while including a limitation clause that provides for conditions of lawful interference with the right. Consequently, any limitation or infringement of the right to property not justified by public interest and not in accordance with appropriate laws is in essence in violation of the right.[19] Furthermore, laws providing

16 *Centre for Minority Rights Development, Minority Rights Group International and Endorois Welfare Council (On Behalf Of the Endorois Community) v Kenya* (2010) ACHPR 276/03 (Endorois case), paras 186–190 referring to the European Court of Human Rights' judgment in *Doğan and Others v Turkey*, European Court of Human Rights, Applications 8803-8811/02, 8813/02 and 8815-8819/02 (2004) and the Inter-American Court of Human Rights' judgment in *The Awas Tingni Case* (2001) <https://www.hrw.org/sites/default/files/related_material/2010_africa_commission_ruling_0.pdf> accessed 30 September 2017.

17 The African (Banjul) Charter on Human and Peoples' Rights (signed 27 June 1981, entry into force 12 October 1986) OAU Doc CAB/LEG/67/3 rev 5, 21 I.L.M. 58, art 14 <http://www.achpr.org/files/instruments/achpr/banjul_charter.pdf> accessed 12 April 2018.

18 African Commission on Human and Peoples' Rights, *Sudan Human Rights Organisation & Centre on Housing Rights and Evictions (COHRE) v Sudan* (2009) ACHPR 279/03-296/05 (Darfur case), paras 192 and 205 <http://www.achpr.org/files/sessions/45th/comunications/279.03-296.05/achpr45_279.03_296.05_eng.pdf> accessed 25 September 2017. See also the United Nations Office of the High Commissioner of Human Rights, 'Basic Principles and Guidelines on Development-based Evictions and Displacement' (2018) Annex 1 of the report of the Special Rapporteur on adequate housing as a component of the right to an adequate standard of living, A/HRC/4/18 which provides the protection provided by procedural requirements applies to all vulnerable persons and affected groups, irrespective of whether they hold title to home and property under domestic law.

19 *Ivorian Human Rights Movement (MIDH) v Cote d'Ivoire* AHRLR 62 (ACHPR 2008), paras 76–78.

for encroachment with the right to property should be in accordance with relevant international standards, should not be arbitrary and should, among other elements, provide for the right to a remedy. Intrusion on the right to property should in those circumstances be the most suitable way of achieving the legitimate interest of the public, with the least possible effect on the related rights of individuals or groups. Hence, limitation should be proportionate with public needs and forced evictions would in principle not meet the requirement.[20] Other appropriate conditions for encroachment, particularly in relation to indigenous land use, include prior environmental and social impact assessment, consultation to seek consent, compensation guaranteeing effective participation and a reasonable share of the benefit or profit.[21] Failure to comply with any of these would, therefore, mean a violation of the right to property.[22]

According to the African Commission's interpretation, article 14 of the Banjul Charter includes the right to undisturbed possession, use, control and access to one's own property.[23] In order to protect those property rights, the state party is obliged to ensure the peaceful enjoyment of property and to protect individuals and groups from arbitrary deprivation of the right. In a couple of cases, the African Commission found the closure and/or search of business premises and the confiscation or seizure of property, in the absence of evidence or proof that such actions were in the public interest, in violation of article 14.[24] Generally and based on the aforementioned discussion, the right to property is an important right recognised under international and regional human rights instruments. Forced eviction/expropriation is an exception only justifiable in limited circumstances.

20 Ibid para 218.

21 Endorois case (no 16) paras 225–228.

22 Ibid para 238 (finding a violation of art 14 because encroachment of Endorois land was not proportionate to public need and not in accordance with national and international law). See also the Darfur case (no 19) paras 192 and 205 ('nothing in the state's obligation, in addition to respect and protect, to regulate the exercise of the right to property in order for it to be accessible to everyone, taking public interest into consideration'). See also UN Basic Principles and Guidelines (no 19) which provide the protection provided by procedural requirements applies to all vulnerable persons and affected groups, irrespective of whether they hold title to home and property under domestic law.

23 *Media Rights Agenda v Nigeria*, ACHPR 224/98, para 77; *Constitutional Rights Project v Nigeria*, ACHPR 102/93, para 54.

24 Ibid.

2.2 *Expropriation/Eviction under International Human Rights Laws*

The term 'expropriation', which is also termed an 'eminent domain' or 'compulsory acquisition' in the common law legal system, has been defined as 'the sovereign power inherent in the states to take private property without the owner's consent for public use upon making just compensation thereof'.[25] This definition is comprehensive in that it contains key elements common in most expropriation laws, both national and international. For instance, the definition imposes a limit on the power of a state while undertaking expropriation, as it puts the state under the obligation to pay 'just compensation' to the owner whose property has been taken.

The 1962 United Nations General Assembly Resolution on Permanent Sovereignty over Natural Resources stated *inter alia* that expropriation 'shall be based on grounds or reasons of public utility, security, or the national interest which are recognised as overriding purely individual or private interest, both domestic and foreign'.[26]

Furthermore, the First Protocol to the European Convention for the Protection of Human Rights prohibits deprivation of property except when in the public interest and subject to the conditions provided for by law and the general principles of international law.[27] In a very similar language, the American Convention on Human Rights prohibits deprivation of property except upon payment of just compensation, for reasons of public utility or social interest, and in the cases and according to the forms established by law.[28]

It is noticeable that legal security of tenure is a basis for the right to housing and other related rights. If a person's house is subject to seizure at any time or is subject to the threat of arbitrary eviction, the person cannot be said to enjoy housing as a right, but rather to reside at another's pleasure. The Committee under the ICESCR explained its stance on forced eviction in its General Comment 7 on the provisions of the Covenant.

According to General Comment 7 of the Committee, forced eviction is said to happen where there are permanent or temporary removals against the will of individuals, families and/or communities from the homes and/or land which they occupy, without the provision of, and access to, appropriate forms

25 Charles S Rhyne, *Municipal Law* (National Institute of Municipal Law Officers 1957).
26 United Nations General Assembly, 'Permanent Sovereignty over Natural Resources' (14 December 1962) 1803(XVII), para 4.
27 Council of Europe, 'First Protocol to the Convention for the Protection of Human Rights and Fundamental Freedoms' (20 March 1952) ETS 9, art 1.
28 ACHR (no 10) art 21.

of legal or other protection.[29] Similarly, by considering international human rights provisions and instruments, the Comprehensive Human Rights Guidelines on Development-Based Displacement on the Practice of Forced Evictions (the Guidelines) come up with a definition of forced evictions that help implement the Guidelines. Accordingly,

> Forced evictions are acts and/or omissions involving the coerced and involuntary removal of individuals, groups and communities from their homes and/or lands and common property resources they occupy or are dependent upon, thus eliminating or limiting the possibility of an individual, group or community residing or working in a particular dwelling, residence or place.[30]

It is apparent that forced evictions constitute violations of human rights as they, directly or indirectly, affect the full spectrum of civil, political, cultural, economic and social rights enshrined in human rights instruments. Among the rights recognised under the UDHR, the right to property[31] can be violated. Similarly, under the ICCPR,[32] the right to life; the right to an effective remedy; freedom from cruel, inhuman and degrading treatment; the right to security of person; freedom of movement and to choose one's residence; the right to non-interference with privacy, home and family; and the right to vote and take part in the conduct of public affairs can be directly or indirectly violated. Moreover, rights recognised and protected under the ICESCR can also be directly or indirectly violated as a result of forced evictions. Among others,[33] the right to work; the right to an adequate standard of living, including the right to adequate housing, food, water and sanitation; the right to health; and the right to education can evidently be violated.

Generally, the violations of different human rights owing to evictions can be directly or indirectly be attributed to:

---

29 United Nations Committee on Social, Economic and Cultural Rights, 'CESCR General Comment 7 – The right to adequate housing (Art. 11(1) of the Covenant)' (1997) E/1998/22, para 8.

30 'The Practice of Forced Evictions: Comprehensive Human Rights Guidelines on Development-Based Displacement' (adopted by the Expert Seminar on the Practice of Forced Evictions, Geneva, 11–13 June 1997), Section 1.2 <http://hrlibrary.umn.edu/instree/forcedevictions.htm> accessed 12 September 2017.

31 UDHR (no 8) art 17.

32 See ICCPR (no 12) arts 2.3, 2.6, 6.1, 7, 9.1, 12.1, 17 and 25.

33 ICESCR (no 12) arts 11, 12 and 13.

- the way evictions are decided (for instance, when there is no consultation or participation, no information, and no recourse mechanisms);
- the way evictions are planned (for instance, when there is an absence of notification, relocation is not available, and compensation is not provided, delayed or subject to unjustified conditions);
- the way evictions are carried out (for instance, when carried out at night or in bad weather, and when there is no protection for people or their belongings);
- the result of eviction (for instance, disruption of children's education, interruption of medical treatment, mental trauma, loss of jobs and livelihoods, inability to vote because of homelessness, no access to basic services or justice because identity and property papers were destroyed during the evictions, etc.)[34]

Looking into the impact of evictions, the former United Nations Commission on Human Rights considered the practice of forced eviction a 'gross violation of human rights, in particular, the right to housing'.[35] Forced eviction undermines the security of tenure, which is the cornerstone of the right to housing under international human rights law.[36] The Committee has stated unequivocally that forced eviction is *prima facie* incompatible with the requirements of the ICESCR and can only be justified in the most exceptional circumstances, and in accordance with the relevant principles of international law.[37]

Owing to the adverse effects of forced or arbitrary evictions, the Committee outlined the normative content of the right to adequate housing and forced evictions, one of which is a legal security of tenure.[38] In unequivocal terms, the Committee has emphasised that all persons should possess a degree of security of tenure, which guarantees legal protection against forced evictions, harassment, and other threats.[39] In that regard, legislation against forced evictions is an important instrument upon which to build a system of effective protection.[40] According to the Committee, states are duty-bound to protect against

34 United Nations Office of the High Commissioner for Human Rights, 'Forced Evictions' (2014) Fact Sheet No. 25/Rev 1, 5 < https://www.refworld.org/docid/5566d6744.html> accessed 12 April 2018.

35 United Nations Commission on Human Rights, 'Forced Eviction' (1993) Resolution 1993/77.

36 '*Global Campaign for Secure Tenure*' UN HABITAT <http://mirror.unhabitat.org/categories.asp?catid=24> accessed 16 December 2017.

37 General Comment 7 (no 29) para 1.

38 General Comment 4 (no 13) para 8(a).

39 Ibid.

40 Ibid para 9.

forced evictions, including control over the disruptive actions of private persons and bodies.[41] For instance, the Committee refers to its earlier General Comment 2, that states 'international agencies should scrupulously avoid involvement in projects which … involve large-scale evictions or displacement of persons without the provision of all appropriate protection and compensation'.[42]

The Committee further indicates that when evictions are undertaken, discriminatory practices should not occur.[43] Furthermore, eviction needs to be proportionate and all due process and procedural safeguards provided in the General Comment need to be vehemently observed.[44] If damage or loss of real or personal property occurs due to forced eviction, adequate compensation must be made to the evictees.[45] Additionally, if evictions are carried out, they should not otherwise affect individual's human rights, particularly by rendering the evictees homeless or vulnerable to the violation of other human rights.[46] Hence, a state has the duty to ensure that adequate alternative housing, resettlement or access to productive land, depending on the case, is available.[47]

Generally, while interpreting the Covenant, the Committee (in 1991 and 1997) stated the following points, which can be considered as guiding principles for when evictions are undertaken:

- eviction should proceed only in exceptional circumstances.
- substantial justification must exist for any eviction.
- all feasible alternatives to eviction must be explored in consultation with the affected persons.
- There must be due process, including:
  a) an opportunity for genuine consultation with those affected;
  b) adequate and reasonable notice;
  c) information on the proposed evictions and, where applicable, on the alternative purpose for which the land or housing is to be used;
  d) government officials or their representatives to be present during an eviction especially where groups of people are involved;
  e) all persons carrying out the eviction to be properly identified;
  f) evictions not to take place in particularly bad weather or at night;
  g) provision of legal remedies; and

---

41 Ibid.

42 Ibid para 17.

43 Ibid.

44 Ibid paras 14–15.

45 Ibid para 13 which relays to ICCPR (no 12) art 2(3) requiring effective remedies for the violation of a person's human rights.

46 Ibid para 16.

47 Ibid.

h) a provision, where possible, of legal aid to persons in order to seek redress from the courts as needed.
- all individuals concerned have a right to adequate compensation for any property, both personal and real, that is affected.
- evictions should not result in individuals being rendered homeless or vulnerable to the violation of other human rights. Where those affected are unable to provide for themselves, the state party must take all appropriate measures, to the maximum of its available resources, to ensure that adequate alternative housing, resettlement or access to productive land, as the case may be, is available.
- Legislation must be enacted to ensure effective protection from forced eviction.[48]

Under the Guidelines, states are obliged to undertake maximum effective protection. Accordingly, states are duty-bound to guarantee the security of tenure for all persons, but special consideration must be given to the rights of indigenous peoples, children and women, and other vulnerable groups. These obligations are further made as of immediate nature and are not qualified by resource-related considerations.[49] In other words, this means that the prohibition of forced evictions is a legal measure that can be taken immediately and is not dependent on the availability of resources.

Under the Guidelines, even if the eviction is justifiable under development-based initiatives, states are required to ensure eviction impact assessments are undertaken before the initiation of any project, in order to fully secure the human rights of all potentially affected persons, groups, and communities.[50] States are further required to refrain from compulsorily acquiring housing or land, except when legitimate, necessary, and designed to facilitate the enjoyment of human rights through measures such as land reform or redistribution. As a last resort, the proceeding of expropriation or compulsory acquisition should be undertaken by considering the following conditions:

a) determined and envisaged by law and norms regarding forced eviction;
b) solely for the purpose of protecting the general welfare in a democratic society;
c) reasonable and proportional; and
d) in accordance with the present Guidelines.[51]

48 See the Committee's General Comment 4 (no 13); the Committee's General Comment 7 (no 29).

49 Guidelines (no 30) para 9.

50 Ibid para 12.

51 Ibid para 17.

Pursuant to the Guidelines, states are duty-bound to adopt legislative measures prohibiting any forced eviction without a court order. Accordingly, the court is also required to consider all relevant circumstances of affected persons, groups and communities and any decision by fully observing the principles of equality and justice and internationally recognised human rights.[52] In this regard, the South African Constitution is almost similar in its content to Paragraph 22 of the Guidelines. Accordingly, the Constitution provides that 'everyone has the right to have access to adequate housing. The state must take reasonable legislative and other measures within its available resources, to achieve the progressive realisation of this right'.[53]

In a very similar wording to the Guidelines, the Basic Principles and Guidelines on Development-Based Evictions and Displacement put states under the obligation to ensure evictions occur in exceptional circumstances and must be, therefore:

a) authorised by law;
b) carried out in accordance with international human rights law;
c) undertaken solely for the purpose of promoting the general welfare; reasonable and proportional;
d) regulated so as to ensure full and fair compensation and rehabilitation; and
e) carried out in accordance with the present guidelines.[54]

The South African courts have played a significant role in ensuring substantive and procedural protections to those facing evictions from their homes. They have repeatedly articulated progressive judgments. Even before the ratification of the ICESCR by South Africa, the courts of the country referred to the ICESCR and the related General Comments as a valuable guide when interpreting Section 26 of the Constitution, as the Constitution requires every court to interpret legislation to be as consistent as possible with international law.[55] The South African constitutional jurisprudence seems to be highly consistent with the international framework, as it gives emphasis to most of the international standards on evictions. The approach taken in the court's decisions is similar

52 Ibid para 22.

53 The Constitution of the Republic of South Africa (signed 18 December 1996, entry into force 4 February 1997) Act No. 108/1996, Section 26.

54 UN Basic Principles and Guidelines (no 18).

55 UN Habitat, Eviction, Acquisition, Expropriation, and Compensation: Practices and Selected Case Studies (Working Paper I, 2013). South Africa is a signatory to ICESCR but ratified the Covenant in 2015. However, the Constitutional Court of the country referred to the ICESCR in its verdict without waiting for its ratification, which is a positive step for the application and enforcement of international human rights instruments.

to that of the Committee, requiring a high level of justification for forced evictions. The courts have further moved to the extent of giving directives to concerned authorities to fulfil their obligations of ensuring the right to adequate housing, especially in the context of eviction.[56]

In South Africa, the landmark verdict in the *Grootboom case*[57] in 2000 has influenced policy. In accordance with the Constitutional Court's decision, the National Housing Programme, Housing Assistance in Emergency Housing Situations was adopted in 2004 to give effect to the ruling of the Court in the *Grootboom case*. The Constitutional Court ordered the state to 'devise and implement within its available resources a comprehensive and coordinated programme progressively to realise the right of access to adequate housing'. The court further added that the programme must include reasonable measures 'to provide relief for people who have no access to land, no roof over their heads, and who are living in intolerable conditions or crisis situation'.[58] The South African experience indicates that courts could play a pivotal role in influencing the government through their rulings to promote the government to come up with policies and programmes for the better protection and enforcement of the right to housing in particular, and human rights in general.

2.3 *Compensation under International Human Rights Law and Standards*

The issue of compensation in connection with the right to property has been a problematic issue for long. Similarly, compensation for losses suffered when a government acquires a piece of land is typically one of the most complex and contentious aspects of compulsory acquisition. However, the 1962 United Nations General Assembly Resolution on Permanent Sovereignty over Natural Resources provided that an owner of a property shall be paid appropriate compensation, in accordance with the rules in force in the state taking such measures in the exercise of its sovereignty and in accordance with international law,[59] when expropriation is ordered on the grounds or reasons of public

56 L Chenwi, 'Putting Flesh on the Skeleton: South African Judicial Enforcement of the Right to Adequate Housing of those Subject to Evictions' (2018) 2 Human Rights Law Review 105.

57 See *Irene Grootboom et al. v the Government of the Republic of South Africa et al.* (2000) CCT 38/00 (Grootboom Case) <www.saflii.org/za/cases/ZACC/2000/14.pdf> accessed 14 April 2018.

58 L Chenwi, *Evictions in South Africa, Relevant International and National Standards* (Community Law Centre, University of the Western Cape 2008).

59 United Nations General Assembly (no 26) para 4.

utility, security, or the national interest.[60] A long-standing principle in many jurisdictions is that compensation should be guided by the objectives of 'equity' and 'equivalence' – that is, the adequacy of compensation should be measured against the goal of ensuring that people are neither impoverished nor enriched.[61] This is the principle also articulated in the Policy on Involuntary Resettlement that states,

> Displaced persons should be assisted in their efforts to improve their livelihoods and standards of living or at least restore them, in real terms, to pre-displacement levels or to levels prevailing prior to the beginning of project implementation, whichever is higher.[62]

However, applying those principles of compensation in practice has always been an extremely complex challenge. In any case, persons who are subjected to eviction have a right to compensation for any loss of land, personal, real or other property or goods, including rights or interests in property not recognised in national legislation, incurred in connection with a forced eviction.[63] The compensation to the victims includes land, access to common property resources and cash payments. According to the Comprehensive Human Rights Guidelines on Development-Based Displacement on the Practice of Forced Evictions, all persons, groups, and communities have the right to suitable resettlement, which includes the right to alternative land, or housing, which is safe, secure, accessible, affordable and habitable.[64] The compensation to be made is for any loss of land, personal, real or other property or goods, including rights or interests in property not recognised in national legislation incurred in connection with a forced eviction.[65] Under the same Guidelines, the compensation should not be restricted to cash payments, but must include land and access to common property resources.[66] The Guidelines furthermore provide all persons with a right to appeal on any judicial or other decisions affecting

60 Ibid.

61 Food and Agriculture Organization of the United Nations, 'Compulsory Acquisition of Land and Compensation' (FAO Land Tenure Studies 10, Rome 2008).

62 World Bank, 'Operational Manual OP 4.12 – Involuntary Resettlement' (2001) <https://policies.worldbank.org/sites/ppf3/PPFDocuments/090224b0822f89db.pdf> accessed 17 April 2018.

63 Guidelines (no 30) para 24.

64 Ibid para 27.

65 Ibid para 24.

66 Ibid.

their rights as established pursuant to the Guidelines to the highest national judicial authority.[67]

Similarly, the UN Basic Principles and Guidelines on Development-Based Evictions and Displacement provide for remedies for forced evictions. Accordingly, appropriate remedies should include a fair hearing, access to a legal counsel, legal aid, return, restitution, resettlement, rehabilitation, and compensation.[68] It further provides details on provision of compensation. Accordingly, when eviction is unavoidable and necessary for the promotion of the general welfare, the compensation to be provided by the state for any losses of personal, real or other property or goods, including rights or interests in the property, must be fair and just.[69] Moreover, it provides that all those evicted, irrespective of whether they hold title to their property, should be entitled to compensation for the loss, salvage and transport of their properties affected, including the original dwelling and land lost or damaged in the process, which also includes losses related to an informal property of slum dwellings.[70] Similarly, the World Bank policy mentioned earlier emphasises that people affected by development projects should be able to improve, or at least be well off after the project as would have been the case without the project. The policy also specifies that the absence of a legal title to land and other assets should not prevent affected people from receiving compensation and that the amount of compensation should be sufficient to replace lost assets, incomes, and living standards.[71] Hence, the World Bank's Operational Policy Statement on

67 Ibid para 23.

68 UN Basic Principles and Guidelines (no 18) para 59.

69 Ibid para 60 further provides for open-ended economically assessable damage such as loss of life or limb; physical or mental harm; lost opportunities, including employment, education and social benefits; material damages and loss of earnings, including loss of earning potential; moral damage; and cost required for legal or expert assistance, medicine and medical services, and psychological and social services. It further provides that cash compensation should under no circumstances replace real compensation in the form of land and common property resources. Where land has been taken, the evicted should be compensated with land commensurate in quality, size, and value, or better.

70 Ibid para 61.

71 The World Bank's criteria for eligibility state, 'Displaced persons may be classified in one of the following three groups: (a) those who have formal legal rights to land... (b) those who do not have formal legal rights to land ... but have a [recognizable] claim to such land or assets ... and (c) those who have no recognizable legal right or claim to the land they are occupying. Persons covered under... (a) and (b) are provided compensation for the land they lose and other assistance... Persons covered under... (c) are provided resettlement assistance in lieu of compensation for the land they occupy, and other assistance, as necessary ... if they occupy the project area prior to a cut-off date...'. See World Bank, 'Gambia – Education Sector Support Project: Resettlement Plan: Resettlement Policy

Involuntary Resettlement underlines the need to identify, understand and mitigate various impoverishment risks (social, cultural, economic, and environment), which may arise because of a development project that entails displacement of people. The three core objectives of the Operational Policy on Involuntary Resettlement are:

a) Involuntary resettlement should be avoided where feasible, or minimised exploring all viable alternative project designs;
b) Whereas it is not feasible to avoid resettlement, resettlement activities should be conceived and executed as sustainable development programmes, providing sufficient investment resources to enable the persons displaced by the project to a share in project benefits. Displaced persons should be meaningfully consulted and should have opportunities to participate in planning and the implementation of resettlement programmes; and
c) Displaced persons should be assisted in their effort to improve their livelihoods and standard of living or at least restore them, in real terms, to pre-displacement levels.[72]

According to the World Bank, compensation must be paid at full replacement cost prior to the actual move, and various sorts of assistance must be provided during the transition period, especially in the resettlement sites. The needs of the poorest groups of claimants must be considered paramount. Community participation in the planning and resettling of claimants is encouraged and resettlers ought to be socially and economically integrated into host communities, to ensure that adverse impacts on host communities are minimised. Land, housing, infrastructure, and other compensations are to be provided to all adversely affected populations without segregation, and absence of legal title to land by such groups should not be a barrier to compensation.[73]

At the African Union level, article 14 of the Banjul Charter is not explicit enough as far as compensation for encroachment on the right to property is concerned. Despite article 14 of the Banjul Charter makes no mention of compensation in case of encroachment on the right to property, it is arguable that the phrase 'appropriate laws' should provide for the payment of adequate, reasonable and just compensation.[74] The Charter's provision for 'the peoples' right to lawful recovery and adequate compensation in case of spoliation of

Framework' (2018) SFG4040 <http://documents.worldbank.org/curated/en/354261518033472605/Resettlement-policy-framework> accessed 15 May 2018.

72 World Bank (no 62).

73 Ibid.

74 Endorois case (no 16).

their wealth and natural resources'[75] indicates that the omission from article 14 may not be purposeful. Hence, states may be required to pay compensation as a remedy to an unjustified interference with individuals' or groups' right to property.

The African Commission has taken important decisions regarding the compensation of the encroached property right. For instance, in the *Modise case*, the Commission found the 'heavy financial loses' of the complainant due to confiscation of his belongings and property by the government of Botswana is an encroachment of his right to property under article 14 and further argued that the Government should compensate him adequately.[76] In another similar case, the Commission found the confiscation and dispossession of property without the provision of adequate compensation is a violation of the right to property.[77] From the decisions of the African Commission, it can be concluded that the right to compensation in case of improper encroachment with property is justifiable and justiciable. Moreover, in the *Endorois case*, owing to eviction, the Endorois' access to land was restricted to the extent they were prevented from practicing their pastoralist way of life. The complainants argued that the Kenyan government violated their right to development since it had 'failed to adequately involve the Endorois in the development process to ensure the continued improvement of the community's well-being'. Hence, the Commission found violations of the Endorois' rights to religious practice, to property, to culture, to free disposition of natural resources and to development citing articles 8, 14, 17, 21 and 22 of the Banjul Charter, respectively.[78] The African Commission then decided that the Kenyan government 'bears the burden of creating conditions favourable to a people's development' and consequently considered that 'the failure to provide adequate compensation and benefits, or provide suitable land for grazing indicates that the respondent state did not adequately engage the Endorois in the development process'.[79] It is, therefore, through the recognition of violations of the right to property, food or cultural life, the Endorois can claim adequate participation rights and remedies for the loss of their land. Generally, it can be concluded from the decisions of the African Commission that the right to compensation in case of improper encroachment with property right is justifiable and justiciable.

75 Banjul Charter (no 17) art 21(2).

76 *Modise v Botswana* (2000) ACHPR 97/93 (Modise case), paras 94 and 98.

77 *Institute for Human Rights and Development in Africa* (IHRDA) *v Angola* (2008) ACHPR 292/04, para 73.

78 Endorois case (no 16).

79 Ibid.

3 The Right to Property, Expropriation/Eviction and Compensation in Ethiopia

Under this section, the right to property, expropriation, and eviction in Ethiopia is discussed by looking into the Ethiopian Constitution and other laws. The sub-sections of this section entertain the normative frameworks that help understand the context of property rights, expropriation/eviction, and compensation, which in turn help to see the challenges facing the Ethiopian legal system concerning the protection of property rights.

3.1 *The Right to Property in Ethiopia*

The Constitution of the Federal Democratic Republic of Ethiopia (FDRE) explicitly recognises the right to property including land.[80] Owing to the federal arrangement, both the Federal Government and the units of the Federation hold respective powers as far as land and other natural resources are concerned. Accordingly, the FDRE Constitution mandates the Federal Government with the power to enact laws for the utilisation and conservation of land and other natural resources, historical sites and objects[81] whereas the Federal States are mandated to administer land and other natural resources in accordance with federal laws.[82] Concerning ownership of land, the Constitution opts for public ownership of both urban and rural land. Hence, land ownership as well as other natural resources are exclusively vested in the state and the Ethiopian people[83] and therefore not saleable. Consequently, private individuals can have only usufruct[84] right on land. Pursuant to the Constitution[85] and the FDRE Rural Land Administration and Land Use Proclamation,[86] Ethiopian peasants have the right to obtain land free of charge. Similarly, Ethiopian

80 Federal Negarit Gazeta, 'The Constitution of the Federal Democratic Republic of Ethiopia' Proclamation No. 1/1995.

81 Ibid arts 51(5) and 55(2)(a).

82 Ibid art 52(2)(d).

83 Ibid art 40(3).

84 'Usufruct' is a civil law term referring to the right of one individual to use and enjoy the property of another, provided its substance is neither impaired nor altered. Hence, an individual has the right to use the land. As a result, the holder of the right may not have the right to sell the property, etc. See *'Usufruct'* The Free Dictionary (2019) <http://legal-dictionary.thefreedictionary.com/usufruct> accessed 30 August 2017.

85 See FDRE Constitution (no 80) art 40(4).

86 Federal Negarit Gazeta, 'Rural Land Administration and Land Use Proclamation' Proclamation No.456/2005, art 5(1)(a).

pastoralists have the right to free land for grazing and cultivation.[87] Private investors, however, have the right to use land only with payment.[88]

As far as the right to property is concerned, the FDRE Constitution recognises to every Ethiopian the full right to the immovable property s/he builds and to the permanent improvements s/he has made on the land with his/her labour or capital.[89] The right includes the right to alienate, to bequeath, and, where the right of use expires, to remove his/her property, transfer his/her title, or claim compensation for it.[90] Here, it can be inferred from the provisions of the FDRE Constitution and other laws that the right to property is recognised and therefore individuals have the right to acquire, to use and to dispose of the property.

3.2 *Expropriation in Ethiopia*

National constitutions and laws typically refer to the compulsory acquisition of property being used for 'public purposes', for 'public uses' and/or in the 'public interest'. In some jurisdictions, these terms have distinct but overlapping meanings. In other cases, these distinctions are blurred or non-existent.[91] When it comes to defining 'public purposes', there is great variety among national laws. In some countries, laws provide a list of land uses that fall within the definition of 'public purpose'; other countries make it general, which could of course lead to abuse by public authorities while expropriating or evicting peoples.[92]

As stipulated under the FDRE Constitution, the right to property in Ethiopia can only be limited by the government through its policy of expropriation of private property for public interests.[93] Pursuant to the wordings of the Constitution,[94] different legislations have been enacted to regulate expropriation and related matters. The legislation meant to regulate the expropriation of landholdings for public purposes and payment of compensation empowers public authorities with the power to expropriate rural or urban land holdings. The public organ exercises its authority of expropriation where it believes that

87 Ibid; FDRE Constitution (no 80) art 40(4);.

88 FDRE Constitution (no 80) art 40(6).

89 Ibid art 40(7).

90 Ibid.

91 Jonathan Mills, 'An Explanatory Note on Issues Relevant for Public-Private Partnerships' 1(3) PPP Insights, 2 <https://library.pppknowledgelab.org/d/1219/download> accessed 13 May 2018.

92 Ibid.

93 FDRE Constitution (no 80) art 40(8).

94 Ibid.

it should be used for a better development project to be carried out by public entities, private investors, cooperative societies or other organs, or where the appropriate higher regional or federal government organ for the same purpose has decided on such expropriation.[95] Similarly, both the Urban Lands Lease Holding Proclamation and the Rural Land Administration and Land Use Proclamation mandate the appropriate body with the power to clear and take over urban land meant for public interest.[96] Generally, both the FDRE Constitution and other subordinate legislations mandate public authorities to expropriate property, including land for public interest.

3.3 *Compensation in Ethiopia*

The FDRE Constitution and other laws of Ethiopia regulate compensation and related matters. Accordingly, the Constitution under article 40(8) stipulates that compensation commensurate with the value of the property to be expropriated due to public interest is to be paid in advance. Similarly, the Constitution stipulates that all persons who have been displaced or whose livelihoods have been adversely affected because of the state's programmes have the right to commensurate monetary or alternative means of compensation, including relocation with adequate state assistance.[97] The Constitution does not, however, define the word 'commensurate', but the Ethiopian Civil Code opts for 'indemnity theory' in determination of compensation. Accordingly, article 1474(1) of the Civil Code provides that the amount of compensation be paid must be equal to the amount of the actual damage caused by expropriation.

The Ethiopian legal system adopts the 'Cost Replacement Method'[98] for valuation of property for which compensation is payable. Accordingly, two types of compensation dependent on the valuation made as per the 'Cost Replacement Method' can be envisaged in Ethiopia. The first one is compensation

95 Federal Negarit Gazeta, 'Expropriation of Land Holdings for Public Purposes and Payment of Compensation Proclamation' Proclamation No. 455/2005, art 3(1).

96 For further details see Federal Negarit Gazeta, 'Urban Lands Lease Holding Proclamation' Proclamation No. 721/2011, arts 25(1)(b) and 26(1); Proclamation No.456/2005 (no 86).

97 FDRE Constitution (no 80) art 44(2).

98 The 'Cost Replacement Method' is the valuation method to estimate the values of real estate developer on the expropriated land by considering the replacement or reproduction cost of the properties developed and the improvements made on the land plus some amount of displacement compensation when the landholder is alienated from the land. See Appraisal Institute, *The Appraisal of Real Estate* (Appraisal Institute 2001) as cited in Abebaw Abebe, Belay 'Expropriation, Valuation and Payment of Compensation: the Law and Practice in Addis Ababa City' (2016) 1(2) International Review of Humanities and Scientific Research 24 <http://www.irhsr.org/papers/1478667516.pdf> accessed 23 December 2017.

to be made for the loss of immovable private property,[99] whereas the second one is compensation to be made to persons displaced by the government's development programmes.[100] Pursuant to article 2(1) of Proclamation No. 455/2005, there are three ways or modes of making compensation to a person affected by expropriation: in cash; in-kind; or in both. As per article 7 of the Proclamation, compensation is payable for each property situated on the land, as well as for permanent improvements made to such land. While compensation for a property is to be fixed based on replacement cost of the property, compensation for permanent improvement is to be fixed based on, and equal to, the capital and labour expended on the land. The amount of compensation payable to an urban dweller may not in any way be less than the current cost of constructing a single room, low-cost house in accordance with the standard set by the concerned region.[101] The cost of removal, transportation, and erection shall be paid as compensation for a property that could be relocated and continue its service as before.[102]

The other way of paying compensation is that compensation payable for displacement is paid in addition to the payment made for the property situated on the land, and for payment improvements made to such land.[103] Accordingly, compensation for the permanent displacement of a rural landholder should be 'equivalent to ten times the average annual income ... secured during the five years preceding the expropriation of the land'.[104] In the case of temporary displacement, the approach is the same with permanent displacement, but it is time-bounded and only payable as long as the displacement continues. Furthermore, it should not exceed the amount that a person would have received had s/he been permanently displaced.[105] In the case of displacement as a result of expropriation made under the Proclamation, the Woreda (District) administration may decide to compensate the displaced person by providing substitute land, which can be easily ploughed and generate a comparable income.[106] In such a case, the compensation payment due to the landholder in cash cannot exceed a one-time payment of the average annual income secured during the five years preceding the expropriation of the land.[107]

99 FDRE Constitution (no 80) art 40.
100 Ibid art 42.
101 Proclamation No. 455/2005 (no 95) art 2.
102 Ibid art 5.
103 Ibid art 8.
104 Ibid art 8(1).
105 Ibid art 8(2).
106 Ibid art 8(3).
107 Ibid.

In urban areas, the landholder whose landholding has been expropriated is entitled to compensation in addition to the compensation paid for the property situated on the land and for permanent improvements made to such land:

- a plot of urban land for the construction of a dwelling (business) house of which the size can be determined by the urban administration; and
- a displacement compensation equivalent to the estimated annual rent of the demolished dwelling (business) house or be allowed to reside (trade), free of charge, for one year in a comparable dwelling (business) house owned by the urban administration.[108]

In addition, when the land is possessed in a lease system, the right to land use can be terminated prior to its expiry date, when it is decided to use the land for other purposes of public interest.[109] In this case, the leaseholder has a right, in addition to the compensation paid for the property situated on the land and for permanent improvements made to such land, to be provided with a similar plot of land. Such a plot can be used for the remaining lease period or longer if the new land is less in size than the former land or if its rent is less than that of the former land.[110] However, if the leaseholder does not want replacement land, s/he has the right to request for and take the balance of the lease payment.[111] Similarly, the Urban Lease Proclamation provides where the leasehold of urban land is terminated for other purposes than of public interest, the leaseholder shall be paid commensurate compensation.[112] In a similar way as with the Expropriation and Compensation Proclamation, the Urban Land Lease Proclamation provides that a person displaced owing to public interest shall be provided with a substitute plot of land within the urban centre.[113] Unlike the Expropriation and Compensation Proclamation, the Urban Land Lease Proclamation has left the determination of the size of the plot of land to be given as a substitute to be effected by the region or the city administration.[114]

As far as the valuation of a property situated on the land to be expropriated is concerned, it is meant to be carried out by certified private or public institutions or individual consultants on the basis of a valuation formula adopted at the regional level.[115] However, the law further provides that until the Ministry

108 Ibid art 8(4).
109 Proclamation No. 721/2011 (no 96) art 25(1)(b). See also Proclamation No. 455/2005 (no 97) art 8(6).
110 Proclamation No. 455/2005 (no 95) art 8(6).
111 Ibid.
112 Proclamation No. 721/2011 (no 96) arts 25(4) and 26(1).
113 Ibid art 26(2).
114 Ibid.
115 Ibid art 9(1).

of Federal Affairs (MFA) ascertains the creation of the required capacity to undertake valuation of property as stipulated under article 9(1) of the Proclamation, such valuation can be carried out by the committees to be established.[116]

4 Challenges Related to Property Rights, Eviction and Compensation in Ethiopia

4.1 *Challenges Related to the Vagueness of Legal Provisions*

In Ethiopia, there is a vague legal provision allowing public authorities to expropriate property to benefit a private company that ultimately fails to fulfil a 'public purpose' objective. In this regard, Karuturi Global,[117] one of the largest foreign holders of land in Ethiopia, is a case in point. It sought to invest in palm oil and food crop production and promised jobs and new infrastructure to the local communities. However, the promises are reported to have remained largely unfulfilled. Moreover, the company pays a low rental rate to the government for the lands used, and many of the peasant farmers that occupied the land were left without compensation.

The other challenge related to 'public purpose' is that those affected by the expropriation cannot challenge the decision of administrative authorities regarding the existence or non-existence of 'public purpose' either before administrative tribunals or regular courts, as can be impliedly inferred from the Expropriation and Compensation Proclamation law.[118]

It means that unlike courts in South Africa,[119] courts in Ethiopia at different levels do not have the power to evaluate the existence or non-existence of 'public purpose'. The Expropriation and Compensation Proclamation only allows lodging of a complaint to the administrative organ established by the concerned urban administration, in order to hear grievances related to urban land holdings on issues pertaining to the meagreness of the amount of

116 Ibid art 9(2).

117 Karuturi Global is an Indian agribusiness company. The Company leased 300,000 hectares of land in Western Ethiopia, Gambella Region in 2008. The Company's farming practice was having visible devastating environmental and demographic impact on the local flora and fauna. As a result, thousands of the displaced local communities were complaining bitterly about the loss of crops and grazing lands. See Alemayehu G Mariam, '*Bye, Bye Karuturistan, Ethiopia!*' Pambazuka News – Voices for Freedom and Justice (26 February 2015) <https://www.pambazuka.org/governance/Bye-Bye-Karuturistan-ethiopia> accessed 6 December 2018.

118 Such prohibition can be inferred from the provisions of the law itself. For further details see Proclamation No. 455/2005 (no 95) art 11.

119 Chenwi (no 58).

compensation.[120] In the rural areas where an administrative organ to hear grievances related to urban landholding is not yet established, a complaint relating to the amount of compensation can be submitted to the regular court having jurisdiction.[121] If the party is not satisfied with the decision of the administrative organ, an appeal is possible to the regular appellate court or municipality appellate court, in which the decision is final.[122]

4.2 *Challenges Related to Valuation of Property and Payment of Compensation*

A further challenge is related to the valuation of the compensation for property to be expropriated and its payment. Since the enactment of the Expropriation and Compensation Proclamation in 2005, land valuation has been undertaken by a committee organised by authorities, but not by an independent consultant. Hence, there is a critique that the property valuation currently undertaken by the committee is not independent from the expropriating public authority and therefore the compensation to be paid in cash and/or in-kind is small, which practically affects the property right of the evictee.[121]

Another challenge of the law is that the single price determined by the expropriating authority has not been updated annually based on the actual market price, although the law requires a market price to be considered while making the valuation of compensation. For instance, the Addis Ababa City Directive on Expropriation Valuation and Payment of Compensation No. 19/2014 provides that compensation to be paid shall not be less than the amount which can build a single saving house.[122] For instance, the current amount which is said to build a single saving house in Addis Ababa City is 111,000 Ethiopian Birr, which corresponds to a value of 4,088.32 USD.[123] According to the views of the

120 Proclamation No. 455/2005 (no 95) art 11(2).

121 Focus group discussion held with members of the Land Valuation Committee in Addis Ababa on 19 January 2017. They further discussed the payment made to the expropriated farmers for each square meter is 2.9 Ethiopian birr according to the current exchange rate of 26 April 2018 (US$ 0.11) whereas the government leases each square meter for thousands of Ethiopian birr. According to the focus group discussant, such an exaggerated difference puts the farmers in a very precarious situation, leading them to be daily laborers and beggars. The names of the members of the focus group discussion are confidential and are on record with the author.

122 See Addis Ababa City Directive on Expropriation Valuation and Payment of Compensation No. 19/2014 as cited in Addis Ababa City Roads and Transport Bureau, 'Resettlement Policy Framework' (2016) Ethiopia Transportation System Improvement Project (TRANSIP) SFG1839, 147 <http://documents.worldbank.org/curated/en/987341468257698361/pdf/SFG1839-RP-P151819-PUBLIC-Disclosed-2-23-2016.pdf> accessed 14 May 2018.

123 The exchange rate between the Ethiopian birr and US$ relates to April 26, 2018.

participants of the focus group discussion, this amount cannot build a single saving house, as the construction materials and labour costs are increasing at an alarming rate, sometimes even on a daily basis.

4.3 *Challenges Related to the Right to Appeal*

A further challenge is related to exercise the right to appeal. The Expropriation and Compensation Proclamation provides that if the aggrieved party is not satisfied with a decision of the administrative organ that first heard the grievance on the insufficiency of the amount of compensation, s/he may appeal to the regular appellate court or municipal appellate court within thirty days from the date of the decision.[124] The Proclamation, however, provides a condition to exercise the right to appeal. Accordingly, the aggrieved landholder served with an expropriation order can only file his/her appeal on the condition that the appeal is accompanied by a document proving the handover of the land to the Urban or Woreda Administration.[125] What further complicates the appeal right of the aggrieved party is that the law provides that the execution of an expropriation order must not be delayed due to a complaint regarding the amount of compensation.[126] Here, it can be inferred from the legislation that grievances on the amount of payment of compensation can only be entertained by a court after the execution of expropriation.

Because of the conditions provided under the aforementioned law, in practice the aggrieved party does not usually take his/her appeal to a court, as he/she is frustrated due to handing over the property to the public authority and likely feeling that it is futile to file an appeal affecting his/her property right.[127] Therefore, the aggrieved party accepts the proposed compensation by the authority even if not satisfied by the compensation amount.[128]

4.4 *Challenges Related to the Right to Housing*

Different studies show that there are serious eviction cases in Ethiopia. Accordingly, thousands of people are evicted from their land and homes throughout the country, most of which are poor farmers whose life is dependent on

124 See Proclamation No. 455/2005 (no 95) art 11(4).

125 Ibid art 11(6). 'Woreda' is an Amharic word and its equivalent meaning is 'District'.

126 Ibid art 11(7).

127 Focus group discussion with evictees in Addis Ababa who received meagre compensation in 2010 and have serious grievances with public authorities. The names of the members of the focus group discussion are confidential and are on record with the author. The group discussion took place on 20 January 2017.

128 Ibid.

subsidy.[129] In particular, there is a large-scale forced eviction of poor farmers, who have often inhabited land in Addis Ababa and its surroundings for centuries. Particularly for the last 25 years, the government has been rooting out poor people to make land available for industries, real estate, and the construction of low-cost housing,[130] usually referred to as condominium housing for the poor.

The fertile farmlands have been leased to investors and real estate developers. Through this, local communities do not have a direct or indirect benefit from the investments. Those farmers who have been forcefully evicted from their ancestral land without being fairly compensated are led to become daily labourers, beggars, and slum dwellers.[131]

Land in urban areas, particularly in Addis Ababa, is very scarce as a result of rapid urbanisation. This problem has further been escalated by challenges related to land management, corruption, and bureaucratic impediments making the provision of land to ordinary residents complex.[132] The increment of the cost of a rental house, the unbearable lease price of land to the poor and the failure of the government to provide housing have forced citizens to ensure that they have a roof over their head at their disposal. These challenges have thus also forced citizens to engage in the construction of houses without a permit.[133]

The urban renewal policy of the government, which is meant for the demolition of slums in different parts of Addis Ababa, has affected the poor living in them despite the communities' relocation to low-cost houses outside the inner city.[134] The transfer has affected their livelihoods and social bonds. The eviction has affected the petty commerce evictees formerly engaged in, has

129 Among others, the Gambella eviction is a case in point. In this case, the Gambella Regional State decided to hand over a forest area to an investor for the purpose of tea farming. The complaint was submitted in May 2011 to the Human Rights Commission of Ethiopia but rejected for lack of jurisdiction. However, there is no provision that prohibits the Commission from investigating the complaint.

130 Despite the government's effort to construct condominiums for the poor due to corruption, those government efforts have stalled. There are Addis Ababa residents who were registered for condominium housing in 2004/5 and saved money with the bank for the purpose of construction, still they have not received housing although more than a decade has elapsed.

131 The researcher's personal observation from the interview conducted.

132 Mohammed Abdo, 'Human Rights Commission of Ethiopia and Issues of Forced Evictions: A Case-Oriented Study of its Practice' in Eva Brems et al., *Human Rights and Development: Legal Perspectives from and for Ethiopia* (Brill 2015) 345.

133 Ibid.

134 Ibid 346.

subjected them to additional transportation cost complexities and intruded into their long-established social schemes such as *Idir* (cultural life insurance) and *Iqub* (cultural saving). Hence, eviction clearly affects the right to protection of property, livelihood, and social and cultural rights.[135]

On another occasion, on 30 June 2016, the government evicted at least 3,000 residents deemed to be 'squatters' in Lafto sub-city, Addis Ababa. The measure was taken during the rainy season, making life cumbersome to the evictees and additionally violating international laws and standards requiring evictions not to take place in bad weather.[136] The government demolished thousands of houses by justifying that the residents lacked legal title, as they were informal settlers building the houses illegally.[137] Evictees on the other hand were arguing that the government already recognised their houses, as it provided infrastructure.[138]

As already discussed, even if the evictees lack legal title, lack of the title should not take away their housing right, as respect for human rights is independent of a particular status, including ownership.[139] The evictees were apparently offered no prior consultation or alternative housing[140] and were given only three days' notice of eviction. While the residents were meeting the local administration to complain, the government taskforce started demolishing their houses. The situation turned violent, resulting in the death of the District Administrator and two police officers.[141] Those who resisted the eviction were subject to arrest, assault, and threats of violence. Particularly, the police arrested all male residents and completed the demolition in the following days.[142]

Similarly, people were not consulted in the Integrated Master Plan (usually referred to as the Master Plan) that was designed to integrate Addis Ababa City

---

135 Ibid.

136 See the Committee's General Comment 4 (no 13); the Committee's General Comment 7 (no 31) for the international laws and standards prohibiting eviction not to be undertaken in bad weather, as the month of June is a rainy season in Ethiopia.

137 This can be deduced from reports made by the government through its media like the Ethiopian Broadcasting Corporation (EBC) in July 2016.

138 Infrastructure like water, electricity, and road were connected to the demolished houses. According to the evictees, this fact entails that there is an implied recognition of the houses by the government. The interviews were conducted on 22 December 2016. The names of the evictees are confidential and are on record with the author.

139 See the Darfur case (no 18); World Bank Criteria for Eligibility (no 71).

140 Pursuant to the Committee's General Comments, the activity of the government constitutes a clear violation of human rights. See the Committee's General Comment 4 (no 13); the Committee's General Comment 7 (no 29).

141 Interviews conducted on 22 December 2016 with three eyewitnesses. The names of the interviewees are confidential and are on record with the author.

142 Ibid.

with the surrounding towns and villages of the State of Oromia.[143] As a result, the Oromo people[144] who would have been adversely affected as a result of the possible expropriation of their land and consequently the implementation of the Master Plan, opposed it while claiming that the action of the government constituted land-grabbing and was against the Constitution and fundamental human rights instruments ratified by the country.[145] Later on, the government suspended the implementation of the Master Plan owing to the fierce protests it faced, which grew into mass protests against the government and eventually led to the recent reforms introduced in Ethiopia.

4.5 *Challenges Related to Public Interest Litigation*

It is apparent that public interest litigation, particularly for poor countries like Ethiopia, is very important, as most citizens may not afford to litigate before a court or any other judicial and quasi-judicial organ. In this regard, the role of non-governmental organisations (NGOs) is indispensable in handling cases on behalf of the poor without proving vested interest/right to standing. However, such a procedure is lacking in the Ethiopian legal system except on environmental issues, for which the law allows public interest litigation.[146] However,

143 The State of Oromia is one of nine member states of the Ethiopian Federation established as per FDRE Constitution (no 80) art 47(1).

144 The Oromos are the largest ethnic group in Ethiopia.

145 This can be inferred from the slogan of the demonstrators. As a result of the unrest in the State of Oromia, according to the 2017 Human Rights Commission of Ethiopia's oral investigation report to the House of People's Representatives, 669 people were said to have been killed together with 63 security personnel, thousands were wounded and properties were destroyed in 2016. Human rights defenders like Amnesty International and Human Rights Watch have criticised the government for committing such atrocities against unarmed and peaceful protestors; they urge the government to refrain from committing such atrocities, and urge for an independent investigation to be undertaken on the incident. The European Parliament has also criticised the government for the killing and detention of thousands of the protesters, party leaders, and journalists. The government, however, denies the allegations coming from every corner, saying that 'those demonstrations are anti-peace and anti-development'; also, the government criticise human rights defenders to the extent of labelling them as 'having a hidden political agenda of destabilizing the country'. See '*Addressing the Pervasive Human Rights Crisis in Ethiopia: Letter to the UN Human Rights Council*' Human Rights Watch (25 May 2017) <https://www.hrw.org/news/2017/06/02/addressing-pervasive-human-rights-crisis-ethiopia> accessed 17 May 2018. See also M Tempest, '*Ethiopian Ambassador: 'Anti-peace elements' took advantage of Oromia, Amhara protests*' EURACTIV (5 October 2016) <https://www.euractiv.com/section/development-policy/interview/ethiopian-government-answers-critics-over-oromia-amhara-protest-deaths/> accessed 5 May 2018.

146 Federal Negarit Gazeta, 'Environmental Pollution Control Proclamation' Proclamation No. 300/2002.

this was later on impliedly repealed by the Charities and Societies Proclamation No. 621/2009. The Charities and Societies Proclamation which only repealed recently hindered the protection and promotion of human rights as it outlawed human rights defenders from engaging in human rights advocacy activities based on the source of their income.[147] As a positive step, the Charities and Societies Proclamation No. 621/2009 was repealed in March 2019 and replaced by a new Proclamation No. 1113/2019. Unlike its predecessor, this proclamation allows human rights defenders to engage in human rights promotion though it has failed to introduce explicitly public interest litigation. The new proclamation needs to be tested in practice at least by allowing human rights defenders to take part in human rights advocacy.

As discussed elsewhere in the chapter, the Ethiopian laws related to property rights, eviction, and compensation deviate from international human rights standards. In conclusion, the Ethiopian laws dealing with property rights, eviction/expropriation and compensation are not compatible with international human rights standards.

5 Conclusion and the Way Forward

5.1 *Conclusion*

International human rights instruments have recognised the right to protection of property, and have made the expropriation of property possible in exceptional circumstances and with fair compensation. Similarly, those international human rights instruments explicitly provide that forced evictions constitute gross violations of human rights, as they affect the full spectrum of civil, political, cultural, economic, and social rights enshrined in human rights instruments. Furthermore, the practice of eviction without consultation or adequate compensation is considered illegal under international human rights law. It is also unjust as it compromises fundamental human rights principles with devastating consequences on those affected by the eviction.

It is obvious that secure rights to land and other natural resources are essential for the livelihoods of people and the basis of their economy; they are often the foundation of their spiritual, cultural, and social identity. However, these rights have been undermined by expropriation and forced eviction for

147 Such limitation can be inferred from art 14's definition clause, which lists in the definition a 'charity' to mean an institution, which is established exclusively for charitable purposes and gives benefit to the public. See for those charitable purposes Federal Negarit Gazeta, 'The Charities and Societies Proclamation' Proclamation No. 621/2009.

development projects, urban expansion and renewal, construction of low-income houses, logging of forests, and the growth of large agribusinesses. Therefore, in Ethiopia, despite the recognition of property rights, the described practices on the ground are absolute infringements of human rights norms and standards.

The compensation of property is paid to strike a 'just and equitable' balance between the interests of those affected and the public. Accordingly, the justifiable reasons why compensation is paid are: first, to protect the citizen from harmful government interference, and second, to distribute the burden of the government interference. The first reason implies that since compensation is required upon expropriation, the government will only expropriate property once it is cost-effective (and therefore efficient) to do so. The second reason implies that in the case of expropriation, an individual is singled out to carry a burden for the public benefit. This would be an unfair burden if compensation was not paid. Compensation is therefore paid to put individuals in the same position they were in before the expropriation. Despite this theoretical foundation, in Ethiopia the expropriation/eviction cases are not actually followed by fair compensation mechanisms as stipulated by the Constitution and other national and international human rights laws and standards. The property valuation to be made for the purpose of compensation is not made by independent consultants but undertaken by a committee not independent from the expropriating public authority. As a result, the compensation to be paid for property loss is meagre, as it does not consider the actual damage sustained and does not replace the lost property, although the expropriator and the developer of the land get enormous benefits.

The government has generously interpreted 'public purpose' to the extent of affecting the property rights of citizens. Furthermore, the Expropriation and Compensation Proclamation of Ethiopia bars the right to appeal on the existence or non-existence of 'public purpose'. Hence, the exclusion of the right violates the right to appeal on any judicial or other decisions affecting rights to the highest national judicial authority provided under the Comprehensive Human Rights Guidelines on Development-Based Displacement on the Practice of Forced Evictions.[148] Here, such an exclusion of the court from entertaining appeal cases is also not in line with the FDRE Constitution, which guarantees to everyone the right to bring a justiciable matter to and to obtain a decision or judgment by a court of law or any other competent body with judicial power.[149] Furthermore, it is not in conformity with the Guidelines, which prohibit any forced eviction without a court order.[150]

148 See the Guidelines (no 30) para 23.
149 FDRE Constitution (no 80) art 37.
150 the Guidelines (no 30) para 22.

Similarly, the condition provided under article 11(6) of the Expropriation and Compensation Proclamation to exercise the right to appeal, in which the aggrieved landholder served with an expropriation order can only file his/her appeal on the condition that his/ her appeal is accompanied by a document that proves the handover of the land to the Urban or Woreda Administration, is not in conformity with international human rights instruments, the FDRE Constitution, or the Proclamation itself. For instance, both the Constitution and the Proclamation respectively require expropriation to be undertaken after the advance payment of compensation is made.[151] Hence, the conditionality of proving handing over land by the landholder to the Urban or Woreda Administration discourages the aggrieved landholder to appeal to the regular courts, as can be seen in actual practice.

It is noticeable that from the human rights perspective, issues of participation, transparency, and accountability are to be given due attention in the implementation of any development agenda in general, and evictions in particular. Although in Ethiopia the Constitution requires transparency and participatory governance,[152] in practice eviction decisions are made behind closed doors. Such an action in effect has led to mistrust of the government and a public perception that evictions are pushing out poor and indigenous landowners to allow the rich or the state to reap major benefits.[153]

Public interest litigation procedure is lacking in the Ethiopian legal system. Public interest litigation obviously helps to challenge the action of a government and/or a private sector when their decisions affect the human rights of citizens, particularly the property right of the poor. Generally, it can be concluded that the legal and actual practice of the protection of property rights, eviction/expropriation, and compensation in Ethiopia is not in conformity with international human rights law and standards.

When it comes to the future of property rights, the protest which began in 2014 in Ethiopia, especially the opposition against the Addis Ababa City Integrated Master Plan, has culminated into a change of leadership in April 2018 when Abiyi Ahmed was elected Prime Minister of Ethiopia. Since his appointment as Prime Minister of the country, he has accelerated a radical reform programme that is overturning politics enormously. Accordingly, his government has been undertaking different reform agendas, including a legal reform. Hence, the current legal reform currently may also consider issues related to

151 See FDRE Constitution (no 80) art 40(8); Proclamation No. 455/2005 (no 95) art 3(1).

152 See FDRE Constitution (no 80) art 12.

153 This can be inferred from the decision of the government to try to implement the Master Plan that meant to integrate Addis Ababa City with the surrounding towns of the State of Oromia without involving the affected community. This led the community to oppose the policy of the government. See Abdo (no 132).

property rights. Furthermore, the new Mayor of Addis Ababa City, Takele Uma, in a televised speech he made on 4 December 2018, vowed not to evict farmers surrounding Addis Ababa City. With the hope that the reform agendas are all-inclusive, the challenges of the country related to property rights, eviction/expropriation and compensation would thereby be resolved.

5.2 *The Way Forward*

As property expropriation is an absolute power of the government in Ethiopia, there are no legal limits on how much and what kind of land the government can expropriate. Hence, the government needs to be sensitive particularly to lands held by the poor and vulnerable groups, such as indigenous and local communities. Accordingly, there should be a law protecting the poor and vulnerable groups from expropriations/evictions.

In order to redress the grievances related to compensation, compensation proceedings must be reconsidered. In this regard, the actual market values of a property need to be accessed by independent property valuation experts. Based on the property valuation made by an independent consultant or expert, the government must pay fair compensation that would help the poor to relocate and rehabilitate themselves. Furthermore, the government should give training to the evictees who have received compensation, in order to help them to save and invest the money.

It has been identified that evictions of property/land in Ethiopia are seriously affecting the poor whose life is dependent on the property/land. Hence, the government must minimise such evictions, especially upon consideration of the impact on evictees. To mitigate its impact, the government should undertake eviction impact assessment before evicting citizens.

In Ethiopia, the concept of 'public purpose' is interpreted widely to the extent of seriously affecting citizens' property right. Hence, the expropriation and compensation law must be revised in the manner that the concept of 'public purpose' be interpreted narrowly to control possible abuses of the executive organ. Similarly, the existence or non-existence of 'public purpose' in the case of expropriation/eviction needs to be evaluated by an independent organ, like courts. Hence, an amendment to expropriation and compensation law must be made to empower courts at a different level to decide on expropriation proceedings.

Policy and legal reforms are inevitable to the extent that they must adopt international standards on expropriation and compensation into domestic laws. Hence, the government should undertake policy and legal reforms that help to adequately protect land tenure, reduce evictions and allow fair compensation to citizens whose property rights are affected as a result of expropriations/evictions.

In Ethiopia, expropriation/eviction decisions are not transparent and participatory, thereby pushing out the poor and indigenous landowners to allow the rich and the state to reap major benefits. Hence, expropriation proceedings must be participatory and transparent, as this would help the government keep the balance between development and its obligation of protecting and promoting human rights. To this effect, the government should establish a public forum in order to consult the affected community.

Finally, public interest litigation procedure, which is almost lacking in the Ethiopian legal system, must be introduced as it helps to challenge the action of a government and of private sectors when decisions affect the human rights of citizens, particularly the property right of the poor.

Cultural Legitimisation of Human Rights: The Case of the Guraghe Ethno-Cultural Community in Ethiopia

Sisay Kinfe

Abstract

With the coming into being of collective and individual national human rights standards in Ethiopia, some ethno-cultural communities at the local level are engaged in transforming their customary laws and practices. This process makes one of their objectives the bringing about of cultural legitimacy of human rights, and in particular women's rights. However, the internal discourse held to transform customary laws and practices is dominated by urban-based male elites and traditional leaders. This has resulted in the selective prohibition of discriminatory and harmful practices against women in community-based customary laws. This could be improved significantly if there was a robust policy on customary local institutions that guides collaborative and integrated working with local government institutions.

Keywords

Cultural Legitimisation – Human Rights – Internal Discourse – Women – Discriminatory and Harmful Practice – Customary Law

1 Introduction

The idea of cultural relativism has been identified as one of the major threats for the notion of the universality of human rights. This led to the reaffirmation of the universality of human rights norms by the United Nations (UN) in 1993.[1] However, while almost all states have recognised human rights as universal values, there is still a wide discrepancy between theory and practice of human rights across jurisdictions. As per the adherents of the relativist approach, the main reason for the discrepancy is the exclusion of non-Western values in the

1 Christina M Cerna, 'Universality of Human Rights and Cultural Diversity: Implementation of Human Rights in Different Socio-Cultural Contexts' (1994) 16 Human Rights Quarterly 740.

 | DOI:10.1163/9789004415966_008

formulation of human rights.[2] Universalists, on the other hand, underline the foundation of human rights as being the human being, while also increasingly recognising the significance of culture and cultural understanding of human rights for its practice.[3] The debate between relativism and universalism has made it clear that the legislative recognition of human rights as being universal at the international, regional or national levels alone is not enough to bring about human rights practices – particularly in the non-Western world.[4]

Scholars widely concur that the main challenge in bringing about human rights practices particularly to non-Western cultures is a lack of sufficient cultural support, rather than the essence of human rights *per se*.[5] To address this challenge, the cultural legitimisation of human rights in every cultural community has been considered a viable strategy,[6] besides the legislative recognition of human rights law. Cultural legitimisation is an on-going process that aims to bring about the internal validity of human rights in a given culture.[7] It is recognised as a means to address the underlying causes of human rights violations in the context of their widespread prevalence, which also supports the efforts of the state in enforcing human rights.[8] As such, it is not a process

2 Eva Brems, 'Enemies or Allies? Feminism and Cultural Relativism as Dissident Voices in Human Rights Discourse' (1997) 19 Human Rights Quarterly 136. To accommodate cultural differences, many human rights conventions have been amended. See Elizabeth M Zechenter 'In the Name of Culture: Cultural Relativism and the Abuse of the Individual' (1997) 53 Journal of Anthropological Research 341; See also Donna J Sullivan, 'Women's Human Rights and the 1993 World Conference on Human Rights' (1994) 88 American Journal of International Law 152.

3 Ann-Belinda S Preis, 'Human Rights as Cultural Practice: An Anthropological Critique' (1996) 18 Human Rights Quarterly 286.

4 Although the international community has a mechanism for the universal recognition of human rights, it lacks proper institutions for universal legal enforcement. See Jack Donnelly, 'The Relative Universality of Human Rights' (2007) 29 Human Rights Quarterly 281.

5 Abdullahi A An-Na'im and Jeffrey Hammond, 'Cultural Transformation and Human Rights in African Societies' in Abdullahi A An-Na'im (ed), *Cultural Transformation and Human Rights in Africa* (Zed Books 2002) 13–37; See also Tore Lindholm, 'Prospects for Research on the Cultural Legitimacy of Human Rights: The Cases of Liberalism and Marxism' in Abdullahi Ahmed An-Na'im (ed), *Human Rights in Cross-Cultural Perspectives: A Quest for Consensus* (University of Pennsylvania Press 1992) 387–426.

6 Cultural legitimacy is defined by An-Na'im as 'the quality or state of being in conformity with recognized principles or accepted rules and standards of a given culture'. See An-Na'im as cited in Beatrix-Ann Nienaber, 'Achieving Culturally Legitimate Human Rights in the Context of HIV/AIDS in South Africa: An Analytical Framework' (MA Thesis, Simon Fraser University 2011) 43 <http://summit.sfu.ca/system/files/iritems1/11715/etd6649_BNienaber.pdf> accessed 14 July 2018.

7 Nienaber ibid 44.

8 An-Na'im and Hammond (n 5) 21.

that substitutes the efforts of the state to protect and promote human rights; rather it is viewed as a supplement to it.

At the local level, the cultural legitimisation of human rights can be achieved through internal discourse.[9] 'Cultural legitimacy can be obtained through the process of contesting, debating or struggling over the legitimacy of human rights in the "culture" in question'.[10] As a social construct, culture is dynamic and susceptible to different interpretations that result in cultural change or transformation. The significance of the cultural legitimisation of human rights also emanates from the sustainability of change from within, rather than from external efforts to bring about change that could be considered as imposition and could be rejected as cultural imperialism.[11] In the cultural legitimisation of human rights, the voices of those in society who are vulnerable to human rights violations, such as women, must be heard to make the process democratically legitimate.[12]

The existence of widespread discriminatory and harmful practices against women in diverse societal settings makes bringing about the cultural legitimacy of women's human rights important for curbing these practices within ethno-cultural communities. This is because the prohibition of discrimination alone cannot fully restrain such practices, which are either performed

9 It is not possible or desirable to argue that international human rights are culturally neutral. However, the claim of the universal cultural legitimacy of human rights is based on a political and moral 'overlapping consensus' among major cultural traditions of the world. See Abdullahi Ahmed An-Na'im, 'States Responsibility Under International Human Rights Law to Change Religious and Customary Laws' in R Cook (eds), *Human Rights of Women, National and International Perspective* (University of Pennsylvania Press 1994) 173. An-Na'im here argues 'in order to engage all cultural traditions in the process of promoting and sustaining such global consensus, the relationship between local culture and international standards should be perceived as genuinely reciprocal global collaborative effort'. See also Bonny Ibhawoh, 'Between Culture and Constitution: Evaluating the Cultural Legitimacy of Human Rights in the African State' (2000) 22 Human Rights Quarterly 838.

10 Beatrix-Ann Nienaber (n 6) 43–46.

11 An-Na'im (n 9) 176.

12 See Monique Deveaux, 'Deliberative Approach to Conflict of Culture' in Avigail Elsenberg and Jeff Spinner-Halev (eds), *Minorities within Minorities: Equality, Rights and Diversity* (Cambridge University Press 2004) 340; See also Minneh Kane Oloka-Onyango J and Abdul Tejan-Cole, 'Reassessing Customary Law System as a Vehicle for Providing Equitable Access to Justice for the Poor' (Conference Paper, Arusha Conference 'New Frontiers of Social Policy', 12–15 December 2005) <http://siteresources.worldbank.org/INTRANETSOCIALDEVELOPMENT/Resources/reassessingcustomary.pdf> accessed 14 July 2018.

underground or are selectively or illegitimately justified by customary local institutions.[13]

Women-based human rights instruments, such as the United Nations Convention on the Elimination of Discrimination Against Women (CEDAW) and the Protocol to the African Charter on Human and Peoples' Rights on the Rights of Women in Africa (Maputo Protocol) impose on state parties the responsibility to take appropriate measures to eliminate all forms of discrimination and harmful practices against women.[14] This implies that guaranteeing the equality of men and women, as well as criminalising harmful practices under national legislation, are both not enough to protect women's rights; instead, efforts to eliminate such practices by the state in cooperation with non-state actors, such as customary local institutions, are encouraged.

This chapter examines the contents and processes of transformation of customary law among the Guraghe community in Ethiopia, following the introduction of federalism in the 1990s. One of the objectives of the transformation of customary law among the Guraghe is bringing about the cultural legitimisation of women's human rights by prohibiting discriminatory and harmful customary practices.[15] In this chapter, the main focus is on investigating how this objective is achieved in the contents of the transformed customary law, as well as during the deliberation and enactment of such normative codes. In analysing the data following Nyamu-Musembi,[16] the author employs a method of looking into human rights in the politics of culture, ie identifying features that are favourable to the cultural legitimisation of women's rights, as well as hindrances to these processes. The chapter also analyses legitimate ways of state intervention to enhance the cultural legitimacy of human rights in communities as part of the state's international and regional responsibility to protect women from all forms of discrimination and harmful practices.

---

13 Bonny Ibhawoh, 'Between Culture and Constitution: Evaluating the Cultural Legitimacy of Human Rights in the African State' (2000) 22 Human Rights Quarterly 838.

14 Convention on the Elimination of All Forms of Discrimination against Women (adopted 18 December 1979, entry into force 3 September 1981) 1249 UNTS 13 (CEDAW), art 2; See also the African Commission on Human and Peoples' Rights, 'Protocol to the African Charter on Human and Peoples' Rights on the Rights of Women in Africa' (Maputo Protocol), arts 2 and 5 <http://www.achpr.org/files/instruments/women-protocol/achpr_instr_proto_women_eng.pdf> accessed 14 July 2018.

15 See Gurage People Self-help Development Organisation (GPSDO), 'The Gurage Customary Law' (Nigd Printing 1998).

16 Celestine Nyamu-Musembi 'Are Local Norms and Practices Fences or Pathways? The Example of Women's Property Rights' in Abdullahi A An-Na'im (ed), *Cultural Transformation and Human Rights in Africa* (Zed Books 2002) 126–127.

The chapter is organised into eight sections, including the introduction and conclusion. In section two, the discussion focuses on the theoretical framework of the study, followed by a brief review of international and regional responsibility of states in eliminating discrimination and harmful practices against women. The main contents of the transformed customary law of the Guraghe community are also discussed in subsequent sections, concentrating particularly on women's rights in the private sphere of family, in which widespread discriminatory and harmful practices have been observed. Finally, the discourses on the transformation of customary law are evaluated. Opportunities and challenges of the cultural legitimisation of women's rights at the local levels in the context of the Guraghe Zone are also identified and elaborated.

2 Human Rights, Culture and Cultural Legitimisation

Human rights as rights of human beings received formal and universal legal recognition with the coming into being of the Universal Declaration of Human Rights (UDHR) in 1948, which was also accompanied by the adoption of several conventions. 'Universalism holds that there is an underlying human unity which entitles individuals, regardless of their cultural or regional antecedents, to certain minimal rights known as human rights'.[17] On the other hand, universalism, which primarily focuses on a dignified life of the individual, faced resistance from cultural relativism based on the grounds that the foundations of these rights are Western cultural contexts. To mitigate this criticism, to accommodate contextual differences of culture and to promote the universal significance of human rights, the development of regional human rights instruments such as the African Charter on Human and Peoples Rights (ACHPR) has been encouraged by the international community.[18] The African Charter, while founded on the fundamental values enshrined in the UDHR, also reflects African cultural experiences of human rights by clearly articulating the inseparability of rights and duties.[19] The African Charter therefore differs from the

17 Zechenter (n 2) 320.

18 Cerna (n 1) 752.

19 The African (Banjul) Charter on Human and Peoples' Rights (signed 27 June 1981, entry into force 12 October 1986) OAU Doc. CAB/LEG/67/3 rev. 5, 21 I.L.M. 58, arts 27–29; See also Makau Mutua 'The Banjul Charter: The case for an African Cultural Fingerprint' in Abdullahi A An-Na'im (ed), *Cultural Transformation and Human Rights in Africa* (Zed Books 2002) 68–107.

UDHR as it 'declares not only that all human beings are equal but also that all people are as well'.[20] Though the ACHPR recognises 'culture' as a means to recognise the unique contexts of Africa, which are also incorporated into the national constitutions of states, there are tensions between cultural practices and universal human rights standards in many African states. This makes investigating the theme of the debate between universalism and relativism more important in order to see both the nexus between human rights and culture, as well as the significance of culturally legitimate human rights in bringing about compliant human rights practices.

Universalism and the universal responsibility of states to enforce human rights emanate from the widespread endorsement of internationally recognised human rights law by states.[21] The acceptance of the universality of human rights by states is based on political grounds rather than on the full convergence of cultural and moral grounds. States, regardless of differences in cultural and moral philosophy, endorse international human rights law because it is increasingly seen as a precondition of full political legitimacy and of the recognition of states being greater powers.[22] Donnelly argues that as a political conception of justice, human rights are legitimately accepted as being universal. However, in practice, there is wide resistance against the notion of the universality of human rights and its enforcement – this mainly emerging from the idea of cultural relativism.[23]

Cultural relativism, which first came into being as a reaction to 'cultural evolutionism',[24] criticises universal human rights for being a reflection of dominant Western culture that defines human beings first and foremost as 'autonomous individual' rights-bearers.[25] Relativism underlines that in the 'non-Western' culture, human beings are defined as having an 'ascribed status as members of a larger group or community such as family, tribe, class, nation or other groups'.[26] This incongruence in the conception of human beings led relativism to contend that universal human rights have limited or no reliability in

20 David Hollenbach 'Solidarity, Development and Human Rights: The African Challenge' (1998) 26 Journal of Religious Ethics 308.

21 Donnelly (n 4) 288.

22 Ibid.

23 Ibid 290.

24 See Zechenter (n 2).

25 Brems (n 2) 145.

26 Ibid.

the non-Western culture.[27] However, it is identified that the ideas of relativism regarding culture and human rights have many flaws.[28]

Relativism is criticised first and foremost for its static and monolithic conceptualisation of culture. 'All forms of cultural relativism fundamentally fail to recognise culture as an ongoing historic and institutional process where the existence of a given custom does mean that the custom is either adaptive, optimal, or consented by a majority of its adherents'.[29] Although there is nothing that can be referred to as one singular culture, even in the egalitarian and non-stratified society or community, cultural relativism warns to respect traditional culture.[30] 'There is no culture in the sense of unitary whole, a bounded entity to which human rights may be said to apply'.[31] Scholars widely concur that culture is social construct that is neither fixed in time nor static. Preis characterises culture as a multi-vocal, multi-dimensional, unpredictable and open-ended process.[32] Culture is also susceptible to different interpretations. It consists of individuals and groups with conflicting agendas, and often the custom of the group is the reflection of the interests of the dominant or powerful section within a community.[33] Power differences within culture lead to conflict, which in turn leads to different interpretations of culture within a given community.[34] This makes the understanding of how culture is constructed and changed or the politics of culture very important in observing human rights across all cultures within a state. This means universal human rights can be practiced if and only if they have been made culturally legitimate. This is due to the fact that 'culture is the framework for understanding human motivation and behavior that underlies political commitment, determination of priorities for allocation of resources and direction of civil society activism'.[35] In other words, human rights practices are determined by culture.

In the politics of culture, cultural norms and institutions are contestable allowing for a variety of interpretations and practices. Culture is contested in a struggle between those who want to legitimise their particular power and

27 Pollis and Schwab as cited in Preis (n 3) 291.

28 Zechenter (n 2) 332–337. Zechenter here identifies four major flaws of the idea of cultural relativism: promotion of self-contradictory idea; static conception of culture; misunderstanding of traditional culture; emphasis on the group at the expense of the individual.

29 Ibid 333.

30 Ibid 336.

31 Preis (n 3) 305.

32 Ibid 306–307.

33 Ibid 305.

34 Ibid.

35 An-Na'im and Hammond (n 5) 18.

privilege, and those who need to change the status quo to redress grievances and protect their rights. 'Since culture needs to respond to different and competing individual and collective needs and aspirations, it tends to combine stability and continues change, offers its adherents a range of options, and seeks to accommodate varying responses to its norms'.[36] According to An-Na'im, this leads to cultural transformation,[37] which makes the processes of cultural change and construction part of the right to self-determination.[38] Making cultural change and reconstruction part of the right to self-determination has a significant place in making human rights culturally legitimate.

The cultural legitimacy of human rights in a given culture can be achieved through 'internal discourse'.[39] Internal discourse within a cultural community helps to legitimately invalidate cultural practices that are against human rights norms through enlightened perceptions and interpretations of cultural values and norms.[40] An-Na'im underlines the significance of looking into human rights norms and cultural practices separately in order to yield culturally legitimate human rights. Normatively, the universality of human rights can only be questioned by those who can disprove the insignificance of a given human rights law through rigorous processes that present a viable alternative.[41] However, culture can be validated or invalidated by members of a given community in response to factors and forces such as the introduction of national human rights standards.

The significance and need for internal discourse to bring about the cultural legitimacy of human rights in African states has been underlined by many scholars. So far, attempts to culturally legitimise human rights in Africa have been viewed based on two contrasting paradigms: the conservative paradigm and the dynamic paradigm of cultural legitimacy.[42] On the one hand, the conservative paradigm is represented by male-dominated, urban-based elites who are inclined towards the main human rights regime within the state. Their perception of cultural legitimisation of human rights focuses on collectivism: the

36 An-Na'im (n 9) 173.

37 Cultural transformation refers to 'the dynamics of change as internal processes of societal adaptation by a variety of actors in response to a wide range of stimuli, at different levels, rather than simply the product of internal hegemony or external imposition'. See An-Na'im (n 9) 13.

38 Ibid 14.

39 An-Na'im (n 9) 174.

40 Abdullahi A An-Na'im (ed), *Human Rights in Cross-Cultural Perspectives: A Quest for Consensus* (University of Pennsylvania Press 1992) 27.

41 An-Na'im (n 9) 172.

42 Ibhawoh (n 13) 850.

retention of cultural initiative on issues of private social relations, such as those concerning family and gender roles.[43] On the other hand, the dynamic paradigm of cultural legitimacy is represented by emerging groups who work for women and minority rights.[44] The dynamic perspective subscribes to the view that universal rights shall be given some form of cultural interpretation; proponents of this perception use the global human rights debate to criticise present cultural practices, which infringe on human rights.

Ibhawoh emphasises that 'the cultural legitimacy of human rights in Africa has tended to focus more on the conservative paradigm'.[45] Little has been done by advocates of the dynamic paradigm of cultural legitimacy.[46] The differences in perspective within a cultural community reflect the conflict between 'the implicit human rights and the importance of collectivism and definitive gender role in most African cultures'.[47] This indicates the need to seek acceptable ways of ensuring the cultural legitimacy of human rights by broadening the internal discourse and dialogue in order to integrate the two paradigms.

States, besides guaranteeing cultural rights in their national constitutions, have the responsibility to establish general conditions conducive to constructive and internal cultural discourses in order to make human rights standards culturally legitimate. In this regard, Ibhawoh states

> It is important to create dialogue between weaker groups within the cultural community and the society at large. Women and minority groups must be able to dialogue over interpretations of cultural values with politicians, officials, traditional leaders, and family heads in both the rural and urban areas. If respect for human rights is to be achieved and made sustainable, human rights must reside not only in law but in the living and be practiced as culture of the people. There is a need, therefore, for dialogue among groups with different paradigms of cultural legitimacy on what role culture should play in legitimising national human rights regimes within African states.[48]

43 Ibid.

44 Ibid.

45 Ibid 851.

46 Ibid 853. The Dynamic paradigm of cultural legitimacy emphasises on the need for human rights work to focus more on traditional systems of support for women; reciprocal relationship between rights and social responsibilities; and traditional methods of conflict resolution.

47 Ibhawoh (n 13) 853.

48 Ibid 855.

Ibhowah suggests a 'cross-paradigmatic' approach to the cultural legitimisation of human rights, which broadens the range of cultural support for human rights by integrating the conservative and dynamic paradigms.[49] This is believed to yield greater opportunities for enforcing cultural legitimisation than either the conservative or the dynamic paradigm. The aim of a cross-paradigmatic dialogue is to promote human rights within prevailing cultural attitudes and institutions, and to make cultural change, adaptation and modification complement human rights through the initiative and involvement of all sections of local community in a manner that creates a sense of ownership of the process.

For sections of society that have been historically dominated, such as women, the realisation of human rights also requires their empowerment and struggles to have a voice in the social [re]construction of 'culture'. 'For women to have a legitimate voice in constructing "culture" by validating or invalidating certain *practices*, some existing value systems must not be eradicated but rather remain intact with a [strategic] emphasis on positive cultural values'.[50] This is because human rights need to manifest a perceived resonance with past and existing cultural values in order to be accepted as culturally legitimate. Hence, to make human rights culturally legitimate, certain types of interpretation of cultural practices that result in the infringement of human rights must be challenged, rather than accepted as a cultural value system *per se*. In such processes, the state, besides legally guaranteeing women's human rights, has the responsibility to support community-based initiatives aimed to eliminate discriminatory and harmful practices in its territory; this applies by virtue of international human rights conventions such as the CEDAW, and regional human rights instruments such as the Maputo Protocol on Women's Rights.

3 Women-based Human Rights Instruments and the Responsibility of States in Eliminating Discriminatory and Harmful Practices

Various components of women's human rights are incorporated under one special human rights treaty framework called the Convention for the Elimination of All forms of Discrimination against Women (CEDAW); it was adopted in 1979 and came into force in 1981.[51] Almost all states of the world, including

49 Ibid.

50 See Nienaber (n 6) 35 (emphasis added).

51 On what makes CEDAW a special human rights treaty, see Cees Flinterman and Catherine Henderson, 'Special Human Rights Treaties' in R Hanski and M Suski (eds), *An Introduction to the International Protection of Human Rights* (Abo Akademi University 1999).

Ethiopia, are a party to this Convention and thus have the obligation to take appropriate measures to eliminate all forms of discrimination.[52]

CEDAW's provisions are directed at bringing about substantive equality over mere formal equality between men and women. First, the Convention acknowledges the 'intersectionality' of gender discrimination with discrimination based on caste, class, disability, ethnicity, sexual orientation etc.[53] Second, it holds that discrimination is socially constructed, and laws, policies and practices can unintentionally have the 'effect' of discriminating against women.[54] Third, women have historically been discriminated against and do not necessarily come into a situation on an equal basis with men by only the guarantee of formal rights.[55] It is also recognised that due to various reasons, many poor and rural women may only have access to the informal justice system rather than state-run formal justice systems – reasons for this include poverty, structural inequalities, pressures from traditional stereotypes, a lack of education and limited awareness of rights.[56] This makes it important to recognise and cooperate with informal (customary) institutions not only to facilitate women's access to justice, but also to end discrimination against women.[57] In this regard, the Convention leaves the obligation on states to give due attention to their own contexts in their policies and laws.

At the regional level, the ACHPR prohibits discrimination based on sex and guarantees equality before the law.[58] In many respects, the ACHPR has incorporated women's rights as enshrined in the CEDAW and has also attempted to incorporate some dimensions of African culture. Yet, despite the existence of the African Charter and the extensive ratification of CEDAW by African states, it became clear that the issue of gender was not seriously considered at the institutional level in Africa.[59] This led to the adoption of a Protocol to the ACHPR relating to the Rights of Women in 2003 (Maputo Protocol). The justification for the adoption of the Maputo Protocol, as reflected in the preamble, is that in

52 CEDAW (n 14) art 2(f); though all states have been party to this convention, there are several reservations on some provisions based on culture and religious interpretation of gender relations in the private sphere, highlighting the fact that finding a common consensus on what constitutes equality will be difficult. See Fareda Banda, *Women, Law and Human Rights: An African Perspective* (Hart Publishing 2005) 88.

53 Naresh Singh 'Legal Empowerment of Women and Girls: Progress and Challenges' (2014) 7 in Segundo Semestre 175.

54 Ibid 176.

55 Ibid.

56 Ibid 179.

57 Ibid 181.

58 ACHPR (n 19) art 18(3).

59 Fareda Banda (n 52) 88.

spite of the existence of international human right instruments, 'women in Africa still continue to be victims of discrimination and harmful practices'.

The Protocol to the ACHPR on the Rights of Women has several similarities with the CEDAW in addressing discrimination against women.[60] It has also its own features that reflect a contextual understanding of African problems. The main points of difference include: first, the Protocol includes 'girls' in its understanding of women, which fills an existing gap in the discussion on women's rights.[61] Second, the Protocol incorporates a comprehensive definition of violence against women.[62] Third, the Protocol contains substantive provisions on reproductive rights. Fourth, the Protocol prohibits harmful practices and confronts the controversial issue of female genital cutting/mutilation.[63] On the issue of culture, the Maputo Protocol under article 17(1) states that 'Women shall have the right to live in a positive cultural context and to participate at all levels in the determination of cultural policies'. The Protocol also obliges state parties to take all appropriate measures to enhance the participation of women in the formulation of cultural policies at all levels.[64] In many respects, the Protocol to the African Charter on Women's Rights is considered a radical document that considers women's rights seriously in the context of Africa, even though the commitment of states in enforcement remains questionable across many African states. For instance, the Protocol is signed but not ratified by several African states including Ethiopia – a fact which may well limit awareness about the Protocol.

4 Culture and National Human Rights Standards in Ethiopia

The Federal Democratic Republic of Ethiopia (FDRE) Constitution has clear provisions that guarantee both collective cultural and family rights, as well as basic individual human rights. The Constitution prohibits discrimination on

60 The similarities between CEDAW and the Maputo Protocol begin with the definition of discrimination against women. For this see CEDAW (n 14) art 1; Maputo Protocol (n 14) art 1(f). Second, similar obligations are put on state parties to incorporate the principle of equality between men and women in their national constitutions and other legislative instruments. For this, see Maputo Protocol (n 14) art 2(1)(a); CEDAW (n 14) art 2(a). Third, state parties also have an obligation to 'take corrective and positive action in those areas where discrimination against women in law and in fact continues to exist'. See Maputo Protocol (n 14) art 2(1)(d); CEDAW (n 14) art 2(f).

61 Maputo Protocol (n 14) art 1(k).

62 Ibid art 1(j). See also Banda (n 52) 80.

63 Maputo Protocol (n 14) art 5 and 5(b), respectively.

64 Ibid art 17(2).

the grounds of sex in all spheres of life and furthermore prohibits the exercise of harmful practices against women.[65] As part of collective cultural rights, every ethno-cultural community in the country has the right to use its customary and religious law in the family arena[66] and also the right to develop its own culture,[67] while respecting the supremacy of the Constitution.[68] The state also has the responsibility to support the development of cultures and traditions that are compatible with democratic norms and human rights standards.[69] In this regard, the federal system in Ethiopia allows for the creation of autonomous local governmental units with the objective of accommodating ethno-cultural diversity, which enable local government institutions to be protectors of cultural rights.[70]

However, in many areas in Ethiopia, customary local institutions and local government institutions function parallel to each other in a manner that delegitimises the role of local government institutions as establishments for the accommodation of diversity. This partly emanates from the narrow understanding of autonomy and democratic norms, as well as from the merely partial recognition given to customary local institutions. Customary local institutions are recognised to function only in personal and family matters (in the arena of civil issues) – although many customary institutions indeed have laws that govern both civil and criminal matters.[71] The absence of policy on customary local institutions in the country can also be seen as another factor for the absence of integration between the two institutions. Due to these, civil society organisations (CSOs) of ethnic communities, such as the Guraghe People Self Help Development Organization (GPSDO), which mainly represents urban-based community elites, understood and used their autonomy to

65 Federal Negarit Gazeta, 'The Constitution of the Federal Democratic Republic of Ethiopia' Proclamation No. 1/1995, art 25 and 35(4).

66 Ibid art 34(4) and 5.

67 Ibid art 39(2).

68 Ibid art 9(1).

69 Ibid art 41(9) and 91(1).

70 Ibid art 39(3); See also Debub Negarit Gazeta, 'Constitution of Southern Nations, Nationalities, and Peoples' Regional State Proclamation' Proclamation 1/1995 (SNNPR Constitution) art 45.

71 Different factors are cited as reasons for the absence of integration and coordination between customary local institutions and local government institutions; typical in this regard is the limited recognition of customary institutions, which are solely confined to family and personal matters even though many ethno-cultural communities have adopted customary laws that cover most aspects of life. See for instance Gebre Yntiso, Assefa Fiseha and Fekade Azeze (eds), *Customary Dispute Resolution Mechanisms in Ethiopia* (The Ethiopian Arbitration and Conciliation Centre 2011).

transform customary laws and practices; they made one of their objectives to bring about the cultural legitimisation of rights of women without seriously taking into account the democratic norms discussed below.

5 The Transformation of Customary Laws and Practices

The Guraghe ethno-cultural community in Ethiopia is one of the multicultural communities within which different community categories, such as the Sebat-bet and Sodo Kistane Guraghes, exercise different forms of culture based on differences in terms of clan, localities, region, and religion. The Sebat-bet Guraghe are numerically the majority in the Guraghe Zone, one of the autonomous local government units in Ethiopian federalism. The focus of this study is on the Sebat-bet Guraghe community (herein after used interchangeably as the Guraghe or Sebat-bet Guraghe). The Guraghe have customary local institutions that served the community for centuries. With the introduction of federalism in Ethiopia, which guarantees the right to self-determination (autonomy) for ethnic communities, the Guraghe ethno-cultural community was inspired to transform its customary law from an oral tradition to a written one,[72] making one of their objectives the cultural legitimisation of the rights of women as enshrined in the federal Constitution.

The transformed customary law document of the Guraghe – also called the 'Guraghe Kitcha' – was published in 1998 following its ratification by the customary local council *Yajok*. It has sixteen chapters and forty-three articles. In Chapter 2, the customary law document deals with rights and duties in the family arena. It prohibits discrimination based on gender, prohibits harmful practices against women, and sanctions trespasses. The prohibited harmful practices are abduction,[73] marriage without the consent of a woman,[74] and

72 Transforming customary laws from unwritten to written ones can be a mere re-statement of customary laws and processes, which basically encompasses reducing the content to writing down and compiling laws and usages into a single document that covers the main areas in which the customary law operates. The factors that inspired the preservation and development of culture/custom in the Guraghe Zone include the introduction of federalism in the country, as well as the need for making customary laws and practices compatible with national human rights standards – particularly with the rights of women as enshrined in the FDRE Constitution; these facts led the author to call the processes 'transformation' rather than a simple 're-statement'.

73 Regarding the different forms of abduction observed among the community and the possible sanctions on the trespasses, see GPSDO (n 15) art 6.

74 Ibid art 3(1).

forcing a woman to get out of her house after a long period of marital life.[75] However, the harmful practices exercised against women among the Guraghe were/are not only those that were prohibited under the customary law document; indeed, there are other harmful practices in the community which are not recognised as such by the customary local council *Yajoka*. A typical example includes the *anqiti*, female genital mutilation, domestic violence (especially wife beating), and the exclusion of women from customary local institutions.

Anqiti is a customary norm and cultural belief adopted by the Guraghe regarding marriage and divorce, which has the purpose of forbidding divorce when requested by a woman.[76] This custom is believed to be the first customary rule that comes with the establishment of the Guraghe customary law system about three hundred years ago. The rationale for such a rule is believed to be rooted in the problem of wife-looting at that time. Although the problem was caused by men, *anqiti* law was established only against women. Since its establishment, the rule has forbidden the Sebat-bet Guraghe woman from divorce and re-marriage without the will of the man she once married or was engaged to. Therefore, if a woman wants to divorce her husband for any reason, she must obtain the husband's consent. Without such consent, the marriage would not be dissolved and the woman would not be allowed to re-marry. On the other hand, the husband is free to divorce his wife at any time, and can also marry as many times as he likes without divorcing the former wife. As per the *aniqit* law, unless the woman who wishes to be divorced obtains the consent of the husband (which entails an established cultural ceremony), it is believed that she will be put under the curse of *anqiti*. This curse allegedly makes a woman infertile, and in case she does give birth to a child, the baby would not grow up or become healthy; according to the belief, the wife may also become unhealthy or may die due to being struck by lightning. Moreover, a woman who chooses to divorce her husband receives almost nothing from the matrimonial property.

The transformed customary law of the Guraghe does not entirely prohibit this customary law on divorce (*anqiti*); rather it sets preconditions for lifting it.[77] The preconditions are: first, if a man takes a woman already married, he must pay birr 10,000 to her former husband; by doing so, the *anqiti* would be

75 Ibid art 5(5).

76 Yewendiwesan Awilachew 'Yajok Kitcha: Sebat-bet Guraghe Customary Dispute Resolution Mechanism' in Gebre Yntiso, Assefa Fiseha and Fekade Azeze (eds), *Customary Dispute Resolution Mechanisms in Ethiopia*, (Ethiopian Arbitration and Conciliation Center 2011) 37–61.

77 GPSDO (n 15) art 5(7).

lifted. Secondly, the *anqiti* is lifted if a man is not able to administer his house economically and the wife asks for divorce. In this case, the woman would have to wait for two years for the *anqiti* to be lifted, with or without the consent of the husband; after two years, she would either be free or the marriage would be dissolved. Through these preconditions, the transformed customary law continues to preserve discriminatory marriage and divorce law, which is against recognised human rights standards. Even though the transformed customary law declares that 'when divorce is inevitable, the rights of the parties to the dispute must be respected equally',[78] it systematically maintains the discriminatory customary divorce law of the *anqiti*.

The contents of the transformed customary law relating to this particular domain make it clear that women's human rights have not yet received full cultural legitimacy. Under the transformed customary laws, it is clear that discrimination and harmful practices against women are prohibited only selectively. This begs the question of why the transformed customary laws maintained the law of *anqiti* – even when historically there have been well-known movements against the law of *aniqit* launched by Guraghe women.[79]

Similarly, questions could be raised as to why the reformed normative order failed to prohibit harmful practices such as the exclusion of women from customary local institutions, the practice of female genital mutilation, as well as wife beating. In order to provide sufficient explanations to such questions, it is important to look into the internal discourses held for the transformation of customary norms, as well as to consider the composition of customary local institutions and particularly the local council *Yajok*.

6 Discourses for the Transformation of Customary Law

As Ibhawoh argues, discourses for the cultural legitimisation of human rights in Africa tend to focus more on the conservative paradigm that is dominated by men, and which emphasises on collectivism, ie the retention of cultural practices on issues of private social relations, such as those concerning family and gender roles.[80] This is also true with regard to the process and outcome of transformation of customary laws among the Guraghe community. While it is

78 Ibid art 5(1).

79 See Bahru Zewde, 'Systems of Local Governance among the Gurage: The Yajoka Qicha and the Gordanna Sera' in Bahru Zewde and Siegfried Pausewang (eds), *Ethiopia: The Challenges of Democracy from Below* (Elanders Gotab 2002).

80 Ibhawoh (n 13) 851.

true that for the deliberation and ratification of the transformed customary law, representatives of the community were elected from both urban and rural areas of the Guraghe Zone to *Yajoka* (the customary legislative council), all members of the council were male traditional leaders and elites, basically excluding women. The discourse on the transformation of customary law of the Guraghe also maintained the interests and views of the dominant section within the cultural community, ie the men, by containing a contradictory provision[81] and by being silent on some wide-spread discriminatory and harmful practices against women, such as the exclusion of women from the customary local council and wife beating.

A legitimate internal discourse for the transformation of culture or customary laws must at least involve the participation of all sections of society – particularly women, who constitute half of the total population of the community and who are vulnerable to discrimination and harmful practices. In this regard, Oloka-Onyango J. and Tejan-Cole state

> It would be important in any discussion of customary law today to ensure that the voices of all the people who are impacted by the laws are heard. Customary laws are not a monopoly to be applied and understood by the few over the many.[82]

Internal discourses that ensure the representation and effective participation of women would create an opportunity for women to debate and to negotiate their interests based on their local contexts and problems. This in turn would bring customary laws of marriage and divorce in line with the rights of women, and would as well prohibit all harmful practices. However, there is little or no effort to ensure the participation of women in the transformation of customary laws of the Guraghe. The exclusion of women from the discourse that aims to bring about the cultural legitimacy of rights of women is by itself paradoxical. This problem could be avoided by the community itself, if there was a policy or law on customary local institutions that functions in collaboration and integration with local governmental institutions, besides the constitutional recognition of customary institutions. The following section discusses the required environment, including constitutional principles essential for achieving

81 For instance, the Guraghe Customary Law document in GPSDO (n 15) art 5(1) states 'when divorce is inevitable, the rights of the parties to the dispute must be respected equally'. However, the same law also systematically preserves the discriminatory customary divorce law of the *anqiti*.

82 Oloka-Onyango J and Tejan-Cole (n 12) 24.

the collaborative and integrative functioning of the two institutions, and how these might help to eliminate discriminatory and harmful practices against women.

7 Opportunities and Challenges of the Cultural Legitimisation of the Rights of Women

To bring about culturally legitimate women's rights within the functioning of ethno-cultural communities in Ethiopia, there are structural opportunities as well as challenges. The opportunities include the introduction of a federal constitution that guarantees cultural rights and autonomy for ethno-cultural communities, which An Na'im states constitutes a sense of a human rights regime as a response to one's own historic injustice.[83] The guaranteeing of cultural rights and autonomy inspired ethno-cultural communities, such as the Guraghe, to engage in internal discourses for the observance of human rights, particularly the rights of women as enshrined in the FDRE Constitution. Traditional leaders of the community come to understand that outlawing some discriminatory and harmful practices against women is necessary to adapt to changing national and international contexts. In other words, there have been enough stimuli to bring about cultural transformation or change within their community.

What is more, the creation of autonomous local governmental units in Ethiopian federalism, such as the Guraghe Zone, which have the purpose of accommodating diversity, is one of the major opportunities although this has not been exploited to its full potential. An autonomous local governmental unit as created for the accommodation of diversity in Ethiopia has three critical features. First, it makes national minorities local majorities, restoring the dignity and pride of such communities in their cultural settings. Second, it leads to the establishment of governmental institutions that exercise political power. Third, there is a devolution of defined competences which are relevant for the protection of the identity and culture of ethnic communities.[84]

With regard to the first feature of autonomy in the Guraghe Zone, the Guraghe communities are now the local majorities in the Zone. The Zone has also established all three branches of government, which exercise political power without contradicting the powers and laws of the federal and regional

83 An-Na'im (n 9) 38–67.

84 Zemelak Ayitenew Ayele, *Local Government in Ethiopia: Advancing Development and Accommodating Ethnic Minorities* (Nomos Verlagsgesellschaft 2014) 248–252.

governments. When it comes to the third feature of autonomy, the federal constitution and regional constitutions indicate competences that can be exercised by every ethnic community in the country.[85] Making use of custom, including making sure that customary laws are recognised cultural rights of all ethno-cultural communities, is endorsed by both the state and federal laws. This makes transforming customary laws a power potentially left to autonomous local governmental units. However, thus far no effort has been made by policy makers to advance the issue of transforming customary laws by using the agency of local government institutions; this is mainly due to the absence of policies on customary institutions that can underpin the integration of the two institutions in making laws for the local community.

If there had been collaboration and integration in the transformation of customary laws, the increasing representation of women in local councils, which nowadays has reached more than 30 percent, could have been employed to help overcome the deficits observed in the customary institutions. In other words, collaboration and integration can help to effectively challenge the exclusion of women from customary institutions or the incorporation of *anqiti* in the local customary law document.

The other virtuous opportunity for the cultural legitimacy of the rights of women is the increasing awareness among women of the community about their rights. Many female informants, both in rural and urban areas of the Guraghe Zone, affirmed their consciousness about the rights of women as enshrined in the FDRE Constitution – although they also remained pragmatic in not applying their rights because of several challenges encountered in patriarchal forces, which punish them using material and socio-psychological powers.[86]

Patriarchal customary beliefs and practices are often seen as the culture of the wider community, even though they negatively affect women's lives. In this regard, the customary law of the Guraghe is underpinned by customary beliefs that undermine the need for cultural transformation, unless such a need was to be encouraged by state policy.

The other challenge that hinders legitimate ways of bringing about the cultural legitimacy of human rights is the absence of laws or policy on customary institutions. In this regard, lessons can be taken from South Africa, who enacted

85 See FDRE Constitution (n 65) art 39(2) and 34(5). See also SNNPR Constitution (n 70) art 39(1) and 34(5), as well as art 81(3) which states that Zonal councils 'shall issue laws on matters uncovered and that are consistent with the state and federal laws'.

86 Regarding the material (economic) and socio-psychological power of intra-group institutions, see Oonagh Reitman, 'Multiculturalism and Feminism: Incompatibility, Compatibility, or Synonymy?' (2005) 5(2) Ethnicities 216.

the 'National Traditional Leadership and Governance Framework Act' in 2003. The Act requires a third of members of the traditional council to be women.[87] In this light, the absence of women's meaningful participation in customary institutions is indicative of the failure of the Ethiopian state to carry out its obligations under international and regional human rights instruments, which require designing appropriate measures to eliminate all forms of discrimination and harmful practices against women.

8 Conclusions

The cultural legitimisation of human rights is understood to have strategic significance to bring about human rights practices within the functioning of ethno-cultural communities. In this regard, the state has the responsibility to support such initiatives at different levels of government. In particular, the state can do so by making internal discourses for the transformation of customary laws and practices inclusive not only of the voices of civil society organisations, but also inclusive of the voices of women themselves. The enforcement of the rights of women, as well as their inclusion in governmental units, can bring about new challenges for the discriminatory and harmful practices towards women as perpetuated by their political representatives.

It is vital to have an overarching policy on customary institutions that underpins the collaboration and integration of customary local institutions with local governmental institutions across all three branches of the government. This would enable the participation of women in the (re)construction of culture by their community, as well as the transformation of discriminatory and harmful practices. In this light alone can the cultural legitimisation of women's human rights within ethno-cultural communities bring about meaningful change.

87 Government Gazette, Republic of South Africa, 'Traditional Leadership and Governance Framework Act' Vol. 465, No. 41/2003 (Cape Town, 19 December 2003) art 3(2)(b).

PART 3

Vulnerable Groups

Legal Empowerment of Women through Property Rights in Ethiopia

Tesfaye Abate Abebe

Abstract

Women in developing countries in general and in Ethiopia in particular are adversely affected by poverty due to the unequal distribution of resources and the unequal division of labour. The legal empowerment of women through property rights is imperative to emancipate women from poverty. Among others, such legal empowerment involves employing legal and institutional means to create rights, capacities as well as opportunities to enable women to escape from poverty. In legal realms, Ethiopia is a party to international human rights instruments such as the Convention on the Elimination of all Forms of Discrimination Against Women (CEDAW), the International Covenant on Civil and Political Rights (ICCPR) and the International Covenant on Economic, Social and Cultural Rights (ICESCR). All these international treaties guarantee women's property rights. Furthermore, the Constitution of the Federal Democratic Republic of Ethiopia (FDRE) and other laws, including the Revised Family Code, incorporate women's property rights as well. The Ethiopian Government has established the Ministry of Women, Children and Youth Affairs (MoWCYA) at the federal level to implement its international commitments. At the regional level, corresponding bureaus have been established. In practice, the legal empowerment of women through property rights is still a challenge to reckon with. The basic objective of this research is to investigate the extent of the legal empowerment of women through property rights, as well as the current situation in Ethiopia. Both qualitative and comparative legal research methods are used; relevant data for the study is gathered through interviews and the analysis of laws, cases and policy documents. The research reveals that despite commendable achievements in adopting laws to empower women, the situation on the ground is not in accordance with the aspirations of existing laws. The number of women who own individual houses is very low, and only very few women own land. As cases decided by courts indicate, the lower courts are not gender-sensitive. The MoWCYA does not have a structure at the kebele level. Therefore, this research recommends for the government to give trainings on the topic to lower court judges in order to strictly apply the law and to discourage bigamy. Further, the study suggests to install structures catering to women, children and youth affairs at kebele level to ensure the implementation of the legal empowerment of women through property rights.

 | DOI:10.1163/9789004415966_009

Keywords

poverty – land law – legal empowerment – women's property rights – women's legal empowerment – Ethiopia

1 Introduction

1.1 *Background*

Women generally do not receive the same chances and opportunities as men when it comes to education, employment, healthcare, etc. This leads to unequal relations between men and women, and gender discrimination.[1] While constituting more than half of the society, women own less than 10 percent of the worlds' property.[2] In many cases, laws in Africa limit women property rights:[3] women do not inherit property, making them have little opportunity to improve their lives. Thus, they depend on men and have little say in decisions revolving around the use of property-generated income or around supporting their families.[4]

According to article 646 of the Ethiopian Civil Code, a wife is bound to attend to all household duties. It is only if her husband is in a position to provide her with a servant that she will have a helper. This makes clear that the husband is not responsible to share the duties of the household, which by definition renders the wife very busy with no time to pursue her own activities, to educate herself, or to generate her own income. Thus, wives are dependent on their husbands. In addition, according to the Civil Code, the husband is given the power to administer common properties other than the wife's earnings,

---

1 EQUILEAP *'Gender Equality and Global Report and Ranking'* (2018) 1 <https://equileap.org/wp-content/uploads/2018/10/Equileap-Gender-Equality-Global-Report-and-Ranking-2018.pdf> accessed 14 February 2019.

2 United Nations Development Programme (UNDP) and Commission on Legal Empowerment of the Poor, 'Making the Law Work for Everyone' (Volume II Working Group Reports, 2008) 77 <https://www.undp.org/content/dam/aplaws/publication/en/publications/democratic-governance/legal-empowerment/reports-of-the-commission-on-legal-empowerment-of-the-poor/making-the-law-work-for-everyone---vol-ii---english-only/making_the_law_work_II.pdf> accessed 15 May 2018.

3 Nadia H Youssef, 'Women's Access to Productive Resources: The Need for Legal Instruments to Protect Women's Development Rights' in Julie Peters and Andrea Wolper (eds) *Women's Rights, Human Rights: International Feminist Perspectives* (Taylor & Francis 1995) 279–280.

4 Naresh Singh, 'Legal Empowerment of Women and Girls: Progress and Challenges' (2014) 4 Estudios Del Desarrollo 157, 185.

salaries and income.[5] The law has thus given the chance to the husband to abuse the common property without consulting his wife.

Nowadays, in modern states around the world, laws have been changed to guarantee women's property rights; however, the custom often remains unchanged. Therefore, there is a mismatch between state laws and customary laws.[6] For example, even though Ethiopia has changed its Civil Code dealing with family, the custom in Ethiopia still considers the wife to undertake all the household duties herself.

Property rights and inheritance often apply differently to men and women, and gender disparities in access to property remain large and significant.[7] Only eleven and 27 percent of land is owned by women in Brazil and Paraguay, respectively. However, their shares of land are smaller than those of men. In many countries, land ownership remains in the hands of men due to customary and modern laws, especially in most African countries and in approximately half of Asian countries. Property rights have indeed begun to improve for women; however, it been proven that the law by itself is insufficient to change women's reality on the ground.[8]

International laws do indeed recognise women's rights to access, own and control land, adequate housing and property; still, discriminatory laws, policies, patriarchal customs, traditions and attitudes negatively affect women in the enjoyment of their rights.[9]

Previous research confirms a strong relationship between property rights, access to finance and business productivity. Women's access to land is linked to gains in family welfare and children's health.[10]

While there have been improvements in women's empowerment in Ethiopia, there are still significant challenges. In the economic sector, for example the agriculture extension service is not yet accessible as expected, which creates a negative impact on the productivity of female farmers. Technologies to increase production in agriculture are not well-accessible for women, the same is true for the availability of credit. There is an absence of procedures to bring

5 Negarit Gazeta, Gazette Extraordinary, 'Civil Code of the Empire of Ethiopia' Proclamation No. 165/1960, art 656(1).

6 Singh (n 4) 186.

7 Ibid.

8 Singh (n 4) 172. For the discussion of women land rights in Africa, see Bina Agarwal, 'Gender, Property, and Land Rights: Bridging a Critical Gap in Economic Analysis and Policy' in Kelly D Askin and Dorean M Koenig (eds), *Women and International Human Rights Law* (International Publishers 2001) 845–872.

9 Ibid 184.

10 Ibid 187.

women from the informal sector to the formal trading sector. Equal pay for equal work is still a problem, particularly in the private sector, and efforts to help small enterprises run by women to grow into middle enterprises are not satisfactory. Furthermore, women's participation in developing and implementing development projects is poor; equally, participation in manufacturing and investment is not up to expectations.[11]

In some regions, the Family Law has not been revised to make it compatible with international and national commitments, and there are still related problems when it comes to early marriage, marriage based on consent, the administration of communal property, and the realisation of fairness in the partition of property at the time of divorce.[12]

Economic empowerment is accepted as one of the instruments to solve gender discrimination.[13] There are several fundamental problems regarding women's empowerment in Ethiopia: attitudinal problems, less commitment of political leaders at all levels, the limitation of capacity of policy implementers at all levels, lack of accountability, unemployment, and limitation of services for empowering women.[14] In addition, the low level of women's literacy and the prevailing community culture are also obstacles.[15] Recently, the Ethiopian Prime Minister, Dr. Abiy Ahmed, has taken encouraging action to empower women in political positions.[16] Still, this does not extend to the economic empowerment of women.

11 FDRE Ministry of Women, Children and Youth Affairs (MoWCYA), 'Ethiopian Women, Development and Change Package' (Addis Ababa, 2017) 7.

12 Ibid 12.

13 EQUILEAP (n 1) 1.

14 MoWCYA (n 11) 12; FDRE National Planning Commission, 'Growth and Transformation Plan II (GTP II) (2015/16–2019/20)' (Addis Ababa, May 2016) 56–57 <https://europa.eu/capacity4dev/file/30510/download?token=efsF8UiP> accessed 14 May 2018.

15 Tefera Assefa Moreda, 'Nature of Women Empowerment in Ethiopia (Constitutional and Policy Provisions)' (Dilla University, 2017) 8 <https://www.researchgate.net/publication/321753588_Nature_of_Women_Empowerment_in_Ethiopia_Constitutional_and_Policy_Provisions> accessed 14 May 2018.

16 Ten out of twenty current state ministers are women. These include: Mufariat Kamil, Minister of Peace; Aisha Mohammed, Minister of Defence; Fetlework Gedre-Egzihaber, Minister of Trade and Industry; Dagmawit Moges Minister of Transport; Dr. Hirut Woldemariam, Minister of Science and Higher Education; Yalem-Tsegay Asfaw, Minister of Women, Children and Youth; Dr Hirut Kasaw, Minister of Culture and Tourism; Mrs Adanech Abeebe, Minister of Revenue. See 'Ethiopia's Abiy Gives Half of Ministerial Posts to Women', BBC *News* (16 October 2018) <https://www.bbc.com/news/world-africa-45881004> accessed 18 February 2019.

1.2 *Research Questions and Objective*

The research investigates the following two questions:

1. What is the extent of women's legal empowerment through property rights in Ethiopia?
2. What does the practice of women's legal empowerment through property rights look like in Ethiopia?

1.3 *Research Methods and Data Analysis*

The writer employs qualitative and comparative legal research methods. To this end, the relevant literature and international legal principles are considered and the relevant Ethiopian laws analysed. Additional data is gathered through interviews and the investigation of relevant primary and secondary sources, including laws, cases, government policy documents, as well as academic literature.

2 Women's Legal Empowerment through Property Rights in General

2.1 *Women's Legal Empowerment*

The term 'legal empowerment' is fluid and subject to different definitions.[17] Legal empowerment is defined both as a process and as an end that results in protections and opportunities. As a process, it confirms economic, social and cultural gains in law. It focuses on the rule of law, property rights, labour rights and business rights. Law might be used as an instrument to help women achieve their full potential.[18]

Legal empowerment is an approach addressing how the law can best serve the poor and other disadvantaged groups, including women.[19] Legal empowerment employs legal and other means in creating rights, capacities, and/or opportunities for the poor, giving them new power to use the law as well as legal tools to escape poverty and marginalisation.[20] Legal empowerment is accepted

17 Rachel M Gisselquist, 'Legal Empowerment and Group-based Inequality' (United Nations University, World Institute for Development Economics Research, WIDER Working Paper 2018/39, March 2018) 2.

18 Singh (n 4) 157.

19 Ibid.

20 JW Bruce and others, 'Legal Empowerment of the Poor: From Concepts to Assessment' (Prepared for the United Nations Agency for International Development, Burlington, 2007) <https://www.usaid.gov/sites/default/files/documents/1866/Legal%20 Empowerment%20for%20the%20Poor%20Guide.pdf> accessed 14 May 2018; Stephen Golub, 'Beyond Rule of Law Orthodoxy: The Legal Environment Alternative' (Carnegie

as a strategy to get out of poverty, overcome economic inequalities, create economic opportunities and get access to credit.[21]

Women's legal empowerment hence refers to using legal and other means in order to create rights, capacities, and/or opportunities for women that give them new power to use the law, as well as legal tools to escape poverty and marginalisation.[22] The legal empowerment of women is a process of systemic change for women to use the law, the legal system, and legal services to protect and advance their rights and interests as citizens.[23] Legally empowered women can exercise their rights and improve their lives.

Empowering women is considered one of the best ways to promote economic growth, peace and social security.[24] The legal empowerment of women enables them to use their rights equally and to seek resources they have been previously denied.[25]

Endowment for International Peace, Working Papers Rule of Law Series No. 41, October 2003) 25 <https://carnegieendowment.org/files/wp41.pdf> accessed 14 May 2018.

21 Dubravka Bojic, Christopher Tanner and Margret Vidar, *Legal Empowerment of Rural Poor: A Pathway out of Poverty* (Food and Agriculture Organization of the United Nations, 2012) 46 <https://worldjusticeproject.org/sites/default/files/legal_empowerment_of_rural_poor_bojic_tanner_vidar.pdf> accessed 14 May 2018; See also Byron M Sheldrich, 'Legal Empowerment, Access to Justice and Poverty Alleviation: Governance Challenges to Linking Legal Structures to Social Change' (2013) 2(1) Canadian Journal of Poverty Law 1.

22 See Mariam Sohail, 'Women Empowerment and Economic Development – An Exploratory Study in Pakistan' (2014) 5(4) Journal of Business Studies Quarterly 210, 212; Women's empowerment is related to the expansion of property rights and capabilities to make strategic life choices. Securing the right to property empowers women. See also Mequanint B Melesse, Adane Dabissa and Erwin Bulte, 'Joint Land Certification Programmes and Women's Empowerment: Evidence from Ethiopia' (2018) 54(10) The Journal of Development Studies, 1759.

23 UNDP and Commission on Legal Empowerment of the Poor (n 2). The aim of women's empowerment is to change the power relations between the sexes. Thus, women should be given equal opportunities in economic, political and legal fields so that they can enhance their development. See also Sohail (n 22) 212.

24 According to the Australian Minister of Foreign Affairs Julie Bishop in 2014. See 'International Women's Day – Joint Media Release' Minister of Foreign Affairs Australia (4 March 2014) <https://foreignminister.gov.au/releases/Pages/2014/jb_mr_140304.aspx?ministerid=4> accessed 14 may 2018.

25 See United Nations (UN) Women, 'The Power of Legislation for Women's Empowerment and Sustainable Development' (Parliamentary Event, 15 March 2016). The four pillars of legal empowerment are: (A) Access to justice and rule of law; (B) Labour rights; (C) Business rights, and (D) Property Rights. See also Gisselquist (n 17) 3; See also UNDP and Commission on Legal Empowerment, 'Making the Law Work for Everyone – Report of the Commission on Legal Empowerment of the Poor' (Volume I, 2008) 31 <https://www.un.org/ruleoflaw/files/Making_the_Law_Work_for_Everyone.pdf> accessed 15 May 2018.

2.2 *Property Rights of Women and Empowerment*

2.2.1 Property Rights and the Legal Empowerment of Women

Property rights as a human right and as part of the legal empowerment of women imply two things: first, the legally enforceable protection of property rights of women; second, the general promotion of access to property by women.[26]

Property rights are defined as 'the liberty or permit to enjoy benefits of wealth while assuming the costs which the benefits entail.'[27] Property rights are abstract social institutions that define privileges and limit the power individuals have over a resource.[28] Property rights stand for a bundle of rights[29] whereby the owner of a property has a right to use his/her property in a manner allowed and expected by the community, and excluding others from interfering with his/her actions. However, his/her actions should not be prohibited by the law. Property rights prevent others, including institutions, from forcibly appropriating what belongs to someone. They thus incentivise owners to voluntarily develop their property.[30]

As Eaton explains, property rights are economic interests protected by law. Regarding real estate, the owner has many significant rights, including the right to hold and use; the right to rent or sell in part or in whole; the right to bequeath; the right to transfer by contract for a specified period of time.[31] From

26 Ibid 73; For the treatment of women rights in general, see Eldalcachew Bayeh, 'Human Rights in Ethiopia: An Assessment on the Law and Practice of Women's Rights' (2015) 3(2) Humanities and Social Sciences 83.

27 Achian and Demsetz (1973) in JM Lusugga Kironde, 'Making Property Rights Work for the Poor in Tanzania' (Working Paper for the National Consultation Conference, Dar es Salaam, 29–30 November 2006).

28 Karol Boudreaux, 'The Role of Property Rights as an Institution: Implications for Development Policy' (Mercatus Policy Series, Policy Primer No. 2, Mercatus Center, George Mason University, May 2005) 4 <https://www.mercatus.org/system/files/Property%20Rights.pdf> accessed 15 May 2018.

29 UNDP and Commission on Legal Empowerment of the Poor (n 2) 73; See also Alison Brown, 'Claiming the Streets: Property Rights and Legal Empowerment in the Urban Informal Economy' (2015) 76(C) World Development 238, 238–239.

30 Kironde (n 27).

31 See WE Tayler 'Property Rights – and Responsibilities? The Case of Kenya' (2004) 28 Habitat International, 275. Property rights are defined as:
Occupancy /Use/Enjoy – the right to occupy without any treat of eviction.
- Restrict – the right to restrict others not to have access to property. This is the right of exclusion.
- Dispose/Buy/ Inherit – the right to give away, to mortgage, to sell, to buy or to inherit.
- Develop/Improve – the right to be able to develop land in some form, for instance through buildings, infrastructure.

a development point of view, an owner should be empowered to decide which rights to retain and which ones to trade away or purchase.[32]

The right to enjoy one's property is one of the property rights of owners. It guarantees the owner the right to use, benefit from, and change the form and substance of the property and to transfer such rights. The very existence of these rights is used as incentive for the owner to use the property in the most productive and competitive way.

Property rights are defined by law. If the law recognises property rights for women, women could be empowered. Law, in this sense, becomes an instrument for the creation of opportunities to exercise property rights and to create entitlements for women.[33]

2.2.2 Empowering Women through Property Rights for Development and Poverty Reduction

The legal empowerment of women is linked to development, poverty alleviation and the growth of women's agency.[34] Women's legal empowerment is related to development[35] and it can be used as an instrument to generate

- Cultivate/Produce- the right to use land to grow food, keep animals, or operate home-based economic entities.
- Sublet – the right to rent out (the land) for a specific duration
- Enforce – the right to have legal remedies in case property rights are violated.
- To access service – the right to enjoy services like roads, drains, open spaces, sewers and social services.
- To access formal credit – the right to use property in financial transactions, which include using the property as collateral.

32 The legal empowerment of women through property right is accepted as an important vehicle for development. See Sheldrich (n 21) 6.

33 UNDP and Commission on Legal Empowerment of the Poor (n 2) 68.

34 Government of India, Department of Justice and the United Nations Development Programme, 'Conference Report International Conference on Equitable Access to Justice: Legal Aid and Legal Empowerment' (New Delhi, 17–18 November 2012) 29 <https://www.undp.org/content/dam/india/docs/DG/equitable-access-to-justice-legal-empowerment-legal-aid-and-making-it-work-for-the-poor-and-marginalised.pdf> accessed 14 May 2018.

35 Lars Waldorf, 'Legal Empowerment and Horizontal Inequalities After Conflict' (United Nations University, World Institute for Development Economics Research, WIDER Working Paper 2017/50, March 2017) 2 <https://www.wider.unu.edu/sites/default/files/wp2017-50.pdf> accessed 14 May 2018; Sébastien Jodoin and Sean Stephenson, 'Introduction: Understanding Legal Empowerment of the Poor in the Context of Sustainable Development' (2013) 2(1) Canadian Journal of Poverty Law, iii; See generally Esther Duflo, 'Women's Empowerment and Economic Development' (National Bureau of Economic Research, Working Paper No. 17702, December 2011) <https://www.nber.org/papers/w17702> accessed 14 May 2018.

change.[36] Goal 5.6 of the 2030 Sustainable Development Goals (SDGs) is devoted to women's empowerment. In addition to eliminating all forms of discrimination, essential goals include property rights, which also encompass undertaking reforms to ensure women's access to ownership and control over land, among others. In such areas, national laws play a pivotal role.[37]

Today, the SDGs have been agreed upon and their implementation has started. At the international level there is a consensus that the SDGs might not be achieved without empowering women in the economy. Hence, the participation of women in the economy and social life is vital for sustainable development.[38]

Securing rural land property and housing are essential property rights to alleviate poverty.[39] Well-defined and transferable property rights are considered a pre-condition for a property owner to take loans. This in turn promotes women's property rights. The importance of property rights, however, is more than their mere use as collateral.

Evidence demonstrates that secured land rights are indeed a pre-condition to land-related investment. Farmers with short-term or insecure land rights do not make long-term investments in the land. They may not exchange their land with others who might be in a better position to develop it. The same applies to urban residents. Land, as well as institutions governing ownership and use are both important for economic growth and poverty reduction. This in turn improves investment climate, access to credit and revenue for the government.[40]

---

36 See Jodoin and Stephenson, ibid ix.

37 United Nations, 'Sustainable Development Goals' (2019) Goal 5.6 <https://www.un.org/sustainabledevelopment/sustainable-development-goals/> accessed 12 February 2019.

38 United Nations Secretary General's High-Level Panel on Women's Economic Development, 'Second Report: Taking Action for Transformational Change on Women's Economic Empowerment' (2017) <http://www2.unwomen.org/-/media/hlp%20wee/attachments/reports-toolkits/hlp-wee-report-2017-03-taking-action-en.pdf?la=en&vs=5226> accessed 14 May 2018.

39 See UNDP and Commission on Legal Empowerment of the Poor (n 2) 77; See Carol S Rabenhorst, 'Gender and Property Rights: A Critical Issue in Urban Economic Development' (prepared for International Housing Coalition and the Urban Institute, July 2011) 4 <http://www.focusintl.com/GD047-%20Gender%20and%20Property%20Rights%20-%20A%20Critical%20Issue%20in%20Urban%20Economic%20Development%20-%20IHC.pdf> accessed 14 May 2018.

40 Ruth Meinzen-Dick and others, 'Women's Land Rights as a Pathway to Poverty Reduction A Framework and Review of Available Evidence' (Environment and Production Technology Division, Poverty, Health, and Nutrition Division, IFPRI Discussion Paper 01663, July 2017) 14 <http://ebrary.ifpri.org/utils/getfile/collection/p15738coll2/id/131359/filename/131570.pdf> accessed 14 May 2018.

Property rights play an essential role in development in the following ways:

1. Property rights help individuals to allocate resources
Individual property rights are a basis for trade and for the market economy. Persons who own resources are empowered to decide how to use and allocate those resources. Owners who have secured property rights have the opportunity to trade voluntarily with others.[41] Trading property gives benefits to the owner, thus trading provides owners with incentives to become entrepreneurs and to act entrepreneurially by employing opportunities to meet the needs of others.[42]
2. Property rights create positive incentives
'Property rights create positive incentives to create, innovate, conserve, and protect property'.[43] In the absence of property rights, individuals may not have incentives to invest in physical or human capital, or technologies. Property rights give reward to the owner and this is an incentive to invest in properties. If a person is free to trade his/her property and retain the profits, s/he is more likely to maintain and improve the property since s/he is likely to be rewarded for the effort made.[44]
3. Property rights promote economic development and alleviate poverty
Markets evolve where property rights are secured for individuals, as persons are free to develop and use property and contract rights. Open trade in a free market economy promotes economic growth. When property rights are secured, persons invest more in property. Where the rule of law is intact and contractual obligations are enforced, economic growth and property will be achieved.[45] Property rights provide the basis for trade and markets. These in turn help to alleviate poverty, making property rights a key ingredient in the struggle for poverty alleviation.[46]
4. Property rights contribute to human flourishing and empowerment
Where individuals are empowered to decide how best to realise their unique capabilities, there will be human flourishing. Individual property rights enable persons to live the best life they can. Property rights decentralise power and create space in which the best life can be pursued.[47]

41 Ibid 11.
42 Ibid 12.
43 Ibid 13.
44 See UNDP and Commission on Legal Empowerment of the Poor (n 2) 73; Rabenhorst (n 39) 13.
45 Rabenhorst (n 39) 14.
46 Ibid 15.
47 Ibid 15.

Ultimately, the legal empowerment of women is about poverty alleviation.[48] Thus, empowering women through property rights means alleviating poverty and malnutrition, keeping in mind that women who earn more spend 'a higher proportion of their income to keep their children healthy and well-fed.'[49] The legal empowerment of women through property plays a role in increasing gender equality and in decreasing poverty, and helps to accelerate progress towards sustainable development.[50] The law is a powerful tool to improve or empower women. The law can create an opportunity for women to claim their rights individually or collectively.[51]

Ensuring women's property rights helps both economic and social empowerment.[52] It also enhances options for livelihood and is vital to decision-making power.[53]

2.3 *Women's Property Rights and International and African Legal Frameworks*

Persons are born with equal rights and dignity.[54] Every person has the right to property,[55] which may not be arbitrarily deprived[56] unless ordered by law. The 1967 Declaration on the Elimination of Discrimination against Women recognises the necessity 'to ensure the universal requisition in law and in fact of the principle of equality of men and women.'[57] Discriminating against women's equality rights is unjust and an offence against human dignity.[58] Women, married or unmarried, have equal rights with men before the law.[59] Particularly,

48 'Poverty alleviation' is narrowly defined as improving material standards of living that addresses income poverty. See Stephen Golub (ed) *Legal Empowerment: Practitioners' Perspectives* (International Development Law Organization, 2010) 203; See also Sohail (n 22) 219.

49 UNDP and Commission on Legal Empowerment of the Poor (n 2) 78.

50 See Golub (n 48) 27, 'Absence, unjust allocation, or insecurity of property rights harm [women] and hinder sustainable development of a society'. See also UNDP and Commission on the Empowerment of the Poor (n 2) 76.

51 Golub (n 48) 203.

52 Ibid 204.

53 Ibid.

54 Universal Declaration of Human Rights (adopted 10 December 1948) UNGA Res 217 A(III) (UDHR), art 1.

55 Ibid art 17 (1).

56 Ibid art 17 (2).

57 Convention on the Elimination of All Forms of Discrimination against Women (adopted 18 December 1979, entry into force 3 September 1981) 1249 UNTS 13 (CEDAW), preamble para 7.

58 Ibid art 1.

59 Ibid art 6(1).

they have the right to 'acquire, administer, enjoy, dispose of and inherit property, including property acquired during marriage'.[60]

As incorporated under the 1979 Convention on the Elimination of All Forms of Discrimination against Women (CEDAW), state parties are required to ensure 'the same rights for both spouses in respect of the ownership, acquisition, management, administration, enjoyment and disposition of property.'[61] State parties are duty-bound to accord women's equality with men before the law.[62] The domestic law of state parties should ensure women's right to administer property.[63] According to CEDAW, women in marriage have equal rights of property; this includes the right to acquisition, management, administration, enjoyment and disposition.[64]

In general, women's property rights are ensured under CEDAW, which is binding upon state parties. State parties are duty-bound to ensure the same rights and equality of men and women, in particular 'the right to bank loans, mortgages and other forms of financial credit.'[65] This provision is important in ensuring women's access to credit, which in turn promotes entrepreneurship. CEDAW gives due attention to women's participation in and benefit from development. Thus, state parties are obliged to take appropriate measures accordingly, particularly in rural development.[66]

State parties must ensure women's participation in development-planning at all levels.[67] Women have the right to access agricultural credits and loans,[68] as well as the right to equal treatment in land and agrarian reform.[69] In addition, they have the right to access appropriate technology[70] to bring about development. The 1995 Beijing Global Platform for Action acknowledges the property rights of women, including land rights.[71] In 2009, a UN General

60 United Nations General Assembly, 'Declaration on the Elimination of Discrimination against Women' (7 November 1967) A/RES/22/2263, art 6 (1)(a).
61 CEDAW (n 57) art 16(1)(h).
62 Ibid art 15 (1).
63 Ibid art 15 (2).
64 Ibid art 16(1)(h).
65 Ibid art 13 (b).
66 Ibid art 14(2).
67 Ibid art 14(2)(a).
68 Ibid art 14(2)(g).
69 Ibid art 14(2)(g).
70 Ibid art 14(2)(g).
71 See 'Beijing Declaration and Platform for Action' (Fourth World Conference on Women, Beijing, 4–15 September 1995) <https://www.un.org/womenwatch/daw/beijing/pdf/BDPfA%20E.pdf> accessed 14 May 2018.

Assembly resolution emphasises the need to ensure land and property rights of women in the context of post-conflict peace-building.[72]

Under the International Covenant on Economic, Social and Cultural Rights (ICESCR), Ethiopia shall ensure equal economic, social and cultural rights to women.[73] To ensure such rights, Ethiopia must adopt legislative measures.[74] Ethiopia must recognise the economic rights of women, such as the right to an adequate standard of living, including adequate food and housing.[75]

At the regional level, the right to property is guaranteed under the African Charter on Human and Peoples' Rights (ACHPR).[76] This right is guaranteed to women as well, as the Charter ensures the equal protection of everyone before the law.[77] Every person is equal and enjoys the same respect and the same rights.[78] Furthermore, the Charter clearly stipulates that the state is duty-bound to ensure discrimination against women is avoided. Beyond that, the state must also ensure the protection of the rights of women as stipulated in international conventions and declarations.[79]

The Protocol to the African Charter on Human and People's Rights on the Rights of Women in Africa provides that a woman has the right to acquire her own property and to manage it freely during marriage.[80] It also stipulates women's rights to share joint property derived from a marriage in the case the marriage is dissolved.[81] The Protocol provides that 'a widow shall have the right to an equitable share in the inheritance of the property of her husband.'[82] Women shall also have the right to inherit equally with men.[83] Considering this, the right to property is guaranteed under African regional law.

---

72 United Nations General Assembly, 'Resolution 1889' (5 October 2009) S/RES/1889 <https://undocs.org/S/RES/1889(2009)> accessed 4 May 2018.

73 International Covenant on Economic, Social and Cultural Rights (adopted 16 December 1966, entry into force 3 January 1976) 993 UNTS 3 (ICESCR), art 3.

74 Ibid art 2(1).

75 Ibid art 11(1).

76 African (Banjul) Charter on Human and Peoples' Rights (signed 27 June 1981, entry into force 12 October 1986) OAU Doc CAB/LEG/67/3 rev 5, 21 I.L.M. 58, art 14.

77 Ibid art 3.

78 Ibid art 19.

79 Ibid art 18(3).

80 African Commission on Human and Peoples' Rights, 'Protocol to the African Charter on Human and Peoples' Rights on the Rights of Women in Africa', art 6(5) <http://www.achpr.org/files/instruments/women-protocol/achpr_instr_proto_women_eng.pdf> accessed 14 May 2018.

81 Ibid art 7(d).

82 Ibid art 21(1).

83 Ibid art 21(2).

3 The Legal Empowerment of Women through Property Rights in Ethiopia

The Ministry of Women, Children and Youth Affairs (MoWCYA) is entrusted to conclude international treaties relating to women and to follow up on their implementation.[84] The international agreements that Ethiopia has ratified are an integral part of the legal regime of the nation.[85] Therefore, the international instruments considered above are understood as part of the national law. These laws are expected to apply to women's property rights in Ethiopia.

The MoWCYA is obliged to submit reports to the concerned bodies regarding the implementation of women's rights in general.[86]

3.1 *Women's Property Rights under the Ethiopian Constitution*

According to the Constitution of the Federal Democratic Republic of Ethiopia (FDRE), women have a right to equality[87] and the same right to property as men.[88] They have equal rights as men in marriage as well.[89] The FDRE Constitution stipulates the property rights of women as having the right to acquire, administer, control, use and transfer property.[90] Special emphasis is put on the right of women to use, transfer, administer and control land in equal terms as men.[91] Furthermore, women have an equal right to the inheritance of property.[92]

3.2 *National Women's Policy*

The objectives of the National Policy on Ethiopian Women include speeding up the equality of women in order to ensure that they can exercise equal

84 Federal Negarit Gazeta, 'Definition of Powers and Duties of the Executive Organs of the Federal Democratic Republic of Ethiopia Proclamation' Proclamation No. 1097/2018, art 28(1)(s).

85 Federal Negarit Gazeta, 'The Constitution of the Federal Democratic Republic of Ethiopia' Proclamation No. 1/1995, art 9(4).

86 Proclamation No. 1097/2018 (n 84) art 28(1)(s). Recently, the Ministry submitted the eighth report regarding the performance of CEDAW. See generally Committee on the Elimination of Discrimination Against Women, 'Eighth periodic report submitted by Ethiopia under article 18 of the Convention, due in 2015' (21 November 2017) CEDAW/C/ETH/8 <https://tbinternet.ohchr.org/Treaties/CEDAW/Shared%20Documents/ETH/CEDAW_C_ETH_8_5939_E.pdf> accessed 14 May 2018.

87 FDRE Constitution (n 85) art 25.

88 See ibid art 35(1).

89 Ibid art 34(1) and art 35(2).

90 Ibid art 35(7).

91 Ibid.

92 Ibid.

property rights.[93] The policy aspires for the advancement of women and for the enjoyment of their human rights.[94] The policy was one of the earliest policies of the Ethiopian government, which was developed after research on the status of women was undertaken.

3.3 *The Growth and Transformation Plan II*

The Growth and Transformation Plan II (GTP II) aspires for the empowerment of women. The Plan envisages the empowerment of women in order to enable their participation in the struggle for poverty reduction.[95] The creation of a conducive environment for women to participate in national development is planned.[96] In addition, the goal is to improve the economic benefits of women and to ensure gender equality as per the 2030 SDGs.[97] To achieve these goals, capacity-building trainings, as well as financial and material support schemes for women are planned.[98] These have the goal of helping the empowerment of women through property, as being able to benefit from the national economy will bring about economic empowerment.

3.4 *The Revised Family Code*

The Revised Family Code of 2000 ensures equal property rights to women both in marriage and at the time of divorce.[99] The private property of spouses is secured in the Revised Family Code. The property of each spouse on the day of their marriage is considered the private property of the respective spouse. Property acquired after marriage by succession or donation remains the private property of the respective spouse.[100] Furthermore, property acquired through the exchange of private property or with money that is either owned personally or derived from the sale of private property, is the private property of the spouse in question.[101] However, the respective spouse has to put a request to a court; the property will be private only in cases in which the court decides so.[102] All the above-mentioned provisions of the Revised Family Code

93 Transitional Government of Ethiopia, '*National Policy on Ethiopian Women*' (Addis Ababa, September 1993) 12.

94 Ibid.

95 FDRE National Planning Commission (n 14) 208.

96 Ibid.

97 Ibid 209.

98 Ibid.

99 Federal Negarit Gazeta, 'The Revised Family Code Proclamation' Proclamation No. 213/2000, arts 62, 63 and 86.

100 Ibid art 57.

101 Ibid art 58(1).

102 Ibid art 58(2).

aim to protect the private property of wives in particular. Thus, the Family Code empowers women (wives) with property rights.

Also, the communal property of wives is guaranteed in the Revised Family Code. In cases where private property is acquired by onerous title during marriage, it is the common property of spouses unless it is made private, as discussed above.[103] In most cases, it is the husband who can acquire properties in onerous title since it is also the husband who generally has more property. Thus, this provision is essential in protecting and empowering the common property rights of women. The law further empowers women through property rights as it considers all income derived by personal efforts of the spouse and from private property as common property.[104] This provision, once again, empowers women through property rights as today it is still mainly the husband who generates income with the labour market generally favouring men. The Revised Family Law has a positive impact in empowering women because they have the opportunity to work outside their homes and to earn an income.[105]

The Family Law presumes a property registered in the name of one of the spouses as common property.[106] Traditionally in Ethiopia, properties are registered in the name of the husband. Therefore, common property registered in the name of the husband is presumed to be common property. However, it noteworthy that an owner of a private property can indeed prove that s/he is the sole owner and thereby disprove the presumption of common property.[107]

3.5 *Land Law*

Ensuring land rights for women increases women's empowerment, particularly in developing countries like Ethiopia in which land is the basic source of economy.[108] Land registration and titling secures the individualisation of the land to a person and creates private property, which the owner can sell or

103 Ibid art 62(2).

104 Ibid art 62(1).

105 See Mary Hallward-Driemeier and Ousman Gajigo, 'Strengthening Economic Rights and Women's Occupational Choice: the Impact of Reforming Ethiopia's Family Law' (Policy Research Working Paper 6695, The World Bank Research Group, November 2011) <http://documents.worldbank.org/curated/en/259861468021600567/pdf/WPS6695.pdf> accessed 15 May 2018.

106 Proclamation No. 213/2000 (n 99) art 63(1).

107 Ibid.

108 See generally Khushba Mishra and Abdoul G. Sam, 'Does Women's Land Ownership Promote their Empowerment? Empirical Evidence from Nepal' (2016) 78 World Development 360–371.

mortgage to the market. This creates the commoditisation of land, which in turn fosters investment.[109]

A registration title is considered as one means of women's legal empowerment, particularly small holders. Women whose land rights are registered can sell or buy their land in a legal manner. By mortgaging their land, they can also borrow money and invest.[110] Registering land secures the holders' use right.[111] In Ethiopia, land certification with the purpose of securing property rights has been implemented.[112] It increases the security of the land use rights. The certification of property enables women to decide which crop to grow on the land of their possession.[113] This also helps women to secure their land rights at the time of divorce.[114]

In Amhara Regional State, the law requires photographs of both the wife and the husband on the land title.[115] This provision protects the land right of the wife, since the husband cannot transfer property rights to others without his wife's consent.[116]

In Ethiopia, a woman who wants to undertake an agricultural activity as a farmer has the right to acquire and use rural land.[117] A woman who is the holder of land use rights must be given a holding certificate 'that indicates the size of the land, land use type and cover, level of fertility and borders, as well as the obligations and right of the holder.'[118]

109 Catherine Boone, 'Legal Empowerment of the Poor through Property Rights Reform: Tensions and Trade-Offs of Land Registration and Titling in Sub-Saharan Africa' (2018) 55(3) The Journal of Development Studies 1, 5.

110 Ibid.

111 Ibid 5–6.

112 MoWCYA (n 11) 22.

113 Lauren Persha, Adi Greif and Heather Huntington, 'Assessing the Impact of Second-Level Land Certification in Ethiopia' (Paper prepared for World Bank Conference on Land and Property, Washington DC, 20–24 March 2017) 14.

114 Interview with Ato Minyamir, Gender Expert in the Ministry of Women, Child and Youth Affairs, Addis Ababa, 3 January 2018.

115 See Askale Teklu, *Land Registration and Women's Land Rights in Amhara Regions – Ethiopia* (IIED 2005).

116 Golub (n 48) 210.

117 Federal Negarit Gazeta, 'Rural Land Administration and Land Use Proclamation' Proclamation No. 456/2005, art 5(1)(c); See also Zikre Hig of the Council of the Amhara National Regional State of the FDRE, 'The Revised Amhara national Regional State Rural Land Administration and Use Proclamation' Proclamation No. 133/2006, art 6(1) cum art 3.

118 Proclamation No. 456/2005 ibid art 6(3); See also Proclamation No. 133/2006 ibid art 24 (2).

The name of both spouses must appear on the holding certificate in cases in which the land is commonly held by both spouses.[119] This provision is good to empower women through land use rights, which provides higher security than the Revised Family Code.[120] This law particularly protects the rights of wives since in most cases it is a husband who transfers property without the wife's knowledge. In this regard, Ethiopian law is praised as being advanced.[121] The Ethiopian land law strengthens the rights of women[122] and ensures co-ownership for spouses,[123] which are important first steps in empowering women.[124] Land holding rights can be transferred to others by gift. However, the wife's agreement is required in cases where the husband wants to transfer common land holding rights.[125]

4 The Practice of Women's Legal Empowerment through Property Rights in Ethiopia

According to Ethiopian law, the MoWCYA shall encourage and support women in organising to implement their rights.[126] It also has the responsibility to lead capacity-building activities.[127]

The MoWCYA is responsible for preparing and implementing a strategy to ensure women's active participation in the economic sector.[128] It also should be studying the labour sectors for women to be beneficiary 'from these opportunities by organizing themselves into cooperative associations'.[129] It facilitates development funds that seek to ensure women's employment opportunities

119 Proclamation No. 456/2005 ibid art 6(4). See also Proclamation No. 133/2006 ibid art 24 (2).

120 Compare this provision to the Revised Family Code (n 99), which does not require property to be registered in the names of both spouses.

121 UNDP and Commission on Legal Empowerment of the Poor (n 2) 46.

122 See Stein Holden, 'From Being Property of Men to Becoming Equal Owners? Early Impacts of Land Registration and Certification on Women in Southern Ethiopia' (Report for UNHABITAT, Shelter Branch, Land Tenure and Property Administration Section, 2 January 2008) 7 <http://mirror.unhabitat.org/downloads/docs/10768_1_594333.pdf> accessed 13 May 2018.

123 Proclamation No. 456/2005 (n 117) art 6(4).

124 Holden (n 122) 7.

125 Proclamation No. 133/2006 (n 118) art 17 (3).

126 Proclamation No. 1097/2018 (n 84) art 28(1)(h).

127 Ibid art 28(1)(b).

128 Ibid art 28(1)(a).

129 Ibid art 28(1)(i).

and make them economic beneficiaries.[130] It is the duty of the MoWCYA to ensure the legal empowerment of women.[131]

The MoWCYA and the relevant regional Women and Children's Affairs Bureaus provide legal advice to women.[132] However, as there is no institutional organisation regarding women at the *kebele*[133] level, and there are problems in the empowerment of women in the development sector, in conducting close supervision and in helping women to implement their rights as per the law.[134] There is a problem of leaders' lacking political commitment when it comes to considering the 'women's development group' which is a basic structure that the ministry has mobilized for the empowerment of women as a key instrument in the country's development aspirations.[135] This indicates that even though the law empowers women through property, the practice is poor.

4.1 *Common Property of Spouses – Relevant Case Law*

One case particularly highlights the issue of distribution of common property. The case started in the Southern Nations, Nationalities and Peoples' Government in the First Instance Court of the town Alaba Kolito.[136]

After the dissolution of the marriage between W/ro Kedija and Ato Haji Mohammed Halis, W/ro Zeineba (who claimed to be the second wife of Haji) lodged a claim for the partition of common property. She indicated that she concluded a marriage to Ato Haji (the defendant in lower court) in 1984 EC and showed that the case would also affect her interests. She petitioned the court to intervene in the case. After examining the litigation and evidence, the First Instance Court of the town reasoned that the property was under the possession of the defendant and the claimant could not prove that she either built it or contributed expenses to it. Hence, the court decided she did not have a right over the property. However, the First Instance Court decided that the defendant and her husband, Ato Haji Mohammed Halis, should partition the property equally.

The claimant (W/ro Zeineba) brought her petition to the Alaba Special High Court and then to the Supreme Court of the Region. However, her petition did not gain acceptance. Therefore, she lodged her petition to the Federal Supreme

130 Ibid art 28(1)(j).

131 See ibid arts 28(1)(a) and (c).

132 Committee on the Elimination of Discrimination Against Women (n 86) 5.

133 'Kebele' is a lower administrative organ in Ethiopia.

134 MoWCYA, *Performance of the Sector during GTP I* (Addis Ababa, March 2015) 13.

135 Ibid.

136 *Zeyneba Kelifa v Kedija Siraj* (2004) Federal Supreme Court Cassation File No. 50489 (Meskerem 24) 11 Federal Supreme Court Cassation Bench Decisions, Addis Ababa, 2–5.

Court Cassation Division. The claimant argued that the house was built by the money sent from Saudi Arabia by the defendant's husband, Haji, and that it should thus be partitioned to her.

The Cassation Division examined the case by framing the issue of whether the claimant is right while at the same time proving that the defendant was indeed the wife and living with the husband.

The defendant (W/ro Kedija), before the cassation court argued that the claimant did not conclude a marriage with Ato Haji Mohammed Halis, that the house was built solely by the defendant's and the husband's common effort, and that this was proven in the court. The defendant argued the claimant contributed nothing to the acquisition of the property, and claimed for the decision of the lower court be upheld.

The Cassation Division examined the case. It was proved that the claimant (W/ro Zeineba) and Ato Haji were indeed married since 1984 EC and had been living in Saudi Arabia; at the same time, W/ro Kedija concluded a marriage with Haji in 1987 EC and requested for divorce due to the fact that despite his living in Saudi Arabia for a long time, he (Ato Haji) failed to keep his promise of bringing her to Saudi Arabia. This makes clear that both the claimant and the defendant concluded a marriage to Haji. No accusation was made regarding bigamy, ie marrying a person despite already being married to another. Thus, both women were married to Haji. The Cassation Division noted that the Family Code did not consider the issue how to partition common property in such a case. However, bigamy is a common societal practice.

The claimant (W/ro Zeineba) argued she spent money together with her husband to build the house in question and claimed for half the house to be partitioned equally between her and Haji, and the other remaining half to be partitioned between Haji and the defendant. The defendant on her part argued that she, with the help of her relatives, built the house together with her husband. The house belongs to her and her husband only. After examining the litigation and evidence, the lower court came to the conclusion that the claimant could indeed not prove property over the house, which would have enabled her to be the only rights-holder. Rather, the defendant could prove she built the house after the marriage with Haji in 1987 and that she possessed it.

The Cassation Court reasoned that in principle, couples upon the dissolution of their marriage should equally partition the common property. The parties have right to take back their private property. They have equal common rights over common property. The claimant (W/ro Zeineba) argued that even if the house was considered the property of Ato Haji, her husband, she would have the right to partition equally.

On the one hand, the Family Code article 62(1) indicates that incomes from private properties of the spouses are common. Although the claimant did not directly contribute to the acquisition of the house, the law indicates that she has common rights over the property her husband acquired. This is because the law presumes that a property not explicitly decided to be a private property by a court is considered a common property by default.

On the other hand, it is accepted that the defendant has a 50-percent right over the house, since she has acquired it directly; at the same time, the claimant should also have the right over the other half of the property, as she has a right over the property acquired by her husband. Thus, the claimant has the right to partition equally over half of the property together with her husband because the marriage between the claimant and Ato Haji was not dissolved on the grounds of bigamy.

Here one can see that the court tried to solve the problem in favour of the second wife, (W/ro Kedija) the defendant, who has a right to half of the property of her husband, Ato Haji. This is important in empowering women because if the court had decided otherwise, the second wife would have lost her property. Thus, the case shows that efforts are indeed made by the Cassation Bench to empower women through property by applying family law.

4.1.1 The Wodere Tachbellie Case

Wodere Tachbellie brought her case to the Council of Constitutional Inquiry (CCI). The case[137] started at the Woreda Court of East Shewa in the Oromia Regional State. The case relates to common properties of the spouses (the wife with her deceased husband). Wodere claimed for the partition of her right to common property including farmland, due to the fact the children of her deceased husband forbade her to use the properties. The Woreda Court decided for the partition of the properties, also including the farmland. An appeal was lodged to the High Court and then to the Cassation of Supreme Court of Oromia, where the Cassation Chilot (Bench) rejected her claim.

Wodere's husband, Ato Mamuye Badeg, died 18 years after their separation. The Cassation Chilot decided that the claim is barred by limitation regardless of the fact that she was using the fruits of the land, which was registered as her and her deceased spouse's common property. The Federal Supreme Court Cassation Chilot also confirmed this decision. The petitioner brought the case to

137 *Wodere Tachbelie v Likie Gurmu* (2009) 2 Constitutional Decisions Journal (March 2009) 96–100.

the CCI by arguing that the decision violates her right to the farmland and not to be evicted, as incorporated under article 37 of the FDRE Constitution.

The CCI recommended to the House of Federation (HoF) that the petitioner has lived in the locality where the farmland is situated and that her husband gave her money for her livelihood. The CCI suggested that the decision violates her constitutional rights.

The HoF investigated the case and reasoned that Wodere's right to use the property was not interrupted, seeing as she had been using it. As per article 6(16) of Proclamation No. 133/2005, the use right is barred if the person does not use the property for two years. Thus, the HoF reasoned that the decision of the courts, namely that the right is barred by limitation, is erroneous. The HoF concludes that the decision violates the rights of farmers not to be evicted from their farmland, as recognised under article 40(4) of the FDRE Constitution. In addition, it violates the property rights of women as provided under article 35(7) of the FDRE Constitution.

This case is an excellent example to show how women face problems regarding their common properties in marriage. Women face problems in showing that the property registered as their common property is indeed also their property in times of contestation.

4.1.2 Ato Adugna Gudeta v Beshadu Gudeta, Banchi Gudeta, Mulu Gudeta

In another court case,[138] which started in Sulilita, the now petitioner was defendant; the first petitioner now was claimant; the second and third petitioners were interveners in the lower court. A piece of land which had previously been under the possession of the Mother of the first respondent, was now under the possession of the defendant. The women claimed for their share of the land to be given to them. The defendant on his part argued that he had been using the land, he had even gotten it registered in his name, and they did not have the right to make such a claim. The Court decided that since the petitioners were living in other places and the defendant was using the land, the land should belong to him. Next, the Higher Court also confirmed the decision. Finally, the Cassation of the Regional Supreme Court decided that the women do have the right to their shares.

138 Petitioner Ato Adugna Gudeta- Respondents (1) W/ro Beshadu Gudeta; (2) W/ro Banchi Gudeta; (3) W/ro Mulu Gudeta, Cassation File No. 108106, Megabit 28 2007EC, Federal Supreme Court Cassation File No. 50489, Meskerem 24 , 2003 EC, Federal Supreme Court Cassation Bench Decisions, Vol 18, pp. 158–161.

The case was subsequently brought to the Federal Supreme Court Cassation Bench. The Cassation Bench examined the case and found that it was proven that the land belonged to the family and the dead (mother) by witness and the letter written by the local government. Thus, the women indeed have a right to claim their shares of the land. Being unable to prove that the women have other income to live off, it would not be fair to decide the man should take all the land and exclude their claims. Accordingly, the Court decided the women indeed have the succession right over the land according to Proclamation 130/2005 and Regulation. No. 151/2005.

From this case it can be derived that the Cassation Court decided by considering what is written in the law; this favours the women and obviously empowers them by ensuring their land rights.

4.1.3 Kelebie Tesfa v Ato Ayelign

Petitioner Kelebe Tesfa[139] made a claim to the Denbiya Woreda Court to annul a land mortgage contract she made on 13 November 2002 with the defendant Ayelign Derbew. She claimed this because she was forced to enter into the contract. The Court dismissed the case by arguing that she was not forced to enter into the contract. The Semen Gondar Zone High Court rejected the appeal and the case was brought to the Amhara Supreme Court Cassation Chilot. The Woreda Court decision was confirmed by arguing that no fundamental error of law was committed.

Following this, the Amhara Women and Children's Bureau assisted Kelebie to bring the case to the Constitutional Interpretation Council (CIC) by arguing that the case violates articles 40(3) and (4) of the FDRE Constitution. The HoF, assisted by the CCI, investigated the case. It considered that the contract made on 13 November 2002 was to replace the mortgage contract made on 26 October 1988, whereby the now petitioner gave away part of her land to ensure the credit payment of 270.00 birr could be made. She then failed to pay back her credit; in the meantime, the former party to the contract died. Then, the now defendant Ato Ayelign entered the picture and they concluded a new contract to replace the former contract. Under this new contract, she was forced to give 8 × 9 metres of land to Ato Ayelign.

The HoF reasoned that this contract contradicts the FDRE Constitution articles 40 (3) and (4). Furthermore, it stated that both the federal and the regional land laws, which provide that land is the common property of nations, nationalities and peoples, ensures that land is not a subject to sell and that

139 W/ro Kelebie Tesfa, The House of Federation of FDRE, (2017) 2 *Constitutional Decisions Journal*, 42–49.

farmers are secured from eviction from their land. Finally, the HoF found the decisions of the courts are inapplicable as per article 9(1) of FDRE Constitution.

This case makes clear that the original contract (and also the later one) are both not fair by any measure, as it is unrealistic such land would be given away for failing to pay 27000 birr. The money is too little and is not worth such land as mortgage.

5 Conclusion

The legal empowerment of women is an approach using legal and other means to create rights, capacities and opportunities for women in order to escape poverty. Property rights are essential to alleviate poverty because they empower women to make appropriate decisions. Women with property rights can decide how and when to use or trade property. The legal empowerment of women through property increases gender equality and decreases poverty; in turn, it accelerates progress towards sustainable development. The law creates opportunities for women to claim their rights.

Various international legal instruments incorporate women's property rights. The International Covenant on Civil and Political Rights (ICCPR), the International Covenant on Economic, Social and Cultural Rights (ICESCR) as well as the Convention on the Elimination of All Forms of Discrimination Against Women (CEDAW), to which Ethiopia is a party, all guarantee women's property rights as equal to those of men. The African Charter on Human and Peoples' Rights (ACHPR) also guarantees the equal rights of women in enjoying property rights. Also, the Protocol to the African Charter on Human and Peoples' Rights on the Rights of Women provides for women's property rights. According to the FDRE Constitution, those international legal instruments ratified by Ethiopia are an integral part of the domestic laws of Ethiopia; hence, Ethiopia is obliged to enforce women's right to property as incorporated in those laws.

Ethiopia has guaranteed women's property rights in the Constitution as well as in several other laws, such as the Revised Family Law. Generally, the Ethiopian laws on the topic can be considered as successful in empowering women through property rights as they guarantee these rights. However, the practice of bigamy remains an obstacle to empowering women through property, as in some cases at least two women are obliged to share common property with their husband. This practice should be discouraged and stopped so as to provide equal rights for women.

In practice, women do not own houses or land in an equal manner to men. The number of women who own individual house or land rights is very low. Indeed, only few women own land while great numbers of women do not own land at all. This indicates that women's empowerment through property rights is not implemented as guaranteed by the law.

The cases decided by Ethiopian lower courts generally reveal the non-existence of gender sensitivity in courts. The Cassation Chilot is more gender-sensitive and rather successful in interpreting women's property rights. Thus, the government should provide trainings for lower court judges on the legal empowerment of women through property rights and their implementation, in order to make them more gender-sensitive than they currently are.

The Ministry of Women, Children and Youth Affairs (MoWCYA) is a governmental organisation responsible for the enforcement of women's human rights in general, including ensuring the empowerment of women through property rights. In addition, the fact that the Ethiopian government appointed women in half of the ministerial positions is a promising sign of political commitment. Yet, a similar structure catering to women, children and youth is non-existent at the *kebele* level, where almost everything is performed under the formal bureaucracy of the government. Therefore, it is imperative for the government to also install this structure at the *kebele* level to fully achieve women's empowerment through property rights.

Ensuring the Compatibility of the Ethiopian Law on Legal Capacity with Article 12 of the Convention on the Rights of Persons with Disabilities (CRPD)

Mehreteab G. Ghebregergs

Abstract

The disability rights agenda has seen a transformation from a medical model to a human rights model. Disabled persons are no longer regarded as persons to be treated and cared for by others. Rather, they are the subject of rights with autonomy and dignity equal with other persons. In line with this shift is the dramatic change on legal capacity. The dichotomy of full capacity and full incapacity is rejected and the universality of capacity and support systems is now the norm. By this, it has moved from a substituted decision-making system to a system of supported decision-making. Disability rights in Ethiopia have made some improvement in terms of accessibility and employment. However, when it comes to legal capacity for all, a positive step to fulfil the requirements of the Convention on the Rights of People with Disabilities (CRPD) is yet to be taken. The Ethiopian legal capacity framework still retains the substituted decision-making model and provides for a system of guardianship and tutorship that gives one person full power over another. This chapter posits that Ethiopia should move towards a supported decision-making system, through which everyone is accepted as a legally capable person but at the same time can enjoy the support s/he needs in decision-making. Support systems can be designed at the personal, community or state level, and state and non-state actors have vital roles to play. However, it is the state that must ensure support is available for any person who needs it.

Keywords

disability – impairment – capacity – incapacity – interdiction – CRPD – human rights of the disabled – Ethiopia

1 Introduction

Disability rights have been one of the international human rights that deserve a separate international regime. Only shortly after the full recognition of

 | DOI:10.1163/9789004415966_010

women as equal holders of rights, disabled persons[1] are a recent addition to the equal recognition of personhood.

Before this shift to equal recognition of such group of persons, disabled people were discriminated against and, in some extreme cases, treated as less than full human beings. Due to this discrimination in law and practice, disabled persons have been denied their rights in the personal, social, political and economic spheres. For example, negative societal attitudes that stem from cultural beliefs and taboos have been sources of obstacles to the participation of disabled persons in societal activities.[2]

In Ethiopia, the rights of disabled persons have been excluded from the enjoyment of rights in law and practice. Disabled persons have been regarded as persons to be treated and cared for due their impairments. This has been expressed in laws and practices in all spheres of life. Even when laws allegedly respect, protect and fulfil the rights of the disabled, they follow the so-called 'welfare model', in which the subject is the recipient of care from state and non-state actors.

This is despite the fact that Ethiopia has ratified the Convention on the Rights of People with Disabilities (the CRPD or the Convention).[3] Some changes to laws have been made to put the legal system in line with the requirements of CRPD, most notably the law on the employment rights of the disabled persons.[4]

One important area that touches on disability rights is legal capacity. The right to legal capacity is not only a right by itself, but also a fundamental right in ensuring that other rights are meaningful.[5] Due to mental illness or mental

1 The author prefers to use the term 'disabled persons' or 'persons with impairment' instead of 'persons with disabilities', as the latter term may signify that the disability is created because of the circumstances of the person, instead of the circumstances in society. See Alex L Pearl, 'Art 12 of the United Nations Convention on the Rights of Persons with Disabilities and the Legal Capacity of Disabled People: The Way Forward?' (2013) 1(1) Leeds Journal of Law and Criminology 1, 4.

2 B Ingstad and L Grut, (2007) 'See Me, and Do Not Forget Me: People with Disabilities in Kenya' (SINTEF Health Research, Oslo, 2007) <http://siteresources.worldbank.org/DISABILITY/Resources/Regions/Africa/LCKenya2.pdf> accessed 31 July 2016.

3 Federal Negarit Gazeta, 'Ratification of Convention on the Rights of Persons with Disability Proclamation' Proclamation No. 676/2010.

4 Federal Negarit Gazeta, 'Right to Employment of Persons with Disability Proclamation' Proclamation No. 568/2008. See also Federal Negarit Gazeta, 'Ethiopian Building Proclamation' Proclamation No. 624/2009 for disability concerns in constructing buildings; see also Federal Negarit Gazeta, 'Higher Education Proclamation' Proclamation No. 650/2009, art 40 on accommodations in higher education institutions for physically challenged students.

5 This has been affirmed by the CRPD Committee in its General Comment No. 1. It states: 'without recognition of the person as a person before the law, the ability to assert, exercise and

or intellectual disability, affected persons might be denied legal capacity or their disability may give rise to legal incapacity.

Ethiopia follows the 'substituted decision-making approach', where a judicially interdicted person is taken care of by a guardian when it comes to his/her person and a tutor when it comes to his/her property. The Civil Code[6] uses a general 'incapacity approach' where it is only possible for a disabled person to perform an act with legal consequences in exceptional circumstances.

This substituted decision-making approach has been challenged in all of its forms and is also formally avoided in the approach taken by the CRPD.

In light of this background, the paper at hand will deal with issues of compatibility of the judicial interdiction system in Ethiopia with the CRPD, particularly with its article 12.[7] It will do so by analysing the provisions related to legal capacity in the Civil Code, the CRPD and literature written on legal capacity. In an attempt to make conclusions and to derive ways forward, the chapter is structured into four sections. Following this introduction, the research will depict the paradigm shift adopted in the CRPD. Part of this paradigm shift is the change in the understanding of legal capacity, which will inform the second section. The third section will deal with the Ethiopian law on legal capacity with its focus on the Civil Code's judicial interdiction provisions. This will be followed by the requirements of supported decision-making in the CRPD and the inclusion thereof into the legal capacity framework in Ethiopia. The paper will conclude by suggesting ways forward.

2 The Shift of Approach from the Medical Model to the Human Rights Model

Disability issues have attracted different and opposed views. The 'medical model' represents the prevalent thinking before Ethiopia's adoption of the CRPD in 2006. The medical model sees disability as an impairment that exists in one's body. Consequently, the affected individual is thought to 'require treatment or care to fix the disability, to approximate normal functioning, or

---

enforce those rights, and many other rights provided for in the Convention, is significantly compromised'. See United Nations Committee on the Rights of Persons with Disabilities, 'General Comment No. 1 (2014) – Article 12: Equal Recognition Before the Law' (2014) CRPD/C/GC/1, IV 31.

6 Negarit Gazeta, Gazette Extraordinary, 'Civil Code of the Empire of Ethiopia' Proclamation No. 165/1960.

7 Convention on the Rights of Persons with Disabilities (signed on 13 December 2006, entry into force on 3 May 2008) 2515 UNTS 3 (CRPD), art 12.

perhaps as a last measure, to help the individual adapt and learn to function despite the disability'.[8]

Because of its focus on curing disability, the model does not recognise that a person with disability has the capacity to fulfil and pursue life choices with that disability. For centuries, the model dictated the world to ignore and exclude disabled persons from the mainstream of education, employment and social cohesion. In tradition, and even in some parts of the world today, disabled persons are considered to be a burden in society and in some way are hidden away from the public. Overall, the most common effect of the medical model is that disabled persons 'feel excluded, undervalued, pressured to fit a questionable norm, and/or treated as if they were globally incapacitated'.[9]

In a dramatic shift from a medical model, the so-called 'social model' unequivocally asserts that disabled persons are capable of performing social functions like others. Proponents of the social model make a sharp distinction between impairment and disability. According to Oliver, 'impairment is, in fact, nothing less than a description of the physical body'.[10] Disability, by contrast, is the 'disadvantage or restriction of activity caused by a contemporary social organization which takes no or little account of people who have physical impairments and thus excludes them from participation in the mainstream of social activities'.[11] Hence, it is not the impairment that restricts disabled persons from participation in the mainstream society, but rather the social structure and constructed environment that makes impairment disabling.[12] In other words, there may be impairments but if barriers are eliminated, there are no disabilities.

The social model locates disability in the social environment rather than in the bodily environment.[13] For example, proponents of the model mention

---

8 A Silvers 'A Fatal Attraction to Normalizing' in Parens (ed) *Enhancing human traits* (Georgetown University Press 1998) <https://www.ncbi.nlm.nih.gov/pmc/articles/PMC4596173/> accessed 14 June 2018.

9 S Goering, 'Rethinking Disability: The Social Model of Disability and Chronic Disease' (2015) 8(2) Current Reviews in Musculoskeletal Medicine 134. <https://www.ncbi.nlm.nih.gov/pmc/articles/PMC4596173/> accessed 14 June 2018.

10 M Oliver, *Understanding Disability: from Theory to Practice* (Macmillan 1996).

11 Ibid.

12 Asia Pacific Forum, 'Human Rights and Disability: A Manual for Human Rights Institutions' (2017) 11 <https://www.asiapacificforum.net/media/resource_file/Human_Rights_and_Disability_Manual_Dec_2018.pdf> accessed 14 June 2018.

13 United Nations General Assembly, 'Declaration on the Rights of Disabled Persons' (9 December 1975) A/RES/3447, art 1 states, 'The term "disabled person" means any person unable to ensure by himself or herself, wholly or partly, the necessities of a normal individual and/or social life, as a result of deficiency, either congenital or not, in his or her

stairs vs ramps; presentation of data using only auditory means vs universal design for communication; restrictive definitions of job requirements vs expansive accommodations for different modes of performing work. The social model calls for an inclusive framework that eliminates all forms of barriers to participation in mainstream society, education, business, employment etc. Hence:

> By placing the 'problem' of disability in the (inaccessible) environment, the solution is to be found there as well. The shift calls for legal, attitudinal and environmental changes. Existing barriers preventing persons with disabilities from being in control of their lives on an equal basis with others needs to be removed, and new systems should be developed enabling persons with disabilities to make choices, live in the community and participate in society.[14]

The 'human rights approach' is basically a consolidation of the social model. Yet, instead of emphasising the distinction between disability and impairment, it accepts impairment as a manifestation of diversity, establishing the value of all persons based on their inherent dignity. Similarly, disability is understood as a universal variation rather than as an aberration: measures should attempt to provide disabled persons the possibility to fully develop their capacities. In describing the fact that the social model is not adequate, Doyle states:

> Yet the application of an 'unembodied' social model of disability is not without its difficulties. The characterization of disability (and the resultant discrimination faced by persons with disabilities) as being solely a consequence of 'social oppression' implicitly denies the existence of any impairment, either physical or mental, and means that such impairments are either ignored or deemed to be irrelevant to the question of substantive equality for persons with disabilities. In particular, the application of the social model to issues of sexuality as they occur in persons with

---

physical or mental capabilities' while the fifth paragraph of the preamble of the CRPD (n 7) states, 'recognizing that disability is an evolving concept and that disability results from the interaction between persons with impairments and attitudinal and environmental barriers that hinders their full and effective participation in society on an equal basis with others'.

14 Council of Europe (CoE), Commissioner for Human Rights, 'Who Gets to Decide? Right to Legal Capacity of Persons with Intellectual and Psychosocial Disabilities' (Issue Paper, 2012) 17 <https://rm.coe.int/16806da5c0> accessed 1 October 2018.

disabilities results in an analysis of the sexual rights of such persons, and in particular the issue of consent to sexual activity, which belies the multifaceted realities of engaging in sexual activity.[15]

3 The Shift from Substituted to Supported Decision-Making

In line with the general paradigm shift in locating the problem in society rather than the individual, the CRPD has also changed the way legal in/capacity is viewed.

In the previous paradigm where impairment is something to be treated and cared for, the disabled person would not have agency in exercising rights. As part of this caring and protection, the disabled person is entrusted to the care of another 'able' person for personal and property affairs whenever the deciding body, mostly courts, believe that the impairment affects the decision-making ability of the person.

Such care by an 'able' person can be in the form of a full guardianship, limited guardianship, guardian-dominated guardianship or disability-dominated guardianship. This was also accepted under international law.[16]

As the previous approach equates impairment with incapacity, it does not acknowledge the person behind the impairment. The assumptions of the substituted decision-making approach have thus been challenged on many grounds.

First, all humans are relational beings and make decisions based on different aspects of relations.[17] This has been supported by contemporary research.[18] Cognitive psychologists have identified experience and support from others as major elements of decision-making. Hence, if the relational aspect is stopped, the capacities of all persons will diminish.[19] Second, not all decisions are rational as expressed in the fact that people, for different reasons, commit the

15 Suzanne Doyle (2010) 'The Notion of Consent to Sexual Activity for Persons with Mental Disabilities' (2010) 31 Liverpool Law Review, 114.

16 United Nations General Assembly, 'Declaration on the Rights of Mentally Retarded Persons' (20 December 1971), A/RES/2856, art 5.

17 Pearl (n 1) 18.

18 Gerard Quinn and Anna Arstein-Kerslake, 'Restoring the "Human" in "Human Rights": Personhood and Doctrinal Innovation in the UN Disability Convention' in Conor Gearty and Costas Douzinas (eds), *The Cambridge Companion to Human Rights Law* (Cambridge University Press 2015) 50 <http://dx.doi.org/10.1017/CCO9781139060875.005> accessed 1 October 2018.

19 Ibid 46.

same mistakes twice or even more often.[20] Third, abilities are a matter of extent as the linear assumption of a dichotomy from full capacity and full incapacity is challenged.[21]

In its general comment, the CRPD Committee noted:

> The concept of mental capacity is highly controversial in and of itself. Mental capacity is not, as is commonly presented, an objective, scientific and naturally occurring phenomenon. Mental capacity is contingent on social and political contexts, as are the disciplines, professions and practices which play a dominant role in assessing mental capacity.[22]

Also, the normative and practical aspects of substituted decision-making have been challenged. Excess protection translates into restrictions of rights and a nullification of the person. Quinn describes substitute decision-making as civil death that 'surrenders personhood of one person to another'.[23]

With decision-making capacity over one's own life taken away, it is difficult to take control of life and to participate in society.[24] Moreover, denial of capacity begets more incapacity and the person loses the opportunity to develop knowledge and skills related to decision-making. The lack of use of one's capacity further degrades incapacities.[25]

In principle, with substituted decision-making given for indefinite time, the approach denies a person's 'right not to be infantilized throughout their lives'.[26] Even with minors, substituted decision-making is justified by the obligation of parents to nurture children's capacities and to gradually empower them to make their own decisions.[27] Hence, paternalism is a gradually diminishing phenomenon, as the system of background support succeeds in imparting the skills and insights needed to exercise autonomy.[28]

---

20 Pearl (n 1) 18.

21 Eilionoir Flynn and Anna Arstein-Kerslake, 'The Support Model of Legal Capacity: Fact, Fiction or Fantasy' (2014) 32(1) Berkeley Journal of International Law, 130.

22 CRPD General Comment No. 1 (n 5) para 14.

23 Gerard Quinn, 'Rethinking Personhood: New Directions in Legal Capacity Law and Policy or How to Put the Shift Back into Paradigm Shift' (Keynote Speech delivered at the University of British Columbia, 29 April 2011) 11 <http://citizenship.sites.olt.ubc.ca/files/2014/07/Gerard_Quinn_s_Keynote_-_April_29__2011.pdf> accessed 15 June 2018.

24 CoE Commissioner for Human Rights (n 14) 5.

25 Quinn (n 18) 42.

26 Asia Pacific Forum (n 12) 69.

27 Quinn (n 18) 43.

28 Ibid.

On the practical side, substituted decision-making teaches the person dependence and helplessness.[29] It reinforces the stereotypes on disabled persons, which in turn deny inclusion and participation.[30] Moreover, research shows that the guardianship system is abused and people can even be locked up for the rest of their life without their will.[31]

Substituted decision-making also violates one core principle of the CRPD and other international human rights instruments, namely the principle of non-discrimination. Legal capacity only comes into question when a person has a mental illness or disability.[32] Applying a standard in its application that would distinguish people based on status can undoubtedly be considered discrimination.[33] Discrimination then is a 'violation of the inherent dignity and worth of the human person',[34] which goes contrary to the purpose of the Convention.[35]

This position is reaffirmed by the CRPD Committee: 'The Committee reaffirms that a person's status as a person with a disability or the existence of an impairment (including a physical or sensory impairment) must never be grounds for denying legal capacity or any of the rights provided for in Article 12'.[36]

With the dramatic shift it has brought, the negotiations on article 12 of the Convention were not easy. The provision brought eleven reservations and declarations. States insisted on retaining substituted decision-making for some persons.[37] This position was even shared by some disability organisations.[38] Also, Arab countries for example accepted the concept of capacity in article 12

29 Bruce Winck, 'The Side-Effects of Incompetency Labeling and its Implications for Mental Health Law' (1995) 1(1) Psychology, Public Policy and Law 6. See also Kenya National Commission on Human Rights and the Open Society Initiative for East Africa, 'How to Implement Art 12 of Convention on the Rights of Persons with Disabilities Regarding Legal Capacity in Kenya: A Briefing Paper' (2013) 15 <http://www.knchr.org/Portals/0/GroupRights Reports/Briefing%20Paper%20on%20Legal%20Capacity-Disability%20Rights.pdf> accessed 1 October 2018.

30 Ibid Kenya National Commission on Human Rights. See also American Bar Association, 'Guardianship' (1978) 2(4) Mental Disability Law Reporter 443, 444.

31 Pearl (n 1) 10.

32 Flynn and Arstein-Kerslake (n 21) 127.

33 Ibid 128.

34 CRPD (n 7) preamble, para (h).

35 Ibid art 1 states, 'the purpose of the present convention is to promote, protect and ensure the full and equal enjoyment of all human rights and fundamental freedoms by all persons with disabilities, and to promote respect for their inherent dignity'.

36 CRPD General Comment No. 1 (n 5) para 9.

37 Pearl (n 1) 14.

38 Ibid 17.

with the declaration that it only applies to capacity to hold rights, not to exercise them.[39]

Some other countries make interpretative reservations indicating that they understand article 12 is written to allow substituted decision-making in exceptional cases. The declarations include interpretative ones that accept substituted decision-making as a last resort, with Canada stating that if this interpretation is wrong, it would make a reservation on the provision. Even in practice, article 12(4) was used by states to allow substituted decision-making in exceptional cases.[40] The disability rights literature has advanced the argument that article 12 allows substituted decision-making with pertinent safeguards.[41]

In its first general comment, the CRPD Committee explicitly declared that supported decision-making does not include substituted decision-making.[42] Previously, the Committee had decided that any restriction of the right to vote on the grounds of disability, even though decided based on individual assessment, violates article 29 and article 12 of the Convention.[43] Hence, the protection-autonomy divide has been settled in favour of full autonomy with the design of support when necessary.

The Convention takes the importance of legal capacity beyond the mere question of decision-making and equates legal capacity with personhood.[44] The move is from regarding disabled persons as objects of care to regarding them as full subjects.[45] Moreover, disabled persons must be regarded as autonomous, ie as able to define how they lead their lives.[46] Through this, the new approach detaches the person from his/her impairment in defining the person.[47]

> The support paradigm requires that the system begins with the assumption that all individuals have a decision-making ability and then determines what support each individual needs in augmenting that ability and expressing her preferences. In this system, no labels are needed;

39 Ibid 16. The CRPD Committee has rejected this interpretation in its General Comment No. 1 (n 5) para 12.

40 CRPD General Comment No. 1 (n 5) para 3.

41 Pearl (n 1) 15.

42 General Comment No. 1 (n 5) para 17.

43 *Zsolt Bujdosó and five others v Hungary*, No. 4/2011, CRPD/C/10/D/4/2011, para 10(2)a.

44 Quinn (n 23) 11.

45 Gerard Quinn and Theresia Degener (eds), 'Human Rights and Disability: The Current Use and Future Potential of United Nations Human Rights Instruments in the Context of Disability' (United Nations Press, 2002) <http://lup.lub.lu.se/search/ws/files/11124103/HRDisabilityen.pdf> accessed 19 July 2016. See also Asia Pacific Forum (n 12) 39.

46 Asia Pacific Forum, ibid.

47 Ibid 69.

> instead, the goal is merely to determine what type of support an individual might need.[48]

'Supported decision-making' emanates from the fact that all individuals require some help in making decisions and expands their capacities to do so.[49] Human beings rely on interdependence among each other and require support.[50] This universality of the support system is one defining point in the Convention, which makes it revolutionary.[51]

The proper question compatible with article 12 of the CRPD is not whether a person has the mental capacity to act or not, but rather what support the person needs in order to act.[52] Hence, the impairment is not grounds to deny capacity but more a fact for consideration in designing support schemes.[53]

Supported decision-making assumes that the support given in disability cases and in ordinary cases is different in extent, not in kind. In a final analysis, it would be similar to the support non-disabled persons would require in making wise decisions, for example like getting assistance from an accountant in making financial decisions. The amount of support required depends on the understanding of the person regarding the issue and the seriousness of the consequence of the decision.

In supported decision-making, courts and other organs provide arrangements to enable Persons with Disabilities (PWDs) to decide for themselves. The support can be in terms of communication, information, additional time to complete a task, legal aid, etc. This obligation falls under the 'reasonable accommodation' obligation of state parties.[54]

> The type and intensity of support to be provided will vary significantly from one person to another owing to the diversity of persons with disabilities. This is in accordance with article 3 (d), which sets out "respect for difference and acceptance of persons with disabilities as part of human diversity and humanity" as a general principle of the Convention.[55]

48 Flynn and Arstein-Kerslake (n 21) 130.
49 Commissioner for Human Rights (n 14) 10.
50 Quinn (n 18) 40.
51 Ibid.
52 M Bach and L Kerzner 'A New paradigm for Protecting Autonomy and the Right to Legal Capacity' (prepared for the Law Commission of Ontario, 2010) 58 <https://www.lco-cdo.org/wp-content/uploads/2010/11/disabilities-commissioned-paper-bach-kerzner.pdf> accessed 1 October 2018.
53 Quinn (n 18) 46.
54 CRPD (n 7) art 5(3).
55 CRPD General Comment No. 1 (n 5) para 18.

However, support cannot be forced on a person. 'At all times, including in crisis situations, the individual autonomy and capacity of persons with disabilities to make decisions must be respected'.[56]

Even people in a coma may have wishes and preferences when it comes to support; in such cases, technological aid that can read brain activities[57] is required to fulfil their preferences. Any means available must be used to determine the individual's subjective will, not an objective best interest.[58]

4 Ethiopian Law on Judicial Interdiction

The Constitution of the Federal Democratic Republic of Ethiopia (FDRE) came into force in 1995, nearly 16 years before the adoption of the CRPD. As such, like other international and domestic instruments before the CRPD, the FDRE Constitution protected the rights of disabled persons through its equality clause, albeit without explicitly mentioning the term 'disability'.[59]

Thus, it is possible to argue that the FDRE Constitution established the equality rights of disabled persons in the phrase 'other status', which, when reading it together with the ratified CRPD, also extends to disability. It follows that the fundamental rights and freedoms enshrined in the Constitution are equally applicable to PWDs. Hence, rights of individuals to life, security and liberty (article 14), honour and reputation (article 24), privacy (article 26), thought, opinion and expression (article 29), association (article 31), movement (article 32), family rights (article 34), access to justice (article 37), property ownership (article 40), employment (article 42), to mention some, equally apply to disabled persons.

The Constitution also provides the obligation of the state to provide rehabilitation and assistance to the physically and mentally disabled.[60]

This is supported by Ethiopia's ratification of the CRPD. Due to its ratification, the Convention has obtained the status of a national law.[61] The law

56 Ibid.

57 Pearl (n 1) 19.

58 Flynn and Arstein-Kerslake (n 21) 131.

59 Federal Negarit Gazeta, 'The Constitution of the Federal Democratic Republic of Ethiopia' Proclamation No. 1/1995, art 25.

60 Ibid art 41(5) reads, '*The State shall, within available means, allocate resources* to provide rehabilitation and assistance *to the physically and mentally disabled,* the aged, and to children who are left without parents or guardian' (emphasis added).

61 According to ibid art 9(4) all international agreements adopted and ratified by Ethiopia are an integral part of the law of the land.

proclaiming the ratification of the Convention gives the mandate to the Ministry of Labour and Social Affairs (MoLSA) to ensure the implementation of the Convention in Ethiopia.[62] The Ministry is also responsible to 'enable persons with disabilities benefit from equal opportunities and full participation'.[63] Still, the issue of disability should be mainstreamed in all ministries and agencies.[64]

The Civil Code, which defines capacities, continues to fall short of the requirements under the FDRE Constitution and the Convention. The Code starts by stating that every person is the subject of rights and duties under the Ethiopian law.[65] However, the right to exercise rights by everyone is just a principle.[66] Some groups of persons, including persons with impairments, can be labelled 'incapable'.[67] The Civil Code applies a general incapacity approach in judicial interdiction, ie once a person is judicially interdicted, s/he cannot perform all juridical acts. Only the court can grant exceptions to the general incapacity.[68]

Once a person is judicially interdicted, s/he is a fully incapacitated person who is in principle deprived of performing all juridical acts. The question shifts from 'what is the interdicted not capable of performing?' to 'what is the interdicted capable of doing?'. The interdicted has no power to enter into marriage, legal representation, write a will, act as a guardian for his/her child, administer property, enter into contracts, participate in commerce, etc.[69] Mental disorder can also be a reason for prohibition of participation in an election.[70]

Legal systems follow different approaches when it comes to defining 'incapacity'. The status approach looks to a person and his/her attached impairment

62 FDRE Convention (n 59) art 3.

63 Federal Negarit Gazeta, 'Definition of Powers and Duties of the Executive Organs of the FDRE Proclamation' Proclamation No. 916/2015, art 34(13).

64 Ibid art 10(4) states, '(each Ministry shall) *create, within its powers, conditions whereby persons with disabilities, the elderly, segments of society vulnerable to social and economic problems and HIV AIDS positive citizens benefit from equal opportunities and full participation*' (emphasis added).

65 FDRE Civil Code (n 6) art 1.

66 Ibid art 192. Capacity is also presumed before any courts and other organs and when a person alleges the incapacity of others, he must prove it (see art 196).

67 FDRE Civil Code (n 6) art 193.

68 Ibid art 371.

69 Reference is made to FDRE Civil Code (n 6) arts 368, 369 and 1678; Federal Negarit Gazetta Extra Ordinary Issue, 'The Revised Family Code' Proclamation No. 213/2000, arts 15 and 243; Negarit Gazeta, Gazette Extraordinary, 'Commercial Code of the Empire of Ethiopia' Proclamation No. 166/1960, arts 11, 52, 218 and 928(3); Negarit Gazeta, Gazette Extraordinary, 'The Civil Procedure Code Decree' Decree No. 52/1965, art 3.

70 Federal Negarit Gazeta, 'Amended Electoral Law of Ethiopia Proclamation' Proclamation No. 532/2007, art 33(3)a states '*a person who is proved to be incapable of making decision due to mental disorder* is not eligible to be elector' (emphasis added).

and concludes that due to the impairment, the person is incapable of performing all acts. A better approach is the 'outcome approach', which concludes disability from an act or series of acts of the person. If a person's act demonstrates irrationality or imprudence, the person is deemed incapable.

The closest approach to the new paradigm of disability is the 'functional approach', which accepts the fact that the extent of inability differs from time to time and from one act to another. This approach identifies particular incapacities of a person and seeks to cure it. This approach does not accept the concept of 'incapacitated persons' but rather accepts the fact that persons can be said to lack capacity to act based on demonstrable evidence.[71]

Ethiopia follows the 'status-based approach'. When a person has a defined status that falls under the Civil Code and that status is believed to prohibit him/her from making a decision, the court may order an interdiction. Once the interdiction is ordered, the court appoints a guardian to take care of the person and a tutor to administer his/her property.[72]

Mainly, the reason for interdiction must be related to an impairment, but is not limited to one of the mind. The nature of the disability in question must be insufficient development of the mind, a mental illness, senility, feeble-mindedness, drunkenness and habitual intoxication.[73] The consequence of this impairment is a lack of the ability to understand the importance of one's actions.[74] When causation is established between the impairment and inability, judicial interdiction might be ordered.

However, substituted decision-making is an option for persons with physical infirmity, who can also 'benefit' from the protection given to the mentally impaired.[75] Application for interdiction can be made by the person with a mental disability themselves or by a spouse, by relatives or by the public prosecutor.[76]

The health of the person and his/her best interests determine whether interdiction must be ordered.[77] It can also be ordered based on the best interests of the heirs of the person.[78] The court must be convinced that the measure of

71 Quinn (n 18) 45.
72 FDRE Civil Code (n 6) art 359(1).
73 Ibid art 339.
74 Ibid.
75 Ibid art 340. Particular mention is given to deaf-mute and blind persons.
76 Ibid art 353(1).
77 Ibid art 351(1).
78 Ibid art 351(2).

interdiction is necessary.[79] Therefore, the court must see the person and evaluate his/her situation.[80]

Judicial interdiction is applied to protect the interest of the interdicted.[81] An appeal on the judgment of interdiction is possible not only by the person in question, but by all others who can apply for interdiction.[82]

An interdiction can be withdrawn by a court upon application by the persons who can apply for interdiction, as well as by the guardian and the tutor.[83] There is an important exception related to the interdicted person him/herself. The assumption is that a withdrawal of interdiction is an act with legal consequences; hence, it is an act an incapable person cannot do. A decision of withdrawal will be given once the court is convinced that the causes of disability have ceased and the person can perform juridical acts by him/herself.[84]

The 'incapacity framework' is not compatible with the CRPD, particularly its article 12. As explained above, the Convention does not allow for substituted decision-making. Moreover, even though the Ethiopian guardianship system is ordered by a court, it is indefinite, general, and with almost no safeguards. When an interdiction is ordered by a court, the person cannot perform juridical acts with the exception of those specified by the court; his/her interdiction has no time limit; the interdiction is not subject to review; and there is no mechanism to check that the 'protection' system is not abused.[85]

In addition to the problems of the organs of protection, Ethiopian laws have also failed to design support systems to enable disabled persons to make decisions for themselves on an equal basis with others.[86] Ethiopia must shift its capacity regime from one of full incapacity to one of full capacity, in order to exercise rights with proper support systems. This support system, which

---

79 Ibid art 354(1).

80 Ibid art 354(2) and (3). The Amharic version uses a stronger phrase "የግድ አስፈላጊ', which can mean 'absolutely necessary'.

81 FDRE, 'Implementation of the UN Convention on the Rights of Persons with Disabilities (CRPD) – Initial Report' (Addis Ababa, December 2012) CRPD/C/ETH/1, note 53 <http://disabilitycouncilinternational.org/documents/CRPD_C_ETH_1_6951_E.doc> accessed 1 October 2018. See also FDRE Civil Code (n 6) art 358.

82 FDRE Civil Code (n 6) art 355.

83 Ibid art 377.

84 Ibid art 378.

85 This has been shared by the United Nations Committee on the Rights of People with Disabilities in 'Concluding Observations on the Initial Report of Ethiopia' (15 August - 2 September 2016) CRPD/C/ETH/CO/1, paras 25 and 26 <http://docstore.ohchr.org/SelfServices/FilesHandler.ashx?enc=6QkG1d%2FPPRiCAqhKb7yhsp2gZdYXWBKA18z%2FSv%2F6lkjfDqI9zs5hd5%2BUAXK5vbPAJ7j6jyrAv5vGf3%2BKDAISC4b6HZ89os5fSRy3geaPEuCRLunudv%2BuislMknxs70mG> accessed 14 June 2018.

86 Ibid paras 27 and 28.

cannot be forced on anyone, should be followed with appropriate safeguards from negative consequences. The following section will briefly deal with the safeguards in supported decision-making as enshrined in article 12(4) of the Convention.

5 Safeguards in Support Schemes

The Convention puts the duty on states to design support mechanisms in order to ensure full legal capacity of all persons. These mechanisms may be implemented by state or non-state actors, however the state must ensure that support is available for those who require it. Support schemes are voluntary and cannot be imposed upon a person.[87]

Whatever the support mechanism designed may be, it should aim at ensuring autonomy, dignity and inclusion on an equal basis. However, some support arrangements can end up having the result of substituted decision-making. For this reason, some safeguards are attached to any support scheme.

First, the equal recognition before the law clause shall also apply in the case of support systems. The support systems shall apply without discrimination and shall not in any way, including their wording, indicate that only mental illness or impairment is the reason for incapacity. In its general comment, the CRPD Committee stated that:

> The provision of support to exercise legal capacity should not hinge on mental capacity assessments; new, non-discriminatory indicators of support needs are required in the provision of support to exercise legal capacity.[88]

Second, the support systems shall at all times respect the rights, will and preferences of the person. This is the overriding safeguard. To go in line with the

87 CRPD (n 7) art 12.3 states 'access to support', the word 'access' indicating that the person is given the opportunity but is not obliged to make use of it. Moreover, CRPD General Comment No. 1 (n 5) para 29(g) states, 'The person must have the right to refuse support and terminate or change the support relationship at any time'.

88 CRPD General Comment No. 1 (n 5) para 29(i). Also, note 13 states, 'Article 12 of the Convention on the Rights of Persons with Disabilities, however, makes it clear that "unsoundedness of mind" and other discriminatory labels are not legitimate reasons for the denial of legal capacity (both legal standing and legal agency). Under Article 12 of the Convention, perceived or actual deficits in mental capacity must not be used as justification for denying legal capacity'.

human dignity of a person, every decision must respect the will and preferences of that person in all circumstances. Hence, the subjective interest of the person must be taken into account in every situation, as opposed to the objective best interest.

When there is a difficulty in identifying the will and preferences of the person, the CRPD Committee states:

> Where, after significant efforts have been made, it is not practicable to determine the will and preferences of an individual, the "best interpretation of will and preferences" must replace the "best interests" determinations. This respects the rights, will and preferences of the individual, in accordance with article 12, paragraph 4. The "best interests" principle is not a safeguard which complies with article 12 in relation to adults. The "will and preferences" paradigm must replace the "best interests" paradigm to ensure that persons with disabilities enjoy the right to legal capacity on an equal basis with others.[89]

The respect for the will and preferences of the person under article 12(4) also includes the right to say no to support systems ab initio or at any time during the time of support.

Third, support systems should not overregulate. Article 12(4) states that the safeguards in supported decision-making shall be proportional to the degree to which such measures affect the person's rights and interests. Hence, the proportionality requirement demands case-by-case decisions about support mechanisms. For better decisions regarding the support system, multidisciplinary evaluation is important.[90]

Fourth, article 12(4) demands the application of support measures for the shortest possible time. Support has the purpose of enhancing the decision-making capacity of a person and once this has been ensured, the support system shall be stopped. Even when substituted decision-making was accepted, the full and indefinite application of incapacitation did not meet the human rights standards of the time.[91]

The fifth safeguard emanates from the fact that capacities are not static; rather, they grow as time goes by and as support is successful. Hence, there must be a 'regular review of measures by competent, independent and impartial

89 Ibid para 21.

90 Thomas L Hafemeister and Bruce D Sales, 'Interdisciplinary Evaluation for Guardianship and Conservatorship' (1984) 8(3/4) Law and Human Behaviour, 350.

91 *Shtukaturov v Russia*, Application No. 44009/05, ECHR 2008, paras 91 and 94.

authority or judicial body'. Furthermore, when there is an application by an interdicted person for a change of the support scheme, it shall be entertained as quickly as possible. Moreover, the burden of proof shall not be high on the applicant.

6 Conclusion and Way Forward

Inherent dignity and equal and inalienable rights of all human beings[92] are the cornerstones of the right to equal recognition before the law. No distinction is made among human beings in the enjoyment of human rights and freedoms.[93]

In responding to the question whether there have been efforts to modify the Civil Code provisions on judicial interdiction, the supplementary report from Ethiopia stated that the Attorney General is working on changing the laws in line with the CRPD.[94]

The first move is to abolish the substituted decision-making. It is only by breaking with this discriminatory scheme that the legal system can move towards the system of inclusive and equally applicable, supported decision-making. The ultimate goal is to support persons in making decisions. Disability is socially created, and if it can be improved, the effects of disability will diminish and a person will be capable.

Hence, challenging old assumptions and accepting new ones is a crucial step. Contemporary research has challenged the assumption of the dichotomy between the rational individual who is capable of deciding on all matters on his/her own, and the incapable person with all their decision-making capacities taken away. For instance, research in the United States (US) showed that the gap of decision-making capacity between a minor and an adult is less than what has been assumed by the law.[95] In our case, we must ask if interdiction fulfils the aim of protection. In many cases, the evidence shows otherwise.[96]

92 Universal Declaration of Human Rights (adopted 10 December 1948) UNGA Res 217 A(III) (UDHR), preamble.

93 Ibid art 2.

94 CRPD Concluding Observations (n 85) note 2.

95 Amita Dhanda, 'Minority and Mental Health: Problematics of an Unproblematic Approach' (1994) 36(4) Journal of Indian Law Institute, 504.

96 Quinn (n 18) 41.

If assumptions are changed, the support system can be designed to take the local context into account. It could be a personal ombudsman system like in Sweden, support networks like in Canada, or any other innovative method.

Article 41(5) of the FDRE Constitution reads, 'The State shall, within available means, allocate resources to provide rehabilitation and *assistance to the physically and mentally disabled*...'.[97] It would be possible to combine both state and non-state resources to make resources available for support systems to be designed. The CRPD Committee adds that the state obligation is to see that support is available, regardless of whether the support is actually carried out by public entities, civil society, family and friends or a mixture of public and private parties.[98]

The Convention has erased the line between civil and political rights and economic and social rights, by stating that only through support and fulfilment it is possible to ensure the respect of rights of disabled persons. The CRPD Committee states:

> "Progressive realization" (art. 4, para 2) does not apply to the provisions of article 12. Upon ratifying the Convention, States parties must immediately begin taking steps towards the realization of the rights provided for in article 12. Those steps must be deliberate, well-planned and include consultation with and meaningful participation of people with disabilities and their organizations.[99]

Limited state services, unemployment, dependence on family, poverty, physical barriers, etc. can be raised as reasons for concern. However, all these factors are considered in determining the appropriate support system Ethiopia can implement.

Government must design ways through which persons can access public facilities; it must also design laws that require private service-providers to make their services accessible to all. This eases the problems in decision-making. For example, a person with a physical impairment may find it difficult to undertake banking transactions, which could be made much easier with modern technology. Government should also ensure accessibility of support when reality shows that it is lacking.[100]

---

97 FDRE Constitution (n 56) (emphasis added).
98 Commissioner for Human Rights (n 14) 22.
99 CRPD General Comment No. 1 (n 5) note 30.
100 Ibid para 29(h).

A repeal of the incapacity system should also start in courts. Courts can apply the Convention to reject incapacity provisions in the Civil Code and design new ways of supported decision-making.

One important point that must be taken note of is to listen to the needs and choices of PWDs. The motto 'Nothing about us without us' is a crucial development in disability rights. The Convention has also stated that consultation with disabled persons and their organisations is an obligation of state parties.[101]

The fact that many issues of mental disability are addressed in informal forums, including monasteries and homes, means that amending the law is just a first step in implementing article 12 of the CRPD. In such informal settings, disabled persons are not allowed and supported to make their own decisions but rather, decisions are made for them without their involvement. Hence, the state must also use the already existing community networks such as religious organisations, *Iddirs*,[102] families, etc. and gear their efforts towards supported decision-making.

The family council of the interdicted person, established under the Civil Code, can also be shifted towards a support network in the supported decision-making system.[103]

Deciding on this specific issue, the CRPD Committee noted:

> Interpreting article 12, paragraph 3, in the light of the right to live in the community (art. 19) means that support in the exercise of legal capacity should be provided through a community-based approach. States parties must recognize that communities are assets and partners in the process of learning what types of support are needed in the exercise of legal capacity, including raising awareness about different support options. States parties must recognize the social networks and naturally occurring community support (including friends, family and schools) of persons with disabilities as key to supported decision-making. This is consistent

101 CRPD (n 7) art 4.3.

102 An 'iddir' is 'an association made up by a group of persons united by ties of family and friendship, by living in the same district, by jobs, or by belonging to the same ethnic group, and has an object of providing mutual aid and financial assistance in certain circumstances'. See Mauri (1987) as cited in Thomas Léonard, 'Ethiopian Iddir Mechanisms: Case Study in Pastoral Communities in Kembata and Wolaita' (Report for Interaide Agricultural Projects, April 2013) <http://interaide.org/pratiques/sites/default/files/iddirs_wolayita-kt.pdf> accessed 1 October 2018.

103 FDRE Civil Code (n 6) art 360(2).

> with the Convention's emphasis on the full inclusion and participation of persons with disabilities in the community.[104]

With more focus and work on the issue and by working from the assumption of capacity rather than incapacity, Ethiopia will surely have a more inclusive and non-discriminatory legal framework when it elaborates its next CRPD country report in August 2020.

104 CRPD General Comment No. 1 (n 5) para 45.

The Right to Mental Health: A Critical Look at the State of Human Rights of the Mentally Ill in Ethiopia

Wondwossen Wakene Frew

Abstract

Unlike other forms of illness that disable the ability to act, mental illness disorganises the actions and thoughts of the individual concerned. As mental illness affects the mind, logical, thoughtful and restrained decision-making is something least to expect. The consequences of such practices pervade the world even though there were legal systems that have been protective over the course of history. It would suffice to mention the Roman law of 'satis furore punitor' where 'the mad are punished by their madness and they should not be punished additionally'. Contemporary practice in many countries is dominated by the act of subjecting persons with mental illness to detention and seclusion. However, the international human rights instruments to which Ethiopia is a party provide different kinds of protections to the mentally ill. These instruments furnish both entitlements and freedoms relating to health, including mental health. Contemporary human rights law strives to ensure health facilities and the protections thereof to be accessible, available, acceptable, and qualitative. This chapter explores the legal protections available under the Ethiopian legal system to persons with mental illness. The study finds that the Ethiopian legal system does not provide sufficient safeguards for affected persons. It is recommended that the government should establish specialised hospitals on mental health and adopt a system and structure of balanced and rights-friendly decision-making under the law.

Keywords

legal protection of the mentally ill – international and national standards – rights of the mentally ill persons, mental illness

1 Introduction

Unlike other forms of illness that only disable actions taken, mental illness disorganises both the actions and thoughts of the individual concerned. As a

 | DOI:10.1163/9789004415966_011

result, the individual may have a tendency of dangerous or violent behaviour, which can have the effect of injuring oneself or others. As mental illness affects the mind, logical, thoughtful and restrained decision-making is something least to expect.

There is ample evidence from historical-anthropological research that reveals the practice of considering the mentally ill as possessed by evil spirits. Based on such premises, many societies used to subject persons with mental illness to cruel and inhumane treatments. Moreover, there are still widespread practices of permanently detaining persons with mental illness to ensure that they will not communicate with the outside world.

Today, the consequential effects of such practices pervade – even though there are some legal systems that have been protective over the course of history. It would suffice to mention the Roman law of '*satis furore punitor*' which holds that 'the mad are punished by their madness and they should not be punished additionally.'[1]

Contemporary practice in several countries is dominated by the act of subjecting the mentally ill to detention and seclusion. In other words, there are many instances of punishing the mentally ill for acts and omissions they are not aware are wrong, even though the proper course of action would have been treatment and medication.

With this being one part of the story, there are also other issues associated with the mentally ill including the question of whether the state has any obligation to provide necessary protection for those who suffer from mental illness. As a general legal framework, international human rights instruments provide different kinds of protections to persons with mental illness. These instruments furnish both entitlements and freedoms to health, including mental health. While the freedom component largely deals with control over one's body and health – including freedom from torture, non-consensual medical treatment and experimentation - the entitlements element of the law is concerned with the existence or otherwise a system of protection for health, especially of equality of opportunity for people to enjoy the highest attainable level of health. In general, human rights law strives to ensure that health facilities and protections are accessible, available, acceptable and qualitative.

This chapter analyses the legal protection available to persons with mental illness under the Ethiopian legal system. The existence of unwarranted pre-trial detentions, along with the nature of the facilities serving as detention centres, is mapped in detail. The fragile system of pre-trial detention of the

1 L O Gostin, 'The Ideology of Entitlement' in P Bean (ed), *Mental Illness: Changes and Trends* (Wiley 1983) 49–50.

mentally ill is also explored. To this end, the sufficiency of such system is evaluated using fundamental rights and freedoms of individuals as point of reference. In general, it is investigated whether the mentally ill have sufficient protection under Ethiopian law and if mental health facilities are available, accessible, acceptable, and qualitative.

2 Definition of Mental Illness

Defining 'mental illness' is a precarious endeavour, not only because the concept is illusive and practically loaded, but also because there are competing definitions to it. Not limited to this, understanding the clear boundaries within the varieties of mental illness remains challenging.[2] As deciding on the definition of mental illness engenders political, economic and social ramifications, the decision must be reserved to a professionally and legally authoritative body.

The definition of mental illness is not intended only for academic discourse; rather, it addresses six controversial issues that the law, policy-makers, institutions and professionals need to attend to.[3] Generally, an authoritative definition of the phrase would be required to determine several issues, including: who is entitled to health care and sick leave; who must be sent to psychiatric care rather than to prison in cases of infringement; when should someone be detained against their will; what is the general role of medicine; who is generally entitled to sympathy of the community.[4]

Mental illness should therefore be appraised in the context of mental health, which in turn requires alignment with the concept of 'health'. For that, the World Health Organization (WHO) rightly notes that 'there is no health without mental health.'[5] According to the WHO, health is defined as 'a state of complete physical, mental and social well-being and not merely the absence of disease or infirmity.'[6] Clearly, one notices mental well-being as constituting an essential component of the definition of health. Upon closer consideration,

2 JC Wakefield, 'The Concept of Mental Disorder On the Boundary between Bio-logical Facts and Social Values' (1992) 47(1) American Psychologist 373.

3 B Brülde, 'On How to Define the Concept of Health: A Loose Comparative Approach' (2000) Medicine, Health Care and Philosophy 305. See also RE Kendell , 'The Distinction between Personality Disorder and Mental Illness' (2002) 180(2) British Journal of Psychiatry 110.

4 Brülde (n 3).

5 World Health Organizaton (WHO), *International Classification of Mental and Behavioral Disorders* (WHO 1992).

6 Ibid.

one finds the specific definition of mental health by the WHO as 'a state of well-being in which the individual realizes his or her own abilities, can cope with the normal stresses of life, can work productively and fruitfully, and is able to make a contribution to community.'[7]

However, this definition still remains loaded. It takes side and overlooks the philosophical controversy between the 'pure value approach' and the 'pure scientific approach'. While the pure value approach argues that mental illness is subjective – hinging on measures and standards of society about acceptable social behaviour - the pure scientific approach analogises mental illness with machine faults, whereby mental illness results from underlying structural or functional abnormalities.[8]

On the other hand, an entirely different approach could be adopted as seen in the definition provided by the Australian Mental Health Strategy, which combines both the value and scientific approaches and defines mental illness as 'health problem that significantly affects how a person feels, thinks, behaves, and interacts with other people … (and) is diagnosed according to standardized criteria.'[9]

Today, mental illness or mental disorder is a clinically diagnosable form of illness that significantly interferes with an individual's cognitive, emotional or social abilities. The diagnosis of mental illness is generally made according to the classification system of the Diagnostic and Statistical Manual of Mental Disorders (DSM) or the International Classification of Diseases (ICD).

3 Background: Conceptions and Practice Relating to Mental Illness

There is ample evidence from historical-anthropological research that reveals the practice of considering the mentally ill as possessed by evil spirits.[10] Based on such premises, many societies have subjected persons with mental illness to cruel and inhumane treatment. Moreover, there are practices of permanently detaining the mentally ill to ensure that they will not communicate with the

7 Ibid.

8 A Murphy and RL Woolfolk, 'The Harmful Dysfunction Analysis of Mental Disorder' (2000) 7(4) Philosophy, Psychiatry, and Psychology 241.

9 '*National Mental Health Strategy*' Australian Government, Department of Health, (17 April 2014) <http://www.health.gov.au/internet/main/publishing.nsf/Content/mental-strat> accessed 14 May 2018.

10 A Scull, *The Most Solitary of Afflictions: Madness in Society in Britain 1700–1900* (Yale University Press 1993).

outside world.[11] Now, the consequential effect of such practice pervades the world although there were legal systems that accorded protective measures during the course of history. It would suffice to refer to the already mentioned Roman law of '*satis furore punitor*'.[12]

Worldwide, approximately 450 million people suffer from a mental disorder at any given time.[13] The 12-month prevalence of mental disorder varies from 6 percent in Nigeria to 27 percent in the United States (US).[14] The Organization for Economic Cooperation and Development (OECD) estimates that 5 percent of the working age population has a severe mental health condition, and a further 15 percent are affected by a more common condition.[15]

Mental illness has a notorious history in Ethiopia. Societal misconceptions, policy directions and legislative choices have all undermined mental illness as negligible concern to the extent that the mentally ill lived in severe and abject conditions.[16]

In Ethiopia, mental illness is the leading non-communicable disorder in terms of burden. Indeed, in predominantly rural areas of Ethiopia, mental illness comprises 11 percent of the total burden of diseases, with schizophrenia and depression included in the top-ten most burdensome conditions, outranking HIV/AIDS. These startling statistics show that mental illnesses have been overlooked as major health priority in Ethiopia and other Low and Middle Income Countries (LMICs); consequently, they underscore the need for public health programmes targeting mental illnesses.[17]

In Ethiopia, severe mental illness is often attributed to supernatural causes, for example spirit possession, bewitchment, or evil eye, rather than as a result

11 U Beck (1992), 'From Industrial Society to Risk Society: Questions of Survival, Social Structure and Ecological Enlightenment' 9(1) Theory, Culture and Society 97, 120.

12 Gostin (n1).

13 D O'Donovan, *The Atlas of Health* (EarthScan 2008).

14 RC Kessler and TB Üstün, *WHO World Mental Health Surveys* (Cambridge University Press 2008).

15 Organisation for Economic Co-operation and Development (OECD) (2014), 'Making Mental Health Count' (OECD 2014) <https://www.oecd.org/publications/making-mental-health-count-9789264208445-en.htm> accessed on 13 May 2018. See also OECD, 'Focus on Health' (OECD 2014) <https://www.oecd.org/els/health-systems/Focus-on-Health-Making-Mental-Health-Count.pdf> accessed on 13 May 2018.

16 ML Baldwin and SC Marcus, 'Stigma Discrimination and Employment Outcomes among Persons with Mental Disability' in I Schultz and ES Rogers (eds), *Work Accommodation and Retention in Mental Health* (Springer 2011) 53.

17 Federal Democratic Republic of Ethiopia (FDRE) Ministry of Health, 'National Mental Health Strategy 2012/13–2015/16' (Addis Ababa, 2012) <https://www.mhinnovation.net/sites/default/files/downloads/innovation/reports/ETHIOPIA-NATIONAL-MENTAL-HEALTH-STRATEGY-2012-1.pdf> accessed 13 May 2018.

of biomedical or psycho-social causes. As a consequence, affected individuals and/or their families often seek help from religious and traditional healers rather than from health facilities. Furthermore, other mental illnesses such as major depression are not well-recognised within the community, and are often explained as being caused by to psychosocial problems, e.g. marital problems or poverty. Help-seeking for depression is often limited to the family or local community, and depression usually remains undetected in general health settings; this leads to the inappropriate prescription of ineffective treatments and represents a missed opportunity for suicide prevention.[18]

While the roots of the problem might be societal misconceptions about mental illness, these very assumptions have been reinforced by states' actions in the form of policy and legal absent-mindedness.[19] The true cost of mental disorder, of course, stems mainly from the untold suffering experienced by patients and their families, in addition to measurable economic and societal costs. When it comes to estimating any of this cost of human suffering in any degree of accuracy, the task is difficult, if not impossible; however, the burden carried by those affected is undoubtedly substantial. This underlines the need to provide treatments that are acceptable, effective and evidence-based to all persons with mental disorder and to extend appropriate support to families and caregivers. This is the dimension examined at length in the chapter.

Generally speaking, resources for mental health – such as beds, staffing and finances - are not only scarce, but are also inequitably distributed and inefficiently employed. This is especially true for LMICs, which are home to more than 80 percent of the world's people but enjoy less than 20 percent of mental health resources.

4 Mental Health, Mental Illness and the Law

4.1 *Mental Health Law*

Mental health law essentially revolves around three matters. The first is concerned with bio-ethics. Bio-ethics emphasises at least four minimum conditions that cannot be discounted. First, it examines the degree of autonomy of the mentally ill in the process of consenting to treatment, even though the capacity to consent might be compromised by mental illness.[20] Second,

18 Ibid.

19 Scull (n 10).

20 LO Gostin, 'Contemporary Social Historical Perspectives on Mental Health Reform' (1983) 10(1) Journal of Law and Sociology 47.

the objective of a mental diagnosis is the treatment of the individual concerned and the protection of others – hence, beneficence.[21] Third, any medical treatment including the treatment of mental illness must strive to avoid doing harm - hence, non-malfeasance.[22] Fourth, there must be a system by which those detained under the guise of treatment must be able to voice their side of the story about the detention.[23] Other bio-ethical issues include the inability of psychiatrists to agree on the kind of treatment a mental patient needs, as well as failure to offer a guarantee that the treatment administered will be effective.[24]

The second concern of mental health law is the general protection available to persons with mental illness. This concern has developed into a full-fledged approach to mental health law.[25] Most of the protections relate to freedom from unjustifiable detention, freedom from pointless medical intervention, and abolition of stigma and discrimination.[26] These areas relate to the most important rights of liberty, dignity and equality. As treating mental illness may necessitate the detention of the patient and the involvement of force, one should be very careful not to jeopardise the interests of the patient; after all, treatment is aimed at benefitting the patient.

Today, ample evidence exists that highlights the widespread practice of arbitrary detention of persons with mental illness.[27] In this regard, many parts in the world – including Ethiopia – remain uncertain about the existence or otherwise of the procedure of admission to detention centres altogether. Moreover, the grounds and the purposes of admission are not yet obvious. It is not even determined in an irrefutable fashion in which circumstances a patient shall be discharged from a facility. Last but not least, mechanisms for solving disputes between assessors in the event of disagreement remain unsolved.[28]

Those protections available to society are equally as imperative to those with mental illness.[29] This forms the third concern in mental health law. In the

21 LO Gostin, *A Human Condition: The Mental Health Act From 1959 to 1975: Observation, Analysis and Proposals for Reform* (Mind Health Association 1975).

22 BJ Winick , 'A Therapeutic Jurisprudence Approach to Dealing with Coercion in the Mental Health System' (2008) 15 Psychiatry, Psychology and Law 25.

23 Gostin (n 12).

24 JQ LaFond and ML Durham, *Back to the Asylum: The Future of Mental Health Law and Policy in the United States* (Oxford University Press 1992).

25 B McSherry and P Weller (eds), *Rethinking Rights-Based Mental Health Laws* (Hart Publishing 2010).

26 Ibid.

27 BK Puri, *Mental Health Law: A Practical Guide* (Oxford University Press 2005).

28 Author's field observation from Amanuel Mental Specialized Hospital (Addis Ababa).

29 McSherry and Weller (n 25).

course of human history, there were instances when mental illness served as a harbour to criminals who abused the gaps in the law and the science of psychiatry in order to ends gain freedom – even when they knew their actions were criminal.[30] At times, 'criminal defendants, making some of the more bizarre claims of mental illness, seemed to be getting away with murder!'[31] This had its own ramifications. At one point, society started asking the *raison d'être* for obeying the law if anyone is to escape punishment under the guise of insanity.[32] Finally, such controversies culminated in the adoption of rigorous criminal laws across jurisdictions, after which it became almost impossible – even to those who indeed suffer from mental illness – to escape criminal punishment.

4.2 *Mental Health and Human Rights: The International Perspective*

Mental health and human rights are bi-directional. While restrictions and violations of human rights may lead to mental illness, the mentally ill might be the subject of human rights restrictions and violations.[33] It is the latter that this study dwells on extensively. This way, protections afforded to persons with mental illness at different levels, both normatively and institutionally, are assessed. For that, international human rights conventions and UN declarations addressing mental health issues are considered. To enable measurement, the salient rights of the mentally ill are investigated and the particular Ethiopian set-up is discussed against this backdrop.

4.2.1 The Universal Declaration of Human Rights (UDHR)

The 1948 Universal Declaration of Human Rights (UDHR) comprises 30 articles, with a preamble which recognises that 'the inherent dignity and ... equal and inalienable rights of all members of the human family is the foundation of freedom, justice and peace in the world'. Further, the UDHR provides that 'it is essential, if man is not to be compelled to have recourse, as a last resort, to rebellion against tyranny and oppression, that human rights should be protected by the rule of law.'[34]

The UDHR also states that 'all human beings are born free and equal in dignity and rights. They are endowed with reason and conscience and should act

30 LaFond and Durham (n 24).
31 Ibid 47.
32 Ibid.
33 McSherry and Weller (n 25).
34 Universal Declaration of Human Rights (adopted 10 December 1948) UNGA Res 217 A(III) (UDHR), preamble.

towards one another in a spirit of brotherhood.'[35] This statement seems particularly relevant to persons with mental illness: does the link the UDHR draws between 'human beings' and being 'endowed with reason' mean that the mentally ill, whose mental disorder may occasionally impair their reason, do not necessarily possess the rights outlined? Such a conclusion would appear contrary to the spirit of the UDHR altogether and especially article 2, which emphasises the universal nature of rights.

Articles 3 to 19 of the UDHR articulate basic principles, including 'the right to life, liberty, and security of a person'.[36] Deprivation of liberty in the context of involuntary psychiatric treatment will therefore not be tolerable.

4.2.2 Convention on the Rights Persons with Disabilities (CRPD)

The human rights backdrop against which capacity and mental health legislation have been developed and have operated has been notably re-shaped with the surfacing of the Convention on the Rights of Persons with Disabilities (CRPD), adopted by the UN General Assembly in December 2006.[37] The CRPD came into effect in May 2008; by June 2014, it had 158 signatories and was ratified by 147 'state parties'. Ethiopia is also a party to the CRPD and has ratified it.[38]

The CRPD is visibly located inside the pre-existing UN human rights agenda and reaffirms 'the universality, indivisibility, interdependence and interrelatedness of all human rights and fundamental freedoms and the need for persons with disabilities to be guaranteed full enjoyment without discrimination'.[39] It emphasises 'the importance of mainstreaming disability issues as integral part of relevant strategies of sustainable development',[40] recognises 'that discrimination against any person on the basis of disability is a violation of the human person',[41] and furthermore underscores 'the importance for persons with disabilities of their individual autonomy and independence, including the freedom to make their own choices'.[42] Most importantly, the CRPD

35 Ibid art 1.

36 Ibid art 3.

37 G Szmukler, R Daw and F Callard, 'Mental Health Law and the UN Convention on the Rights of Persons with Disabilities' (2014) 37(1) International Journal of Law and Psychiatry 245.

38 Federal Negarit Gazeta, 'Convention on the Rights of Persons with Disability Ratification Proclamation' Proclamation No. 676/2010.

39 Convention on the Rights of Persons with Disabilities (signed on 13 December 2006, entry into force on 3 May 2008) 2515 UNTS 3 (CRPD), preamble (c).

40 Ibid preamble (g).

41 Ibid preamble (h).

42 Ibid preamble (n).

acknowledges the social context of disability, highlighting 'the fact that the majority of persons with disabilities live in conditions of poverty' and recognising the 'critical need to address the negative impact of poverty on persons with disabilities'.[43]

Starting with the general principles, the CRPD encompasses eight basic principles under its article 3. These are: respect for dignity, autonomy (including freedom to make one's own choices) and independence, non-discrimination, full and effective inclusion and participation in society, respect for difference and acceptance of persons with disabilities as part of humanity and human diversity, equality of opportunity for all, accessibility, equality between women and men, respect for the right of children with disabilities to preserve their identities, and respect for the evolving capacities of children with disabilities. Although it fits in the domain of persons with mental illness, the issues of dignity, autonomy, non-discrimination and inclusion particularly come to the foreground with regard to mental illness.

The CRPD's provisions relating to liberty and disability are among the most imperative and contentious. The CRPD requires that state parties 'shall ensure that persons with disabilities, on an equal basis with others: (a) enjoy the right to liberty and security of person; (b) are not deprived of their liberty unlawfully or arbitrarily, that any deprivation of liberty is in conformity with the law, and that the existence of disability shall in no case justify deprivation of liberty.' This is juxtaposed with the widespread practice of detaining and institutionalising persons with mental illness just for being mentally ill. Persons with mental illness are detained by their relatives and families, by the police and by health institutions. The CRPD pays attention to this and abolishes the practice of arbitrary deprivation of liberty. The unlawfulness and arbitrariness are measured by the subjectivity in the reasons of detention, as well as by the absence of consent on the part of the person who is deprived of liberty. Challenging preventive detention as paternalistic and against the CRPD, the UN High Commissioner for Human Rights noted:

> ...authorizing the institutionalization of persons with disabilities on the grounds of their disability without their free and informed consent must be abolished. This must include the repeal of provisions authorizing institutionalization of persons with disabilities for their care and treatment without their free and informed consent, as well as provisions authorizing the preventive detention of persons with disabilities on grounds such as the likelihood of them posing a danger to themselves or others, in all

43 Ibid preamble (t).

> cases in which such grounds of care, treatment and public security are linked in legislation to an apparent or diagnosed mental illness.[44]

The CRPD also states:

> …if persons with disabilities are deprived of their liberty through any process, they are, on an equal basis with others, entitled to guarantees in accordance with international human rights law and shall be treated in compliance with the objectives and principles of the present Convention, including by provision of reasonable accommodation.[45]

Another area that calls attention is article 25 of the CRPD. In this regard, the CRPD recognises the right to health of persons with disabilities. As the common outlines of the right to health of persons with disabilities under the CRPD are gender-sensitivity and rehabilitation, state parties are specifically obliged to provide non-discriminatory services, targeted services, and to ensure the accessibility of services (requiring health professionals to provide the same quality services to persons with disabilities as provided to others), as well as to avail health insurance in non-discriminatory fashion, and finally to prevent a discriminatory denial of health care.

In the mental health context, medical torture and ill-treatment are prevalent in many jurisdictions. The CRPD appears to have taken note of the dark side of medical history. The medical profession has a downside in relation to persons with disabilities, which had its peak expression in the eugenics movement that called for sterilisation and culminated in their systematic murder during the Nazi era. Psychiatrists were active participants in the selection of patients for purposes of killing and euphemised the killings as 'treatments'.[46]

44 United Nations Office of the High Commissioner for Human Rights (OHCHR), 'Annual Report of the United Nations High Commissioner for Human Rights and Reports of the Office of the High Commissioner and the Secretary General: Thematic Study by Office of the United Nations High Commissioner for Human Rights on Enhancing Awareness and Understanding of the Convention on the Rights of Persons with Disabilities' (26 January 2009) A/HRC/10/48, para 49 <https://www2.ohchr.org/english/bodies/hrcouncil/docs/10session/A.HRC.10.48.pdf> accessed 13 May 2018. For implications of the Convention on legislations that legalise psychiatric detention, see BD Kelly (2014), 'An End to Psychiatric Detention? Implications of the United Nations Convention on the Rights of Persons with Disabilities' (2014) 204(3) British Journal of Psychiatry 174.

45 CRPD (n 39) art 14(2).

46 L Lapon, *Mass Murderers in White Coats: Psychiatric Genocide in Nazi Germany and the United States*(Psychiatric Genocide Research Institute 1986).

Hence, for years, the field of psychiatry remained demonised with regard to persons with mental illness. In particular, the field has been marked by a search for 'great and desperate cures', unchecked by the subjective suffering of the patients involved.[47]

4.2.3 UN Principles for the Protection of Persons with Mental Illness and the Improvement of Mental Health Care (UNMI Principles)

In 1991, the UN introduced the Principles for the Protection of Persons with Mental Illness and the Improvement of Mental Health Care (UNMI Principles), the first substantial declaration of rights to focus specifically on people with mental disorder.[48] The Principles emphasise that all people are entitled to receive the best mental healthcare available and to be treated with humanity and respect. In addition, there shall be no discrimination on the grounds of mental disorder: all persons with mental disorder have the same rights to medical and social care as other people, as well as the rights to live, work and receive treatment in the community, as far as possible.

The twenty-five MI Principles include wide-ranging commitments relating to: standards of care and treatment, including the right to least restrictive environment; the right to medication; consent to treatment; the treatment of minors and criminal offenders; the review of involuntary admissions; access to information; complaints, monitoring, and remedies; and others. The MI Principles take a strong and positive position with regard to community integration, recognising, inter alia, the right of every person with mental illness to be treated and cared for, as far as possible, in the community in which he or she lives. While some of the MI Principles recognise important rights and standards, others are controversial and are considered to offer inadequate protections, notably on the issue of informed consent.

The MI Principles state that mental healthcare shall be based on internationally-accepted ethical standards, and not on political, religious or cultural factors, and that the treatment plan for each patient shall be reviewed regularly with the patient. Mental health skills and knowledge shall not be misused, and medication shall meet the health needs of the patient (ie medication shall not be administered for the convenience of others or as a punishment). For voluntary patients, no treatment shall be administered without

---

47 ES Valenstein, *Great and Desperate Cures: The Rise and Decline of Psychosurgery and Other Radical Treatments for Mental Illness* (Basic Books 1986) 23–44.

48 OHCHR, UN Principles for the Protection of Persons with Mental Illness and the Improvement of Mental Health Care' (17 December 1991) A/RES/46/119 <https://www.un.org/documents/ga/res/46/a46r119.htm> accessed 13 May 2018.

their informed consent, subject to some exceptions (eg patients with personal representatives empowered by law to provide consent). For involuntary patients, every effort shall be made to inform the patient about treatment. Physical restraint or involuntary seclusion shall be used only in accordance with official guidelines. The Principles also require that records are kept of all treatments and that mental health facilities are structured and resourced appropriately. Finally, an impartial review body shall, in consultation with mental health practitioners, review the cases of involuntary patients.[49]

5 Mental Health and Mental Illness in Ethiopia: Normative and Institutional Overview

5.1 *The Prevalence of Mental Illness in Ethiopia*

According to the Central Statistical Agency of Ethiopia (CSA), of the total population in Ethiopia, there are 58,726 persons with mental illness.[50] In terms of gender, 35,198 are male and 23,528 female.[51] The age distribution also shows significant variation. Mental illness is prevalent between the ages of 15 and 34, accounting for a total of 27,377 persons; this clearly shows that the problem attacks the roots of the productive population. Regionally, the Oromia National Regional State (ONRS) tops the list with 21,039 people having mental illness, followed by the Amhara National Regional State (ANRS) with 13,277 people. The South Nations, Nationalities and Peoples Regional State (SNNRS) stands third with 11,772 persons.[52]

5.2 *The Normative Landscape at the National Level*

The Ethiopian mental health law regime requires investigation based on the three big concerns of mental health law raised earlier, namely bio-ethics, the general protection of the mentally ill, and the general protection of society – keeping in mind and emphasising on a human rights regime that corresponds to mental health.

49 BD Kelly, *Dignity, Mental Health and Human Rights Coercion and the Law* (Ashgate Publishing 2015).

50 Central Statistical Authority, '2007 Population and Housing Census of Ethiopia' (2007) <http://unstats.un.org/unsd/censuskb20/Attachment489.aspx?AttachmentType=1> accessed 13 May 2018.

51 Ibid.

52 Kelly (n 49).

Ethiopia does not have a systematised mental health law.[53] One must bring together the pieces to determine the mental health law system. The history of psychiatry, however, supports the unique importance of dedicated mental health legislation, rather than a general law or a non-binding regulation for protecting the rights of the mentally ill. While there were substantial advances in the articulation of human rights standards for the general population throughout the early twentieth century, the plight of the mentally ill remained bleak until much later in most jurisdictions, suggesting the need for specific and dedicated measures to protect their rights.[54]

5.2.1 The FDRE Constitution

The Constitution of the Federal Democratic Republic of Ethiopia (FDRE) provides various protections to persons with mental illness, although not very explicitly. Most of the protections the FDRE Constitution furnishes and that are subsequently discussed are not intended to address the vulnerabilities of the mentally ill only. They are protections and rights one enjoys simply because one is a human being. However, because mental illness disposes one towards possible violations presupposed by the FDRE Constitution, one could say the rights and protections serve persons with mental illness most.

The first protection for the mentally ill relates to human dignity. Article 24 of the FDRE Constitution stipulates that 'everyone shall have the right to his human dignity and good reputation.' Mental illness is degrading by itself. History is also full of degrading episodes to persons with mental illness. The mentally ill have been treated in a sub-standard and sub-human manner. They were not recognised as a person and have been subjects of violations by fellow human beings. The FDRE Constitution addresses this problem and clearly recognises human dignity as one aspect of human rights.

Another important guarantee the FDRE Constitution puts forward relates to equality. As per article 25, equality is guaranteed for everyone and discrimination on whatever grounds is out-rightly prohibited. There is ample likelihood for the mentally ill to be subject to discrimination because of their status and disability; the law therefore affords them protection in this regard.

---

53 The WHO explicitly states that countries may address some or all of these mental health issues in general legislation (eg equality legislation), other forms of (not legally binding) regulation, or mental health policy, rather than specific mental health legislation. See WHO, *WHO Resource Book on Mental Health, Human Rights and Legislation*, (WHO 2005) <https://ec.europa.eu/health/sites/health/files/mental_health/docs/who_resource_book_en.pdf> accessed 14 May 2018.

54 Ibid.

In addition to these umbrella protections, specific guarantees are also included in the FDRE Constitution. Under article 18, for instance cruel, inhuman and degrading treatment is outlawed. Under article 17, the FDRE Constitution guarantees the liberty of individuals and outlaws arbitrary deprivation of liberty. Building on this, article 19 stipulates the rights of arrested persons including that of habeas corpus. Even though the applicability of this provision to individuals detained because of their mental illness is doubtful, article 19 guarantees arrested persons' rights to court appearance and court review, among others. As a passing remark, it is also wise to take into account the remand and custody of an arrested person. While article 19(4) authorises a court to remand an arrested person into custody in the interest of justice, it is not clear what happens when an arrested person raises insanity as an issue before the charges are framed and read to them.

The FDRE Constitution also tries to regulate the treatment of persons while in custody. Under article 21, it stipulates a humane and dignified treatment while one is in custody. In addition, those in custody have a right to communication 'with and be visited by spouse(s), close relatives and friends, medical attendants, religious and legal counselors.'

It is only under article 41 that the FDRE Constitution makes direct reference to the mentally ill. It aspires for the rehabilitation of the physically and mentally handicapped. Apart from this, the modalities of rehabilitation and the conditions and framework thereof are bypassed – this simply indicating a broader constitutional approach on the subject.

Nevertheless, the constitutional stipulations notwithstanding, it is evident that the progressive realisation and conditional application of the right based on availability of resources will likely have an effect on the successful implementation of this constitutional aspiration in many instances.

5.2.2 The Civil Code of Ethiopia (1960)

A neglected and yet important law that deals with civil status of persons with mental illness is the Civil Code of Ethiopia. To begin with, it should be noted that the Civil Code extensively discusses 'insane' and 'infirm' persons. Under article 339, the Civil Code defines the 'insane' as 'one who, as a consequence of his being insufficiently developed or as consequence of mental disease or of his senility, is not capable to understand the importance of his actions.' As such, insanity is a status arising from biology, epidemiology or age with the effect of disabling the person to appreciate their conducts.

More intriguing is article 341 of the Civil Code. Rather than defining 'notorious insanity' in other terms, it translates the effects of insanity as composing elements of the same. It reads 'a person shall be deemed by law to be notoriously insane where by reason of his mental condition, he is an inmate of a hospital…' Hence, this entails that the mere fact that someone is institutionalised brings about the designation as being insane. Even more problematic is what has been provided under article 342, which deals with the presumed insanity of persons in rural communes, where the family can decide on the condition of the person.

5.2.3 The Criminal Code and the Criminal Procedure Code

Mental illness has served as one of the defences against criminal liability for centuries.[55] Crime stands by its elements. Of the three elements of crime, one has direct bearing on the mental state of a person. The mental element of crime presupposes the sanity of the accused person. The logic is that there is no criminal liability in the absence of the mental element (ie either intention or negligence, depending on the case). However, in which particular cases could one indeed say that the mental element is absent?

There are three ways of approaching the subject of irresponsibility in criminal law. One of these approaches holds that irresponsibility arises from biological reasons causing a physical defect and hence a consequential irresponsibility for action.[56] On the other hand, in light of the psychological method, regardless of the causes, irresponsibility is presumed if a person is incapable of understanding the nature of their acts.[57] Finally, there exists an approach that combines the two and can be termed the 'bio-psychological approach'. This approach understands irresponsibility as a combination of biological causes of incapability, rendering someone incapable of understanding the consequences of his actions, as is the case under article 48 of the FDRE Criminal Code.[58]

The Criminal Code regulates what happens to people with mental illness. Mental illness is not simply about one's exoneration from criminal liability. It is also about what happens to the accused once they are found irresponsible for their acts. After ascertaining that the accused is fully or partially irresponsible, the Criminal Code prescribes for the court to resort to two courses of action. The first, under article 130, states that if the court deems that the accused, because of their conditions, is a threat to public safety and order or persons

55 This contrasts the idea of some scholars who argue that criminality is by itself a mental health problem. See R Brancle, 'Diagnostic Techniques in Aid of Sentencing' (1958) 23(1) Law and Contemporary Problems 442.

56 RF Schopp, *Automatism, Insanity, and the Psychology of Criminal Responsibility: A Philosophical Inquiry*, (Cambridge University Press 1991).

57 Ibid.

58 P Graven, *An Introduction to Ethiopian Penal Code* (Addis Ababa Haile Selassie I University Press 1965).

living with them, it may order the confinement of the accused in a suitable institution. On the other hand, under article 131, the Criminal Code holds that where a criminal is suffering from a mental disease or deficiency, deafness and dumbness, epilepsy, chronic alcoholism, narcotic and psychotropic substances, intoxication due to the abuse of narcotics, or from any other pathological deficiency and requires to be treated or placed in a hospital or asylum, the court shall order their treatment in a suitable institution or department of an institution.

Here, the Criminal Code focuses on the causes of irresponsibility, while under article 130 it focuses on the consequences of the mental illness. This is the reason why the Criminal Code recommends for treatment in the latter case and for confinement in the former. However, the Criminal Code holds confinement dearly, as it is only under exceptional circumstances that the mentally ill are allowed to follow up treatment as an out-patient.[59] In all other cases, the mentally ill must remain confined in hospital or an asylum as an in-patient. Not only this, an order of confinement or treatment is made for an indefinite duration,[60] implying that the mentally ill might spend the rest of their life in confinement. Experts involved in assisting the court with its decisions remain unaccountable for possible ill-advice. The Criminal Code has not provided for any mechanism of review of decisions to confine or treat a mentally ill person. Whether the consent of the accused is required remains undecided.

5.2.4 The National Mental Health Strategy (2012/13–2015/16)

Ethiopia's first organised normative intervention to the problem of mental illness is articulated by the National Mental Health Strategy (NMHS). The Strategy stands on three pillars. In its first part, the NMHS provides a general introduction about the document and discusses the burden mental illness poses to the community. The need to have a mental health strategy is justified in this part.[61] In the second part, the NMHS maps the prevalence and impact of mental illness in Ethiopia – asserting that mental illness has become a major public health problem. In addition, the cultural outlook of the community towards mental health is presented. Finally, the NMHS reviews major developments in the area of mental health in terms of facilities and human resources, plainly establishing that mental health is not to be neglected and under-served.[62]

59 Federal Negarit Gazette Extraordinary Issue, 'Criminal Code of Ethiopia' Proclamation No. 414/2004, art 131 (2).

60 Ibid art 132.

61 FDRE Ministry of Health (n 17).

62 Ibid.

When one looks at the foundations and directions of the NMHS, integrating mental health services into primary health care is considered as one target. Patient-centred care, community, family and patient participation, quality services, de-institutionalisation, decentralisation and integration, accessibility and equity, efficiency, continuity and sustainability, human rights and the mentally ill, recovery and rehabilitation, and inter-sectoral collaboration all make up the core of the outlined principles and values.[63] Moreover, the NMHS lays down objectives, areas of priorities, institutional models, mental health financing, human rights in relation to the mentally ill, mental health research, and focuses especially on vulnerable populations.

While adopting a national strategy is commendable, the instrument falls short in certain areas. The NMHS is not oriented in a spirit of human rights and does not pursue the human rights approach. The human rights of persons with mental illness are merely mentioned as a passing remark. Moreover, legislative intervention comes last in the list of its priorities. Apart from mentioning human rights as one area of concern, the NMHS does not indicate the mechanisms of implementation.

5.3 *The Institutional Set-Up*

Combined with the normative framework, an effective and robust institutional set-up promotes the protection of persons with mental illness. The policies and laws, as well as values and principles, are likely to be futile paper-tigers in the absence of well-functioning and structured institutions.

When looking into the institutional set-up, we must take into account the availability of institutions dedicated to coordinating the efforts of protecting and promoting the well-being of the mentally ill, as well as the availability and accessibility of institutions, professionals and resources to serve the mentally ill.

Mental health efforts are coordinated by the Federal Ministry of Health. There is a section within the Ministry dedicated to overseeing and coordinating efforts related to mental health. However, it remains vague whether or not regions are also looking after the mentally ill in their respective jurisdictions.

So far, there is only one dedicated psychiatric hospital in Ethiopia – Amanuel Specialized Mental Hospital. This Hospital is located in Addis Ababa and is destined to serve patients from all over the country. It has 268 beds.[64] In a country where one out of every five persons might be affected by mental

63 Ibid.
64 Ibid.

disorder,[65] the number of hospitals and beds made available is a harsh mockery. Furthermore, a mental health hospital that was supposed to be built and completed by the end of 2013 has not yet been realised.

At the same time, the number of psychiatrists available in Ethiopia evidences another under-served area. There are only 40 practicing psychiatrists in the country, ten of whom are in the regions and 30 of whom are in Addis Ababa. This means that there is only one psychiatrist per six million people.[66] Prevalence for mental health disorders is estimated to be at 15 percent for adults and at 11 percent for children. Most patients admitted to Amanuel Specialized Mental Hospital come from Addis Ababa, with a rate about 20-fold higher than for the rest of the country.[67] This is compatible with findings that demonstrate that the proximity to health facilities is an important factor in determining whether patients seek support in an emergency and during chronic illnesses.

6 Pre-trial Detention of the Mentally Ill: The Ethiopian Practice

Having so far investigated the normative and institutional frameworks of mental health and its governance, the following sections will consider the specific challenges faced by persons with mental illness in Ethiopia – making use of the 'freedom approach' and' 'entitlement approach' of the right to health as adopted under UN General Comment No. 14.[68]

6.1 *The Right to Health: The Freedom Dimension Focusing on the Admission of the Mentally Ill to an Institution*

One area in which the vulnerability of persons with mental illness surfaces relates to the institutionalisation of a mentally ill person. In this regard, the overall procedure of admitting the mentally ill to institution and whether such a system conforms to accepted legal standards is worthy of consideration.

Admitting a mentally ill person to an institution is not an easy endeavour. While voluntary admission somehow reduces legal friction, one encounters

65 K Yimam, Y Kebede and T Azale, 'Prevalence of Common Mental Disorders and Associated Factors among Adults in Kombolcha Town, Northeast Ethiopia' (2014) 7(1) Journal of Depression and Anxiety.

66 WHO (n 53).

67 A Fekadu et al., 'A Descriptive Analysis of Admissions to Amanuel Psychiatric Hospital in Ethiopia' (2007) 21(2) Ethiopian Journal of Health Development 173.

68 United Nations Committee on Economic, Social and Cultural Rights (CESCR), 'General Comment No. 14: The Right to the Highest Attainable Standard of Health (Art. 12 of the Covenant)' (11 August 2000) E/C.12/2000/4 <https://undocs.org/E/C.12/2000/4> accessed 13 May 2018.

that involuntary admission raises many more questions than it promises to answer. Some, however, contend that compulsory admission and treatment on health grounds are acceptable, provided the intervention was limited and aimed at restoring the person to a position of health and social stability.

Even in such levels, it is argued that institutionalising a person without providing treatment and for the mere fact of detaining them is simply unacceptable.[69] The WHO recommends for procedural safeguards to be put in place in order to protect against the overuse and abuse of involuntary admission and treatment.[70] In addition, countries that subscribe to involuntary admission put forward various safeguards against potential abuse. For instance, in England and Wales, it is only when the mentally ill do not have the capacity to express their consent that involuntary admission will be made under strict scrutiny.[71] Moreover, because the international human rights regime reserves certain areas of compromise for arbitrary arrest and detention, many countries continue to detain people on the grounds of mental illness.

In principle, no one shall be deprived of liberty, and arbitrary arrest and detention are both unacceptable.[72] According to UN General Comment No. 8, article 9(1) 'is applicable to all deprivations of liberty, whether in criminal cases or in other cases such as mental illness, vagrancy, drug addiction, educational purposes, immigration control, etc.'[73]

When the International Covenant on Civil and Political Rights (ICCPR) reproves arbitrary detention, it does so in two ways. One, the deprivation of liberty must be on the basis of the law, and two, even arbitrary legal mandates of deprivation may not be valid.[74] Hence, detention must not only be lawful but also reasonable and necessary. This holds firmly for persons with mental illness. Mental illness cannot be grounds for arbitrary and illegal detention. All

69 LO Gostin, 'Contemporary Social Historical Perspectives on Mental Health Reform' (1983) 10(1) Journal of Law and Society 47.

70 WHO (n 53).

71 G Richardson, 'Autonomy and Risk: A Failure of Nerve in England and Wales?' (2007) 30(71) International Journal of Law and Psychiatry 71.

72 International Covenant on Civil and Political Rights (adopted 16 December 1966, entry into force 23 March 1976) 999 UNTS 171 (ICCPR), art 9.

73 UN Secretariat, 'United Nations Compilation of General Comments and General Recommendations Adopted by Human Rights Treaty Bodies' (27 May 2008) HRI/GEN/1/Rev.9, 179 <https://www.legal-tools.org/doc/58d740/pdf/> accessed 17 May 2018.

74 See *Gridin v Russian Federation* (18 July 2000) U.N. Doc. CCPR/C/69/D/770/1997, para 8.1 <http://hrlibrary.umn.edu/undocs/session69/view770.htm> accessed 13 May 2018. See also *A.W. Mukong v Cameroon* (26 February 1991) U.N. Doc. CCPR/C/51/D/458/1991 <http://hrlibrary.umn.edu/undocs/html/vws458.htm> accessed 13 May 2018. The communications assert that absence of grounds of detention in the legal system and inappropriate, unjust and unpredictable grounds of deprivation form violations against art 19 of the ICCPR.

the criteria required for detention under article 9 of the ICCPR should be observed for the mentally ill as well.

The regional human rights systems have been favourable to such strict interpretation of the exceptions to liberty. For instance, the European Court of Human Rights (ECtHR) follows a stricter modicum. In one of its decisions concerning the detention of a mentally ill person, the Court held that '…except in emergency cases, the individual concerned must be reliably shown to be of unsound mind, that is to say, a true mental disorder must be established before a competent authority on the basis of objective medical expertise; the mental disorder must be of a kind or degree warranting compulsory confinement; and the validity of continued confinement depends upon the persistence of such a disorder…'[75]

A person may not be involuntarily admitted to an institution simply because they do not have the capacity to consent. The mere fact that a mental health problem is detected by a psychiatrist will not suffice to institutionalise a person with mental illness. The diagnosis leading to detention must be carried out as per internationally-accepted standards.

In the United Kingdom (UK), where there are clearly laid down grounds and procedures of admission to a mental health institution, a patient is admitted if they are suffering from mental disorder of a nature or degree that warrants detention in a hospital for assessment (or for assessment followed by a medical treatment) for at least a limited period; *and* the patient ought to be so detained in the interests of their own health or safety; *or* the patient ought to be so detained with a view to the protection of other people.[76] Elaborating on the procedures for admission, the Mental Health Act (MHA) holds that the application for admission is preferably made by an approved social worker or by the nearest relative of the patient; following the application, two registered medical practitioners must examine the patient within five days of each other and give their signed, written recommendations on the appropriate form.[77] In addition, the MHA fixes the duration of stay to be 28 days – provided that a situation that warrants the person's detention occurs in the first place.

In Ethiopia, one finds gaps in the laws with regard to admission. There is no single authoritative legal regime that regulates the detention of a mentally ill person on the grounds of mental illness. The detentions are mostly

75 *Case of X. v the United Kingdom* (5 November 1981) Application No. 7215/75 ECtHR, para 40 <https://www.npm.rs/attachments/CASE%20OF%20X[1].%20v.%20THE%20UNITED%20KINGDOM.pdf> accessed 14 May 2018.

76 Mental Health Act 1983, Section 2.

77 Ibid.

administrative and some are even orchestrated by families and relatives of the person concerned. Psychiatric institutions do not have clearly-articulated admission and discharge guidelines. Some admit patients because the police brought them there, while others admit patients because families asked for it.[78] Considering the absence of admission criteria, psychiatrists do not check and evaluate why family members or the police brought a person to the hospital. For example, there is no preventive mechanism for healthy persons who may be admitted to the hospital pending a diagnosis on a personal vendetta or due to exclusionary measures of family members. This is also reinforced by the law, as the Civil Code mandates the community and family members to authoritatively label someone as mentally ill – this consequentially can result in one's alienation from family and from property rights.

A court order constitutes another grounds for admission. Courts might remand a patient to a mental health institution pending diagnosis and recommendation of psychiatrists in a criminal investigation. One of the possible objections to a charge that the accused may raise during a criminal trial is that they are not responsible for the act committed.[79] When this is the case, the court may order for the relevant evidence be presented without delay.[80] One of the objections that the accused might raise with regard to responsibility relates to insanity. Whilst the accused may claim they are mentally ill and could not appraise their act when committed, the court must order that the mental state of the accused be evaluated and expert evidence presented without delay. This is the point at which the accused will be referred to a mental hospital for a diagnosis to be made and for evidence to be presented to the court.

The challenge Ethiopian courts face today relates to the responsiveness of mental hospitals. When courts order the only specialised mental hospital in Addis Ababa to make an assessment of the mental condition of an accused person, the hospital must make the decision to either admit or not to admit the person on the basis of the beds it has available. As mental health diagnosis involves much observation and little laboratory work, the accused person must be admitted to the hospital and must stay there so that psychiatrists can conduct diagnosis by close observation.

However, the specialised medico-legal ward of the Amanuel Specialized Mental Hospital hosts only eleven beds, one of which is devoted to a female

78 Yitbarek Hizekeal, 'Exploring Challenges and Opportunities of Geferssa Mental Health Rehabilitation Center in its Rehabilitation Program in Oromia Regional State' (Unpublished Thesis, Addis Ababa University, 2015).

79 Negarit Gazeta, 'Criminal Procedure Code of the Empire of Ethiopia' Proclamation No. 185/1961, art 130(2)(g).

80 Ibid art 131(3).

and the remaining ten devoted to male patients. Given such dearth and the number of patients referred to the hospital and in the absence of clear, fair and accountable admission procedures, mentally ill persons sent to be diagnosed at the hospital will fail to receive proper service. Because accused persons all over the country are referred to the hospital for forensic psychiatric purposes, the hospital obviously cannot accommodate all referred persons with the eleven beds devoted to this purpose. The hospital admits persons only when there are vacant beds. Hence, in most cases, the date of admission is not likely to be any sooner than after a year of waiting time.[81] In a criminal trial, therefore, there is a chance for an accused person to be remanded to prison pending mental diagnosis. In one particular case, the East Gojam Zone High Court could not do anything but say that 'though it has been repeatedly ordered that the accused be diagnosed and results be sent to the court, this was not possible; the accused had been deprived of his liberty and his human rights [had been] violated.'[82] In this particular instance, the accused to-be-diagnosed person was detained for a little less than two years pending his diagnosis simply because the hospital was not admit able to him earlier. This means that not only was someone detained in prison without any consideration of the mental condition in which he is, but detaining someone in prison together with persons of better health also constitutes a violation.[83]

This practice goes against the liberty of the accused; his constitutional right to be presumed innocent is also at stake. The delay in diagnosis negatively affects the trial because the diagnosis is unlikely to be carried out objectively or by taking into account what the mental state of the accused person looked like when the act was actually committed. The accuracy of evidence will be in jeopardy as time passes without the basic diagnosis being made.

Apart from the flaws in the admission process and consequentially also the flaws in detention practices, there is also a huge gap when it comes to discharging a patient from hospital. Many jurisdictions regulate the span of time one

81 Aberash Dhugassa, 'The Role of Mental Health Court in the Protection of Human Rights of Persons with Mental Disability in Ethiopia' (LL.M. Thesis, Unpublished Addis Ababa University, 2015).

82 Criminal File No. 1967, East Gojam Zone High Court (2002).

83 The European Court of Human Rights has once held that detaining someone with mental illness in a regular prison amounts to inhuman and degrading treatment, finding in particular that the nature of the applicant's psychological condition made him more vulnerable than the average detainee and that his detention might have exacerbated his feelings of distress, anguish and fear. See *Case of Dybeku. v Albania* (18 December 2007) Application No. 41153/06 ECtHR <http://hudoc.echr.coe.int/app/conversion/pdf/?library=ECHR&id=001-84028&filename=001-84028.pdf&TID=thkbhnilzk> accessed 13 May 2018.

stays in a mental hospital. They also spell out who has authority to decide on the discharge from an institution or on the prolongation of stay in a mental institution. Clarifying the grounds of confinement and discharge, Gostin builds on three necessary grounds.[84] The first relates to the existence of mental illness as objectively established by a psychiatrist.[85] Secondly, the mental condition of the person must warrant compulsory confinement;[86] as confinement must be for the purpose of protecting the public and treating the mentally ill, persons with untreatable mental disorders should not be confined.[87] Finally, if the person with mental illness attains better health, they must be automatically discharged.[88]

In Ethiopia, there is no mechanism that allows for a patient or their relatives to ask for the discharge of a patient from hospital. At the same time, there is also no review mechanism under which refusal to discharge or delay in discharge might be appraised. Except for the verdict of the psychiatrist who might choose to lengthen the stay of the patient in hospital, the frequency of prolongation decisions and the minimum and maximum thresholds of stay have not been formally set.

In this particular chapter, two fundamental issues were investigated in evaluating the amount of time a patient spends in detention. First, the period a detainee should spend in a detention centre is clearly set out under Ethiopian laws. Second, in the absence of such standards, detainees are forced to spend more than one and a half years on average in detention and prison centres without being sentenced to serve prison terms. Even when the patient is admitted to hospital, it will spend an average of 71 days there.[89] What happens when a person referred to a hospital by a court is diagnosed with a mental illness remains a grey area in the Ethiopian legal arena.

6.2 *The Right to Health: The Entitlements Dimension Focusing on Availability, Accessibility, and Acceptability*

The right to health of persons with mental illness poses a three-pronged concern. First, there is the concern that mental health policy and legislation affect human rights. This is to imply that governments may positively promote the

84 LO Gostin, 'Human Rights, Judicial Review and the Mentally Disordered Offender' (1982) 1 Criminal Law Review 779, 782.

85 Ibid.

86 Ibid.

87 Ibid.

88 Ibid.

89 Interview with Dr. Melkamu Agonafir, former Medical Director, Amanuel Specialized Mental Hospital, Addis Ababa (2017).

right to mental health by introducing practices that promote autonomy, bodily integrity, privacy, property and liberty of persons with mental illness. This could be done positively by providing access to mental health care. Negatively, governments might engage in discriminatory and inhumane practices against the mentally ill.[90]

Second, human rights violations may result in mental illness. Severe human rights violations like torture, rape, genocide, and inhuman and degrading treatment affect the mental health of individuals.[91] Human rights abuses have a pervasive and far-reaching impact not only on the victim of abuse but also family members and the community at large. The interdependence of the right to health with other human rights has also been clearly identified by the Committee on Economic, Social and Cultural Rights.[92]

Third, mental health and human rights bear on one-another. The betterment of one's mental health promotes well-being and welfare, as well as dignity and self-development. Disease and disability are thought to disable one's active political and economic participation.[93] On the other hand, respect for human rights secures one from harm and restraint so that free and reasonable opinions will ultimately be formed, leading to self-development of the individual.[94]

Article 12.1 of the International Covenant on Economic, Social and Cultural Rights (ICESCR) provides that state parties recognise 'the right of everyone to the enjoyment of the highest attainable standard of physical and *mental* health.' The CESCR's General Comment No. 14, providing for the most authoritative interpretation of the right to health, confirms that the right is not simply about being healthy. It is a right to facilities, goods, services, and conditions that are conducive to the realisation of the highest attainable standard of physical and mental health. The Comment articulates a framework of norms and obligations that make up the right to health. This includes, inter alia, freedoms,

90 LO Gostin, 'The Human Rights of Persons with Mental Disabilities: A Global Perspective on the Application of Human Rights Principles to Mental Health' (2004) 63 Medical Law Review 111.

91 AE Goldfield, 'The Physical and Psychological Sequelae of Torture: Symptomology and Diagnosis' (1988) 259(28) Journal of the American Medical Association 2725.

92 OHCHR, 'CESCR General Comment No. 14: The Right to the Highest Attainable Standard of Health (Art.12)' (11 August 2000) E/C.12/2000/4 <https://www.refworld.org/pdfid/4538838d0.pdf> accessed 13 May 2018.

93 N Daniels, *Just Healthcare* (Cambridge University Press, 1985) 32–35.

94 D Rosenthal and LS Rubinstein, 'International Human Rights Advocacy under the Principles for the Protection of Persons with Mental Illness' (1993) 16(3–4) International Journal of Law and Psychiatry 257.

entitlements, non-discrimination and equality, participation, international assistance and cooperation, and monitoring and accountability.

The right to health includes entitlement to a system of health protection, including healthcare and the underlying determinants of health, which provides equality of opportunity for people to enjoy the highest attainable standard of health. Crucially, care and support services as well as medical attention play a vital role in ensuring the health and dignity of persons with mental disabilities.[95]

In this regard, the Committee submits the protection one deserves by defining the right to health in an inter-related manner. In particular, the Committee draws attention to state parties' obligations in terms of availability, accessibility, acceptability and quality. In terms of availability, the Committee stresses that public health and health care facilities, goods and services, as well as programmes must be available in sufficient quantity. The underlying determinants of health – including safe and potable drinking water, adequate sanitation facilities, hospitals, clinics and other health-related buildings, trained medical and professional personnel and essential drugs - all fill the circle of availability.[96]

With regard to accessibility, the Committee underscores non-discrimination and physical, economic and informational accessibility as defining elements. Thus, health care must be available especially to those who are vulnerable and marginalised without any discrimination. Health facilities, services and goods must be within safe physical reach. Apart from this, health facilities, good and services must also be affordable for all. Finally, health-related information must be accessible and all must have the right to seek, receive and convey information and ideas concerning health issues.[97]

Acceptability, on the other hand, hinges on the respectfulness and cultural appropriateness of health facilities, goods and services. The culture of individuals also merits respect.[98] Finally, health facilities, goods and services must also be scientifically and medically appropriate and in good quality.[99]

Reflecting on health conditions of the mentally ill in Ethiopia, one finds that most aspirations and stipulations of the international human rights regime are not realised. The mental health institutions in the country do not live up to the expectations of the ICESCR in terms of numbers. There is only one mental

95 Gostin (n 84).
96 General Comment No. 14 (n 92).
97 Ibid.
98 Ibid.
99 Ibid.

hospital supposed to serve all persons with mental illness all over the country. The availability of medical professionals remains a noteworthy challenge. So far, there are only 40 psychiatrists for a population of about 100 million. Accessibility, required treatment and care are often provided far from the homes and workplaces of persons with mental disabilities, while at the same time there is also lack of community-based support services.[100] This denies persons with mental illness their rights to live, work, and be treated and fully supported, as far as possible, in their communities.

Information asymmetry is another challenge that the mentally ill in Ethiopia face. There is the widespread institutional and individual perception that the mentally ill lack the capacity to make rational decisions and to participate in their treatment and rehabilitation scheme. Hence, the approach is paternalistic and labelling, where society marks the mentally ill person as being irresponsible and unworthy. The state does not address the information asymmetry that persists with regard to mental health; awareness and promotional works are not worth mentioning as they simply do not exist.

Acceptability is another ill-served area. The cultural dimension of mental illness has not been addressed in Ethiopia. Modern medicine does not encourage community-based and regulated traditional healing and rehabilitation arrangements. Medical ethics is not respected in most instances. As one of the underlying elements of medical ethics is consent, persons with mental illness are subjected to involuntary admission and treatment and there is no system that accommodates individuals that do not have the legal capacity to consent to their treatment.[101]

7 Ameliorating the Problem through Diversion Programmes

In the preceding sections, an attempt has been made to show that the treatment of persons with mental illness in Ethiopia falls short of international and domestic human rights principles. A great majority of the mentally ill are unable to access the immediate treatment interventions they require. Very often, they are detained in a mental hospital unnecessarily. Sometimes, individuals are sent to prison instead of to a mental hospital, even though they have a

100 A Fekadu and G Thornicroft *'Global Mental Health: Perspectives from Ethiopia'* (2014) 7(25) Global Health Action, 447.

101 For the legal requirement of procurement of consent before treatment, see Federal Negarit Gazette, 'Food, Medicine and Health Care Administration and Control Council of Ministers Regulation' Regulation No. 299/2013, art 52(1).

mental illness. The criminal justice system in Ethiopia faces challenges in addressing the demands of the mentally ill on a daily basis. The police do not fully know what to do when a mentally ill person violates the law. The prosecution rather prefers to pass over the mentally ill to judges than to confront the demands of the mentally ill. Judges put their trust in doctors in mental hospitals and wait for final dispositions of a medical professional on questions related to persons with mental illness. Doctors have few resources to cater to cases involving the mentally ill and simply make decisions – often ordering the police to take back such patients altogether. The police then keep such patients in the nearest prison facility. The accused must wait for at least one year in prison before they are admitted to a hospital. This simply entails a vicious cycle of dehumanising actions towards persons with mental illness in Ethiopia.

Still, Ethiopia is not unique when it comes to this status quo. Many countries all over the world encounter similar predicaments – although in varying degrees. In this context, mentally ill persons are more likely to be arrested or detained because they cannot post even very low bails, they are charged with more serious crimes, they have stiffer penalties imposed, they spend 2–5 times longer in prison and are involved in more fights, infractions and sanctions.[102]

Many jurisdictions have taken steps to ameliorate the situation and have indeed improved because they recognised the problem, acknowledged its consequences and planned for ways out. One such way out relates to the reduction of the prison population by lessening the incidence of mentally ill persons going to prison. This practice is called diversion. Let alone prisons, also mental health institutions are condemned by many to not be good places to send mental patients. Society must improve when it comes to taking care of its mentally ill members.[103]

An organised international response to prison over-crowding and the rehabilitation of some members of society is provided by the United Nations under the banner of the United Nations Standard Minimum Rules for Non-custodial Measures (The Tokyo Rules), adopted by General Assembly Resolution 45/110 on 14 December 1990. In recognition of the fact that the traditional prison system is failing in meeting the basic objectives of punishment, and that in some

102 J Massaro (2005), 'Overview of the mental health service system for criminal justice professionals' (Technical Assistance and Policy Analysis Center for Jail Diversion, 2005) <http://schizophrenia.com/pdfs/criminaljustice.pdf> accessed 13 May 2018.

103 There are extensive practices of diverting the mentally ill from the ordinary court system and mental health treatment schemes into less formal and more relaxed court systems and treatment institutions. See B McAsey, 'A Critical Evaluation of the Koori Court Division of the Victorian Magistrates Court' (2005) 10(2) Deakin Law Review.

circumstances, the traditional criminal justice machinery might not be successful in meeting its objectives while facing certain kinds of individuals, the international community has come together to introduce non-custodial measures as alternatives to incarceration. Article 3 of the Tokyo Rules embodies twelve fundamental principles. To state a few, the system must furnish a legal regime that deals with non-custodial measures; there must be established criteria based on the nature and gravity of the offence, personality and background of the offender, as well as purposes of sentencing; the offender's consent needs to be taken into account before deciding on non-custodial measures; the dignity of the offender must be respected at all times; privacy of the offender must be respected, and the confidentiality of the records of the offender must be protected.

There is a growing body of research describing a complex array of socio-economic factors contributing to offending behaviour. Acknowledging that these factors may require social or therapeutic responses rather than legal solutions underlies an emerging trend to situating justice processes firmly within (rather than above or outside) the broader social context.[104] This is particularly the case given the low level of empirical support for the effectiveness of punitive sanctions as deterrent of future offending.[105]

Mentally ill persons are better treated outside than inside prisons. If possible, they should continue living in their communities.[106] Should they themselves call for treatment in a mental health facility, it should also be as near to their homes as possible. It should never be a prison.[107]

Mental health diversion and support aims to improve well-being and to reduce re-offending in people whose mental illness significantly contributes to offending behaviour. The aim is to provide interventions and, targeted to their illness and related problems, to support the person in place of, alongside, or integrated with other criminal justice system processes.[108]

Many countries have installed various forms of diversion programs that constitute best practices to learn from. These interventions range from the

---

104 DS Nagin, 'Imprisonment and Reoffending' in M Tonry (ed), *Crime and Justice: An Annual Review* (University of Chicago Press, 2009) 115–200.

105 P Villetaz and M Killias 'The Effects of Custodial vs Non-Custodial Sentences on Re-offending' (2006) 13 Campbell Systematic Reviews <http://library.college.police.uk/docs/Killias-custodial-2006.pdf> accessed 13 May 2018.

106 OHCHR (n 48).

107 Ibid principle 7.2.

108 Villetaz & Killias (n 105).

Psychiatric Emergency Response Team,[109] to the Magistrates' Court Diversion Program,[110] the Mental Health Court,[111] and the Koori Court.[112]

There are also other models of intervention. The widely-accepted model is the Sequential Intercept Model developed by Munetz and Griffin.[113] This involves five stages of interception for mentally ill people who might possibly violate the law. The first, called the 'ultimate intercept model', argues that access to adequate, appropriate, comprehensive and integrated community-based treatment services should be the alternative to incarceration.[114] Intercept 1 holds that police are mandated to take corrective measures when facing a mentally ill offender.[115] Intercept 2 involves initial detention and hearings wherein police and prosecution may undertake early screenings for the presence of mental illness, as well as linkages to appropriate treatment and use of information management systems to identify individuals currently using community-based treatment services.[116] Intercept 3 works to further filter what Intercept 1 and Intercept 2 have failed to; as a post-booking measure, diversion staff establish a treatment plan and coordinate with attorneys and judges to arrange for release from custody.[117] Intercept 4 attempts to increase communication between correctional institutions and community treatment providers in order to promote the successful transition back into community.[118] Finally, there is the 'community corrections stage', Intercept 5, whose goal

109 K Hartford, R Carey and J Mendonca, 'Pre-Arrest Diversion of People with Mental Illness: Literature Review and International Survey' (2006) 24(6) Behavioral Sciences and the Law 845.

110 M Burvill et al., 'The Management of Mentally Impaired Offenders within the South Australian Justice System' (2003) 26(1) International Journal of Law and Psychiatry 13.

111 E Richardson, 'Mental Health Courts and Diversion Programs for Offenders with Illnesses: the Australian Context' (Paper presented at 8th Annual International Association of Forensic Mental Health Services Conference, Vienna, 14–16 July 2008).

112 B McAsey, 'A Critical Evaluation of the Koori Court Division of the Victorian Magistrates' Court' (2005) 10 Deakin Law Review 654.

113 MR Munetz and PA Griffin (2006), 'Use of the Sequential Intercept Model as an Approach to Decriminalization of People with Serious Mental Illness' 57(4) Psychiatric Services 544.

114 Ibid.

115 Ibid.

116 NY Delmar (2007), '*Practical Advice on Jail Diversion: Ten Years of Learnings on Jail Diversion from the CMHS National GAINS Center*' (CMHS National GAINS Center, 2007) <http://www.pacenterofexcellence.pitt.edu/documents/PracticalAdviceOnJailDiversion.pdf> accessed 13 May 2018.

117 AR Gilbert et al., 'Reductions in Arrest Assisted Outpatient Treatment in New York' (2010) 61(10) Psychiatric Services 996.

118 K Heilbrun, 'Community-Based Alternatives for Justice-Involved Individuals with Severe Mental Illness: Review of the Relevant Research' (2012) 39 Criminal Justice and Behavior 351.

is to effectively address mental illness to prevent reoffending and/or return to incarceration due to technical violations or failure to adhere to the conditions or supervision.[119]

The Ethiopian diversion practice must be viewed against this backdrop. Ethiopia adheres to the traditional criminal justice practices of screening persons with mental illness very late after the commission of a crime and during trial. It is only for purposes of criminal adjudication that mental illness becomes part of the discussion. There is no organised attempt to mitigate the effects of mental illness before or after the commission of crime.

The latest organised, institutional attempt to deal with this affair in Ethiopia relates to the establishment of the Mental Health Court (MHC) under the Federal First Instance Court, in partnership with the Health Science College, Psychiatry Department of Addis Ababa University (AAU), which serves as a pilot test.[120] While the court furnishes the structural basis, the Department of Psychiatry provides the technical and professional support. The MHC is not established through a directive of any kind and therefore lacks working guidelines, mandates and operational techniques. Issues of accountability and procedural safeguards also remain unattended. Currently, the MHC looks into cases of fitness for trial, bail and diversion.[121]

The MHC, in addition to lacking an institutional and legal basis, also lags behind in incorporating the models and principles of diversion considered above. The MHC does not take care of the mentally ill before they come to court or after they stop coming. The community integration, rehabilitation, treatment and non-custodial measures are not included in its operational manual. This is solely because the MHC is established as a project and not as a scientifically-demanded and legally-reinforced institution.

On the other hand, it should be noted that the National Mental Health Strategy preaches for de-institutionalisation, community participation, and rehabilitation.[122] Further promising on de-institutionalisation, the NMHS advocates for the elimination of mental health hospitals on the grounds that their management is expensive and that institutionalisation needs to be discouraged. In furtherance of the de-institutionalisation endeavour, the NMHS caters to fully integrating mental health into primary and general health care,

---

119 V Hiday and B Ray, 'Arrests Two Years after Exiting a Well-Established Mental Health Court' (2010) 61 Psychiatric Services <https://ps.psychiatryonline.org/doi/full/10.1176/ps.2010.61.5.463> accessed 13 May 2018.

120 Memorandum of Understanding between the Federal First Instance Court and Addis Ababa University Health Science College, Department of Psychiatry (unpublished, 2015).

121 Aberash (n 81).

122 FDRE Ministry of Health (n 17).

to bringing mental healthcare close to home in a restrictive setting, to the integration of community-level treatment, and to prioritising community level treatment over inpatient care.

Unfortunately, the MHC system does not live up to expectations of the NMHS, which advocates for a more liberal mental health treatment scheme. What is more, the MHC sets aside stipulations of the FDRE Criminal Code. While the Code determines the fate of the mentally ill after trial, the MHC appears to side-line the measures forwarded by the Code under articles 129–133. Article 130 contemplates for the confinement of the mentally ill in a suitable institution, and article 131 talks about the order of treatment of persons with mental illness in a suitable institution. Article 132 makes confinement and treatment indefinite, even though it might be reviewed every two years.

Although the Criminal Code's positions are contestable on the face of the NMHS, which calls for de-institutionalisation and for out-patient mental health services, the MHC remains retracted from those minimum protections the FDRE Criminal Code gives to the mentally ill.

8 Conclusion and Recommendations

Generally, the following remarks can be made in relation to the findings of this research.

First, the number of people referred to the Amanuel Specialized Mental Hospital in Addis Ababa to undergo mental diagnosis is significant, and the number of people who will pass through diagnosis continues to be low; this contributes to the arbitrary pre-trial detention of accused persons, which is very concerning.

Second, courts remain passive in safe-guarding the rights of accused persons, even when the accused person's rights are clearly violated.

Third, the Ethiopian legal system has not provided for sufficient safeguards for the accused who await the results of a mental diagnosis.

Fourth, Amanuel Specialized Mental Hospital does not have clear procedures for the admission and release of a patient.

Fifth, no practical measures have been taken on the part of the Ethiopian state to make mental health facilities accessible and available to the masses. There is only one specialised mental hospital in the country admitting patients to a specialised medico-legal ward, which operates with only eleven beds.

Sixth, no system has been put in place to combat the possible abuse of power against those who are entitled to make decisions on the admission or dismissal of the patient.

In light of these findings, the following key recommendations are offered.

First, the government should exert maximum efforts to increase the number and to improve the quality of hospitals specialising in mental health, in order for them to become both available and acceptable.

Second, a well-articulated, balanced and rights-friendly standard of decision-making system and structure should be put in place in all institutions.

Third, prosecutors and judges should play their constitutional duty of obeying and enforcing the FDRE Constitution, especially focusing on Chapter Three of the Constitution, which has direct ramifications on the rights and welfare of the mentally ill.

Fourth, offices accepting and treating medico-legal conditions should be established at courts all over the country in order to enable making preliminary observations and recommendations on the mental status of accused patients.

Fifth, a system of bio-ethics and disciplinary standards should be enshrined under the laws of the country to particularly deal with the treatment of persons with mental illness.

Exploring Tax Incentive Mechanisms to Strengthen the Inclusion of Persons with Disabilities in the Private Workforce in Ethiopia

Gebrehiwot Hadush and Biniam Mekonen

Abstract

The Convention on the Rights of Persons with Disabilities (CRPD), which Ethiopia ratified in 2010, requires a private business to provide reasonable accommodation in order to create an enabling environment for persons with disabilities. This could involve work rescheduling, the structural re-adjustment of offices, walkways, and office benefits such as transport, among others. Unarguably, such changes would require employers to incur additional costs even if they get more returns in the long run. As such, it would be naive to ignore the issues of cost recovery or cost sharing mechanisms in the realm of employment of persons with disabilities. The tax incentive mechanism is a growing positive measure, which has strong potential to encourage employers to increase the hiring of persons with disabilities. This is in agreement with the concluding observations of the CRPD Committee, which requires member states to put in place incentive mechanisms either separately in their own right or as complementary to other affirmative actions, such as quota rules. An exploratory analysis on the availability and limitations of tax incentive mechanisms in the promotion of the CRPD in Ethiopia, this research posits that in addition to increasing the employment rate of persons with disabilities, tax incentive mechanisms could be instrumental in creating values on the freedom and dignity of persons with disabilities that are on an equal footing with persons without disabilities.

Keywords

Tax incentive mechanisms – persons with disabilities – CRPD – private workforce in Ethiopia

1 Introduction

The Convention on the Rights of Persons with Disabilities (CRPD), adopted on 13 December 2006, recognises the fundamental rights of persons with

 | DOI:10.1163/9789004415966_012

disabilities and encompasses their inclusion into the workforce without discrimination on the basis of disability.[1] The Convention is grounded on the human rights principle of equality and freedom for all.[2] It considers persons with disabilities not just as 'objects of charity' and 'medical treatment and social care', but as 'subjects with the same human rights as everybody.'[3]

The Convention brings together civil and political rights and economic, social and cultural rights in one treaty instrument.[4] In principle, the CRPD applies the existing human rights normative framework to the particular circumstances of persons with disabilities. As such, it is also viewed as an 'implementation convention.'[5] Yet, it should be noted that the CRPD is not only a restatement of existing human rights; it has also reformulated these rights and clarified the context in which they apply to persons with disabilities. The CRPD also unravels the specific experience of persons with disabilities, which cannot be taken into account adequately by the general human rights instruments.[6] With special regard to the particular challenges persons with disabilities face in the workforce and other sectors, the CPRD therefore introduces two human rights principles: 'the principle of accessibility' and 'the means of reasonable accommodation', both of which can be used to protect the human rights of persons with disabilities.[7]

Like all other human rights conventions, the obligation to implement the CRPD lies solely with the state. As such, individuals cannot bring human rights cases or violations of the Convention against individuals or non-state actors in general. The CRPD requires states to put in place legislation that could effectively implement the rights of persons with disabilities.[8] The CRPD also encourages states to take 'positive measures', including employment quotas, funding, or tax incentive mechanisms to promote the employment of persons

1 G Quinn, 'A Short Guide to the United Nations Convention on the Rights of Persons with Disabilities' (2009) 1 European Yearbook of Disability Law 89, 95 <https://intersentia.com/en/european-yearbook-of-disability-law-27231.html> accessed on 16 January 2018. See also Convention on the Rights of Persons with Disabilities (signed on 13 December 2006, entered into force on 3 May 2008) 2515 UNTS 3 (CRPD), Articles 3 and 27.

2 Convention on the Rights of Persons with Disabilities (signed on 13 December 2006, entered into force on 3 May 2008) 2515 UNTS 3 (CRPD), Article 3.

3 M Hirschberg and C Papadopoulos '"Reasonable Accommodation" and "Accessibility": Human Rights Instruments Relating to Inclusion and Exclusion in the Labor Market' (2016) 6(1) Societies 3, 4 <https://www.mdpi.com/2075-4698/6/1/3> accessed 23 March 2017.

4 Ibid.

5 Quinn (n 1).

6 Ibid.

7 Hirschberg and Papadopoulos (n 3) 1.

8 CRPD (no 2) Article 4.

with disabilities in the private sector.[9] States enjoy relative freedom regarding their approaches to taking positive measures. States may choose a punitive model or an enabling model in their pursuit to implement the CRPD obligations. On the one hand, the punitive model emphasises the compliance of the employer with meeting rules on reasonable accommodation or quotas for a percentage of employees with disabilities.[10] On the other hand, the enabling model focuses on motivating the employer and creating value, based on the understanding that persons with disabilities will perform and be productive in the labour market.[11] This may include access to public funding, limiting an insurance premium, and most importantly, a tax reduction for providing reasonable accommodation to include persons with disabilities in the workforce.[12]

The quota-based positive measure and the tax incentive mechanism fundamentally vary, both in the means and in the outcome they seek to achieve. Hence, they can hardly complement each other. While the quota system puts the compulsory employment rate of persons with disabilities to a certain percentage, the tax incentive mechanism is motivational in that it aims to encourage the employer to value the employment of persons with disabilities both in the short-term as well as in the long-term corporate plan.[13] There is no sufficient empirical claim that establishes the comparative advantages of one over the other. There are, however, growing claims that as a pro-active approach, the tax incentive mechanism has stronger potential in changing the attitudes of employers and thereby also in enhancing the employment of persons with disabilities than its counterpart, the quota system.[14]

A more rigorous analysis of the benefits and disadvantages of both mechanisms could not be pursued in this research simply on account of spatial considerations. Hence, except for some brief cross-references to the quota-based positive measures, this chapter primarily focuses on the availability and importance of the tax incentive mechanism in increasing the employment of persons with disabilities in the private workforce in Ethiopia.

9 Ibid Article 27(h).

10 P Sargolia 'Strategies and Incentives for Matching Disability Workers with Jobs: Lessons for Italy from the United States' (2009) Comparative Domestic Policy Paper Series 4 German Marshall Fund of the United States <http://www.gmfus.org/sites/default/files/files/CDPSarogliaStrategies_and_Incentievs_for_Matching_Disabled_Workers_with_Jobs.pdf> accessed 25 March 2017.

11 Ibid.

12 Ibid.

13 Ibid.

14 Ibid.

The chapter is generally organised into three sections. The first section elaborates on principles of accessibility and reasonable accommodation under the CRPD. The second section further analyses these principles in light of the relevant Ethiopian laws. The third section deals with the tax incentive mechanism as it applies to the current tax system in Ethiopia.

2 Access and Reasonable Accommodation

2.1 *Access to the Labour Market*

The right to work is variously recognised as a fundamental human right under the Universal Declaration of Human Rights (UDHR), the International Covenant on Economic, Social and Cultural Rights (ICESCR), the International Covenant on Civil and Political Rights (ICCPR), and subsequent conventions such as the Convention on the Elimination of all Forms of Discrimination Against Women (CEDAW).[15]

The CRPD reasserts the right to work with a strong emphasis on the inclusion and participation of persons with disabilities in the mainstream labour market. According to Article 27,

> States parties recognize the right of persons with disabilities to work, on an equal basis with others; this includes the right to the opportunity to gain a living by work freely chosen or accepted in a labour market and work environment that is open, inclusive and accessible to persons with disabilities.[16]

Article 27 further requires states to 'promote the employment of persons with disabilities in the private sector through appropriate policies and measures, which may include affirmative action programmes, incentives and other measures.' It also requires state parties to ensure that reasonable accommodation is provided to persons with disabilities in the workplace.[17]

However, the implementation of the Convention still remains a source of big concern.[18] Persons with disabilities still face both physical and attitudinal barriers that limit their inclusion in the workforce. 'In many cases, neither are employers prepared for inclusion nor is this issue considered as strategically

15 Hirschberg and Papadopoulos (n 3). See also Quinn (n 1).
16 CRPD (no 2) Article 27(1).
17 CRPD (no 2) Article 27(1)(g) and (h).
18 Quinn (n 1) 95.

necessary.'[19] According to the International Labour Organization (ILO), the unemployment rates of persons with disabilities in developing countries are sometimes as high as 80 percent.[20] The OECD Report in 2010 revealed that 'the average employment rate of persons with disabilities across the OECD countries is 40 percent compared to 75 percent of persons without disability.'[21] According to the Office of the United Nations High Commissioner for Human Rights (OHCHR), there are physical, attitudinal, information and communication, as well as transport-related barriers that prevent persons with disabilities from seeking, obtaining and maintaining work.[22] The World Report on Disability (WRD) also lists the lack of access to formal education and relevant training as central barriers for persons with disabilities in entering the labour market.[23]

2.2 *Positive Measures for Enhancing the Employment of Persons with Disabilities in the Private Workforce*

With its emphasis on the equalisation of opportunity and inclusiveness of the labour market, the CRPD recognises that positive measures, which are necessary to accelerate or achieve the substantive equality of persons with disabilities, do not constitute discrimination.[24] In view of this, Article 27 (e) requires state parties to 'promote the employment of persons with disabilities in the private sector through appropriate policies and measures.' In this context, it is submitted that positive measures, which aim to improve the participation of persons with disabilities in the workforce, are not prohibited. This is consistent with the concluding observation of the United Nations Committee on the Rights of Persons with Disabilities (CCRPD), which often refers to the necessity

19 Hirschberg and Papadopoulos (n 3) 3.

20 International Labour Organization (ILO) Fact Sheet Fact Sheet, 'Inclusion of Persons with Disabilities in Ethiopia' (2013) <https://www.ilo.org/skills/pubs/WCMS_112299/lang--en/index.htm> accessed 27 April 2017.

21 Organisation for Economic Co-operation and Development (OECD), *Sickness, Disability and Work: Breaking the Barriers: A Synthesis of Findings across OECD Countries* (OECD Publishing 2012).

22 World Health Organization (WHO), *World Report on Disability* (WHO 2011) 237. <https://www.who.int/disabilities/world_report/2011/report.pdf?ua=1> accessed 15 April 2017.

23 United Nations Human Rights Council, 'Thematic Study on the Work and Employment of Persons with Disabilities – Report of the Office of the United Nations High Commissioner for Human Rights' (2012) A/HRC/22/25, para 26 <https://www.ohchr.org/Documents/HRBodies/HRCouncil/RegularSession/Session22/A-HRC-22-25_en.pdf> accessed 13 April 2017. See also Committee on the Rights of Persons with Disabilities, 'Convention on the Rights of Persons with Disabilities General comment No. 2 (2014)' (2014) CRPD/GC/2, para.7 <https://undocs.org/CRPD/C/GC/2> accessed 20 April 2017.

24 CRPD (no 2) Article 5(4).

of establishing programmes to enhance disability employment both in the public and private sector.[25]

The CRPD does not limit the nature and type of positive measures that member states may pursue to stimulate the employment of persons with disabilities in the workforce. As stated above, positive measures may take the form of quotas or tax incentive mechanisms. The quota system is the oldest and most commonly applied system in many countries.[26] The ILO, in its Recommendation No. 99 on Vocational Rehabilitation, has recommended the 'engagement by employers of a percentage of disabled persons.'[27] The CCRPD noted that many countries that have signed and ratified the CRPD had already put in place different quota systems even before the adoption of the CRPD.[28] In general, the CCRPD stated the quota system is not inconsistent with the Convention rights.[29] However, it was noted that the quota system is most often limited to employment in the public sector.[30] Moreover, the CCRPD expressed its concern that the quota system has not been effective in many countries.[31] Critics also disapprove of the quota system, arguing that it reinforces social prejudices instead of integrating the disabled employee into the workforce on an equal footing with persons without disabilities.[32] Likewise, critics of the system claim that the quota targets only 'quantity not quality.' This is to say that employers can easily meet employment quotas by offering jobs with a

25 The United Nations Committee on the Rights of Persons with Disabilities (CCRPD) gave similar recommendations in its concluding observations to member states such as Belgium, Paraguay, Peru, and Mexico. See United Nations Committee of the Rights of Persons with Disabilities, 'Concluding Observations on the Initial Report of Belgium' (2014) CRPD/C/BEL/CO/1, paras 38f; United Nations Committee of the Rights of Persons with Disabilities, 'Concluding Observations on the Initial Report of Paraguay' (2013) CRPD/C/PRY/CO/1, paras 63f; United Nations Committee of the Rights of Persons with Disabilities, 'Concluding Observations on the Initial Report of Peru' (2012) CRPD/C/PER/CO/1, para 41; United Nations Committee of the Rights of Persons with Disabilities, 'Concluding Observations on the Initial Report of Mexico' (2014) CRPD/C/MEX/CO/1, para 52(d).

26 L Waddington, 'Positive Action Measures and the UN Convention on the Rights of Persons with Disabilities': Case Note: Communication No. 9/2012 A.F. v. Italy, UN Committee on the Rights of Persons with Disabilities, 19 May 2015 (2016) 2(3) International Labor Rights Case Law 396.

27 Ibid.

28 See CCRPD (n 25).

29 Ibid.

30 Ibid.

31 Ibid.

32 Einat Albin 'Universalizing the Right to Work of Persons with Disabilities: An Equality and Dignity Based Approach' in V Mantouvalou (ed) *The Right to Work: Legal and Philosophical Perspectives* (Hart Publishing 2015).

lower title or positions with less salary.[33] The quota system is a group right that addresses the disability population as a class. As such, individuals are entangled to invoke quota laws with a view to enforcing their employment rights. For example, in *A.F v Italy*, the author, relying on the Quota Law No. 68/99, submitted a communication to the CCRPD stating that his right to work under Article 27 had been violated.[34] The author complained that the University of Modena declined to employ him in spite of the quota law, which requires at least half the positions recruited via competitive exams in the public sector to be filled by registered disabled persons.[35] The government argued that the University of Modena agreed with the provincial government that it would fulfil its quota requirement (7 percent) in other ways than through recruitment via competitive exams.[36] The CCRPD found there was no violation of Article 27. The CCRPD in particular noted that the 'author did not provide any element which would enable the Committee to conclude that the provisions of the legislation and its application amounted to a violation of his *individual rights* under the Convention.'[37] The CCRPD, in assessing A.F, did not ponder whether individuals can claim a quota law based on Article 27. Yet, it held 'it is doubtful that individuals can base claims based on Article 27 obligations that relate to disability policy or positive action more generally.'[38] Incentive mechanisms encompass both tax and non-tax benefit packages. They were also known in the pre-CRPD era, following the enactment of the famous American Disability Act (ADA).[39] Under the ADA, the federal government took robust measures such as the provision of funding for providing reasonable accommodation, limiting insurance premiums, and tax reductions.[40] Incentive mechanisms target prejudices and barriers on the part of employers. Contrasting the quota system, incentive mechanisms focus on incentivising employers to hire persons with disabilities with the belief that persons with disabilities will perform on an equal footing with persons without disabilities.[41] As such, the issue for the employer is not whether the disabled applicant is qualified for the job compared to other applicants without disability, but rather whether the

33 See Waddington (n 26) 97.
34 Ibid 398.
35 Ibid.
36 Ibid.
37 Ibid.
38 Ibid.
39 P Sargolia (n 10) 5.
40 Ibid.
41 Ibid.

employer can provide reasonable accommodation having considered the available incentive mechanisms. It also places higher moral obligations on the employer, who is unlikely to find reason to decline a qualified person with disabilities when the government provides mechanisms for cost recovery.[42]

By and large, the incentive mechanism is unexploited and has not spread well into other countries on a comparable scale to how it works in the US.[43] Yet, it is hardly doubted that incentive mechanisms, particularly in the form of tax reductions, are more attractive to employers than the compulsory quota system. The initial state reports to the CCRPD also show that incentive mechanisms have been successful.[44]

2.3 *Reasonable Accommodation*

The most common excuses raised by employers for excluding persons with disabilities from the mainstream workforce is that the organisation in question is not fit for the needs of persons with disabilities.[45] As such, the inability of an organisation to adjust to the needs of the persons with disabilities was almost taken for granted without any scrutiny. Against this background, the CRPD consciously introduced the concept of 'reasonable accommodation' as a key weapon to eliminate discrimination on the basis of inability or failure to adjust one's environment to the needs of persons with disabilities. Article 2 of the CRPD defines the concept of 'reasonable accommodation' as follows:

> Necessary and appropriate modifications and adjustments not imposing a disproportionate or undue burden, where needed in a particular case, to ensure to persons with disabilities the enjoyment or exercise on an equal basis with others of all human rights and fundamental freedoms.[46]

Reasonable accommodation is specifically envisaged under Article 24 (the Right to Education) and Article 27 (the Right to Work). Both provisions warn that

---

42 Ibid.

43 Ibid.

44 United Nations Committee of the Rights of Persons with Disabilities, 'Concluding Observations on the Initial Report of Argentina' (2012) CRPD/C/ARG/1, para 513.

45 Quinn (no 1) 95. See also Leticia de Campos Velho Martel, 'Reasonable Accommodation: The New Concept from an Inclusive Constitutional Perspective' (2011) 8(14) Sur International Journal on Human Rights, 103 <https://papers.ssrn.com/sol3/papers.cfm?abstract_id=2000291> accessed 13 March 2017.

46 CRPD (no 2) Article 2.

'denial of reasonable accommodation' constitutes a form of discrimination.[47] Consequently, the provision of reasonable accommodation is read as an obligation that has to be fulfilled immediately.

It should be noted that reasonable accommodations are individualised measures that meet the special needs of persons with disabilities.[48] Reasonable accommodation goes beyond formal equality to achieve substantive equality; it requires ensuring that persons with disabilities can reach the same level of opportunities as other persons. This means, for example, that buildings and offices must be accessible, transportation to the workplace available, communication technologies installed, and teaching support measures like braille, bold notes, sign language and personal assistants provided.[49]

Reasonable accommodation should be provided by both the public and the private sector. Yet, it is the role of the state to guarantee that the private sector does so.[50] The most commonly raised question is when accommodation may be considered 'reasonable'. Unfortunately, there is no definite and objective answer. Normally, it has to be determined on a case-by-case basis.[51] In its ordinary use, it can be submitted that accommodations are reasonable if they do not create an undue burden. Hence, 'there may be a burden, which means that efforts are required, but this burden may not be undue.' Certainly, this involves 'analysis of costs and possibilities of compensation either in the form of tax relief or grants or benefits, including advantages for parties other than those for whom the measures are taken.'[52] The CCRPD in its concluding observation on Spain elaborated on 'reasonableness' as 'the result of an objective test that involves an analysis of the availability of resources, as well as the relevance of the accommodation, and the expected goal of countering the CRPD rights.'[53]

47 CRPD (no 2) Articles 2 and 27.

48 Leticia de Campos Velho Martel, 'Reasonable Accommodation: The New Concept from an Inclusive Constitutional Perspective' (2011) 8(14) Sur International Journal on Human Rights, 104 <https://papers.ssrn.com/sol3/papers.cfm?abstract_id=2000291> accessed 13 March 2017. See also Hirschberg and Papadopoulos (n 3) 10.

49 Ibid.

50 CRPD (no 2) Article 27.

51 Leticia (n 48).

52 Ibid.

53 United Nations Committee on the Rights of Persons with Disabilities, 'Concluding Observations on the Initial Report of Spain' (2011) CRPD/C/ESP/CO/1, para 44.

3 Employment Rights of Persons with Disabilities: Ethiopian Laws and Policies

Ethiopia ratified the CRPD in June 2010 – but not the optional protocol. As such, the CRPD guides disability laws and policies in Ethiopia. The following paragraphs will discuss disability laws and policies that specifically deal with the inclusion of persons with disabilities in Ethiopia.

3.1 *Disability Rights under the FDRE Constitution*

The Constitution of the Federal Democratic Republic of Ethiopia (FDRE) was adopted in 1995, nearly 16 years before the adoption of the CRPD. Like the pre-CRPD international and domestic human rights instruments, the Constitution protected the right of persons with disabilities through its equality clause but without mentioning the term 'disability'. The equality clause under Article 25 provides:

> All persons are equal before the law and are entitled without any discrimination to the equal protection of the law. In this respect, the law shall guarantee to all persons equal and effective protection without discrimination on grounds of race, nation, nationality, or other social origin, color, sex, language, religion, political or other opinion, property, birth or *other status*'.[54]

The phrase 'other status' has been construed widely to include persons with disabilities and on this basis, it can be argued that the FDRE Constitution established the equality rights of persons with disability. It follows that the fundamental rights and freedoms enshrined in the Constitution and other rights established through subsidiary laws are equally applicable to persons with disability – a category of persons in society who could not be discriminated against based on their status of disability. On the other hand, the Constitution has also specifically established the obligation of the state to provide rehabilitation and assistance to the physically and mentally disabled.[55] This is open for debate. One can argue that this appears to be advancing the medical model predicated on the assumption that disabled people are prevented from accessing the labour market due of their impairment, which has to be cured or adjusted in a way that fits the existing settings of the labour market. On the other

54 Federal Negarit Gazeta, 'The Constitution of the Federal Democratic Republic of Ethiopia' Proclamation No. 1/1995. (emphasis added)

55 Ibid Article 41(5).

hand, it can be construed as complementary to the equality clause, which establishes the equality of all persons.

Be that as it may, the equality clause of Article 25 and the rehabilitation and assistance requirement under Article 41 are not sufficiently broad and clear enough to specifically address the various challenges of persons with disability as covered under the CRPD. Nonetheless, we should not forget that the FDRE Constitution is forward-looking as it opens a gateway for the immediate domestication of international treaty agreements through the ratification process.[56] The CRPD is the only other international human rights instrument next to the Convention on the Rights of the Child (CRC), which was published in the Federal Negarit Gazette by the Legislature as Proclamation No.676/2010.[57] This proclamation confers to the Ministry of Labour and Social Affairs (MoLSA) the mandate to ensure the implementation of the Convention in Ethiopia.[58] The 'Definition of Powers and Duties of the Executive Organs' Proclamation (2015, as revised) made the MoLSA responsible to 'enable persons with disabilities to benefit from equal opportunities and full participation'.[59] The Proclamation further requires that the issue of disability shall be mainstreamed in all ministries and agencies.[60]

3.2 *Regulation of Employment of Persons with Disability in Ethiopia*

There are general and specific legislations and polices that regulate the employment rights of persons with disabilities in Ethiopia. The first specific milestone legislation is the 'Right to Employment of Persons with Disabilities' Proclamation No.568/2008.[61] This legislation came two years after the adoption of the CRPD (in 2006), although it was only ratified by Ethiopia in 2010. Thus, it would not be surprising to see similarity in terms and contents between the Convention and this Proclamation.

In its preamble, the Proclamation states that negative social perceptions about persons with disabilities are deeply-rooted in Ethiopian society. Looking at the Proclamation as a whole, one can submit that its contents are influenced by the social model. It unequivocally provides that a person with disabilities

56 Ibid Article 9(4).

57 Federal Negarit Gazeta, Convention on Rights of Persons with Disability Ratification proclamation No.676/2010.

58 Federal Negarit Gazeta, 'Convention on the Rights of Persons with Disabilities Ratification Proclamation', Proclamation No. 676/2010, Article 3.

59 Federal Negarit Gazette, 'Definition of Powers and Duties of the Executive Organs of the Federal Republic of Ethiopia Proclamation' Proclamation 916/2015, Article 34(13).

60 Ibid Article 10(4).

61 Federal Negarit Gazeta, 'Right to Employment of Persons with Disability Proclamation' Proclamation No. 568/2008.

shall have equal employment rights without any discrimination based on such status.[62] It outlaws any forms of discrimination that impairs the equal employment opportunity of disabled persons (Article 5(1)) with the exception of jobs, which cannot be performed by qualified persons with disabilities even if reasonable accommodation is provided.[63] Furthermore, it stipulates that affirmative action intended to create equal employment opportunities to persons with disabilities shall not be regarded as discrimination.[64]

Like the CRPD, the Proclamation also states that the denial of reasonable accommodation is a form of discrimination, unless the required accommodation puts an undue burden on the employer. According to Article 2 (6), an undue burden occurs when an action by the employer 'entails considerable difficulty or expense' to be assessed in light of the nature and cost of adjustments, the size and nature of the business, the cost of its operation and the number and composition of its staff.[65] Obviously, this would trouble many employers who have to make safe decisions while considering all subjective elements required to determine what constitutes an undue burden. As no jurisprudence is developed domestically regarding the standard of assessment, it may confuse persons with disabilities as well in their pursuit of jobs in the private sector. Yet, it should be noted that the ratification of the CRPD in 2010 has afforded Ethiopian courts with possibilities to follow and apply interpretations of the CRPD Committee.

On the other hand, Article 6 (2) provided for an absolute guarantee that the 'assignment of an assistant for an employee with disabilities shall not, under any circumstance, constitute an undue burden to an employer.'[66] This is a very bold measure, which can promote the employment of persons with disabilities who rely on personal assistants for performing their job. It shall be cherished for taking milestone steps in the promotion of disability rights, which has not been explicitly required even under the CRPD itself.

As discussed above, Proclamation No.568/2008 applies both at federal and state levels. It also governs employment in the public and private spheres. Thus, as far as the rights of persons with disabilities are concerned, it could be labelled as an important source of trust along with the CRPD.

62 Ibid Article 4.
63 Ibid Article 2(8).
64 Ibid Article 5(4).
65 Ibid Article 2(6).
66 Ibid Article 6(2).

3.3 *Employment Policy and Strategies*

Prior to the ratification of the CRPD, the Ethiopian government progressively promoted disability inclusion through policies and strategies. The 2009 Employment Policy and Strategy of Ethiopia is a typical example of such advanced government measures. This instrument recognises the special situation of persons with disabilities and makes promises for strategies towards protecting persons with disabilities by addressing issues from skills development to employment service provision. With employment-related entitlements in mind, therefore, the document outlines specific strategies, which include improving and expanding training and other skill development services suited to the special needs of persons with disabilities, as well as promoting and making the formal private sector community aware of and sensitive to the causes of persons with disabilities.[67] Subsequent to the ratification of the CRPD, Ethiopia adopted a National Plan of Action for Inclusion of Persons with Disabilities[68] – further evidencing the government's focus on disability mainstreaming. All sectors of the economy – health, education, labour – should have a role to play in its implementation, promoting a better standard of living, equal rights and full participation of disabled persons in society. Moreover, the National Human Rights Action Plan has pledged to solve this problem by crafting different disability-centred projects aimed at creating job opportunities for persons with disabilities.[69]

The disability issue is also well-covered under the Growth and Transformation Plan (GTP). The GTP, in its social welfare policy component, provides that:

> [o]n the course of promoting the economic and social development of the country, the social welfare's main emphasis lies in protecting rights and facilitating conditions which will enable persons with disability and older people to use their abilities as individuals or in association with others to contribute to the development of society as well as to be self-supporting in the political, economic and social activities of the country.[70]

---

67 Federal Democratic Republic of Ethiopia, 'National Employment Policy and Strategy of Ethiopia', Ministry of Labour and Social Affairs (Addis Ababa, 2009) 2.3.5.8.1.

68 Federal Democratic Republic of Ethiopia, 'National Plan of Action for Inclusion of Persons with Disabilities, 2010–2020' Ministry of Labour and Social Affairs (Addis Ababa, 2012).

69 Federal Democratic Republic of Ethiopia, 'National Human Rights Action Plan 2013–2015' (Addis Ababa, 2013) 77.

70 The Federal Democratic Republic of Ethiopia, 'Joint IDA-IMF Staff Advisory Note on the Growth and Transformation Plan (GTP) 2010/11–2014/15', Report No. 63592-ET, 8.3.1

The GTP also promises that programmes that are going to be implemented for people with disabilities should be:

> 'programs that aim in preventing disability and providing education and training for persons with disability by rehabilitating them and have equal access and opportunities as well as by providing information about disability'.[71]

4 Availability of Tax Incentive Mechanisms for Hiring Persons with Disabilities in the Private Sector in Ethiopia

4.1 *General Overview*

Although it may seem like a new concept in many countries, the CCRPD in its concluding observations has noted the significance of incentive mechanisms as a separate option and/or as complimentary to affirmative actions, such as quotas. Virtually, the United States of America (USA) are an exception due to the enormous experience in exploiting tax incentive mechanisms, mainly after the enactment of the ADA in 1990. The USA tax incentive mechanisms serve two interrelated purposes: first, to support modifications and accommodations designed to enhance the accessibility of the workplace and productivity of workers with disabilities; and second, to motivate employers to increase the hiring persons with disabilities.[72] With the purpose of increasing the inclusion of persons with disabilities in the labour market, therefore, the USA provides tax incentives that fall under three categories: Work Opportunity Tax Credit (WOTC), Disabled Access Credit, and architectural/transportation Tax deduction. WOTC is available for employers who hire 'targeted low-income groups' such as disabled veterans and disabled persons who are completing or have completed rehabilitative services.[73] The Disabled Access Credit supports small businesses that incur costs in removing barriers and making their business and work environment accessible to persons with disabilities.[74] Specifically, Disabled Access Credit is provided for employers who:

<http://documents.worldbank.org/curated/en/796761468255282515/pdf/635920PRSP0P120e00nly0900BOX361530B.pdf> accessed 15 April 2017.

71 Ibid.

72 '*Tax Incentives for Employers*' United States Department of Labor, Office of Disability Employment <https://www.dol.gov/odep/topics/TaxIncentivesForEmployers.htm> accessed 17 April 2017.

73 Ibid.

74 Ibid.

- remove barriers that prevent a business from being accessible to or usable by individuals with disabilities;
- provide qualified interpreters or other effective methods of making audio materials available to individuals with hearing impairments;
- provide qualified readers, taped texts, and other methods of making visual materials available to individuals with visual impairments;
- acquire or modify equipment or devices for individuals with disabilities.[75]

Architectural/transportation tax deduction is dedicated to support positive measures that remove barriers in the construction of buildings as well as in transportation. Examples include making parking accessible, installing ramps and curb cuts, making telephones, water fountains and restrooms accessible, and widening walkways.[76]

4.2 *Tax Incentives for Employers of Persons with Disabilities in Ethiopia*

The FDRE Constitution provides that the Federal Government and the Federal States shall collect taxes and share revenue, taking the federal arrangement into account. Accordingly, revenue sources (tax powers) are divided into four categories: federal power of taxation, regional power of taxation, concurrent power of taxation, and undesignated power of taxation.[77]

As far as the collection of the revenues is concerned, each level of government collects its own tax while the Federal Government, additionally, collects the joint revenues with a possibility of delegation whenever it deems it necessary.[78]

In pursuance of their respective constitutional powers, both federal and regional governments have provided various tax incentive schemes to businesses,[79] albeit for different socio-economic reasons. These incentives are formulated in the form of tax holidays, tax exemptions, tax deductions, tax credits and loss carryforward. To mention some, the following tax incentives are granted to businesses/employers under various tax legislations:

75 Ibid.

76 Ibid.

77 FDRE Constitution (n 54) Article 94.

78 Ibid Article 94.

79 Generally, employers as owners of business are liable to pay income tax under schedule C of the Federal Income Tax Proclamation. Tax payers under this schedule are classified into three categories. Category C: business with annual turnover of less than 500,000 birr; Category B: business with annual turnovers between 500,000 birr to 1,000,000 birr; and Category A: business with annual turnover is above 1,000,000 birr.

- various cost-recovery schemes for capital and non-capital expenditures (including deduction, depreciation and tax credits);[80]
- tax exemptions on social, economic and health grounds;[81]
- customs duty exemptions of up to 100 percent on imports of capital goods for eligible areas of investment;[82]
- income tax exemptions for a period ranging between one and nine years, depending on the specific activity and location of the investor;[83]
- loss carryforward for businesses that suffer losses during the income tax exemption period for half of the tax exemption period;[84]
- with the exception of a few products, no export tax is levied on Ethiopian export products;

Having considered the recognised list of tax incentive mechanisms above, it is important to make an enquiry on whether such incentives can be exploited to stimulate employers to hire persons with disabilities. This can be approached from two perspectives: whether the general rules on deduction, exemption and tax credits can be used as an opportunity to recover extra costs of an employer who hire persons with disabilities; and, whether there are specific tax incentive schemes for employers with disabled employees.

According to Proclamation No.568/2008, an employer is duty-bound to provide materials and assign an assistant to enable a disabled employee to perform his/her duty.[85] Undoubtedly, by providing such necessary materials and assignment of assistants, the employer benefits from the work of a qualified person with disabilities. As such, such provisions are indispensable tools needed for running a business as long as the business hires and relies on the work of the person with disabilities. Thus, it can be safely argued that the provision of necessary materials and assignment of assistants to persons with disabilities

80 See Federal Negarit Gazette Extra Ordinary Issue 'Federal Income Tax Proclamation' Proclamation No. 979/2016, Articles 22–27 on deductible expenses for non-capital expenses and depreciation allowance for capital goods.

81 See Federal Negarit Gazeta, 'Value Added Tax Proclamation', Proclamation No. 285/2002, Articles 8 and 16; Federal Negarit Gazette Extra Ordinary Issue 'Federal Income Tax Proclamation' Proclamation No. 979/2016, Article 65.

82 See Article 12 and 3 of Federal Negarit Gazeta, 'Re-establishment and Modernization of Customs Authority Proclamation' Proclamation No. 60/1997 and Federal Negarit Gazeta, 'Re-establishment and Modernization of Customs Authority (amendment) Proclamation' Proclamation No. 368/2003, respectively.

83 Federal Income Tax Proclamation No. 979/2016 articla 65.

84 See Federal Negarit Gazette Extra Ordinary Issue 'Federal Income Tax Proclamation' Proclamation No. 979/2016, Article 26.

85 Federal Negarit Gazeta, 'Right to Employment with Disability Proclamation' Proclamation No. 568/2008, Article 6(1)(c).

are deductible expenses permitted under Article 22(1)(a) of the Income Tax Proclamation, which makes 'any non-capital expenses incurred to drive, secure and maintain the business income a deductible expense'.[86]

Moreover, employers can invoke Article 25(1) of the same Proclamation, which provides depreciation allowance as a cost recovery method for structural adjustment expenses by an employer.[87] Under sub-article (7)(c) of the same article, structural adjustment is defined to mean 'a building or any other addition or alteration to immovable property that becomes part of or permanently affixed to the immovable asset including a road, drive way, car park fence or a wall'.[88] It follows that if an employer improves a building to make it accessible to disabled employees, it shall be considered as falling into depreciation allowance.

It should also be noted that an employer who hires persons with disabilities is exempted from the payment of income tax for expenses listed under Article 65 of the Income Tax Proclamation, including amounts spent to cover the cost of medical treatment, transportation and salaries of employees.[89]

While the income tax law regime can be exploited as discussed above, the Value Added Tax (VAT) Proclamation is explicit with regard to tax incentive schemes. Under the VAT Proclamation, an employer is entitled to tax reduction provided that more than 60 percent of his/her employees are persons with disabilities.[90] This legislation came into force four years before the adoption of the CRPD in 2006. As such, it symbolises the understanding on the part of the government that tax incentive mechanisms are necessary to stimulate employers to hire more persons with disabilities. Yet, it remains unclear how the government really intends to fulfil the purpose considering the fact that a very high threshold has been set under the law with regard to the percentage of disabled employees to be employed in private businesses. In other words, it would be very hard to imagine a single private business or even a government enterprise to engage a number of employees with disabilities that constitutes 60 percent of the total employee workforce. The threshold is unarguably too high and unrealistic.

Moreover, as persons with disabilities will choose some and ignore other businesses in the same vein occupational choices are made by persons without

86 CRPD (n 2) Article 22.
87 Ibid Article 25 (1).
88 Ibid Article 25 (7)(c).
89 Ibid Article 65.
90 Federal Negarit Gazeta, 'Value Added Tax' Proclamation No 285/2002, Article 8(2). See also Federal Negarit Gazeta, 'Council of Ministers Value Added Tax Regulation', Council of Ministers Regulation No.79/2002, Article 32.

disabilities, employers may not be able to meet the 60 percent ceiling even if they wish to. In terms of costs, too, some persons with disabilities may require less assistance than others. In such a case, the cost of the support required could be higher for an organisation that hired fewer persons with disabilities than it would be for another organisation that hired many, hence this would also raise issues of unfairness.

Overall, the tax incentive mechanism as it appears under the income tax laws in general terms, and under the VAT laws with direct reference, is less likely to induce employers to hire persons with disabilities. Except for female disabled employees with regard to whom employers are required to take affirmative actions, there is no quota rule for the employment of persons with disabilities. As such, it appears from the foregoing reading of the relevant legislations that the government relies on rules that barely require private employers to hire persons with disabilities on an equal footing with persons without disabilities. Although such position is not wrong by itself, the CRPD has taken a meticulous move by requiring member states to take positive measures that include quotas and tax incentive mechanisms. The CCRPD has also repeatedly emphasised the importance of positive measures to ensure access to the increasingly competitive labour market.

It is suggested in this research that a tax incentive mechanism, which is also supported by the CCPRD, has huge potential to stimulate the employment of persons with disabilities in the private sector in Ethiopia. For limitations associated with the quota system discussed in this chapter, it is also argued that the tax incentive mechanism provides a stronger platform not only to increase the number of disabled employees, but also to create value and to ensure that qualified persons with disabilities are placed into the right employment positions. As tax incentive mechanisms apply to the employment of qualified disabled employees, they can also be useful to change employers' behaviour, at least on the long run. As such, it is recommended in this study that the government shall revisit its scant tax incentive options and make the regime strong enough to assist private employers in providing reasonable accommodation and thereby in enhancing access opportunities to the labour market for persons with disabilities.

5 Conclusions

The chapter considered that the CRPD recognises the fundamental rights of persons with disabilities, encompassing inclusion into the workforce without discrimination on the basis of disability. The CRPD also underscores that denial of providing reasonable accommodation by itself is considered discrimination, unless the employer shows that providing reasonable accommodation entails an undue burden. Reasonable accommodation is individualised and may vary depending on the needs of the individual person with disabilities. As such, it shall be determined on a case-by-case basis.

The CRPD requires states to take positive measures that can stimulate and enhance the employment of persons with disabilities in the private sector. The CRPD has not limited the nature and type of such positive measures. However, it stipulates that positive measures shall not be used to reinforce prejudices and stereotypes that counter the Convention rights.

Member states have designed positive actions, which take the form of quota rules or incentive mechanisms either with or without other complementary incentive mechanisms, such as access to public funding or legal guarantees against an increase of insurance premiums. The quota system is the most common measure in many jurisdictions. It obliges employers to hire persons with disabilities up to at least a legally fixed percentage. On the other hand, tax incentive mechanisms focus on motivating the employer and on creating value, based on the understanding that persons with disabilities will perform and be productive in the labour market.

There is no sufficient empirically-investigated claim that establishes the comparative advantages of the quota system over tax incentive mechanisms or vice versa. Critics deny that a quota could bring meaningful impact on the employment of persons with disabilities. They also criticise quota rules stating that they may negatively influence employers to offer lower jobs with lower salaries only for the purpose of meeting the quota percentage on employees with disabilities. In its concluding observation, the CRPD Committee has noted that many states have not applied quota rules in the private sector. As such, the Committee recommends that quota rules shall be complemented with incentive mechanisms.

At the same time, there is a growing claim that the tax incentive mechanism as a pro-active approach has stronger potential to change the attitudes of employers and thereby to enhance the employment of persons with disabilities, as opposed to the quota system.

Through the adoption of Proclamation No.568/2008, the Ethiopian government has made a legislative adjustment that very much goes in line with the CRPD. The precise scope of the normative interface and difference between the Proclamation and the CRPD has yet to be studied. Still, as is the case with the CRPD, the Proclamation requires private employers to provide reasonable accommodation, which includes the provision of materials including hiring assistants to 'enable a person with disabilities to perform his/her work.' It also requires that persons with disabilities shall be prioritised in case of a tie in competitive recruitment exams. Moreover, it requires private employers to take affirmative measures to increase the employment of women with disabilities.

However, the Proclamation does not provide strong mechanisms to ensure or stimulate the compliance of private employers with its stipulations. Employers are only fined up to 5000 Ethiopian birr (approximately 155 Euros) for violating disability rights established under the Proclamation. It is submitted here that such a penalty amount is negligible and may even encourage employers to avoid hiring persons with disabilities into their workforce. It is also a notable void in the legislative architecture that the Proclamation does not mention any tax incentive mechanisms that could induce the private sector to hire persons with disabilities.

Except for the VAT Proclamation, therefore, the Ethiopian tax regime does not provide explicit tax incentive mechanisms geared towards hiring persons with disabilities. Even under the VAT Proclamation, only employers who hire persons with disabilities constituting more than 60 percent of their employee workforce are eligible for VAT exemption. This is a threshold that can hardly be met considering the social prejudice and stereotypes that prevail in Ethiopian society. Based on the foregoing analyses, it can be concluded that there are no real and effective tax incentive mechanisms in Ethiopia that motivate private employers to provide reasonable accommodation and incentivise them to hire persons with disabilities.

PART 4

Institutional and Remedial Issues

From 'Rights in Law' to 'Rights in Action': Towards an Effective Remedy for Human Rights Violations through Constitutional Complaint Procedures in Ethiopia

Yemane Kassa Hailu

Abstract

Compared to its predecessors, the Constitution of the Federal Republic of Ethiopia (FDRE) could be labelled as more progressive in recognising an extensive set of fundamental rights and freedoms under its Chapter 3, and for entrenching the same as can be discerned from the rigorous amendment procedures established by the Constitution in relation to human rights provisions. However, textual recognition of fundamental rights and freedoms alone serves no grand purpose unless the rights are effectively enforced. Rights could be claimed to have a true constitutional guarantee only if there is a robust enforcement mechanism and therefore also a worthy custodian of human rights against undue infringement by government actions.

The Constitution entrusts the House of Federation (HoF) as the guardian of its supremacy – including constitutional rights – by making it the ultimate umpire in the determination of constitutional disputes, which quite frequently also involve human rights complaints. This chapter argues that the HoF is far too remote to be considered the appropriate custodian of human rights matters, supposedly being capable on the one hand of transforming them from mere rhetorical ideals to tangibly consumable claims, and on the other hand of acting as an institutional forum for ensuring access to effective remedy through constitutional complaints. Its suitability is questionable not only because of issues related to its institutional competence and lack of political insulation but also because of the timid and human rights restrictive interpretations expounded in its jurisprudence in relation to various claims submitted to its jurisdiction. The analyses in the chapter will present a systemic appraisal of the various decisions of the HoF on human rights issues submitted to it and will engage in comparative scrutiny of the relevant jurisdictions. The main objective of the research at hand is to indicate options for possible legal and institutional reforms to be taken regarding the realisation of the right to an effective remedy for human rights violations through constitutional complaint procedures.

 | DOI:10.1163/9789004415966_013

Keywords

Human Rights – Constitutional Complaint – the House of Federation – Ethiopia

1 Introduction

> In Britain we have no Bill of Rights; we merely have liberty according to law; and we think – truly, I believe – that we do the job better than any country which has a Bill of Rights or a Declaration of the Rights of Man.
>
> Sir IVOR JENNINGS

It was in 1958 that Jennings very succinctly expressed his belief in the vitality of the common law in protecting and enforcing human rights as quoted above.[1] It is not the aim of this piece to discuss the British tradition of valuing liberty or the protection and enforcement of the Bill of Rights. It is rather to show that his statement triggers any rational being to pose a question relevant to the topic: is a constitutional entrenchment of the Bill of Rights enough when we talk about rights and states' commitment of their duty under international human rights instruments? Constitutional recognition of the Bill of Rights, no matter how strong it appears to be, would mean little unless there is a strong and effective enforcement mechanism, and appropriate custodians against possible violations by government branches. A constitutional commitment to human rights is firmly established if there is a robust enforcement mechanism by and through institutions established for that purpose – particularly by and through those institutions empowered to interpret the constitution.

In addition to recognising individual human rights, international human rights law also imposes an obligation on states to ensure, secure or guarantee the effective enjoyment of human rights within their jurisdictions. Such obligation imposed on states is enshrined in so many international human rights treaties and confirmed in state practice and international jurisprudence, that it can be considered to have attained the status of customary international law.[2] Yet, it is a settled fact that domestic legal systems take precedence over international human rights systems in terms of their effectiveness in the

1 W Ivor Jennings, *The Approach to Self-Government, Cambridge* (Cambridge University Press 1958) 20.

2 International Commission of Jurists (ICJ), 'The Right to a Remedy and to Reparation for Gross Human Rights Violations – A Practitioners' Guide' Practitioners' Guide Series No. 2 (International Commission of Jurists, 2006) 23 <https://www.refworld.org/docid/4a7838b42.html> accessed 12 June 2018.

protection of human rights. This is because domestic systems offer a more concrete and accessible forum for victims of violations and have more effective enforcement mechanisms.

In Ethiopia, constitutional rights are not only broadly recognised, but also entrenched; this can be inferred from the more stringent amendment procedure required in comparison to other provisions of the FDRE Constitution.[3] However, it is also evident that the realisation and practical enforcement of such rights go beyond constitutional recognition and entrenchment, and therefore does not seem to be an easy undertaking.

Under the existing arrangement, the position of the ultimate supreme custodian of the federal Constitution, that is responsible for ensuring the enforcement of human rights, is vested in the House of Federation (HoF). This chapter raises the recurring question of whether the HoF could indeed be the most appropriate institutional platform for ensuring the protection and enforcement of human rights recognised under the Constitution and other international and regional human rights instruments to which Ethiopia is a party. The chapter intends to make a modest inquiry into the institutional arrangements existing in Ethiopia in ensuring the protection of human rights in light of the country's obligation under international and regional human rights instruments; it focuses on constitutional complaint procedures as means for realising the *right to an effective remedy* for human rights violations.

In analysing the efficacy of the existing institutional arrangements, the discussions involve both normative and empirical approaches. Normatively, the focus is on a comparative discussion of the domestic enforcement mechanisms of human rights through constitutional complaint processes. Empirically, the appraisal involves the scrutinisation of different cases decided at different times by the HoF and the Council of Constitutional Complaints (CCI) – the objective is thereby to showcase the jurisprudence on constitutional litigation involving human rights violations.

To this end, the chapter is organised into six sections. Preceded by the introductory part, part two presents a brief discussion on the concept of the right to an effective remedy as developed in international, regional, and national human rights regimes in general, and its enforcement through constitutional complaint procedures in particular. By looking into the experience of certain jurisdictions, section three investigates the right to an effective remedy for human rights violations through constitutional complaint procedures. Section four looks at the institutional set-up of constitutional adjudication in Ethiopia.

3 Federal Negarit Gazeta, 'The Constitution of the Federal Democratic Republic of Ethiopia' Proclamation No. 1/1995 (FDRE Constitution), art 105 (1).

Section five indulges in the appraisal of cases adjudicated by the HoF/CCI and endeavours to establish how the institutional design of constitutional adjudication affects the substantive right to an effective remedy for human rights violations in Ethiopia. The chapter concludes by positing that the Ethiopian system for constitutional adjudication is hardly suited to ensuring the right to an effective remedy for human rights violations. The author thus puts forward a possible reform of the institutional design.

2 Enforcement Mechanisms: Access to an Effective Remedy as a Right

International, regional and national human rights regimes commonly impose on states the duty to ensure human rights. This duty entails a multi-dimensional obligation on states which, *inter alia,* includes the duty to adopt necessary legislative measures, the duty to prevent violations, and to respect, protect and promote human rights. In this regard, the relevant human rights institutions, particularly the United Nations (UN) Human Rights Committee, the European Court of Human Rights (ECtHR) and the African Commission on Human and Peoples' Rights (ACHPR) similarly held that states have a duty to take legislative and other measures to give effect to rights, investigate human rights violations and provide effective remedies against violations.[4] The different obligations of states are complementary and not substitutive.[5]

2.1 *The Right to an Effective Remedy: Conceptual Framework*

Conceptually, the evolution of the right to an effective remedy is not limited to the development of international instruments on human rights law. It rather has its roots in the development of an important ideal of constitutional and

4 United Nations (UN) Human Rights Committee (HRC), 'General Comment No. 31 – The Nature of the General Legal Obligation Imposed on States Parties to the Covenant' (21 April 2004) CCPR/C/74/CRP.4/Rev.6 <https://www.refworld.org/docid/478b26ae2.html> accessed 12 June 2018; *Case X and Y v the Netherlands,* Application no. 8978/80 (26 March 1985), para 27 <https://www.coe.int/t/dg2/equality/domesticviolencecampaign/resources/x%20and%20y%20v%20the%20netherlands_EN.asp> accessed 14 June 2018; Case of *Aksoy v Turkey,* 100/1995/606/694 ECtHR (18 December 1996) para 98 <https://www.refworld.org/cases,ECHR,3ae6b67518.html> accessed 12 June 2018; Case of *The Social and Economic Rights Action Center and the Center for Economic and Social Rights v Nigeria* (2001) Communication 155/96, ACHPR, paras 44–48 <http://www.achpr.org/files/sessions/30th/comunications/155.96/achpr30_155_96_eng.pdf> accessed 12 June 2018.

5 ICJ (n 2) 25.

political theory: the rule of law. The need for an effective remedy, when rights and freedoms are violated, has been at the table of constitutional law scholarship at least since the end of the nineteenth century, where Albert V. Dicey, a renowned English liberal, came up with a leading constitutional law account on the rule of law.[6] The rule of law, according to Dicey, was a product of the multitude and totality of 'judicial decisions determining the rights of private persons in particular cases brought before the Courts.'[7] Thus, while the academic debate on the exact meaning of rule of law is still alive, the least common denominator of the ideal, both in its formal and substantive conception, is that there must exist an independent tribunal before which an aggrieved individual requires a remedy for harms and injuries earned due to illegal acts of government.[8]

The significance and development of the term 'remedy' has increased with the evolution of international human rights law. However, the term also features ambiguity to its meaning and scope. This is because it is variedly used by different regional and international human rights instruments and institutions; some limit its meaning only to procedural remedy while others refer to both procedural and substantive remedy. For instance, the American Convention on Human Rights (Pact of San José) and the European Convention of Human Rights (ECHR) guarantee the procedural right to remedy and the right to reparation (substantive remedy) – the focus is put on the procedural aspect of the term.[9] Yet, it can refer to both a procedural as well as a substantive remedy, such as reparation. On the other hand, the right to an effective remedy is recognised under article 2 (3) of the International Covenant on Civil and Political Rights (ICCPR) and interpreted by the Human Rights Committee (HRC) as

6 Brian Z Tamanaha, 'The Dark Side of the Relationship between the Rule of Law and Liberalism' (2008) 33 Journal of Law & Liberty, 534.

7 Ibid. See also Brian Z Tamanaha, *On the Rule of Law: History, Politics, Theory,* (1st edn, Cambridge University Press 2004) 67.

8 For the debate on the formal and substantive conception of rule of law, see Paul Craig, 'Formal and Substantive Conception of the Rule of Law: Analytical framework' in Richard Bellamy (ed), *The Rule of Law and Separation of Powers* (2nd edn, Routledge 2005); see also FA Hayek, 'Freedom and the Rule of law,' in Richard Bellamy (ed), *The Rule of Law and Separation of Powers* (2nd edn, Routledge 2005); see also Joseph Raz, 'The Rule of Law and Its Virtue,' in Richard Bellamy (ed), *The Rule of Law and Separation of Powers* (2nd edn, Routledge 2005).

9 European Convention on Human Rights (signed 4 November 1950, entered into force on 3 September 1953) ETS 5 (ECHR), arts 13 and 41; American Convention on Human Rights 'Pact of San José, Costa Rica' (signed 22 November 1969, adopted 18 July 1978) 1144 UNTS 123, arts 25 and 63, respectively.

entailing the right to reparation, which requires substantive obligation to provide compensation, satisfaction, restitution and rehabilitation.[10]

According to M. Antkowiak, the procedural component of remedy refers to a victim's access to judicial, administrative or other appropriate authorities so that the claim of a right's violation may be fairly heard and decided. The substantive aspect, on the other hand, constitutes the result of those proceedings – that is, the redress or relief afforded to the successful claimant.[11] Be this as it may, the concept of remedy comprises substantive and procedural elements, and both are universally guaranteed. This can be inferred from the jurisprudence developed by regional and international human rights bodies and is depicted in the subsequent section.

2.2 *Right to an Effective Remedy under Regional and International Human Rights Law*

While it is disputed whether the individual's right to remedy for state abuses has attained the rank of customary international law,[12] this right is nevertheless expressly guaranteed by numerous global and regional human rights agreements. The major international and regional human rights treaties all demand an 'effective' remedy or recourse – although they do not provide specific guidance as to how states should undertake measures to redress violations of any character.[13] Consequently, state parties that violated the human rights of individuals within their jurisdiction are required to provide such persons with an appropriate remedy.

While such instruments require an 'effective remedy' or 'just satisfaction,' most fail to stipulate what 'just satisfaction' or 'effective remedy' precisely demand and to what extent such violations should actually be redressed. This, therefore, necessitates a look at the jurisprudence of the relevant institutions regarding the interpretation and/or application of the human rights instruments.

---

10 HRC (n 4) para 16.

11 Thomas M Antkowiak, 'Remedial Approaches to Human Rights Violations: The Inter-American Court of Human Rights and Beyond' (2008) 46(2) Columbia Journal of Transnational Law, 355–356.

12 Ibid.

13 See for instance, the Universal Declaration of Human Rights (adopted 10 December 1948) UNGA Res 217 A(III) (UDHR), art 8; Pact of San José, Costa Rica (n 9) art 25; International Covenant on Civil and Political Rights (adopted 16 December 1966, entry into force 23 March 1976) 999 UNTS 171 (ICCPR), art 2(3); see also the Convention Against Torture and Other Cruel, Inhuman or Degrading Treatment or Punishment (signed 10 December 1984, entry into force 26 June 1987) 1465 UNTS 85; see also ECHR (n 9) art 13.

To begin with the jurisprudence at the global level, there are some UN human rights bodies that examine individual petitions as part of their compliance monitoring functions, which are relevant for determining what an effective remedy refers to. For example, the views of the HRC on the interpretations of article 2 (3) of the ICCPR state that the right to an effective remedy necessarily entails the right to reparation, which in turn requires a substantive obligation to provide compensation, satisfaction, restitution and rehabilitation.[14] In the case of *Birinci Bithash Wiwa and E Tshisekedi Wa Mulumba v Zaire*, the HRC considered the state had to provide the applicants with an effective remedy under article 2(3) of the ICCPR, and 'in particular to ensure that they can effectively challenge these violations before a court of law.'[15] More specifically, the HRC held that mere disciplinary or administrative sanctions are not sufficient in case of serious violations and that the remedy had to be judicial in nature.[16]

Apart from international bodies, the jurisprudence by regional human rights institutions also reveals a trend towards a broader understanding of the right to an effective remedy. At this point, a look at the progressive jurisprudence of the Inter-American Court of Human Rights (IACtHR) is worthy of consideration. Relying on the right to judicial remedy as enshrined under article 28 of the American Declaration of the Rights and Duties of Man (the Bogota Declaration) and articles 25 and 8 (1) of the American Convention on Human Rights, the IACtHR held that victims must have a right to judicial remedies, and 'remedies that must be substantiated in accordance with the rules of due process of law.'[17] In its opinion on the requirements of an effective remedy, the IACtHR ruled that a remedy is ineffective,

> ...when the judicial power lacks the necessary independence to render impartial decisions or the means to carry out its judgments; or in any other situation that constitutes denial of justice, as when there is an

14 HRC (n 4).

15 *Birinci Bithash Wiwa and E Tshisekedi Wa Mulumba v Zaire* (1989) CCPR/C/37/D/241/1987, para 14 <http://www.worldcourts.com/hrc/eng/decisions/1989.11.02_Birhashwirwa_v_Zaire.htm> accessed 19 June 2018.

16 *Nydia Erika Bautista v Colombia* (1993) CCPR/C/55/D/563/1993, para 8.2 <http://hrlibrary.umn.edu/undocs/session55/vws56355.htm> accessed 14 June 2018; *José Vicente and Amado Villafañe Chaparro et al. v Colombia* (1997) CCPR/C/60/D/612/1995, para 8.2 <http://hrlibrary.umn.edu/undocs/612-1995.html> accessed 14 June 2018.

17 *Velásquez Rodríguez v Honduras* (1987) Case 7920, IACtHR, para 91 <http://www.corteidh.or.cr/docs/casos/articulos/seriec_04_ing.pdf> accessed 12 June 2018.

> unjustified delay in the decision; or when, for any reason, the alleged victim is denied access to judicial remedy.[18]

In a similar fashion, the African Commission on Human and Peoples' Rights (ACHPR) interpreted the right to an effective remedy in its Principles and Guidelines on the Rights to Fair Trial and Legal Assistance in Africa and considers that an effective remedy means a judicial remedy. It stated that '[e]very one has the right to an effective remedy by competent national tribunals for acts violating the rights granted by the constitution, by law or by the Charter, notwithstanding that the acts were committed by persons in an official capacity.'[19]

The interpretation of the concept of effective remedy is another jurisprudential source in dealing with the right to an effective remedy. With a slight difference from the ACHPR and the IACtHR, the European Court of Human Rights (ECtHR) held that the right to an effective remedy under article 13 of the ECHR did not require in all instances a judicial remedy and that the scope of the remedy varies with the nature of the right.[20] By requiring that in all cases the remedy must be practical and effective and not illusory, the ECtHR has in practice developed about seven requirements which ultimately correspond to a judicial remedy.[21] First, the remedy must be effective, prompt and accessible. In the case *Airey v Ireland*, the court stated that an effective remedy means that the remedy must not be theoretical and illusory, but provide practical and real access to justice.[22] Second, it must be a remedy before an independent

18 Inter-American Court of Human Rights (IACtHR), 'Advisory Opinion OC-9/87 – Judicial Guarantees in States of Emergency (Arts.27(2), 25 and 8 American Convention on Human Rights)' (6 October 1987) No 9, para 24 <http://www.corteidh.or.cr/docs/opiniones/seriea_09_ing.pdf> accessed 19 June 2018.

19 African Commission on Human and Peoples' Rights (ACHPR), 'Principles and Guidelines on the Right to a Fair Trial and Legal Assistance in Africa,' Principle C(a) <http://www.achpr.org/files/instruments/principles-guidelines-right-fair-trial/achpr33_guide_fair_trial_legal_assistance_2003_eng.pdf> accessed 19 June 2018; see also the case of the *Social and Economic Rights Action Center and the Center for Economic and Social Rights v Nigeria* (n 4) para 61 in which the Commission considered that the State had to ensure 'legal remedies.'

20 *Silver v the United Kingdom*, No. 6205/73, [1983] ECHR, para 113 <https://swarb.co.uk/silver-and-others-v-the-united-kingdom-echr-25-mar-1983/> accessed 18 June 2018. See also *Chahal v the United Kingdom*, Application no. 22414/93 [1996] ECtHR, para 150–51 <https://www.asylumlawdatabase.eu/sites/default/files/aldfiles/Chahal.pdf> accessed 16 June 2018.

21 ICJ (n 2) 55–56.

22 *Airey v Ireland* (1979) 2 EHRR 305, para 24 <https://www.escr-net.org/caselaw/2006/airey-v-ireland-32-eur-ct-hr-ser-1979-1979-2-ehrr-305> accessed 14 June 2018.

authority with no interference by authorities against which the complaint is brought.[23] Third, the victim should have access to legal counsel and if necessary also to free legal assistance that makes the system simple and accessible for those in need of remedy.[24] Fourth, the remedy must be capable of leading to relief, including reparation and compensation. Fifth, the right to remedy must be prompt, effective and attended by an impartial investigation. Sixth, the remedy must be expeditious and enforceable by competent authorities. Finally, the remedy must be judicial in case of gross human rights violations.

3 Right to Effective Remedy through Constitutional Complaint

As discussed above, international human rights law imposes a duty on states to ensure the effective enjoyment of human rights which entail, among others, that the state must adopt all necessary legislative and other measures to give effect to the rights guaranteed.[25] Thus, establishing an effective institutional and legal arrangement that ensures a remedy for human rights violations at the national level is at the heart of discharging such duty by states.

Even though human rights norms have been largely internationalised, their effective implementation remains almost exclusively national. In fact, there are only a few relevant international courts and tribunals when it comes to redressing human rights violations. However, one may still question whether a universalised system of human rights remedies, which apply uniformly at both the national and international levels, is likely or desirable. This is due to the fact that international courts and tribunals differ from national authorities in their powers, structure, resources and context, not to mention also that they differ from one another.[26] Moreover, contemporary international and regional human rights regimes are more supervisory mechanisms that monitor relations

23 There are some instruments that explicitly put forward such a requirement, such as International Convention for the Protection of All Persons from Enforced Disappearance (signed 20 December 2006, entry into force 23 December 2010) 2716 UNTS 3, art 13 or the Vienna Declaration and Programme of Action (adopted 25 June 1993), art 27 <https://www.ohchr.org/EN/ProfessionalInterest/Pages/Vienna.aspx> accessed 18 June 2018.

24 HRC, 'Concluding Observations of the Human Rights Committee – Poland,' (2 December 2004) CCPR/CO/82/POL, para 14 <https://www.refworld.org/docid/42ce96324.html> accessed 18 June 2018.

25 ICJ (n 2) 23.

26 Gerald L Neuman, 'Bi-Level Remedies for Human Rights Violations' (2014) 55(2) Harvard International Law Journal, 324–325.

between states and citizens, thus they are not alternatives to a fundamentally state-related conception of human rights implementation.[27]

As a result, remedy options at international and regional forums have their own problems. Unlike domestic courts, international and regional human rights tribunals generally lack coercive powers to ensure obedience to their orders – with a noted exception of the ECtHR. Furthermore, they impose a greater procedural cost on victims throughout the stages leading to the entry of the tribunal's remedial order.[28] It is established, at least in principle, that domestic human rights regimes are preferred over international human rights systems in terms of effectiveness in the protection of human rights; they offer a more accessible forum for victims of violations and are endowed with more effective enforcement mechanisms.

Given also the requirement that the victim must exhaust domestic remedies, or must show that exhaustion would be futile before an international tribunal adjudicates on a case,[29] it is obvious that the existence of vigorous institutional and legal arrangements at the national level should be the priority for pursuing an effective remedy in cases of human rights violations.

Taking the main theme of this chapter on constitutional complaint mechanisms, the mere existence of an institution by itself does not suffice unless the scope of the remedies is adequate enough for the protection and enforcement of human rights. In this regard, the Constitution of South Africa clearly provides for a remedy that any person might receive from the constitutional court. In addition to declaring any law or conduct inconsistent with the Constitution as being invalid to the extent of the inconsistency, the court is also empowered, when doing so, to make any order that is 'just and equitable.' This includes an order limiting the retrospective effect of a declaration of invalidity or suspending a declaration of invalidity for any period and on any conditions to allow the competent authority to correct the defect.[30]

Furthermore, decisions rendered by the ECtHR reveal that restricting the legal scope of a remedy through a constitutional complaint mechanism may make it ineffective in certain circumstances. In the case *Savics v Latvia*, the

27 The state-related inception of human rights can also be inferred from the substance of recognised rights, where the implementation of some rights, such as rights related to political participation, obligation to provide education, social insurance, etc. are virtually applicable to citizens only. For more on this, see Jack Donnelly, *Universal Human Rights in Theory and Practice* (2nd edn, Cornel University Press 2003) 34.

28 Neuman (n 26) 324–325, 337.

29 Ibid 337.

30 The Constitution of the Republic of South Africa (signed 18 December 1996, entry into force 4 February 1997) Act No. 108/1996, section 172 (1) a & b.

ECtHR stated that a remedy offered by a constitutional court in relation to individual complaints was ineffective where the alleged violation resulted not from the unconstitutionality of an applied legal provision as such, but from an erroneous application or interpretation of a provision whose content was not unconstitutional.[31]

Moreover, general remedies furnished through constitutional complaint procedures must be effective, sufficient and accessible. Regarding this, the ECtHR held that a general remedy by way of a constitutional complaint, the scope of which is limited to points of law alone, would be ineffective for it 'results in an actual bar to the examination of the applicant's substantive claims' by the constitutional court.[32]

4 The Right to an Effective Remedy and Constitutional Complaint Mechanisms in Ethiopia

Human rights are most securely protected in two scenarios: where they are entrenched as fundamental norms of a supreme constitution through a comprehensive Bill of Rights with strict amendment requirements, and where they are enforceable by courts of law or similar tribunals. The Ethiopian Constitution recognises a fairly broad catalogue of human rights (encompassing economic, social, cultural, civil and political rights) under Chapter Three; the contents of the rights protected as fundamental rights and freedoms are more or less similar to internationally recognised standards of protection of human rights, with the Constitution, in some instances, offering a more progressive normative order than the international system.[33] This is, in particular, true with regard to the right to self-determination, the right to sustainable development, and the rights to a clean and healthy environment. It also includes secession – thereby making it, according to one author,[34] the only African constitution with a right to self-determination. The Constitution further incorporates economic, social and cultural rights both generically (under article 41) and in substantive detail, covering family, marital, personal, property, labour and developmental rights.

31 *Savics v Latvia* (2012) Application No. 17892, para 113–115 <http://31.24.192.35/downloadetclawfile/758> accessed 15 June 2018.

32 *Zborovsky v Slovakia* (2012) Application No. 14325/08, paras 51–54 <https://dejure.org/dienste/vernetzung/rechtsprechung?Gericht=EGMR&Datum=23.10.2012&Aktenzeichen=14325/08> accessed 12 June 2018.

33 FDRE Constitution (n 3) Chapter 3, arts 14–44.

34 Adem Kassie Abebe, 'Towards More Liberal Standing Rules to Enforce Constitutional Rights in Ethiopia' (2010) 10 African Human Rights Law Journal 408.

It is important to note that the constitutional entrenchment of human rights is clearly established, as inferred from the strict amendment procedures distinctly applicable to Chapter Three of the FDRE Constitution.[35] The Constitution also recognises a broad list of socio-economic rights under chapter 10 dealing with 'National Policy Principles and Objectives' although their enforcement would indeed require a compassionate government.[36] These objectives, among others, entail the government to promote self-rule and equality of the people, to formulate policies that ensure equal economic opportunities and benefits, and to adopt policies that aim at providing access to public health and education, clean water, housing, food and social security to the extent the country's resources permit.[37]

Moreover, article 13 (1) of the FDRE Constitution establishes the duty of all federal and state legislative, executive and judicial organs to respect and enforce fundamental rights and freedoms. In line with this, article 9 of the Constitution declares the Constitution as the supreme law of the land and furthermore stipulates that any law, customary practice or decision of an organ of state or a public official who contravenes it, shall be of no effect.

However, while the elevation of norms might generally create deterrence, such constitutional recognition or protection of human rights cannot on its own fully guarantee that human rights are well-entrenched in terms of enforcement. Thus, a detailed inquiry into the available enforcement of the Bill of Rights through constitutional complaint procedures offered under the Constitution and other relevant laws becomes imperative.

Constitutional complaints are generally subsidiary because applicants are often required to first exhaust accessible and effective remedies available before courts of law; however, some countries provide an exception to this rule.[38]

35 FDRE Constitution (n 3) art 105 (1).

36 This is because they are deemed to be non-justiciable. In fact, there are contending views on the justiciability of socio-economic rights among scholars: some argue that they are not wholly out of the reach of courts and may also be used as tools that guide the interpretation of fundamental rights and freedoms. See Sisay Alemahu, 'The Justiciability of Human Rights in the Federal Democratic Republic of Ethiopia' (2008) 8(2) African Human Rights Law Journal, 277. See also Tsegaye Regassa, 'Making Legal Sense of Human Rights: The Judicial Role in Protecting Human Rights in Ethiopia' (2009) 3(2) Mizan Law Review.

37 FDRE Constitution (n 3) arts 85–92.

38 For instance, an exception to the general rule is provided when its application would cause serious and irreparable harm to the applicant in countries such as Azerbaijan, Germany, Latvia, and Slovenia or in particular types of complaint, such as excessive length of proceedings before ordinary courts as in, for example, Croatia and Serbia. See Council of Europe (CoE), 'Guide to Good Practice in Respect of Domestic Remedies

Still, it should be noted that even this general rule does not seem to be conceivable in the Ethiopian context. This is because constitutional adjudication (largely but not exclusively focusing on testing the constitutionality of government actions or inaction) remains within the exclusive mandate of the HoF. Courts of law as such do not have such far-reaching power.[39] Thus, the constitutional complaint procedure remains the most important mechanism for ensuring access to an effective remedy when the constitutionality of government actions or inaction is questioned – especially in relation to the violation of recognised human rights. This is of course not to say that constitutional adjudication and the quest for redress of human rights violations are triggered only in connection with challenging the constitutionality or otherwise of government actions; a host of private relationships with an impact on constitutionally guaranteed rights could as well provide grounds for constitutional disputes and be litigated both before courts of law as well as the HoF.

In relation to procedures availed by the HoF, therefore, the main issue is how effective the remedy that individuals receive through constitutional complaint procedures is when human rights are violated either by laws or government actions or the conduct of other private individuals. This requires an investigation of the whole system in Ethiopia – taking into account key factors that would help in the determination of the effectiveness of remedies in the conventional sense. This includes rules relating to standing, complaint procedures, and the nature and scope of a remedy that individuals eventually have. A modest inquiry in this chapter will focus on the last part alone – involving the institutional set-up and jurisprudence of the HoF and the CCI.[40]

4.1 *The Institutional Framework: The HoF as the 'Ultimate Custodian of Human Rights'*

It is submitted above that the remedies availed in the context of constitutional complaints submitted to the HoF show a general character. For any remedy to

(adopted by the Committee of Ministers on 18 September 2013)' (Directorate General – Human Rights and Rule of Law, 2013) 47–48 <https://www.echr.coe.int/Documents/Pub_coe_domestics_remedies_ENG.pdf> accessed 14 June 2018.

39 See FDRE Constitution (n 3) cumulative readings of art 62 (1), art 83 (1) and art 84 (2). In fact, the jurisdictional boundary of courts vis-à-vis the HoF regarding constitutional interpretation has been a subject of academic debate in the Ethiopian discourse on constitutional law . For details on this, see Yemane Kassa, 'The Judiciary and Its Interpretative power in Ethiopia: A Case study of the Ethiopian Revenue and Customs Authority' (Addis Ababa University, November 2011) 54–69 <https://chilot.me/wp-content/uploads/2013/01/the-judiciary-and-its-interpretive-power-in-ethiopia.pdf> accessed 15 June 2018.

40 For details on complaint procedures and standing rules on constitutional complaints, see Abebe (n 34).

be effective, it has to guarantee, among others, the right to vindicate one's right before an independent and impartial body, with a view to obtaining recognition of the violation, a cessation of the violation if it is continuing, and adequate reparation.[41] It also guarantees access to an independent authority which has the power to decide whether a human rights violation has taken place or is taking place and can offer an appropriate remedy in the sense of ordering cessation or reparation.

4.1.1 The Nature and Identity of the HoF as a Neutral Umpire

The nature and identity of the HoF are contentious, which inevitably poses a question of whether the HoF is an organ capable of delivering an effective remedy for violation of human rights. The main issue that recurs in this regard involves the question of whether the HoF, generally regarded as the second chamber under the Constitution, could as well be portrayed as a neutral umpire in constitutional adjudication proceedings. The questions are framed by looking at the powers it has, its composition, selection procedures of the members, the interest the HoF represents, and the identity of members of the HoF.

Looking at the powers, the HoF is not, strictly speaking, a second legislative chamber in the federal arrangement; yet, it is vested with key political, policy and occasional/indirect legislation-related functions which are not only uncommon but also do not prevail in the experience of other organs wielding constitutional adjudication powers in many parts of the world. For instance, the HoF is granted the power to participate in the amendment of the Constitution as well as in the determination of undesignated taxation powers, it can recommend to the House of Peoples Representatives (HoPR) the enactment of laws on civil matters, order federal intervention in regional states, and prepare the allocation formula on the federal subsidy given to states and the division of revenue from joint tax sources.[42]

The HoF's composition is also based on the proportional representation system whereby all nationality groups are guaranteed automatic representation – with those nationality groups with a larger population being given more seats;[43] this makes it a deviant institutional platform in terms of one of the most common objectives of constitutional dispute resolution organs, that is, serving as a counter-majoritarian institution.

41 ICJ (n 2) 43.

42 FDRE Constitution (n 3) arts 104 and 105, art 99, art 55 (6), art 62 (9), and art 62 (7), respectively.

43 Ibid art 61 (2).

The selection of members of the HoF entirely depends on the wish of political institutions: the state councils of each of the regional states in the Federation.[44] The interest the HoF represents is the 'Nations, Nationalities, and Peoples' of Ethiopia, an anthropological conception that focuses on group rights, and not individual rights.[45] Furthermore, the Constitution does not provide who is eligible to be a member of the HoF. In practice, however, almost all members come from the political parties administering the federal and state governments and include presidents of regional states, speakers and vice-speakers of regional state councils, as well as federal and regional ministers.

From this it follows that it would be very difficult to consider the HoF as a neutral interpreting organ capable of ensuring an effective remedy for human rights violations. This holds particularly true when considering that such violations are perpetuated by agencies linked to various layers of governments at the national and regional levels. The HoF is rather a political institution which mostly renders a political interpretation of the Constitution in constitutional adjudication processes. While human rights values and norms may inform its decisions depending on the nature of each particular case and the parties to a dispute, in most cases – including in some instances where private disputes involving individual citizens are considered, the HoF has demonstrated clear proclivity to base its decisions on pragmatic political exigencies. Such an approach in the disposition of constitutional disputes is exhibited not only in the readings of individual decisions rendered so far, it is also clearly provided in the Minutes of the Constitutional Assembly. The Minutes highlight that the HoF is not a perfect fit within the power structure of the three branches of government and has to interpret the Constitution as 'representative' of the Nations, Nationalities and Peoples of Ethiopia.[46] Based on this factual setting alone, it suffices to hold that the HoF's institutional suitability and credibility as independent and impartial constitutional arbiter capable of offering an effective remedy for human rights violations is inevitably undermined.

Generally, the same could be submitted in relation to the Constitutional Commission of Inquiry (CCI) as well. The CCI gives technical legal support to the HoF and is composed of eleven members, nine of whom are appointed through the recommendation and designation of two political institutions; the

44 Ibid art 61 (3).

45 Ibid art 61 (1).

46 'Minutes of the Constitutional Assembly of the Transitional Government of Ethiopia' Version 5 (1–4 December 1994), discussions on art 62 (1) as cited in DB Wagasa, 'All about Words on the Procedure of Constitutional Interpretation in Ethiopia: A Comment on Melaku Fanta Case' (2015) 4(1) Oromia Law Journal 207, 213 <https://www.ajol.info/index.php/olj/article/download/120620/110070> accessed 14 June 2018.

HoPR (six members) and the HoF (three members).[47] Given that Ethiopia follows a parliamentary system wherein legislative and executive powers are blended, and considering that currently all parliamentary seats are taken by the Ethiopian People's Revolutionary Democratic Front (EPRDF) and its affiliates, the huge role played by the two houses in selecting members of CCI is likely to rather be based on party loyalty than on professional competence and moral standing of nominees, as required under the Constitution.[48] This, in turn, poses uncertainty and raises serious concerns as to whether the CCI interprets cases involving human rights violations based on human rights values and norms or on political exigency/expediency. This obviously has far-reaching implications on the effectiveness of remedies provided through constitutional complaint procedures.[49]

4.1.2 Institutional Efficacy

Notwithstanding issues of impartiality and independence, the institutional strength of the HoF to discharge its constitutional mandate is also important when dealing with the right to an effective remedy for human rights violations. As a comparative study reveals, the task of constitutional interpretation and adjudication, whether such is carried through the agency of constitutional courts, supreme courts or constitutional counsels, is a full-time occupation that requires substantial devotion, commitment and knowledge of the law. This is simply because the institutional set-up and efficacy has a strong bearing in ensuring the protection of human rights and rule of law, and in shaping the constitutional jurisprudence of a given country. The institutional efficacy of an umpiring organ may be manifested in different ways, including, among others,

47 FDRE Constitution (n 3) art 82 (2).

48 If one looks at members of the CCI based on the cases decided from 2014 to 2016, it can be noted that many are either party members or closely affiliated to the ruling party. To mention some, Getachew Ambaye (member of the Ethiopian People's Revolutionary Democratic Front (EPRDF), Attorney General of the Federal Government), Demitu Hambisa (EPRDF member, former Minster of Science and Technology Minister, currently Minister of Cabinet Affairs), Hashim Towfiq (EPRDF member, former Minister at the Ministry of Justice), Fasil Nahum (Advisor of the Prime Minister since the adoption of the Constitution), Eshetu W/semayat (Former Attorney General of the Ethiopian Revenues and Customs Authority).

49 The possibility of the legislature's influence over the system of constitutional adjudication can also be inferred from the fact that the legislature (HoPR) is the one who enacted the two laws that detailed the constitutional mandates of the CCI and the HoF on constitutional interpretation. An organ that is going to be checked by the HoF for constitutionality of its acts, enacts the procedures, rules, and principles of interpretation the HoF must follow.

by looking at the level of expertise of judges/members on the subject matter of constitutional litigation, the scope of the institution's mandate, and the procedures adopted for discharging the mandates.

A brief look at the jurisprudential trajectory in Ethiopia seems to reveal that the levels of efficiency expected from the HoF and the CCI in discharging a constitutional interpretation in general, and an adjudication of human rights violations in particular, seems to be very contestable. Three key factors can be stated for this. First, the task of constitutional interpretation in Ethiopia is a part-time undertaking. This is because, for one thing, almost all members of the HoF and the CCI are full-time employees in other government positions. Second, members of the HoF and the CCI are required to only meet two to four times a year, respectively.[50] In particular, given that the HoF has other constitutional mandates, it is hardly easy for it to speedily and properly dispose of constitutional complaints by convening twice a year. This inevitably affects the right to an effective remedy for human rights violations not only because its accessibility is limited, but also because the quality of decisions and deliberations on constitutional complaints is also compromised.

Furthermore, the level of expertise the HoF possesses does not seem to be adequate enough to accomplish such complicated tasks as are entailed in constitutional interpretation and adjudication; members of the HoF are not required to be educated in law or political philosophy. While it is true that the CCI is established to give support to the HoF on the legal technicalities of constitutional interpretation and adjudication, it is equally evident that the CCI's role is extremely limited to only giving recommendations,[51] not to mention that its political insulation is also contestable. Since the final say is reserved to the HoF, which passes decisions through majority rule,[52] it is also plausible to raise the concern that valid constitutional reasoning rendered by the CCI may be overshadowed by majority decisions that are solely motivated by political and policy interests of the government. This ultimately puts access to an effective remedy in constitutional adjudications in an utter state of uncertainty.

50 Federal Negarit Gazeta, 'Consolidation of the House of Federation and the Definition of its Powers and Responsibilities Proclamation' Proclamation No. 251/2001 (HoF Proclamation), art 13 (1).

51 FDRE Constitution (n 3) art 84 (1); See also Federal Negarit Gazeta, 'Council of Constitutional Inquiry (CCI) Proclamation' Proclamation No. 798/2013 (CCI Proclamation), art 3 (1) and art 12 (1 b).

52 The HoF Proclamation (n 50) art 46 (3).

5 The Jurisprudence on Constitutional Complaints of Human Rights in Ethiopia

In the preceding sections, an attempt was made to present an analysis of the institutional context of constitutional interpretation in Ethiopia and how such context affects decisions involving human rights issues. As a follow-up, this section investigates cases of constitutional complaints on human rights entertained by the HoF/CCI. To demonstrate whether or not the jurisprudence on constitutional interpretation is adequate enough in ensuring an effective remedy for human rights violations, one important, albeit not exclusive factor is considered: the techniques of constitutional interpretation the HoF adopts when human rights are said to have been violated; this largely focuses on whether or not the HoF follows a generous or a human rights-restrictive approach.

In reality, a constitutional interpretation involves various theories, principles and approaches depending on the specific contexts of the constitutional systems. However, this piece is interested in seeing only the approaches adopted by the HoF/CCI when interpreting government actions and laws that derogate or limit human rights – hence, another branch of constitutional adjudication that involves private parties is left out. Particularly in Ethiopia, such government actions may manifest in the form of making rights non-justiciable, by enacting laws with finality clauses, by imposing actions that directly or impliedly violate/restrict protected rights, and by a broad delegation of law-making powers to the executive.

Human rights are not absolute and they may be restricted in various ways including suspension, restriction or derogations and for various legitimate reasons. The rights may be subject to limitation for the better enforcement of other rights or to achieve a greater social good.[53] The problem is, however, the way such limitations are imposed or exercised by concerned authorities, which often raise issues related to the constitutional legitimacy of the limitations in the first place. This becomes a pressing problem when a constitution does not contain basic standards through which the power to impose limitations may be justifiably exercised, which is also known as a 'general limitation clause,'[54] or when a constitution provides specific grounds but fails to also offer standards for evaluating the proportionality or necessity of such limitations. The Constitution of South Africa is illustrative in this regard as it provides that any

53 Regassa (n 36) 313–314.

54 General limitation clauses are 'limits to limitations' that require the fulfilment of certain prescribed standards before exercising the power to limit rights. See ibid 314.

limitation on the exercise of fundamental rights should be made only to the extent it is reasonable and justifiable in an *open democratic society* based on human dignity, equality, freedom and on considerations of other relevant facts.[55]

According to the jurisprudence on constitutional adjudication, when the constitutionality of government action is questioned for limiting or derogating human rights, one of the core standards applied is whether or not there are better policy choices for the legislature with the least impact on the enjoyment of the right, other than the law that has already been adopted.[56] This is just one aspect of the series of stringent safeguards developed by the HRC and the ECtHR to assess legality, proportionality and necessity in adopting any restrictive human rights laws or measures. If limitations on fundamental rights are to be legitimate, they must achieve a benefit that is proportional to the costs of the limitation. However, if there *are less restrictive*, but *equally effective* alternatives other than the chosen methods, the limitation is not proportionate, and hence unacceptable.[57]

Such an approach of strict interpretation of laws that purports to pose limitations on fundamental rights is adopted by the South African Constitutional Court. In *S v Zuma*, the Court adopted a pro-right and strict interpretation of any limitations on rights saying '…[an interpretation of the Bill of Rights should be] "generous" and "purposive" and "give…expression to the underlying values of the Constitution."'[58] This is in line with the South African Constitution, which requires the common law and customary law to be developed and all legislation to be interpreted to 'promote the spirit, purpose and objectives of the Bill of Rights.'[59]

---

55 Under Section 36 of the Constitution of South Africa (n 30), it is provided that limitation on rights can only be exercised by taking into account the extent of the right to be limited, the importance of the purpose of limitation, the nature and extent of the limitation, the relation between the limitation and the purpose, and less restrictive means to achieve the purpose. For details on this, see Yemane Kassa, 'Executive Override of Judicial Power: In Search of Constrained Exercise of Delegated Legislations in Ethiopia' (2015) 27(1) Journal of Ethiopian Law (emphasis added).

56 See J De Waal, I Currie, and G Erasmus, *The Bill of Rights Handbook* (4th edn, Lansdowne 1999) 144–162.

57 Ibid (emphasis added).

58 As employed by the Court, the term 'generous' interpretation is interpretation in favour of rights and against their restrictions.' Whereas 'purposive' interpretation is 'aimed at teasing out the core values that underpin the listed fundamental rights in an open and democratic society…;' See ibid 148–150.

59 Constitution of South Africa (n 30), section 39 (2).

The interpretation approach the HoF/CCI adheres to not only lacks any systemic orientation and consistency, but it also seems to be questionable as it tends to be human rights-restrictive – often undermining the very objective of the Constitution and essence of the constitutional Bill of Rights. In one of the most recent cases, *Agency for Government Houses v Ayele Habteyes,* the HoF/CCI passed a decision that clearly contradicts the equality clause provided under article 25 of the Constitution under a debatable guise.[60] The case arose when the Agency terminated a lease contract it had with the respondent for the reason that the latter violated his contractual obligation. Article 5 (4) of the contract between the parties states that 'a person who leased a business house from the Agency has a duty to inform the agency in person when he wants to lease or assign his business to a third party.'[61] Accordingly, the Agency terminated contracts it had with many tenants who leased their businesses to other people without informing the Agency.

Following the measure, the tenant (respondent) lodged a case to courts against the Agency by asserting two important arguments. First, the applicant did not only lease the house (building) to the third party, but in addition to his business also his business license, business name, goodwill, machineries and other equipment relevant for the business. Second, the clause in the contract on which the Agency relied to terminate the contract is void for it contradicts article 145 (1) of the Commercial Code, which clearly contains contractual clauses that prohibit tenants from leasing, selling or assigning their business. The case reached the Federal Supreme Court Cassation Division where the Court decided by confirming the tenant's claim that he did not lease the house, but rather his business and stating that '*business lease, by its nature, content, and legal effect, is quite different from lease of a business house.*'[62] Accordingly, the Court decided the Agency's unilateral termination of the contract by relying on a precondition written in the contract is unlawful because inserting such precondition is prohibited under the Commercial Code,[63] which states:

---

60 *Agency for Government Houses v Ayele Habteyes*, Decision of the HoF (unpublished, 15 Ginbot 2008).

61 *Agency for Government Houses V Ayele Habteyes*, File No.96786, Federal Supreme Court Cassation Division (unpublished, 18 Miazia 2007) (author's own translation from Amharic).

62 The Court asserted that what was leased is a business, which is clearly compatible with the definition given to 'business' under the FDRE Commercial Code; See Negarit Gazeta – Gazette Extraordinary, 'Commercial Code of the Empire of Ethiopia' Proclamation No. 166/1960, arts 124, 126 and 127. See also ibid.

63 The Court stated that freedom of contract is legitimate to the extent that its objects (terms and conditions) are not contrary to what is provided under the FDRE Civil Code which states, 'The object of a contract shall be freely determined by the parties subject to

> Notwithstanding the provisions of Art.2959 of the Civil Code, any provision in the contract of lease which prevents the lessee from assigning the contract of lease or from sub-letting the premises to the person who buys his business, or which makes such assignment or sub-lease dependent on the lessor's consent, *shall be of no effect.*[64]

The Agency appealed to the HoF by providing complicated claims, which can be briefly summarised as follows: The Agency is mandated through its establishment Proclamation to 'give and execute expulsion orders to tenants of government houses who have breached their obligations under their lease contracts…'[65] To this end, the Agency issued directives which require tenants to inform the Agency when they lease their business, with a view of controlling those tenants who further or sub-lease a house they rented from the Agency to third parties by increasing the lease price, yet without adding any value to the house. This ultimately amounts to a so-called 'rent-seeking' transaction. Thus, the decision by the Court not only prevents the government's policy and commitment to fighting rent-seeking; in effect, it also violates the constitutional mandate of the legislature by undermining the powers given to the Agency under the Establishment Proclamation.[66]

The HoF approved the recommendation given by a majority of members of the CCI and invalidated the decision given by the Cassation Division because of its unconstitutionality.[67] The main reasons of the final decision can be summarised as follows:[68] First, one of the rationales for the adoption of Proclamation No. 555/2007 is fighting rent-seeking practices. To this end, the Agency is entrusted under article 6 (3) of the Proclamation to administer government houses, which includes leasing houses to individual persons. It is in line with this that the Agency enacted a directive and took measures against tenants that sub-lease houses without informing the Agency. Such act of tenants is considered rent-seeking, for they sub-leased houses by adding price and yet

such restrictions and prohibitions as are provided by law.' See Negarit Gazeta – Extraordinary Issue, 'Civil Code of the Empire of Ethiopia' Proclamation No.165/1960, art 1711.

64 FDRE Commercial Code (n 62) (emphasis added).

65 Federal Negarit Gazeta, 'Agency for Government Houses Establishment Proclamation' Proclamation No. 555/2007 (Establishment Proclamation), art 6 (3).

66 The Agency claimed the decision violates its mandate given pursuant to the Establishment Proclamation (ibid) and alleges that this disregards the constitutional mandate of the HoPR to make laws, and therefore requires constitutional interpretation.

67 It is important to note that four of the eleven members of the CCI registered their dissenting opinion upholding the decision of the Cassation Division with very strong arguments.

68 *Agency v Ayele Habteyes* (n 60).

without adding value. Thus, the decision of the Cassation Division quashing the action of the Agency is contrary to the government policy of *fighting rent seeking practices* in the economy.

Second, Proclamation No. 555/2007 is a recent and specific law in terms of governing the issue at hand and the Commercial Code is too old to rely on when there is contradiction between the two legislative frameworks. Thus, it is wrong for the Court to rely on the Commercial Code to address the case in its docket. Third, the HoPR enacts laws in order to *enforce government policy,* of which this Proclamation is one. Therefore, it is a big mistake of the Cassation Division to ignore such a Proclamation and thereby to undermine the constitutional mandate of the legislature, which the Constitution declared as the *highest organ of the federal government* (parliamentary supremacy) under article 50 (3).

Finally, rejecting the directives and quashing the measure taken by the Agency based on readings of the Commercial Code while knowing that there is a new law (proclamation) that empowers the Agency to do so violates the judicial mandate under article 79 (3), where judges are required to exercise their functions in full independence and directed solely by the law.

The decision of the HoF could be contested on the basis of various grounds. First, the key arguments on which the HoF relied to make its final decision are new and politically-crafted. For instance, claims which portray the decision of the Court as contrary to a directive issued by the Agency and undermine the government's policy and commitment of fighting rent-seeking practice were not part of the appeal brought before the Cassation Division. Second, the decision can be questioned based on the Constitution itself and the basic principles and theories often adopted in constitutional interpretation. In this regard, it would be adequate to rely on the dissenting opinion, which provides strong arguments against the final decision made by the majority of the CCI members. From the very beginning, there was no need for constitutional interpretation for two main reasons. First, the issues are confined to the interpretation of laws – especially as to whether or not the Directive can repeal article 145 (1) of the Commercial Code and whether there is any contradiction between the two legislations (Proclamation No. 555/2007 and the Commercial Code).[69]

69 On both questions, the dissenting opinion stated the Agency does not have any authority to enact a directive that will have the effect of repealing a pre-existing higher law (the Commercial Code), which is specifically relevant to the issues at hand. Furthermore, there is no contradiction between the two legislations for the Commercial code is equally applicable to all commercial transactions, whether such is made between private individuals or a government agency and individuals. Nor does the Establishment Proclamation (n 65) provide for any indication of amending the specific provision of the Commercial

Furthermore, it is unacceptable to give a constitutional interpretation not only for making a general assumption that there are rent-seeking tenants that sub-lease a house by increasing rent price, but also the very issue of rent-seeking cannot be an issue worthy of constitutional interpretation.[70] Furthermore, the Agency does not, in its constitutional complaint, specifically mention which constitutional provision is violated and why constitutional interpretation had become necessary in its context.

It could be contended that the above decision reveals the HoF/CCI did not develop or adhere to any standards or theories of constitutional interpretation. In the absence of specific guiding tools, it seems the HoF only made a political interpretation of the issues at hand and applied the same to the Constitution, which can be established in three ways. First, the interpretation is backed by political motives, not only for relying on the political economy concept of 'rent seeking,' but for the fact that the measure by the Agency was taken as a consequence of the government's campaign of fighting rent seeking at that specific time.[71] Second, it admitted the case without following the proper complaint procedure for constitutional interpretation. This is to say, as mentioned previously, that the question of the rent-seeking act by the tenant (respondent) was never an issue before the Cassation Division. Thus, a constitutional complaint based on such a cause of action could not be pursued as challenging the constitutionality of the Court's decision on an issue which the Court did not address in the first place.[72]

Moreover, the decision is a clear indication that the HoF is re-endorsing parliamentary supremacy in a way that challenges the supremacy of the Constitution itself. This is particularly true when considering one of the reasons submitted for quashing the decision of the Court, which says 'It is, therefore, a big mistake for the Cassation Division to ignore such Proclamation which ultimately violates the Constitutional status of the legislature which the Constitution declared as the *highest organ* of the federal government.'[73] Such reasoning,

Code. The argument seems to be plausible if one notes that Proclamation No. 555/2007 (n 65) is a Proclamation which only provides for the establishment of the Agency together with its mandates.

70 *Agency v Ayele Habteyes* (n 60).

71 Today, rent-seeking gets the most prominent space in the politics of the nation – especially by the ruling party, the EPRDF.

72 This is because, the complaint procedure requires that of cases entertained by a court of law, only legal issues necessary for constitutional interpretation shall the party concerned submit to the CCI/HoF. Thus, the CCI/HoF not only failed to employ sound interpretation approaches, it also violated its own rules of complaint procedure. See the CCI Proclamation (n 51) art 4 (4).

73 See *Agency v Ayele Habteyes* (n 60).

coupled with the statement above and portraying the Court as renegading from its judicial mandate,[74] is not only a wrong accusation of the judiciary and its institutional independence; it also embarrasses the judges involved in the case – and may well constitute intervention on personal independence of the judiciary.

Apart from the technical inappropriateness in interpretation, the decision by the HoF/CCI also violates one of the fundamental rights provided under the Constitution: the right to equal protection.[75] As discussed above, the Commercial Code and relevant provisions of the Civil Code govern any contracts related to commercial transactions irrespective of the identity of the parties (government agencies or private individuals). However, the decision of the HoF clearly violates the equal protection clause by invoking political and policy grounds to favour an unwarranted measure taken by the Agency against the right to equal protection that tenants are entitled to.

While it would be wrong to make far-reaching conclusions based on the reading of a few cases in constitutional interpretation and adjudication, the extent to which the CCI and the HoF are exposed to political influence or are guided by such considerations when interpreting the Constitution can be established from other cases as well. Particularly, it could be noted from the jurisprudence that the HoF/CCI have held different decisions on similar constitutional claims depending on whether the government is the applicant or the defendant.

For instance, very recently, the HoF/CCI applied a generous interpretation of human rights in the case of *Federal Ethics and Anti-Corruption Commission (FEAC) v Melaku Fenta* merely because the unconstitutionality of provisions of the Federal Courts Proclamation and the Revised Federal Ethics and Anti-Corruption Commission Special Procedure and Rule of Evidence Proclamation are contested by the FEAC. According to the two laws, any proceeding related to corruption crimes falls within the first instance jurisdiction of the Federal High Court – except those where federal ministers are among the list, which are required to fall within the first instance jurisdiction of the Federal Supreme Court.[76] The issue arose when the Commission contested the constitutionality on the grounds that provisions in these Proclamations, which make the prosecution of higher officials (including ministers) for corruption offences

74 Ibid.

75 FDRE Constitution (n 3) art 25 stipulates that all persons are equal before the law and are entitled without any discrimination to equal protection of the law.

76 See Federal Negarit Gazeta, 'The Revised Anti-Corruption Special Procedure and Rules of Evidence Proclamation' Proclamation No. 434/2005, art 7 (1) and Federal Negarit Gazeta, 'Federal Courts Proclamation' Proclamation No. 25/1996, art 8 (1).

to fall under the first instance jurisdiction of the Federal Supreme Court, violate the constitutional right to equality (article 25) and the right to bail (article 20 (5)) of the defendants.

On the other hand, the defendant (Melaku Fenta) claimed that the High Court should not see his charges since he was a minister; in such cases, the law clearly states that the Supreme Court shall have first instance jurisdiction on the matter. This objection by the defendant was not endorsed by the FEAC and hence a counter-objection was submitted. The key essence of the objection by the FEAC was predicated on the fact that there are other thirty co-defendants (along with Melaku Fenta) whose cases were pending at the Federal High Court; in the FEAC's submission, trying defendants accused over the same cause of action in different courts (venues) would create inconvenience in the proceedings – especially in hearing evidences where many of them are applicable to defendants. Based on this theory, the FEAC questioned the constitutionality of the laws for two reasons which, if only incidentally, provided a golden opportunity for elaborating on the conceptual framework and application of fundamental human rights in constitutional interpretation and adjudication proceedings.[77] First, the FEAC reasoned that determining the jurisdiction of courts based on the status of the accused persons is against the equality clause under article 25 of the Constitution. Second, and related to this, prosecuting the defendant in the Supreme Court with first instance jurisdiction violates the right to appeal of accused persons (article 20 (6)) for there is no appellate court thereafter.[78]

The case was then referred to the HoF by the Federal High Court requesting constitutional interpretation on both issues. Both the CCI and the HoF made a very liberal interpretation of human rights by referring to specific provisions of the Constitution and relevant international human rights instruments ratified by Ethiopia. To mention some, the inviolability and inalienability of human rights (article 10), the duty of every government organ to enforce and protect fundamental rights and freedoms recognised in the Constitution (article 13 (2)), the right to equality (article 25), the right to bail (article 20 (6)), the need to use international human rights treaties as guiding instruments while interpreting human rights (article 13 (1)), as well as the need to uphold the supremacy of the Constitution – were addressed and covered in the decision. After making a thorough deliberation on such provisions, the HoF finally decided

77 *Federal Ethics and Anti-Corruption Commission* (*FEAC*) *v Melaku Fenta*, File No. 141356, Federal Supreme Court Cassation Division (unpublished, 11 Hedar 2006).

78 It is important to note that the defendant (Melaku Fenta) wanted his case to be litigated at the Supreme Court.

that the contested provisions under the two Proclamations are unconstitutional and hence null and void.[79]

Though, these specific rights were not claimed by the defendant, the interpretation and reasoning was extremely pro-human rights, and in such context, the HoF's enterprise must be recognised. However, the question remains as to whether such an approach was adopted because the HoF cares about the human rights of the defendant, or because such a line of argument suits the position adopted by the government agency, which is a party to the proceedings. Considering that the HoF has acted quite differently in many other cases where similar claims have been submitted, one has but to suspect the sincerity of the decision in this particular case as well. A mention of one recent case of constitutional complaint where the applicant coincidentally happened to be the same person (Melaku Fenta) is critical to showcase where the HoF really stands and to demonstrate the human rights-restrictive and political nature of constitutional interpretation in Ethiopia.

In the case of *Melaku Fenta v FEAC*, the applicant was accused of corruption for the abuse of powers vested in the Director General (the applicant) to settle certain customs related offences through administrative measures as provided under the various customs proclamations.[80] While the case was pending, a new Customs Proclamation was issued repealing the previous laws and downgrading acts which were considered to be criminal offences under the former laws to administrative transgressions; this included those acts which gave rise to the accusation of the applicant for abuse of power.[81]

However, the new Proclamation dubiously states that the abolishment of those acts that were considered criminal offences is not applicable to cases already pending before a court, stating that 'without prejudice to the provisions of other laws, cases pending before the effective date of this Proclamation shall be disposed in accordance with previous laws.'[82]

When the applicant requested to the court to no longer be prosecuted for crimes which are repealed under the new law, the prosecutor counter-argued that the new Proclamation would not be applicable to pending cases. On the

79 *Federal Ethics and Anti-Corruption Commission (FEAC) v Melaku Fenta* (2009) 2 HoF – Journal of Constitutional Decisions.

80 The Proclamations which were said to have violated and given rise to corruption charges against the applicant are Federal Negarit Gazeta, 'The Re-Establishment and Modernization of Customs Authority Proclamation' Proclamation No. 60/1997 and Federal Negarit Gazeta, 'Re-establishment and Modernization of Customs Authority (amendment) Proclamation' Proclamation No. 368/2003.

81 Federal Negarit Gazeta, 'Customs Proclamation' Proclamation No. 859/2014, art 181 (1).

82 Ibid art 182.

other hand, the applicant argued that the exclusionary provision in the new Proclamation, which bars the application of the new law to pending cases, is unconstitutional for it violates article 22 (2) of the Constitution, which states 'Notwithstanding the provisions of sub-Article 1 of this Article [non-retroactivity of criminal law], a law promulgated subsequent to the commission of the offence shall apply if it is *advantageous to the accused or convicted person*.' Following such a claim, the case was referred to the HoF for constitutional interpretation.

Quite surprisingly, both the CCI and the HoF decided that the specific provision under the new Proclamation does not violate the Constitution. In its decisions, the CCI completely relied on *policy rationales for the enactment of the new law* and the annulment of acts previously considered criminal offences, stating '...when laws are not clear and ambiguous in meaning, their interpretation shall be made in line with the *general purposes of the proclamations and our law making procedure*.'[83] It further stated that:

> ...the change in the new laws is made to rectify problems in the previous proclamation, *not to benefit accused persons per se*...the exception for retroactive application of criminal laws under Art.22 (2) of the Constitution is applicable *only if the new law makes the accused persons beneficiaries of the same*. However, since the Art.182 of the Proclamation *clearly excluded accused persons from benefitting under the new law,* the applicant cannot claim retroactive application of the law, and therefore the matter at hand does not require constitutional interpretation.[84]

It is not clear why the CCI did not try to interpret the rationale of article 22 (2) of the Constitution, which allows for the application of subsequently-adopted criminal laws when they are advantageous to the accused or convicted person. Its over-reliance on policy justifications of the Proclamation [and thus parliamentary politics] instead of the Constitution, demonstrates not only the utter inconsistency of the mechanisms in the defence of human rights, but it also quite alarmingly reveals how easily constitutional guarantees of human rights could be restrictively understood, applied and swept away in pursuance of momentary government policies. In the two cases of constitutional adjudication where the parties are the same but adopted different positions and interpretation approaches, the final outcomes varied – with negative implications on the

83 *Melaku Fenta v the Federal Ethics and Anti-Corruption Commission* (FEAC), Decision of the CCI, File No. 1421 (unpublished, 17 Hamle 2015).

84 Ibid.

availability and effectiveness of remedies in such procedures. At least in these proceedings, it appears very obvious that what mattered in constitutional interpretation was the identity of the parties. While risking over-generalisation, it seems that when a law violating human rights is challenged by any government agency, it is likely quashed; however, if such a challenge comes from individuals against the government, the HoF/CCI upholds the constitutionality of the laws.[85] This ultimately underlines that in Ethiopia the right to remedy for violation of human rights by government actions is not only ineffective, but the practice also reinforces an unwarranted dichotomy between 'parliamentary Supremacy' and 'Supremacy of the Constitution' in favour of the former.

The practice of interpreting constitutional disputes by the HoF/CCI in a way that restricts human rights and aggrandises the supremacy of the Parliament is not new. For instance, in *Ashenafi Amare et al. v Ethiopian Revenues and Customs Authority*,[86] the CCI clearly endorsed that Parliament is supreme where the legitimacy of its actions cannot be checked through constitutional adjudication. The claim by the complainants stated that article 37 (2) of the Regulation for the Administration Employees of the Ethiopian Revenue and Customs Authority is contrary to the constitutional right of access to justice as provided in the Constitution. The Regulation states:

1. Notwithstanding any provision to the contrary, the Director General may, without adhering to formal disciplinary procedures, dismiss an employee from duty whenever he has suspected him of involving in corruption and lost confidence in him.
2. An employee who has been dismissed from duty in accordance with sub article 1 of this Article may not have the right to reinstatement by the *decision of any judicial body*.[87]

85 There are also other cases where the unconstitutionality of legislations because of violation of constitutional right were initiated by individuals to the HoF, but decisions were finally made upholding the legislations. See for instance, the complaint directly lodged to the HoF by Dr. Negasso Gidada challenging the constitutionality of Proclamation No. 255/2001, which states that the benefits and privileges that ex-presidents of the federation shall cease if a former president subsequently joins any political party. The applicant challenged the law for its retroactive application and restrictions on democratic and political right provided under arts 29, 30, 31 and 38 of the FDRE Constitution (n 3). See Negasso Gidada, Direct Constitutional Compliant (2009) 2 HoF – Journal of Constitutional Decisions.

86 *Ashenafi Amare et al. v Ethiopian Revenues and Customs Authority* (*ERCA*), Decision of the CCI, File No. 101 (9 February 2010).

87 Federal Negarit Gazeta, 'Administration of Employees of the Ethiopian Revenues and Customs Authority Council of Ministers Regulation' Regulation No. 155/2008.

In this case, the CCI did not address the main issue of delegation; the Regulation was issued beyond the scope of delegation given by the legislature;[88] yet, the CCI remained timid in discharging its task of interpretation. The CCI, in its opinion, provided:

> ...the HoPR is the highest legislative organ in our Constitution; and within the constitutional boundary, it has an absolute power to do whatever it deems necessary. The power to decide as to what type of laws it should adopt is within its discretion; and in so far as it does not exceed the constitutional limit, it can adopt any type of policy choice from among available alternatives when issuing legislations. To decide whether or not the adopted law is appropriate is *not the mandate of the Council*.[89]

Moreover, the CCI ruled that since the judiciary is established within a parliamentary system, it is up to Parliament to decide which issues shall be justiciable and which shall not, provided that it acts in line with the constitutional limit. It further stated that 'regarding the issue of whether or not [a] matter is justiciable, the decision of the legislature made *according to the Constitution* saying this matter is justiciable and that is not, is correct even though it could be said that *it constricts judicial power*.'[90] In this light, the CCI concluded that the Regulation's effects, making claims of reinstatement non-justiciable and excluding judicial review of the Authority's decision, are both valid.

If one reads the above-mentioned ruling in light of widely advocated principles and theories of constitutional adjudication, several issues can be framed to contest the soundness of the decision.[91] At this juncture, however, the discussions would be limited to two important issues relevant to the topic under consideration. First, if deciding on the constitutional appropriateness or otherwise of a law adopted by the legislature is not the mandate of the CCI, who can therefore exercise this function? Second, if determining which matters are justiciable and which are not is within the mandate of the legislature, can one claim that human rights recognised in the Constitution have a constitutional

88 What is delegated to the executive by the primary legislation is the power to enact a regulation regarding the administration of employees of the Authority, not to make a law that have the effect of excluding the right of access to justice. See Federal Negarit Gazeta, 'Ethiopian Revenues and Customs Authority Establishment Proclamation' Proclamation No. 587/2008, art 19(1)b.

89 *Ashenafi Amare et al. v ERCA* (n 86) (emphasis added).

90 Ibid (emphasis added).

91 For more detail on this, see Kassa (n 55).

guarantee against undue restrictions by the legislature, by making them non-justiciable any time it wishes to do so?

If anything, the above lines reveal a very bizarre reasoning forwarded by such a body with the power of constitutional interpretation – which is also entrusted to ensure that the supremacy of the Constitution is upheld by all government branches.[92] In this regard, the discussion by the Constitutional Assembly on the issue provides that '…generally, a person should not be left without a say when he/she is aggrieved by a decision of government institution; rather he is entitled to bring his grievance to another government institution and get remedy.'[93]

In reality, the rights-restrictive approach of interpretation by the HoF is also attributable to the very design of the Constitution itself. The Constitution does not provide for a general limitation clause, which would have prevented illegitimate restrictions on human rights through legislations. Although there is no clear constitutional limitation on the power of the legislature to limit rights (such as the less-restrictive means criteria), the CCI should have relied on those implied limitations that the Constitution enshrined, of which the rule of law and values relevant to human rights are important. In this connection, it is said that if the Constitution is to be the highest law, a law that controls state actions and its interpretations must be constrained by the rule of law.[94] Apart from the implied constitutional standards, the CCI would have also resort to international human rights instruments and conventions that Ethiopia has adopted, for they also serve as guidelines in interpreting the human rights provisions of the Constitution and the legitimate and acceptable grounds on the basis of which limitations could be introduced.

However, the stand of the HoF/CCI gives the impression that the legislature is at no duty to see and choose better solutions from available alternatives or to consider stringent requirements pronounced, for instance, by the Human Rights Committee; this reading gives it a blank cheque to adopt, by any means, limitations on fundamental rights and exclusions of judicial review procedures. Both institutions failed to make a delicate balance between the two competing interests, limiting rights and achieving the goals of the Authority as intended by the law maker. The task of determining which matters are justiciable and which are not is also left to the mercy of the legislature. This is

92 This is to say that even though the CCI is not considered to be a bearer of any of the power divisions in the constitutional structure, its functions are far too important; it is only through its rulings and decisions (subject to approval by HoF) that the act of the 'supreme' legislature can be kept constrained.

93 Minutes of the Assembly (n 46), discussion on art 37.

94 Richard Post, 'Theories of Constitutional Interpretation' (1990) 30 Law and the Order of Culture, 19.

true when considering the decisions of the HoF/CCI where legislations which provide for the *finality* of the decisions of government agencies are interpreted as if they mean that the subject matter is 'non-justiciable.'[95] This creates confusion on human rights in Ethiopia and raises issues of whether they are legislative privileges or constitutionally entrenched claims.

The aforementioned readings notwithstanding, it should be noted that there were instances where the HoF/CCI have decided cases in favour of certain fundamental rights and freedoms. Recently, the HoF expanded its scope of interpretation, in which international human rights treaties were also well-considered. For instance, in *Wosene Alemu et al v Amhara National Regional State Judicial Training and Research Institute,* the HoF ruled the decision that excluded blind lawyers not to be appointed as judge merely because of visual impairment is contrary to article 41 (2) and article 25 (right to equality) of the Constitution. In this case, the HoF undertook a thorough investigation of the Convention on the Rights of Persons with Disabilities (CRPD), which Ethiopia ratified.[96]

There are also some decisions in which the HoF invalidated decisions rendered by Regional Supreme Court Cassation Divisions – especially on matters related to women's right to equality. For instance, *in Halima Mohammed v Adem Abdi,* in *Mamitie Seble v Mulu Gurmu,* and in *Wederie Tachbelie v Lkie Gurmu,* the HoF quashed decisions of regional Cassation Divisions affirming women's right to equality of using and administering rural land.[97] Nonetheless, these cases are different from the ones discussed in the preceding paragraphs both in terms of the lower decision being challenged and the parties involved in the proceedings. What the HoF quashed are decisions of regional governments, not of the federal government. In addition, most of them also evolved from claims of land use rights between individuals.

6 Conclusions and the Way Forward

The task of constitutional interpretation is not a matter only relevant to the protection and enforcement of human rights. It is also important in shaping and realising other important values of modern constitutional democracies,

95 For more on how the finality clauses and the concept of justiciability are interpreted to restrict access to justice and the right to effective remedy, see Yemane Kassa, 'Dealing With Justiciability: In Defense of Judicial Power in Ethiopia,' (2015) 3(1) Mekelle University Law Journal.

96 *Wosne Alemu et al. v Amhara National Regional State Judicial Training and Research Institute,* Decision of the HoF, File No. 019/2008 (unpublished, 2 Tikimt 2009).

97 For details on each case, see (2009) 2 HoF – Journal of Constitutional Decisions.

including constitutionalism, the rule of law, and democracy. Thus, any problem related to the effectiveness and legitimacy of the system of constitutional interpretation will inevitably and negatively affect the fundamental values and principles of modern constitutionalism and constitutional democracy. This gives rise to potential authoritarian and unlimited government where there is a constitution but the government functions without constitutionalism.

The constitutional adjudication system in Ethiopia is hardly adequate – especially in delivering effective remedies for the violation of human rights perpetuated by various functionaries of the government. The institutional set-up and various cases decided by the HoF/CCI reveals that the existing system of constitutional adjudication in Ethiopia falls far below the minimum threshold required of states to establish adequate mechanisms that ensure an effective remedy for the violation of human rights. The following reasons are adduced as justifying this conclusion. First, the fact that the HoF and the CCI are not politically insulated makes the interpretation of the Constitution and the adjudication of human rights claims highly susceptible to political bias.

Second, the composition of members of the HoF, their incompetence in legal and constitutional jurisprudence, and the assumption of such a task being merely a part-time pre-occupation creates complications and further shows that the level of attention accorded to the system of constitutional adjudication is only secondary.

Third, the jurisprudence on constitutional decisions also demonstrates that the HoF/CCI often adopted human-rights restrictive approaches – especially when issues related to the constitutionality of government laws and actions, which also entail violation of human rights – are raised. As can be deduced from the practice so far, the institutions' interpretational approaches have relied more on momentary government policies as manifested in the contested legislations, instead of adhering to universally-accepted rules of constitutional interpretation and fundamental values of the Constitution that are relevant to human rights. The right to an effective remedy is also seriously undermined simply because the remedy that one receives from the HoF in any given setting is unpredictable. In particular, the interpretations made regarding the constitutionality of legislations, finality clauses and issues of justiciability seem to endorse parliamentary supremacy over supremacy of the Constitution, potentially transforming constitutional rights to legislative or government privileges.

The findings disclose that the remedies received in constitutional adjudication are largely ineffective; this ultimately violates the Constitution's aspiration of ensuring the protection and enforcement of human rights and Ethiopia's commitment under international human rights instruments. As a way forward, therefore, a change in the institutional set-up of constitutional adjudication must be engineered in a way that addresses, at least, the interrelated problems outlined below.

First, the particular nomenclature of the umpiring organ notwithstanding, reform has to focus on guaranteeing its political insulation particularly when it comes to the enforcement of human rights, so that the legitimacy and credibility of the organ vested with the ultimate task of upholding the supremacy of the Constitution can be well-established. This is also true for the composition of the CCI, which is considered to be the main gateway and clearing house in constitutional interpretation.

Second, the HoF/CCI must develop solid principles of constitutional interpretation that generously promote the protection and enforcement of constitutionally-guaranteed human rights claims, and at the same time ensure the predictability in the outcome of cases. Doing so would require getting rid of approaches that over-rely on policy and political ends at the expense of fundamental rights and freedoms. Otherwise, the problem would not only be limited to the enforcement of human rights, but also to a choice between two contradicting values: a system based on the rule of law or on rule by law.

Enforcement of Constitutional Bills of Rights in the Regional States of Ethiopia

Mekonnen Fisseha and Gebrehiwot Hadush

Abstract

The Constitution of the Federal Democratic Republic of Ethiopia guarantees a cluster of fundamental rights and freedoms, many of which are verbatim reproduction of the rights enunciated in the international bill of rights. In the same vein, all these rights are enshrined in all regional constitutions. Nevertheless, the human and democratic rights chapters under the federal Constitution and regional constitutions do not explicitly provide remedies for violations and the process of making claims before courts of law, other than in the broader framework of a right of access to justice. On the one hand, it is argued that courts and other constitutional institutions, such as the House of the Federation (and its regional counter-parts), are apparently given 'competing' powers that negatively impact the enforcement of constitutional bills of rights. As such, it is commonly held that courts are divested of their 'inherent' power to apply human rights provisions of the constitutions so much that only rare references are made to the constitutional bill of rights in their decisions. On the other hand, several scholars criticise courts for not being proactive in the interpretation and application of constitutional bill of rights. This article investigates the enforcement of constitutional human rights by courts in the regional states of Ethiopia, taking the State of Tigray as a case study. Grounded in empirical inputs, the researchers argue that despite a comprehensive recognition of rights in the federal and regional Constitutions, there is little space or institutional proclivity in the enforcement of a constitutional bill of rights by courts in Tigray. The practice of courts in the region reveals that constitutional bills of rights are invoked very rarely and extremely selectively, this being evidenced by the little reference made to constitutional provisions by courts of law in proceedings and decisions. This gives way to a concerning jurisprudential dearth in constitutional rights litigation in the State of Tigray, although, on the contrary, an increasing trend of constitutional rights-based claims submitted before the Constitutional Commission is also found.

Keywords

Human Rights – Constitutional Bill of Rights – Judicial Enforcement of Bill of Rights – Tigray – Ethiopia

 | DOI:10.1163/9789004415966_014

1 Introduction

Although there is no clear definition of the constitutional bill of rights phrasing, the epistemology of the concept is corollary with the emergence of bills of rights in several constitutions. It is based on the principle of entrenchment of rights, as opposed to legislative protection of rights or the informal set-up bills of rights. While bills of rights are used in some constitutions, such as the Republic of South Africa and the United States of America (USA), they can interchangeably be referred to as fundamental rights and freedoms, as is the case in Ethiopia.

Bills of rights cover a wide range of rights documents, ranging from short manifestoes to constitutionally entrenched and legally enforceable instruments.[1] In the modern sense, bills of rights are embodied in major constitutions as a formal commitment to rights that bind not only the executive but also the legislative organ.[2] Since 1945, the phrase 'human rights' has become the preferred language for bills of rights in the international legal order through the United Nations (UN) Charter and the Universal Declaration of Human Rights (UDHR).

The Ethiopian approach is based on entrenchment, wherein rights are duly recognised in the supreme law of the land as per the Constitution of the Federal Democratic Republic of Ethiopia (FDRE Constitution). The FDRE Constitution is one of the most modern constitutions that gives prominence to human rights in a detailed fashion. Nearly a quarter of the Constitution's coverage is devoted to fundamental human and democratic rights.[3] What is more, by virtue of article 13(2) and 9(4) of the Constitution, international human rights instruments ratified by Ethiopia do form part of the law of the land.

Given the context of the federal structure, similar rights are also protected under regional constitutions. Hence, the federal system in Ethiopia provides a double guarantee of rights functioning at two tiers of administration.

While the FDRE Constitution stipulates human rights as common obligations of all organs of the state on the federal and regional levels, not much can be said on the provision of actual enforcement mechanisms articulated in the constitutions, especially at the regional levels. Most of Chapter Three of

1 Charles Manga Fombad, *African Bills of Rights in a Comparative Perspective* (UNISA Press, 2011) 35.

2 Philip Alston, 'Framework for the Comparative Analysis of Bills of Rights' in Philip Alston (ed), *Promoting Human Rights through Bills of Rights: Comparative Perspectives* (Clarendon Press 1999) 7.

3 Federal Negarit Gazeta, 'The Constitution of the Federal Democratic Republic of Ethiopia' Proclamation No.1/1995 Chapter 3Three, arts 13–44.

the bill of rights does not explicitly provide for remedies, nor does it indicate the process for making claims before law enforcement bodies, particularly the judiciary and other entities with judicial competence. This raises strong contention as to whether the FDRE Constitution offers a genuine rights protection mechanism.

In this article, it is argued that despite a comprehensive recognition of rights under the FDRE and regional constitutions, there is narrow space for the enforcement of constitutional bill of rights by courts of law. Equally, the jurisprudential dearth on constitutional bills of rights in Ethiopia explains the lack of enforcement mechanisms for the constitutional bill of rights.[4] This situation is reflected both at the federal and regional levels, with more nuanced faults in the regions.

Scholars have often criticised those who framed the constitution for what is widely referred to as 'divesting' judicial power on constitutional interpretation matters. There is also an ongoing debate that courts and judges have 'retreated' from taking any meaningful role in the promotion and implementation of fundamental human rights recognised in the constitution.[5] However, there are few research works that critically examine the actual role and function of state courts in relation to human rights-based empirical investigations and involving, for example, the perception of key stakeholders like judges and other law enforcement organs on the subject.

The investigation in this chapter focuses on the practice of the enforcement of constitutional bills of rights by courts in the regional states of Ethiopia, taking the State of Tigray as a case study. Due to lingering debates over the justiciability of socio-economic and cultural rights, the discussion shall be limited to examining the enforcement of civil and political rights. The issues are approached from the point of the judicial enforcement organs, as well as the remedies availed for violations of these rights.

2 Methodological Approach and Organisation

In conducting this study, the researchers employed a qualitative research methodology complemented by modest case studies and reviews. This

4 At the federal level, very few cases have been brought before the Council of Constitutional Inquiry (CCI) and the House of Federation (HoF). For discussions of some of the cases, see Getahun Kassa, 'Mechanism of Constitutional Control: A Preliminary Observation of the Ethiopian System,' (2007) 20(1–2) Africa Focus 75.

5 For details, see Tsegaye Regasa, 'Making Legal Sense of Human Rights: The Judicial Role in Protecting Human Rights in Ethiopia' (2009) 3(2) Mizan Law Review 288 <https://www.ajol.info/index.php/mlr/article/download/54014/42556> accessed 15 January 2016.

approach was chosen in order to truly identify and understand whether there exists a pattern of institutional experience, which can support or challenge the authors' claims regarding the role of courts in the protection of human rights. To this end, randomly selected cases were used involving thirty pertinent cases from the Mekelle Woreda Courts, the Zonal High Court, and the Supreme Court of Tigray. A total of thirteen judges, both from the civil and criminal benches, including presidents directly involved in the handling and assignment of cases, as well as fifteen practicing lawyers and eight public prosecutors took part in semi-structured interviews. Particular focus was accorded to case analyses of the Council of Constitutional Inquiry (CCI) and the Constitutional Commission.

The level of analysis in this study involved two stages: first, the practice of constitutional rights litigation as an avenue for pursuing independent claims, both substantively and procedurally (referred to as the 'direct application'); and second, the practice of adherence to and reasoning in light of human rights norms in court decisions (referred to as the 'indirect application').

To this end, the study is organised into three general thematic sections. The first section highlights the fundamental human rights recognised under the FDRE Constitution and elaborates on important concepts, such as justiciability and standing. It also presents the long-standing debates on the role of judges in protecting and promoting human rights under the FDRE Constitution. The second thematic section discusses the protection of fundamental human rights at the sub-national level with particular emphasis on the Revised Constitution of Tigray. The third section analyses the remedies provided for violation of rights and the judicial (with some reference to non-judicial) practices in the Regional State of Tigray.

3 Framework of Fundamental Rights and Freedoms under the Ethiopian Constitution

In the contemporary setting, it has become somewhat self-evident that human rights are universal standards endowed to all individuals, against which the behaviour of states and non-state actors shall be measured.[6] Entrenching fundamental rights and freedoms in constitutions has thus become the standard practice of virtually all modern constitutions, most importantly also in post-conflict societies. The FDRE Constitution was adopted following years of

6 The inherence of rights is embodied in the first international human rights instrument, Preamble of the Universal Declaration of Human Rights, 1948. See Universal Declaration of Human Rights (adopted 10 December 1948) UNGA Res 217 A(III) (UDHR).

struggle for freedom and equality.[7] Thus, as a post-conflict constitution, it incorporates several individual as well as group rights and freedoms. The makers of the FDRE Constitution emphasised popular sovereignty, political equality and pluralism.[8] As part of the international constitution-making process of the post-1990s, the Constitution is said to have benefitted from the rights guaranteed in major international human rights systems.[9] In addition, the Constitutional Drafting Commission considered the practice of different countries in laying out the framework of the provisions that deal with fundamental rights.[10] For example, on the right to self-determination, the normative organisation and practices of Canada and the USA were considered, although this does not necessarily imply that the same substantive format as in both countries was eventually adopted in the constitution.[11] Similarly, in drafting the provisions that deal with the rights of women, the practices of Bangladesh, Egypt, England and Norway were considered.[12]

In general, it should be noted that the historical development of the bill of rights under the FDRE Constitution has drawn together several elements of similar evolutionary growth, including international documents, historical facts of repression and injustice at the local level, and practices of other countries. Nonetheless, it appears as though there was greater focus on the history of discrimination that subsisted in the country for decades.[13] As the minutes on the preparatory works of the Constitution reveal, the national context of the historical infringement of rights, as well as the overall setting of the country

7 For discussion on human rights during the Emperor and Derg Regimes, see Minasse Haile, 'Comparing Human Rights in Two Ethiopian Constitutions: The Emperors and The "Republics" – Cucullus Non Facit Monachum,' (2005) 13 Cardozo Journal of International Law And Comparative Law 1; Andargachew Tiruneh, *The Ethiopian Revolution 1974–1987: A Transformation from an Aristocratic to a Totalitarian Autocracy* (Cambridge University Press 1993).

8 Andreas Eshete, 'Implementing Human Rights and a Democratic Constitution in Ethiopia' (1993) 21(1/2) A Journal of Opinion 8 <https://www.jstor.org/stable/i249400> accessed 12 May 2016. See also Kinfe Abraham, *Ethiopia: From Empire to Federation* (EIIPD Press 2001).

9 Constitutional Drafting Commission, 'Minutes of the Commission' 54th Session, 29 October 1994.

10 Ibid.

11 On the position of rights during the Charter and in the making, see for example Tsegaye Regassa, 'The Making and Legitimacy of the Ethiopian Constitution: Towards Bridging the Gap between Constitutional Design and Constitutional Practice' (2010) 23(1) Afrika Focus 85.

12 Constitutional Drafting Commission (n 9).

13 Adem Kassie, 'Human Rights under the Ethiopian Constitution: A descriptive Overview' (2011) 5(1) Mizan Law Review 42.

in the accommodation of rights and freedoms, had in fact received greater attention as key drivers in the Commission's work on the subject.[14]

Substantively, the FDRE Constitution could be considered a major normative development in terms of the scope of human rights recognition at constitutional levels.[15] One of the cornerstones of the Constitution is the 'full respect of individual and peoples' fundamental freedoms and rights.'[16] The Constitution also recognised human rights as one of the fundamental principles of the Constitutional framework. Article 10(1) provides that 'Human rights and freedoms, emanating from the nature of mankind, are inviolable and inalienable. Human and democratic rights of citizens and peoples shall be respected.'[17] Although both human and democratic rights are considered fundamental, the Constitution noticeably takes differential treatment of the two terms; it holds that human rights are regarded as inviolable and inalienable, while democratic rights of citizens and people shall be respected. However, this only has little practical bearing as far as the standing of these rights is concerned.

One of the defining features of the FDRE Constitution is its comprehensive coverage of all categories of rights, which are traditionally labelled as first, second and third generation rights. Chapter Three of the Constitution is dedicated to 'Fundamental Rights and Freedoms.' The Constitution categorises fundamental rights into 'Human Rights and Democratic Rights,' and focuses on the application of some democratic rights, such as the right to property, the right to self-determination, and economic, social and cultural rights as suitably pertinent to citizens. Although hardly scientifically-based and with little precedence elsewhere, the Drafting Commission took the position that human rights are entitlements granted for all by virtue of being human, while democratic rights are rights claimed as a result of being a member of a political community (citizens).[18] However, constitutionally speaking, except for some voting rights, many of the so-called democratic rights are framed as belonging to 'everyone' or 'every person.'

The provisions dealing with economic, social and cultural rights outline the duty of the government to ensure these rights, rather than guaranteeing individual rights directly. This duty obliges the state, within its available resources, to take necessary measures to fulfil these rights. This duty-based formulation of

14 See Kassa (n 4) 78–79.

15 Eshete (n 8) 43.

16 FDRE Constitution (n 3) Preamble.

17 Ibid art 10 (1).

18 Tsegaye Regasa, 'Making Legal Sense of Human Rights' 3(2) Mizan Law Rev 288, 303. See also 'the Explanatory Note for the Draft Constitution' (adopted by The House of Peoples Representatives, 28 October 1994) 15.

rights (rather than guaranteeing individual rights directly) creates a difficulty in knowing the rights protected and the scope of protection. It also makes the determination of justiciability of these rights difficult.

However, it can be argued that these rights are justiciable even under the current Constitution of Ethiopia. One argument is that since the Constitution does not expressly declare non-justiciability of these rights, the rights are justiciable before the House of the Federation (HoF).[19] The provisions dealing with these rights can also be interpreted in line with the National Policy Principles and Objectives, which require the government to formulate policies and objectives to insure the social needs of people as provided under Chapter 10 (articles 85 to 92) of the Constitution. Although the status of the National Policy Principles and Objectives is not clear, it seems that they represent a duty of the state and therefore do not automatically create rights of the individual to bring claims against the government. Different experiences also show different approaches with regard to the degree of enforceability of such rights. The South African Constitutional Court adopts the 'reasonable measure' criteria, while the Committee under the International Covenant on Economic, Social and Cultural Rights (ICESCR) devised the 'minimum core obligation' rule.[20] In addition to the basic rights guaranteed under the Constitution, Ethiopia is a party to most international human rights instruments.[21] As explained above, the Constitution has clearly stated under article 9(4) that international instruments, including international human rights laws, are an integral part of the laws of the land. Moreover, the interpretation rule of the Constitution provides authoritative guidance on how the rights outlined in Chapter Three should be interpreted. Article 13(2) states: 'The fundamental rights and freedoms specified in this Chapter shall be interpreted in a manner conforming to the principles of the Universal Declaration of Human Rights, international covenants on human rights and international instruments adopted by Ethiopia.'

On the other hand, article 9(1) of the FDRE Constitution provides: 'The Constitution is the supreme law of the land. Any law, customary practice or a decision of an organ of state or a public official which contravenes this

19 Eshete (n 8) 54.

20 Office of the High Commissioner of Human Rights, 'CESCR General Comment No. 3: The Nature of States Parties' Obligations (Art. 2, Para. 1, of the Covenant)' (Adopted at the Fifth Session of the Committee on Economic, Social and Cultural Rights, on 14 December 1990) <https://www.refworld.org/pdfid/4538838e10.pdf> accessed 13 June 2016.

21 Reference was made to the body of international human rights instruments during the drafting process of the FDRE Constitution. See 'Explanatory Note for the Draft Constitution' (adopted by The House of Peoples Representatives, 28 October 1994) 15.

Constitution shall be of no effect.' Article 9(1) upholds the supremacy clause of constitutional provisions over any other laws and government practices.

When reading articles 9(1), 9(4) and 13(2) in combination, the exact status of international human rights instruments under the FDRE Constitution may appear to be less straight-forward. Three lines of arguments could generally be advanced on this issue. The first argument holds Chapter Three rights supreme and international human rights subsidiary. This argument is faintly based on the supremacy clause of article 9(1), which is read by many as heightening the Constitution and anything it contains to a higher normative ground. The second most commonly endorsed argument holds that international human rights instruments prevail over Chapter Three rights mainly because of, among others, the treaty obligations of Ethiopia under the Vienna Convention on the Law of Treaties (VCLT). The third argument puts international human rights instruments on equal status with Chapter Three of the Constitution.[22] The argument in support of this assertion is based on the belief that since ratified international agreements are an integral part of the law of the land as per article 9(4) and the constitutional provisions dealing with fundamental rights must be interpreted in conformity with international instruments adopted by Ethiopia as per article 13(2) of the Constitution, international instruments adopted have a status equal to the Constitution.

A lot of ink has gone into literature trying to expound the status of international human rights in Ethiopia and hence, there is no need to replicate the arguments here. For the purpose of this article at hand, it suffices to hold that the interpretative provision of article 13(2) is not to create a hierarchy of human rights norms between international instruments and Chapter Three rights. Article 13(2) may well be termed a reference provision, which is invoked when there is ambiguity in the specific provisions of Chapter Three or when the contents thereof need to be explained in light of normative developments and understandings at the international level. For example, article 18 of the Constitution prohibits inhuman and degrading treatment. However, what constitutes the elements of cruel, inhuman and degrading treatment or torture is provided in substantive details under the UN Convention Against Torture (UNCAT) to which Ethiopia is a party. Similarly, article 25 of the Constitution provides the right to equality and non-discrimination; yet, what constitutes discrimination is provided in greater depth under the Convention for Elimination of All Forms of Discrimination Against Women (CEDAW) and the

22 Ibid 47.

subsequent general comments furnished by the Treaty Monitoring Committee. Therefore, one should refer to these instruments and the interpretative understandings of the respective Committees in applying constitutional provisions in specific contexts.

The same reasoning can be applied to other Chapter Three rights of the Constitution where, based on interpretative clauses, reference for clarity on the content and application of the rights is sought using international human rights standards. After all, Chapter Three rights are by and large taken from the international human rights instruments. Thus, instead of arguing one is superior over the other, it is desirable to construct rights more broadly by utilising positive interpretation techniques so as to better-advance liberty. In the event of unlikely conflict or normative incompatibility between both tiers of human rights orders, it can be held that the wider set of protection provided under international instruments shall be upheld, although there are still authorities who argue that the Constitution's stipulations shall have paramount importance, as the rights are considered to be the direct expressions of the will of the people.

As far as the application of the fundamental rights and freedoms is concerned, the FDRE Constitution, unlike the South African Constitution, does not clearly extend to private actors. While it appears that article 13(2) of the Constitution limits the scope of application of Chapter Three rights to legislative, executive and judicial organs at both levels, its wider application to private actors as duty bearers could be defended through constructive and purposive interpretation. This is not to mention that under article 9(2), a horizontal application is explicitly sought when the Constitution provided that 'All citizens, organs of state, political organisations, other associations as well as their officials have the duty to ensure observance of the Constitution and to obey it.'[23]

On the other hand, in relation to specific modalities, similar to the international model of protection, the FDRE Constitution adopts a two-stage approach: the first is protection (through legislative, administrative or judicial measures) and the second is limitation and/or derogation. The Constitution does not specifically require the state organ that shall legislate or the type of legislation (whether a proclamation or regulation), which shall be employed to define the limitations or derogations. This is expressed by the very generic phrase 'as prescribed by law.'

23 FDRE Constitution (n 3) art 9(2).

4 Procedural Guarantees and Remedies for Violations of Rights: 'Indeterminacy' of the Constitutional Bill of Rights in Ethiopia

4.1 *Justiciability*

Article 37 of the FDRE Constitution guarantees access to justice as a one of the fundamental rights and freedoms. It is contended that the application of access to justice is not limited to fundamental rights and freedoms provided in Chapter Three of the FDRE Constitution. It can be applied to other cases, such as administrative measures and civil law matters involving for example contract law, tort and family law cases. The Constitution's provision reads that 'Everyone has the right to bring a justiciable matter to, and to obtain a decision or judgment by a court of law or any other competent body with judicial power.'[24]

While a few court cases have incidentally treated the concept, the Constitution does not define what constitutes a justiciable matter, nor has the HoF given an authoritative definition through constitutional interpretation. At the federal level, the Cassation Bench in its recent decisions has vaguely listed out certain elements of access to justice.[25]

In the context of the discussion at hand, what perhaps becomes problematic is that the Constitution does not mention which of the fundamental rights and freedoms are justiciable and which are not. This invokes possible arguments about whether constitutions are supposed to provide such specifics notwithstanding the practice. However, a deeper reading of the fundamental rights and freedoms reveals that some rights are justiciable and some are not; this is mostly attributed to the inherent nature of the rights per se. For example, the prohibition against inhumane and degrading treatment can give rise to automatic implementation and hence is justiciable. Other rights of individual nature such as the right to life, liberty and security can be directly claimed before a competent judicial organ or other tribunal. Rights, such as the right to self-determination, are also justiciable in a different context on the condition that the required procedural minimum is fulfilled as provided under article 39 of the Constitution. The more pressing question will be whether all rights recognised in the Constitution can be justiciable.

Evidently, a detailed protection of the fundamental rights covered under the Constitution could be pursued through primary legislations such as labour law, family law, criminal law, tort law, and property law. Such legislation either

24 FDRE Constitution (n 3) art 37(2).

25 For example, see Federal Supreme Court, 'Cassation Bench Decisions' vol 18–20 on access to justice.

can promote the protection of the rights or, at the minimum, be framed in a manner that is compliant with the Constitution's stipulation of the rights and freedoms. In the context of the protection of rights, of course, one may question the wisdom of trying to ensure the protection of rights merely through piecemeal primary legislations and the impact thereof on constitutionally guaranteed rights. One plausible argument is that such legislations neither replace nor avoid constitutional rights litigation; they rather supplement rights protection in a concrete manner. The other argument could be that rights in the constitution should be actionable only through further legislation and until then, they shall remain unenforceable. It may be held that the purpose of the inclusion of rights in the Constitution serves as an authoritative guide for legislations. This way, constitutional rights inform private and public law litigation. However, one may ask what the concept of 'rights' would really mean if such rights are not enforced in their own as stand-alone rights.

When considering the experience of other countries, the constitutional protection of rights gives rise to constitutional rights litigation, having its own processes and institutions of enforcement/adjudication. Rights litigation can also arise during the application of either private law litigation, such as property rights in private properly law, contract, tort law, or labour laws and cases. In summary, it could be concluded that under the Ethiopian legal system, the Constitution does not explicitly provide for a provision that guarantees a mechanism of claiming any rights violations, except for cases pursued within the framework of constitutional disputes.

4.2 *Standing*

In the context of human and constitutional rights, standing constitutes the core of procedural guarantees for rights-related claims. Standing as part of access to justice is regulated under the FDRE Constitution, which provides:

1. Everyone has the right to bring a justiciable matter to, and to obtain a decision or judgment by a court of law or any other competent body with judicial power.
2. The decision or judgment referred to under sub-article 1 of this Article may also be sought by:
   (a) Any association representing the collective or individual interest of its members; or
   (b) Any group or person who is a member of or represents a group with similar interests.[26]

26 FDRE Constitution (n 3) art 37.

As discussed above, access to justice in general and standing in particular is not limited to claims based on Chapter Three of the FDRE Constitution; it can apply to other civil claims as well. Before the adoption of the FDRE Constitution, the governing law of standing was the Civil Procedure Code (1965). According to article 33(2) of the Ethiopian Civil Procedure Code, the requirement of 'vested interest' is a precondition to institute a case against a certain person.[27] The question, then, is whether the standing requirement provided for in the Civil Procedure Code is consistent with the FDRE Constitution.

Obviously, the readings of the texts of the Code and the Constitution foretell that article 37 of the FDRE Constitution is much broader than article 32 of the Civil Procedure Code. Standing under the Constitution governs not only matters pertaining to human rights, but also any other justiciable subject matter including private law-based claims.

When it comes to standing, though, there are many who submit that the usage of the term 'every person' under article 37(2) of the FDRE Constitution should not be read as authorising anyone without any stake to take a case to courts of law.[28] The vested interest requirement appears to be implied under article 37(1).[29]

Other provisions of the Constitution provide rules for standing in relation to specific rights claims. For example, article 39 of the FDRE Constitution stipulates that questions relating to self-determination can only be initiated by each nation, nationality and people in question. Such requirement excludes individuals to bring claims for self-determination.[30] The main governing constitutional provision on standing before the Council of Constitutional Inquiry (CCI) and the HoF in constitutional disputes is provided under article 82 (2) of the Constitution, which states 'Where any federal or state law is contested as being unconstitutional and such a dispute is submitted to it [the Council] by any court or interested party, the Council shall consider the matter and submit it to the House of the Federation for a final decision.'[31]

27 Under the Civil Procedure Code, there are also other mechanisms for bringing a case such as class action or representation.

28 Adem K Abebe, 'Towards More Liberal Standing Rules to Enforce Constitutional Rights in Ethiopia' (2010) 10 African Human Rights Law Journal 417. Some argue that article 37(1) allows anybody to bring constitutional claims, including non-governmental organisations (NGOs). For a detailed discussion on the subject see YM Badwaza 'Public Interest Litigation as Practiced by South African NGOs: Any Lessons for Ethiopia?' (Unpublished, LLM thesis, University of Pretoria 2005).

29 Ibid 417.

30 Ibid 424–425.

31 FDRE Constitution (n 3) art 84(2).

According to the constitutional provision above, there are two parties that can bring a case before the CCI and HoF. These involve referrals by courts/appeals from court decisions or submission by an interested party. The Constitution neither defines the type and level of courts, nor the nature of the interested party, but a close reading of the same provision implies that the reference is to courts established in accordance with the Constitution and having judicial powers as expressed in article 79 of the FDRE Constitution.[32] In this light, therefore, constitutional disputes from courts, Sharia courts, and quasi-judicial organs with judicial powers can be brought before the CCI and HoF.[33] Detailed procedures of constitutional adjudication are set out in the Council of Constitutional Inquiry Proclamation No.250/2001.

The second modality of standing in relation to constitutional disputes is that whosoever submits claims must be an interested party, as discussed above. The Constitution does not define what a constitutional dispute entails. In the context of constitutional bills of rights, in the authors' opinion, constitutional disputes can arise from two perspectives. The first is a question raised in relation to the constitutionality of federal and state laws. The second is when rights are violated and a case alleging human rights violations is instituted. As will be discussed below, there is confusion as to where a case for violation of rights by public authorities can be instituted. A restrictive approach of bringing a constitutional claim is however provided under article 23 (1) of the Council of Constitutional Inquiry Proclamation No.250/2001, which states: 'Any person who alleges that his fundamental rights and freedoms have been violated by the final decision of any government institution or official may present his case to the Council of Inquiry for constitutional interpretation.'

Furthermore, the law on standing is defined in other legislations, such as the proclamations adopted to define the powers and duties of the HoF and the CCI, and to regulate environmental matters. Such laws provide specific requirements for standing.[34] Otherwise, it suffices to note that the debates relating to whether to the Constitution could be regarded as recognising public interest litigation, a common practice in India and South Africa, remains large in the contemporary discourse in Ethiopia.[35]

32 FDRE Constitution (n 3) art 79.

33 Ibid.

34 For a detailed discussion of standing before the CCI, HoF, Human Rights Commission and Ombudsman, see Abebe (n 28).

35 See Sisay Alemahu Yeshanew, 'The Justiciability of Human Rights in the Federal Democratic Republic of Ethiopia' (2008) 8(2) African Human Rights Law Journal 291. See also Mehreteab Ghebremekel, 'Realization of Human Rights in Ethiopia through Public Interest Litigation' 111–122 in Wolfgang Benedek and others (eds), *Ethiopian and Wider African*

5 Jurisdiction: Procedural and Institutional Safeguards

It goes without saying that states ratify human rights treaty agreements to enforce them and to behave accordingly. The general globally trend has been that states over-commit in terms of adoption and ratification of international human rights instruments, while respect and enforcement of human rights remains abysmal across jurisdictions. The enforcement mechanism put in place domestically is, therefore, one indication of genuine state commitment to comply with human rights standards.

The international bill of rights, and notably the International Covenant on Civil and Political Rights (ICCPR), provides due process of law and procedural guarantees in relation to property rights, liberty, freedom of expression, freedom of religion, and other rights embodied in the Convention. It also establishes the Human Rights Committee (HRC) 'whose main purpose is to enhance mechanisms of accountability through its authority to monitor and receive state reports that are due on regular basis.' More directly, the Committee is conferred through the First Optional Protocol with a court-like power to consider individual complaints against own governments.

The ICCPR is not the only international treaty instrument on civil and political rights. The European Convention on Human Rights (ECHR), the American Convention on Human Rights (ACHR), and the African Charter on Human and Peoples' Rights (ACHPR) also provide procedural guarantees for the enforcement of civil and political rights envisaged under the respective instruments, which are largely similar to the ICCPR.

The ECHR in particular requires contracting parties to provide effective remedies against the violation of human rights protected by the Convention. The European Convention is unique in its design of the enforcement mechanisms. The convention creates the European Court of Human Rights (ECtHR) and a political body, the Committee of Ministers, composed of representatives from each of the member states of the Council of Europe. While the ECtHR adjudicates human right violations, the Committee of Ministers oversees and monitors the enforcement of the convention rights including the decisions of the ECtHR.

By and large, the civil and political rights from the ICCPR are imported into the FDRE Constitution. In fact, the Constitution imposes responsibility and duty to respect and enforce provisions of the Constitution at all levels of the federal and state legislative, executive and judicial bodies.

Perspectives on Human Rights and Good Governance (Neuer Wissenschaftlicher Verlag 2014).

The FDRE Constitution also requires that appropriate institutional mechanisms should be in place as a means for implementing the human rights laws of the country. To mention some, the House of Peoples Representatives has a constitutional obligation to establish a National Human Rights Commission and the Institution of the Ombudsman. As a result, both institutions were established with powers to take measures necessary for human rights protection and the building of good governance in the country.[36]

As stated above, under the Constitution the key enforcement organs of the constitutional bills of rights are the legislative, executive and judiciary bodies both at the federal and regional levels, and the National Human Rights Commission and the Institution of the Ombudsman at all levels of the country.

The application of constitutional human rights provisions can be direct (applied to cases in court proceedings) or indirect (in which the Constitution's provisions indirectly influence laws, decisions, actions, and practices).[37] In these contexts, the human rights Chapter of the Constitution serves as a framework of understanding, a tool of interpretation, and a guide to public decision-making.[38] This implies that the constitutional bill of rights functions as standard against which the constitutionality of laws, decisions, actions and practices are measured.

In the context of federalism, the FDRE Constitution establishes three types of courts at the federal and regional levels.[39] These are the Federal Supreme Court, the Federal High Court, and the Federal First-Instance Court; and the State Supreme Court, the State High Court and the State First-Instance Court. The Constitution also provided for cassation powers of the Federal Supreme Court in relation to fundamental errors of law from any court decision, and the cassation power of state courts for fundamental errors of law from any court decision of state matter. The State Supreme Court and the State High Court shall also have delegated judicial power for the Federal High Court and the Federal First-Instance Court, respectively.

The Proclamation establishing federal courts, Proclamation No.25/1996, details the respective jurisdictional competence of federal courts as common

36 The Ethiopian Human Rights Commission and the Institution of the Ombudsman are established pursuant to Proclamation No.210/2000 and Proclamation No. 211/2000 respectively. Federal Negarit Gazeta, 'Ethiopian Human Rights Commission Establishment Proclamation' Proclamation No.210/2000; Federal Negarit Gazeta, 'Institution of the Ombudsman Establishment Proclamation' Proclamation No.211/2000.

37 Kassie (n 13) 311.

38 Ibid 313.

39 FDRE Constitution (n 3) arts 78 and 79.

jurisdiction, civil jurisdiction and criminal jurisdiction.[40] Cases arising from the federal Constitution and international agreements are the common jurisdiction of federal courts. From this provision, it seems that human rights cases of the federal Constitution would constitute the common jurisdiction of federal courts. However, in further inquiry one would not find adequate explanation regarding the question of which of the three types of federal courts as such entertain human rights claims, except for cases of *habeas corpus*.

As far as the implementation and enforcement of rights through other civil and criminal cases are concerned, courts should still have to make sense of the fundamental rights and freedoms guaranteed under the FDRE Constitution and other human rights instruments to which Ethiopia is a party. Similarly, other quasi-judicial organs are under obligation to enforce constitutional rights in their respective decisions. Nevertheless, it may well be noted that enforcement of constitutional human rights based on subsidiary legislation may not bring about sufficient protection of rights.[41]

Given the clear constitutional provision empowering the HoF and the CCI to settle constitutional disputes, there has been an ongoing debate on whether or not there is anything left for courts to 'interpret' in the Constitution, in a sense that impacts the understanding and application of human rights provisions in specific settings. There are two basic lines of argument. The first argument submits that based on article 84 (2) of the FDRE Constitution, the HoF has the power to adjudicate constitutional issues concerning 'legislation' enacted by both federal and state legislative organ; courts shall have power to adjudicate the 'executive' acts of both federal and state governments.[42] This is because the term 'law' covers federal and regional laws enacted by respective legislatures in their primary legislative powers. As a result, it can be said that courts in Ethiopia have not necessarily lost all their powers of interpreting the Constitution and hence can feature whenever there is inconsistency between executive actions and the Constitution.

The second line of argument is based on Proclamation No.251/2001, which states that courts do not have any power left to interpret the Constitution, since the Proclamation under article 2(2) defines the term 'law' so broadly and includes 'regulations and directives issued by the federal and state government institutions which shall also include international agreements that have been

---

40 Federal Negarit Gazeta, 'Federal Courts Proclamation' Proclamation No.25/1996. (as amended).

41 Cases on labour law, family law, and property law are said to be impliedly protected rights at subsidiary level.

42 Assefa Fiseha, 'Constitutional Adjudication in Ethiopia: Exploring the Experience of the HoF' (2007) 1(1) Mizan Law Review 1, 3.

ratified by Ethiopia.' Therefore, if such law is said to include acts of the executive organs of federal and state governments, nothing will remain for courts and it can be concluded that courts only have the power to implement and enforce the Constitution, and not to interpret the provisions of the Constitution. This implies that following the adoption of Proclamation No.251/2001, the jurisdictional power to interpret all legislation enacted by the federal and state legislative organs and all executive actions conducted in such way is vested solely in the hands of the HoF. In a reverse predisposition, the said legislation further complicated constitutional rights litigation by stating that if 'the constitutional case submitted to the House pertains to the fundamental rights and freedoms enshrined in the Constitution, the interpretation shall be made in a manner conforming to the principles of the UDHR, ICCPR and other instruments.'

Whether this particular law is constitutional or not is beyond the scope of this research. On a possible way to remedy the defect either in the design or ambiguity of the practice, however, it is submitted that the ideal way would be to base human rights cases on international human rights instruments. This is not common and it is not clear how courts or other human rights enforcing bodies might react.

6 Remedies for Violations of Rights

In rights analysis, substantive protection of rights is one important thing. However, protection of rights without an effective remedy is simply meaningless. The maxim is that where there is no remedy, there is no right; effective human rights protection is more than just a question of how many rights are recognised and protected in the bill of rights.[43]

Thus, it is imperative that rights must have a corresponding mechanism of redressing or remedying violations. As stated above, the FDRE Constitution does not have an explicit provision that deals with remedies for human rights violations. The Constitution merely provides everyone access to courts or other competent bodies to obtain a decision or judgment concerning any 'justiciable matter,' without setting in place specific remedial mechanisms.[44] As discussed above, violations of human rights can occur in two ways. The first is infringement of rights through legislation, and the second is infringement of

43 Manga Fombad (n 1) 49.

44 FDRE Constitution (n 3) art 37.

rights by official or individual actions. The remedy for the first violation is nullification of the law by the HoF which, unless otherwise decided, is effective as of the date of the decision.[45] Remedy for the second type of violations is not provided in the FDRE Constitution or any other law except as may be impliedly addressed in civil and public law litigation.

From a human rights perspective, it is still possible to argue that remedy for violation of rights is possible through interpretation using article 13(2) of the FDRE Constitution, where international human rights instruments to which Ethiopia is a party require effective remedy for violations of human rights. In this connection, for example, use could be made of article 8 of the UDHR, which stipulates that 'Everyone has the right to an effective remedy by the competent national tribunals for acts violating the fundamental rights granted him by the constitution or by law.' Likewise, article 2 of the ICCPR provides that each state party to the present Covenant undertakes:

(a) To ensure that any person whose rights or freedoms as herein recognized are violated shall have an effective remedy, notwithstanding that the violation has been committed by persons acting in an official capacity;
(b) To ensure that any person claiming such a remedy shall have his right thereto determined by competent judicial, administrative or legislative authorities, or by any other competent authority provided for by the legal system of the State, and to develop the possibilities of judicial remedy;
(c) To ensure that the competent authorities shall enforce such remedies when granted.

From the reading of the above in relation to article 13(2) of the FDRE Constitution, one can construct possible remedies for the violation of human rights in Ethiopia by referring to the international covenants and other human rights instruments to which Ethiopia is a party. Major types of constitutional remedies include the declaration of invalidity, prohibitory and mandatory reliefs like injunction, deferential reliefs like suspended declaration of invalidity, and awards of damages. Such remedies for rights violations may be expressed in a constitution or under separate legislations. In the Ethiopian case, there is no remedy in the Constitution; such are only provided ambiguously in an array of legislations.

45 Federal Negarit Gazeta, 'Proclamation to Define the Powers of the House of Federation' Proclamation No.251/2001.

7 Protection of Rights at the Sub-National Level: Institutions and Process of Rights Adjudication in the Tigray Region

7.1 *Sub-National Constitutionalism and the Protection of Rights*

It is true that the scholarly discourse of human rights gains more important attention when looked at from the federal school of thought, which is based on diversity rather than assimilation.[46] An important question to ask in such setting would be what federalism implies for the protection of rights at sub-national levels.

At the sub-national level, there are constitutional protections of human rights, although the mandate of the institutions and processes of human rights enforcement might not be sufficiently clear. The FDRE Constitution provides corresponding obligations on legislative, executive and judicial organs at both levels, imposing the duty to respect and protect fundamental rights and freedoms. Regional states as crucial actors in the enforcement of human rights have constitutional obligation to this effect.

At a glance, duplicate protection mechanisms of rights at the national and sub-national levels might provide evidence, where it occurs, of sub-national constitutionalism.[47] Where a supreme national constitution already provides express protection for a right, the provision of protection of the same right in a sub-national constitution appears at first glance to be superfluous. Yet, it could be contended that mechanisms of sub-national protection of human rights may have many advantages. First, they could be easily available as a means of addressing questions. Second, they would reduce the practice of resorting to extra-constitutional and extra-legal redress. Third, they would supplement the growing emphasis in many parts of the world on supranational and international regimes as primary protectors of human rights. Instead of a single regime of rights protection implemented at the national level, sub-national protection of human rights can allow room for the creation of a second, and to some degree competing and completing regime of rights protection.

For Gardner, there are two ways in which sub-national constitutions might protect the liberty of individuals in a state. The first and most obvious scenario is that sub-national constitutions might protect liberty directly, through the identification and explicit protection of rights or its equivalent. Second,

46 In federations, power is distributed both vertically between federal government and state governments and horizontally between the three organs; namely legislative, executive and judiciary.

47 See Tsegaye Regassa, 'Sub-National Constitutions in Ethiopia: Towards Entrenching Constitutionalism at State Level' (2009) 3(1) Mizan Law Review 33, 51.

sub-national constitutions might protect liberty indirectly, by granting sub-national governments affirmative powers, sufficient to permit them to shield their citizens from abuses of centralised power at the national level.[48] Such mechanisms of protection of human rights thus allow sub-national units to use their autonomy to protect the rights of their citizens, either by identifying and protecting rights in enforceable sub-national constitutional rights, or by using other powers to block rights-invading actions of the national authorities. Hence, sub-national rights protection opens a room for wider protection of rights at the regional level.[49]

7.2 *Framework of Rights, Institutions and Remedies for Violations of Rights in the Tigray Region*

7.2.1 The Framework of Rights

Tigray is one of the nine regional states of Ethiopia. It is located in the northern part of the country. According to article 50 (2) of the FDRE Constitution, the Regional State of Tigray shall have legislative, executive and judicial bodies. Pursuant to article 50 (3) of the Constitution, the 'State Council is the highest organ of State Authority.' What is more, the 'State Council has the power of legislation on matters falling under State jurisdiction,' which includes the drafting, adopting and amending of state constitutions.[50] Within the framework of the FDRE Constitution, the Tigray Regional State (TNRS) has enacted its own constitution, which has since undergone a series of revisions from the transitional Constitution of 1993,[51] to Proclamation No.1/1987 (E.C.), and to the Amended Constitution of Tigray Proclamation No.45/1994 (E.C.), which in turn is amended by Proclamation No.105/1998 (E.C.).[52]

Following the FDRE Constitution, the Revised Constitution of Tigray guarantees fundamental rights and freedoms of the people under Chapter Three. Being a member of the Ethiopian Federation, the previous discussions on rights under the FDRE Constitution are extremely relevant. Thus, the nature of

48 James A Gardner, 'In Search of Sub-national Constitutionalism' (Paper prepared for 7th World Congress, International Association of Constitutional Law, Athens 2007) 5.

49 Christophe Van der Beken, 'Sub-National Constitutional Autonomy in Ethiopia: On the Road to Distinctive Regional Constitution' 1. (Paper submitted to the IXth World Congress of Constitutional Law 'Constitutional Challenges: Global and Local,' Proceedings, Oslo, 2014) <http://www.jus.uio.no/english/research/news-and-events/events/conference/2014/wccl-cmdc/wccl/papers/Ws2/W2-Vanderbeken.pdf> accessed 22 August 2015.

50 FDRE Constitution (n 3).

51 The Tigray Transitional Constitution was enacted following the Transitional Charter of 1991. It was first enacted on June 20, 1993.

52 'The Constitution of the Federal State of Tigray' (as amended) Proclamation No.45/1994 E.C (and its amendment Proclamation No.105/19998 E.C.).

rights, their limitation, the system of adjudication and its problems, and the remedies for human rights violations shall *mutatis mutandis* apply to the regional context as well.

For instance, article 16 of the Revised Constitution provides that 'Everyone shall have the right to protection against bodily harm.' Article 18 (1) provides 'Everyone has the right to be protected against cruel, inhuman or degrading treatment and punishment.' In principle, international human rights are also directly applicable to regional states, but there is no clarity as to how international human rights could be enforced in the regions. The confusion regarding the enforcement of constitutional rights at the federal level is more or less replicated in the regions with far-reaching consequences.

In summary, it is held that as far as the formulation and protection of substantive rights is concerned, the Revised Constitution is very similar to the FDRE Constitution except for a few provisions. It is also evident that the protection of rights under the Revised Constitution occurs at two levels. The first mechanism is through the immediate effect of federal constitutional rights and international human rights instruments in the region, by virtue of article 13(1), article 9(4) and article 13(2) of the FDRE Constitution. The second mechanism of protection is through regional constitutional guarantees.

7.2.2 Procedural Guarantees and Remedies for Violations of Rights

The institutional frameworks for the protection of rights in the TNRS are courts, the CCI, the Constitutional Commission, and other quasi-judicial bodies. In fact, the Tigray Regional State has established similar institutions that are directly or indirectly related to human rights enforcement. The first important organ is the judiciary, involving both ordinary courts and quasi-judicial courts such as the Tax Appeal Commission and Civil Service Tribunal. The Woreda Court is the lowest court structure in the region as far as ordinary courts are concerned. The FDRE Constitution establishes a dual court structure at the federal and state levels.[53] Similar to the FDRE Constitution, therefore, the Revised Constitution establishes three levels of courts.[54] Thus, the judicial structure in the TNRS is composed of the State Supreme Court, the State High Court (Zonal Court), and the State First-Instance Courts (Woreda Court).

The State Supreme Court is the highest judicial organ of the Region, which is located in Mekelle. There are three benches at the Regional Supreme Court.

53 FDRE Constitution (n 3) art 78 (1 and 2).

54 Proclamation No.251/2001 (n 45) art 65.

These are the Cassation Bench, the Criminal Bench, and the Civil Bench.[55] Zonal Courts are middle level Courts; at the zonal level, there are 15 Zonal Courts, each having both civil and criminal benches.[56] In Tigray, there are 94 Woreda Courts, which entertain both criminal and civil matters in holistic benches, although the Revised Constitution Establishment Proclamation requires separate civil and criminal benches.[57] The other types of courts in the TNRS are Social Courts, which assume quasi-judicial functions. Since the Revised Constitution anticipates only three tiers of court structures, one can safely conclude that Social Courts are not really within the purview of the hierarchy of regular courts.

On the other hand, parallel to the federal institutions of the HoF and the CCI, the Region has established two constitutional institutions, namely the regional Council of Constitutional Inquiry and the Constitutional Commission.[58] The two institutions were established only in 2012, 17 years since the adoption of the regional Constitution. To date, both institutions have not been furnished with their own secretariat and offices. The Chairperson of the Constitutional Commission is the Speaker of the Regional Council.

The mandate of the two institutions is very similar to that of the two federal institutions, the CCI and HoF. Hence, the discussions on the competence and operation-related problems of the CCI and the HoF apply *mutatis mutandis* to the regional institutions as well. Yet, the following differences can also be observed: first, the mandates of the Constitutional Commission and the Council of Constitutional Inquiry are limited to the Tigray Constitution, proclamations, regulations, directives, and issues of constitutionality raised in such connection. Since their establishment, the institutions have not decided more than twenty cases. In recent times, there has been an increase in the number of cases being submitted to their jurisdiction, many of them related to land rights.

Evidently, the fact that regional states have the obligation to enforce the FDRE Constitution and the fact that those constitutional disputes under the FDRE Constitution are brought before the HoF may have created jurisdictional confusion, and hence may create competing platforms and encourage forum shopping by applicants.

---

55 Ibid art 14 (1).

56 Ibid art 14 (2).

57 Ibid art 14 (4).

58 Federal Negarit Gazeta, 'Council of Constitutional Inquiry' Proclamation No.229/2006 (E.C.) and Federal Negarit Gazeta, 'Constitutional Commission Proclamation' Proclamation No.228/2205 (E.C.).

Similarly, the establishment of regional sub-national institutions parallel to the Human Rights Commission and Ombudsman instituted at the federal level is worth considering. Under the FDRE Constitution, regional states are authorised to 'establish regional government and other administrative levels they [states] deem necessary.'[59] The FDRE Constitution is not however clear on whether states can also establish regional institutions, such as the Human Rights Commission and Ombudsman. It is however evident that the regions are free to set up their internal administrative functions, which may well include the establishment of such democratic and human rights institutions. In fact, for regions to meaningfully carry out their responsibility and duty under the federal Constitution in relation to human rights, the establishment of human rights institutions would be an imperative undertaking.

Thus far, the discussions have focused on the different institutions involved in the enforcement of human rights in Ethiopia and the TNRS. In the following sections, the respective jurisdictional competencies of courts will be investigated in the regional setting.

8 Empirical Evidence

As stated above, human rights can be enforced either as stand-alone cases having their own processes and institutions, or through further legislation such as criminal law, labour law, tort law, property law. This research investigated a total of thirty cases: twenty of them are civil cases and the other ten cover criminal matters drawn from the Mekelle, Alamata, Adigrat and Shire zonal courts. The objective is to understand and discern a pattern of enforcement of human rights provisions of the Constitution through the employment of different parameters.

8.1 *Analysis of Cases*

In all the court cases investigated, the research found that none of the applications were predicated on human rights claims submitted as separate and independent rights. Out of the thirty cases examined, courts made mention of the constitutional bill of rights established under the FDRE only in one civil and one criminal matter.

59 FDRE Constitution (n 3) art 50 (4).

The civil case involves a dispute over land between *Amete Gebresilassie v Abadi Gebresilassie* and a third-party defendant, Shishay Gebregziabher.[60] The case was brought before the Ayder Woreda Court. The plaintiff argued that enjoyment of her right to use the land that she lawfully possesses has been hindered by the defendant and the third party. Essentially, the Court relied on the Civil Code in rendering its decision. However, the Court explicitly stated that the plaintiff has the right to use and enjoy the fruits of his property as enshrined under articles 40 (1) and (2) of the FDRE Constitution. Yet, the Court refrained from indicating whether the defendant and the third party were responsible for violation of the constitutional rights of the plaintiff. This approach was not meaningful, since it is pointless for the Court to mention the Constitution and not to make any one responsible for its violation. On the other hand, in the *Prosecutor vs. Birhane T/mariam et al* case, the Court gave a decision based on the right to personal security guaranteed under article 16 of the FDRE Constitution.[61] The case was entertained by the Mekelle Zonal Court. The defendants were charged for violating various provisions of the Criminal Code. Along with relevant provisions of the Criminal Code, the Court mentioned article 16 of the FDRE Constitution, stating that the defendants have violated the right to personal liberty and security.

A cursory review of the cases sampled for the purpose of this study demonstrates that the constitutional bill of rights is invoked only rarely as informing private and criminal law litigation in Tigray. However, when a party argues based on the higher law, the issue has a very high likelihood of ending up as a matter of constitutional dispute.

Similarly, the decision-making process of the Constitutional Commission looks very informal, highly politicised, and hardly legal. All cases analysed show a perceptible pattern. The following are some of the cases decided by the Constitutional Commission, split into two groups. The first three cases relate to individual cases, and the fourth is related to group identity.

In a constitutional dispute between *Amine Berwo v Justice Office*, the claimant submitted a constitutional question to the Council of Constitutional Inquiry to invalidate a regional law, Regulation No.10/1992 (E.C.) that the Justice Office based its decision on. The claimant argued that the Regulation violates his constitutional rights set out under the FDRE Constitution, including article 25 (right to equality), article 37 (access to justice) and article 9 (supremacy clause). He first submitted his case to the Council of Constitutional Inquiry,

60 *Amete Gebresilassie v Abadi Gebresilassie* and a third-party defendant Shishay Gebregziabher, File No.04795, Ayder Woreda Court.

61 *Prosecutor v Brhane T/mariam and others*, File No. 04262, Ayder Woreda Court.

which dismissed the case on the ground that the Regulation in question does not violate the rights stated under the federal Constitution and hence there is no need for constitutional interpretation. An appeal was taken to the Regional Constitutional Commission, which upheld the decision rendered by the Council of Constitutional Inquiry. The Commission similarly reasoned that the Regulation does not violate any of the rights set out in the Constitution.

The second case was referred to the Ayder Woreda Court in an instance involving land rights between private persons (land use rights). The dispute that gave rise to the constitutional issue was concerning the transfer of a title for the sale of free land. The Constitutional Commission decided that there is a need for constitutional interpretation, as the case raises a constitutional matter. The Commission reasoned that free land cannot be the subject of sale or any other mode of exchange as per article 40 (3) of the Regional Constitution. Hence, the contract entered into between the seller and the buyer was unconstitutional and no right to transfer had existed during the making of the contract.

In a similar case, the Constitutional Commission received a constitutional complaint from the Semien Woreda Court, where the Court ordered the Semien Sub City Administration to transfer free land rights to a head of Church called Gebremesekl Hindeya. The Sub City Administration brought a constitutional dispute before the Council of Constitutional Inquiry and the Council gave its recommendation for constitutional interpretation. The Commission approved the recommendation of the Council, reasoning that the complainant has no right over free land that is the property of the state.

In a different case, the Constitutional Commission rejected a constitutional claim of identity of one *qushet* (*sub-kebele*) called Adi Sheik Adem. A *kebele* is the smallest administrative unit in Ethiopia, similar to a ward or neighbourhood, whereas a *qushet* is the lowest unit of administration in Tigray. The representative of the Qushet Adi Sheik Adem brought the identity claim to the Council of Constitutional Inquiry, requesting a right to be administered under the Afar Regional State based on article 39 of the FDRE Constitution and Tigray Constitution. The *qushet* had previously been administered as a *kebele*, but relegated to *sub-qushet* status due to administrative reorganisation. The representatives also raised that the whole *qushet* speaks the language of Afar and that their geographic setting, religion and culture is the same as that of the Afar people. The Council of Constitutional Inquiry decided that there is no need for constitutional interpretation and dismissed their claim. An appeal was taken to the Constitutional Commission, which on its part decided that the people in question have the right to self-administration under the *qushet*. They have the right to use and promote their language, identity and religion within the regional state of Tigray. Accordingly, their right to 'secede' from Tigray and join the Afar Regional State was rejected. An attempt to take the matter to the House of the Federation was not successful.

This case involving the group's identity claim raised interesting legal issues. Whose mandate is it to entertain identity rights claims under the Ethiopian federal structure? As per the Proclamation that established the Constitutional Commission, identity cases should first be brought before the relevant bodies in the regions. The requirement of exhaustion of local remedies is a key procedural requirement stated in said Proclamation.

8.2 *Analysis of Qualitative Data*

In order to examine and understand the perception of judges, police, public prosecutors, lawyers/attorneys, the public and arrested persons, a semi-structured interview was prepared and conducted with each of the selected respondents, focusing on their respective powers and how they make sense of the enforcement of human rights. The observations of the data collectors and researchers are summarised in the following section. Four Zones in the region were selected for the interview. These are the North Western Zone, the Central Zone, the Eastern Zone and the Southern Zone. From the judiciary, a total of thirteen judges from civil and criminal benches, including presidents who are directly involved in the handling and assignment of cases, were purposefully selected. A total of fifteen practicing lawyers and eight public prosecutors was also interviewed. The selection method of the public prosecutors was purposive sampling, wherein those who are directly involved and had supervised criminal cases were chosen. Practicing lawyers were randomly chosen when they were in the court compounds or because their offices happened to be near to the courts. The method of selection of police officers followed a purposeful sampling approach, where those in the commanding positions were interviewed. To get general information on the level of awareness of the public in relation to the processes and institutions of human rights adjudication, focus group discussions were also conducted with arrested persons (approximately forty persons in Shire Endaselassie and fifty persons in Axum). The following section summarises the interviews and draws conclusions based on the information gathered.

8.3 *Summary of Results of Interviews with Judges*

The judges were asked about their experience of litigation that involved the constitutional bill of rights. All of them responded that there was no case submitted before their benches explicitly predicated on the violation of rights recognised under the Constitution(s). They further responded that a case could be submitted before their jurisdiction only if the claim could be supported by a specific legal provision. When asked whether they had in mind human rights provisions as stipulated under the Constitution(s), almost all responded that they did not, except in few instances involving bail rights, rights of arrested/detained persons, and article 40 of the FDRE Constitution on property-related disputes. The judges were also asked what they would have done if they had received cases alleging human rights violations as covered under the Constitution(s); they responded that in such cases, they would refer the case to the police if it is related to a crime, and to local authorities if the case relates to private rights. However, they all responded that there is no 'human rights-related adjudication' as such, the only forums available being limited to the criminal and civil benches. Thus, there is no 'stand-alone' or sufficient protection of rights provided by the judiciary, except when a human rights violation case is pursued within the framework of other specific laws.

8.4 *Summary of Results of Interviews with the Police*

Police officers were asked whether they received violations of constitutionally guaranteed rights either from individuals or from public authorities. All reported that they did not receive specific claims of violations predicated on human rights. All submissions pursued claimed commission of a criminal offence in violation of the FDRE Criminal Code such as homicide, rape, arson etc. In such cases, they said, the cases merely proceed as a criminal matter and the investigations are conducted on such basis.

The police were also asked whether they received complaints against police officers, alleging violations of constitutionally protected rights. Very few (two of the respondents) said they received formal complaints on such basis and, in fact, one police officer stated that a dismissal and criminal prosecution of an officer (in the North Western Zone) resulted from a complaint of transgression committed by the police officer.

8.5 *Summary of Results of Interviews with Public Prosecutors*

Public prosecutors were asked on how they protect the rights of individuals during their work. All of them stated that during criminal investigations and prosecutions, they only refer to the relevant parts of criminal law. However, they also mentioned that they undertake visits to prisons to check on the status of arrested persons and to monitor instances of abuse in police stations. As far as a specific mentioning of human rights in criminal proceedings is concerned, all said that they hardly remember any cases where human rights were explicitly invoked on the basis of the Constitution(s).

8.6 *Summary of Results of Interviews with Attorneys*

Likewise, practicing lawyers were asked whether they received human rights-related cases, either as stand-alone cases or related to other cases. All responded that they did not receive alleged rights violations except for one, who did not take the case up with a court. All interviewed attorneys stated they hardly argue cases based on constitutional provisions, although mention of occasional references could be made.

8.7 *Summary of Results of Interviews with Arrested Persons*

A large number of focus group discussants said the police did not inform them that they had the right to remain silent. Many also said they were not promptly informed about the reasons of their arrest. Similarly, many complained about failure and abuses on the part of the police. Bringing these claims before courts could take many days, sometimes even weeks. One arrested person said he did not appear before the court for more than twenty days. Two Eritreans, who escaped from refugee camps and were arrested in Axum police station, were held for a long time without any charge. When the police commander was asked why, he responded that they were detained not because of the commission of a crime. However, until they were sent back to their camps, an obvious instance of flagrant violation of constitutional safeguards and misunderstanding in the enforcement of human rights occurred.

Other arrested persons also complained that their rights were grossly violated, especially by police officers. When asked where they took their cases in the event of violations, many responded that they did not have such opportunity at all. Complaints lodged with police officers at police stations rarely receive proper attention. When asked where else they could take their cases complaining against police abuses, most of them said courts would be the preferred platforms.

9 Conclusions

This chapter investigated the practice of enforcement of constitutional bills of rights in regional states in Ethiopia through the jurisprudence of courts and other constitutional organs. The Region of Tigray was taken as a case study. The discussions mainly dwelled on civil and political rights, due to the less controversial nature of these rights as opposed to socio-economic and cultural rights. The paper involved a two-tiered approach: normative discourse together with a practical analysis of court practices and other constitutional organs. For this, constitutional-legal analysis and qualitative empirical research methods were employed.

The FDRE Constitution recognises fundamental human and democratic rights. In identical terms, the Tigray Revised Constitution recognises fundamental human and democratic rights. Both Constitutions stipulate the highest judicial power (in the region) is vested in the Tigray Supreme Court. Parallel to the set up and mandates of federal institutions like the HoF and the CCI, the Revised Constitution established two constitutional institutions, namely the regional Council of Constitutional Inquiry and the Constitutional Commission.

The issue of the promotion and enforcement of fundamental human rights by courts is a rather significant point of concern. Judicial practice reveals that courts hardly apply the Constitution's human rights safeguards in practical settings. Stand-alone claims relating to the violation of human rights are virtually non-existent. It was found that out of the thirty cases analysed, courts in Tigray invoked the constitutional bill of rights in only one civil case and in one criminal case. Even in the particular civil case mentioned, while the judges had mentioned the constitutional bill of rights, the court failed to indicate the party that was in fact responsible for violation of the rights. This meant that the courts ignored the relevant section of the bill of rights when it was evident that the judgment would not be based on the Constitution as such. From this, it is concluded that the two cases could not be used to support the argument that judges apply the constitutional bill of rights in their cases. The investigation also revealed that practicing lawyers do not make human rights arguments based on the Constitution(s) a part of their strategy in advancing the interest of their clients.

In conclusion, in spite of the incorporation of fundamental human and democratic rights both under the FDRE Constitution and under the Tigray National Regional State's Revised Constitution, it appears courts have kept the position that they are not the right avenue to promote and enforce these rights. The findings of the paper reveal that notwithstanding the ratification of international human rights instruments and the constitutional recognition of fundamental rights and freedoms, there is little to no practice of their enforcement before courts of law. Courts mention constitutional bills of rights only in passing, merely to give weight to their decisions. The pattern is not fundamentally different in other constitutional bodies, such as the Council of Constitutional Inquiry and the Constitutional Commission.

As a result, it can safely be concluded that constitutional rights litigation as a stand-alone procedure is wholly underdeveloped. Any meaningful protection of rights requires credible institutions and clear procedures, as well as remedies in the absence of which no true protection of rights can be imagined. Future discourse must therefore focus on revitalising the roles of such institutions so that the objectives of the Constitution(s) in safeguarding fundamental rights can be pursued meaningfully and more effectively.

Assessing the Ethiopian House of Federation in the Light of the Exhaustion of the Local Remedies Rule under the African Charter

Mulu Beyene Kidanemariam

Abstract

Human rights monitoring bodies at the regional and global levels are typically accessible to individual complainants. However, for petitions to be considered there is a usual condition that domestic remedies, among others, be exhausted first. This requirement is qualified in all systems in order to not frustrate the very purpose of availing people with international protection. For instance, for local remedies to be exhausted as a condition for admissibility under the African Charter for Human and Peoples' Rights (the Charter), such remedies need to be available, effective and sufficient in the first place. The actual content of these qualities, however, is not easy to pin down. Moreover, ascertaining these qualities in actual cases requires a closer look at the operations of the organ under review and the prevailing context within which it works. The purpose of this chapter is to highlight how these qualifications are being applied in the growing jurisprudence of the Charter. It does so by taking a recent decision from the African Commission on Human and Peoples' Rights (the Commission) in which the Ethiopian House of Federation (HoF) and its constitutional review mandate was scrutinised vis-à-vis the stated qualities of the Exhaustion of Local Remedies Rule. The chapter considers whether the HoF qualifies as an organ that offers remedies worthy of exhaustion for the purpose of admissibility before the Commission. It is identified that the Commission has left out important considerations of the rule from its own jurisprudence. If these had been duly considered, they might arguably have changed the final ruling in a particular case in which a complaint was found to be inadmissible. It is argued that if a proper and holistic assessment was made, the HoF and more precisely the remedies that it provides fall short of qualifying for the requirements of the Commission.

Keywords

African Commission on Human and Peoples' Rights – House of Federation – Exhaustion of Local Remedies Rule – Charities and Societies Proclamation – Ethiopia

 | DOI:10.1163/9789004415966_015

1 Introduction

Addressing this particular research problem requires a three-tiered analysis. First, the content, or indicators of the qualities of the rule need to be established. Second, the extent to which the African Commission on Human and Peoples' Rights (the Commission) applied these tests to the case mentioned is scrutinised. In a way, this is a question of consistency. The third and more nuanced part of the investigation will focus on the Commission's characterisation of the House of Federation (HoF) and the Council of Constitutional Inquiry (CCI) to the extent that it informed the ultimate decision made.

1.1 *General Essence and Rationale of the Rule*

Traditionally understood as a norm in the sense that a '[s]tate should be given the opportunity to redress an alleged wrong within the framework of its own domestic legal system before its international responsibility can be called into question,'[1] the Exhaustion of Local Remedies Rule (the Rule) is now provided for in virtually all international and regional human rights instruments as a condition for admissibility.[2] The Rule is said to have originated in the context of the diplomatic protection of aliens, where the host state was allowed to settle the matter internally before international mechanisms were invoked.[3] Particularly since the 1950s, it also emerged in the realm of human rights.[4] However, the different nature of human rights, focusing on the protection of individuals rather than the reputation of states, means that a realistic approach of exhaustion of local remedies must be followed, marked by absence of mechanical or rigid application.[5]

1 Cancado Trindade, *The Application of the Rule of Exhaustion of Local Remedies in International Law: Its Rationale in the International Protection of Individual Rights* (Cambridge 1983) 1.

2 Frans Viljoen, 'Communications under the African Charter: Procedure and Admissibility' in Malcolm Evans and Rachel Murray (eds), *The African Charter on Human and Peoples' Rights: The System in Practice, 1986–2000* (2nd edn, Cambridge University Press 2008) 111; See also Ebenezer Durojaye, 'An Assessment of the Decision of the Committee of Experts of the African Children's Charter in the Nubian Children Communication' (2012) 12 African Human Rights Law Journal 570.

3 Viljoen (no 2) 111 citing CF Amerasinghe, *Local Remedies in International* Law (2nd edn, Cambridge University Press 2004).

4 Silvia D'Ascoli and Kathrin Maria Scherr, 'Rule of Prior Exhaustion of Local Remedies in the Context of Human Rights Protection' (2006) 117 Italian Yearbook of International Law, 127.

5 Trindade (n 1) 49.

The African Charter on Human and Peoples' Rights (the Charter), like other human rights instruments, provides for the exhaustion of local remedies as one of the conditions for communications to be considered by the Commission. The Rule applies for both the inter-state as well as the individual complaint system, which has dominated the works of the Commission.[6] Given the differences in the nature of the communications, the forums and manners with which the remedies are to be exhausted also differ, as is clearly noted in the Commission's Rules of Procedure.[7] As for the purpose of this research, the focus is on the individual complaint system under the Charter; it is to be noted that the exhaustion rule is only one of the seven cumulative admissibility requirements under article 56 the Charter.[8]

The Commission has frequently expressed that the Rule is the most important condition for admissibility and one that is 'in almost all the cases, the first requirement looked at by both the Commission and the states concerned.'[9] Indeed, the Commission considers the Rule as 'the cornerstone of the Commission's adjudicatory function.'[10] This may have occurred for several reasons. For once, it is heavily used by states and the Commission must deal with it in almost every communication it seizes.[11] The other possible explanation is that it is a condition that closely relates to the very purpose of having an international/regional system; the Rule is one way of monitoring whether member states have put in place a system that enables them to implement the Charter rights. This is as the Rule 'entails a state's duty to maintain the legal basis for

6 See the African (Banjul) Charter on Human and Peoples' Rights (signed 27 June 1981, entry into force 12 October 1986) OAU Doc CAB/LEG/67/3 rev 5, 21 I.L.M. 58, arts 50 and 56(5), respectively.

7 For the 'interstate communications,' see African Commission on Human and Peoples' Rights (ACHPR), 'Rules of Procedure' (20–26 May 2010, Banjul, The Gambia), rule 87 (2(b)) <http://www.achpr.org/files/instruments/rules-of-procedure-2010/rules_of_procedure_2010_en.pdf> accessed 5 May 2018. For 'other communications,' see the African Charter (n 6) art 56(5) and ACHPR Rules of Procedure (n 7) rules 93(2, i) and 106.

8 The other six are: providing full author information, compatibility with the Charter (complaints only against state parties and the need to show a prima facie violation); use of decent language in writing a complaint; application not being exclusively based on media reports (the need to corroborate allegations); that a complaint is brought within reasonable time to the Commission; and that it is not settled or is under consideration in other forums.

9 *Sir Dawda K Jawara v The Gambia*, Communications 147/95 and 149/96 (Jawara case), para 30.

10 *Crawford Lindsay von Abo v The Republic of Zimbabwe*, Communication 477/2014, para 66.

11 Takele Soboka Bulto, 'Exception as Norm: Local Remedies Rule in the Context of Socio-Economic Rights in the African Human Rights, System' (2012) 16 The International Journal of Human Rights, 560.

the domestic protection of treaty-based rights as well as to provide effective and sufficient remedies in case of their violation.'[12]

Closely related to this, the Rule is usually discussed in relation to the right to fair trial or right to effective remedy, when this is provided. For instance, the Commission held that article 56(5) 'must be applied concomitantly with Article 7, which establishes and protects the right to fair trial.'[13] Further, in its Fair Trial Guidelines, the Commission notes that the right to an effective remedy includes access to justice, reparation for the harm suffered, and access to the factual information concerning the violations.[14] It is submitted that the Charter does not provide the right to effective remedy as a free-standing right.[15] However, three provisions in the Charter would establish the right indirectly.[16] First, it is argued that the right is a constituent element of the general obligation that requires state parties to give effect to the norms of the Charter.[17] In addition, the duty 'to guarantee the independence of the Courts and … allow the establishment and improvement of appropriate national institutions entrusted with the promotion and protection of the rights and freedoms guaranteed by the present Charter'[18] signifies a core of the right to effective remedy. As hinted above, the right to fair trial, as enshrined under article 7 of the Charter is the other normative basis for effective remedy.

With regard to its rationale, different reasons are offered explaining the application of the Rule in human rights monitoring bodies. The Commission has highlighted a number of them in its decisions. These reasons seem to be crafted in a way that they address the interests of the state concerned, the Commission, and complainants. From the perspective of a state that is accused of violating a Charter right, the Rule emanates from the need to give it a notice of human rights violation and thereby an 'opportunity to remedy matters through

12 Ibid 561.

13 *Amnesty International* [*et*] *al./Sudan,* Consolidated communications 48/90, 50/91, 89/93, para 31.

14 See African Commission on Human and Peoples' Rights, 'Principles and Guidelines on the Right to a Fair Trial and Legal Assistance in Africa,' part C (b) <http://www.achpr.org/instruments/principles-guidelines-right-fair-trial/> accessed 5 May 2018.

15 For this it has been criticised. See for instance, Godfrey M Musila, 'The Right to an Effective Remedy under the African Charter on Human and Peoples' Rights' (2006) 6 African Human Rights Law Journal, 447.

16 See Nsonguruaj Udomban, 'So Far, So Fair: The Local Remedies Rule in the Jurisprudence of the African Commission on Human and Peoples' Rights' (2003) 1 American Journal of International Law, 9–10.

17 African Charter (no 6) art 1.

18 Ibid art 26.

its own local system.'[19] Such an opportunity is supposed to help an accused state 'save its reputation' by acting before an allegation reaches the external world.[20] To Viljoen, '[i]t is only fair that a State must be afforded full opportunity to give effect to its international law obligations, something it has consented to do.'[21] In line with this, the Commission has considered some communications admissible in cases where the states' awareness of the violations was obvious or is proven. For instance, in earlier joined cases that involved the then Zaire (now the Democratic Republic of Congo), the Commission explained that 'the government had ample notice of the violations' in considering the complaint admissible despite the fact that domestic remedies were not exhausted.[22] Similarly, in a more recent case, the Commission had to say the following in rejecting the government's admissibility defence based on article 56(5):

> In the instant case, the international community in general and the African Commission paid particular attention to the events that took place in the run up to the referendum in Zimbabwe in February 2000 right up to the end of and after the Parliamentary elections of June 2002. The Respondent State was *sufficiently informed and aware of the worrying human rights situation* prevailing at the time.[23]

Apart from the issue of fairness to the respondent state, it is also observed that the requirement of exhaustion of local remedies conforms with the principle that international law is subsidiary to national law,[24] meaning rights are supposed to be enforced at the national level, and the international procedures would set in only if the former is not up to the task. To this state-centric justification of the Rule, one can add that the Rule also gives national institutions the chance to be challenged and thus to practice ways of safeguarding rights.

19 See for instance the Jawara case (n 9) para 31. Related to this, the Commission's Rules of Procedure dictate that complaints should include, among others, information regarding 'any public authority that has taken cognizance of the fact or situation alleged.' See ACHPR Rules of Procedure (n 7) rule 92(2(f)).

20 *Anuak Justice Council v Ethiopia,* Communication 299/05 (Anuak case), para 47.

21 Viljoen (n 2) 111.

22 *Free Legal Assistance Group and others v Zaire,* Communications 25/89, 47/90, 56/91, 100/93, para 36.

23 *Zimbabwe Human Rights NGO Forum v Zimbabwe,* Communication 245/02, para 69 (emphasis added).

24 Viljoen (n 2) 111. The Commission also opined that the rule reinforces 'the subsidiarity and complementarity relationship of the international system to that of internal protection'. See, the Anuak case (n 20) para 48.

From the standpoint of the Commission, the Exhaustion of Local Remedies Rule spares it from becoming a court of first instance, which is not tenable as a matter of realism and principle. In the words of the Commission, the application of the Rule enables it to 'avoid playing the role of a court of first instance, a role that it cannot under any circumstances arrogate to itself.'[25] Lastly, the Rule has also been approached from the perspective of complainants. In this regard, the Commission would argue that local remedies are 'normally quicker, cheaper, and more effective than international ones.'[26] Explaining the relative advantage of domestic procedures over international mechanisms, the Commission reasoned that in the domestic arena, 'an appellate court can reverse the decision of a lower court, whereas the decision of an international organ does not have that effect, although it will engage the international responsibility of the state concerned.'[27] In a way, the message is that the rule is in place not only in reverence to state parties' reputation, but also in consonance with complaints' interests.

1.2 *The Scope of the Rule: Available, Effective and Sufficient*

Having introduced the essence of the Rule in general, let us now briefly sketch its content under the Charter as developed in the jurisprudence of the Commission. To begin with the relevant provision, it reads that communications shall be considered if they 'are sent after exhausting local remedies, if any, unless it is obvious that this procedure is unduly prolonged.'[28] This tells little about the nature of the remedy that needs to be exhausted to satisfy the admissibility requirement; it has been described as 'well established but inadequately defined.'[29] It is clear that complainants should exhaust procedures that are not unduly prolonged and inefficient. It is important to consider the question as to what other substantive characteristics a remedy should possess in order for it to serve as an admissibility requirement under article 56(5) of the Charter.

The leading case, where the Commission set out these characteristics for the purpose of the rule is the *Sir Dawda* case.[30] Accordingly, for a remedy envisaged under article 56(5) to warrant exhaustion, it must be 'available, effective and sufficient.' Further, '[a] remedy is considered available if the petitioner

25 *Malawi African Association and Others v Mauritania,* Communications 54/91, 61/91, 98/93, 164–196/97 and 210/98, para 80.

26 Anuak case (n 20) para 48.

27 Ibid.

28 African Charter (no 6) art 56(5).

29 Silvia and Scherr (n 4) 118 citing PC Jessup, *A Modern Law of Nations* (Cambridge 1956) 104.

30 Jawara case (n 9).

can pursue it without impediment, it is deemed effective if it offers a prospect of success, and it is found sufficient if it is capable of redressing the complaint.'[31] These three characteristics have been further analysed by the Commission in subsequent communications.

It appears that it suffices for a complainant to show that either of the features is missing to get away with the requirement. That being said, making a distinction among them has been difficult, including in the jurisprudence of the Commission. According to Viljoen, 'they are often entangled and not usefully separable.'[32] Furthermore, the Commission in one case stated that the 'likelihood of the complainant succeeding in obtaining a remedy that would redress the situation complained of in this matter is so minimal as to render it unavailable and therefore ineffective,'[33] stressing how connected the features are. In short, the three elements and the reasonable time requirement have been considered constitutive elements of an effective remedy.[34]

Furthermore, the Commission gave some indications of what these requirements separately mean in real cases. To begin with the availability of a remedy, which is also implied with the use of 'if any' under article 56(5), it generally implies that the remedy at hand is readily accessible as a matter of practical reality.[35] For instance, challenging the constitutionality of laws for complainants from poor economic background was considered inaccessible and thus a remedy was unavailable to them.[36] Procedures that may otherwise redress violations are also adjudicated as unavailable to people who flee their countries out of genuine fear of persecution.[37] Other instances in which the Commission found remedies as not being available include situations where the jurisdiction of courts is ousted in such a way that it would have no means of checking the executive.[38] It also encompasses situations when a potential finding of violation by the Commission would potentially add nothing or little to the

31 Ibid paras 31 and 32.

32 Viljoen (n 2) 117. Similarly, it is noted that the similarity between effectiveness and sufficiency go 'sometimes even to such an extent that it [is] virtually impossible to make a distinction between the two.' See Udomban (n 16) 32.

33 *Lawyers of Human Rights v Swaziland,* Communication 251/02, para 27.

34 Musila (n 15) 446.

35 Viljoen (n 2) 117, citing cases the Commission disposed of.

36 *Purohit and Moore v The Gambia,* Communication 241/01.

37 See the Jawara case (n 9).

38 See for instance *Constitutional Rights Project* (*in respect of Zamani Lakwot and six others*) *v Nigeria* Communication 87/93,. It is noted in this regard that the Commission found violations of articles 7 and 26 of the Charter in those cases, where the jurisdiction of courts has been ousted, strengthening the link between the requirement and substantive rights of the Charter. See Henry Onoria, 'The African Commission on Human and Peoples'

applicant, such as the execution of an applicant amidst the consideration of a complaint by the Commission.[39] In such cases, the idea of exhausting remedies becomes illogical, according to the Commission. However, notwithstanding these indicative elements of the 'availability' requirement it needs to be noted that a mere (subjective) doubt by complainants about the availability of a remedy, as such, is not sufficient.[40] This means that if there are some avenues that might render justice despite limitations, complainants are supposed to attempt bringing their complaint to such avenues before they approach the Commission.

Turning back to effectiveness, a remedy is considered not effective, for instance, when complainants are asked to challenge a ruling on clemency[41] and the government has discretionary power to deport aliens.[42] Also the fact that a remedy is not of a judicial nature, such as a plea for pardon that cannot be vindicated as a right, is ruled as ineffective and thus does not need to be exhausted.[43] Remedies that give way for the executive branch of a government to influence the result have also been particularly scrutinised by the Commission as being remedies of non-judicial nature and thus ineffective.[44] However, the mere fact that a remedy is inconvenient, unattractive, or that it did not produce a result favoured by an applicant, does not render it ineffective.[45]

The Commission has also set sufficiency as a stand-alone test. Generally, sufficiency is understood as a capacity of a remedy to redress a complaint.[46] The expectation is that the type and magnitude of a redress should be, to the extent possible, proportionate to the violation at hand. Additionally, the Commission in a certain case has considered a remedy that only 'meets parts of a claim as understood by the Respondent State' as being not sufficient.[47] It is also observed that the Commission obviates the requirement in cases where

Rights and the Exhaustion of Local Remedies under the African Charter' (2003) 4 African Human Rights Law Journal 1, 10.

39 See for instance *International PEN, Constitutional Rights Project, Civil Liberties Organisation and Interights (on behalf of Ken Saro-Wiwa Jnr.) v Nigeria,* Communication, 137/94–139/94–154/96–161/97 where the military regime in Nigeria executed the complainants despite a provisional measure from the Commission for a stay of the same.

40 Viljoen (n 2) 118.

41 *Zimbabwe Human Rights NGO Forum v Zimbabwe,* Communication 245/02, para 67.

42 *Kenneth Good / Republic of Botswana,* Communication 313/05, para 89.

43 Onoria (n 38) 6.

44 Ibid 7.

45 *Michael Majuru v Zimbabwe* (2008) Communication 308/05, ACHPR (Majuru Case), para 102.

46 Udomban (n 16) 32.

47 *Crawford Lindsay von Abo v the Republic of Zimbabwe,* Communication 477/14, para 87.

massive violations can be established prima facie.[48] This is premised on the understanding that the state in such circumstances must have had ample opportunity to rectify violations and that it is unreasonable to demand the exhaustion of local remedies in the face of massive violations. This, therefore, renders the remedy impractical or undesirable.[49] It is also implicit that in such cases, the remedy that domestic procedures can offer is only limited and thus should not bar international protection. Regarding the procedure, the Commission has developed a three-step test.[50] Accordingly, the initial burden of proof rests with the complainant. As such, the complainant needs to set out what has been done to exhaust local remedies.[51] If the complainant contends that the remedy is unavailable/ineffective, s/he should prove it.[52] If this is satisfied, the responsibility shifts to the respondent state. If the state claims there is an untried remedy which is effective and adequate to redress the violation alleged, it needs to prove it.[53] If this is so proven, the claimant would get a chance to reply. This is the standard procedure as can be seen from many communications. However, at times claimants or respondent states fail to respond or present additional information that the Commission requests in the course of a ruling on admissibility. In these cases, the Commission rules against the party who fails to respond.[54] At last, it is worth noting that under the Rules of Procedure[55] and the jurisprudence of the Commission, there is a possibility of resubmitting a communication to the Commission after it was initially ruled inadmissible. This is provided that new evidence is presented, including the exhaustion of remedies that were not tried before filing the complaint to the Commission.

2 Communication 445/13 – *Human Rights Council and Others v Ethiopia*

Reviewing a recent case decided by the Commission will help investigate how the House of Federation of Ethiopia (HoF) performs against the indicators of 'available, efficient and sufficient' remedies. To this end, it is imperative to first

48 See for instance, *Open Society Justice Initiative v Côte d'Ivoire*, Communication 318/06.
49 Udomban (n 16) 24.
50 Viljoen (n 2) 113.
51 Ibid.
52 Ibid.
53 Ibid.
54 See Udomban (n 16) 18.
55 ACHPR Rules of Procedure (n 7) rule 107(4).

provide a summary of the case that the Commission decided. Following this, some aspects of the decision the author believes need more investigation and which might have changed the final ruling of the Commission will be examined. In doing so, the jurisprudence of the Commission on exhaustion of local remedies will be used as a framework. In addition, the functions and context within which the HoF works will be assessed, as they have played a crucial role in the decision of the Commission in the case at hand. The recent reform attempts and its promises will also be taken into account in the analysis. It should be noted that this particular Communication is only one of a handful but growing number of complaints against Ethiopia before the Commission.[56]

2.1 *Background*

The complaint, Communication 445/13 – *Human Rights Council and Others v Ethiopia*, was filed to the Secretariat of the Commission on 13 April 2013 by the Ethiopian Human Rights Council (the Council) against the Federal Democratic Republic of Ethiopia (FDRE), a state party to the Charter since 15 June 1998.[57]

56 Well before Ethiopia became signatory to the Charter on 15 June 1998, seven communications were lodged to the Commission against it. As they were duly considered as not receivable, they were simply dismissed – no public information is available about the cases. Since then, five communications have been submitted on which information is provided on the Commission's website, namely: *Interights v Ethiopia* and *Interights v Eritrea* (1999), which was postponed as the matter was seized in another international forum; *Anuak Justice Council v Ethiopia* (ruled inadmissible on account of local remedy rule); *Interights v Ethiopia* (2009) (also inadmissible for the same reason); *Heregewein and IHRDA v Ethiopia* (decided on merit and the Commission found Ethiopia in violation of various aspects of the right to fair trial during the Red Terror Trials); and *Human Rights Council v Ethiopia* (inadmissible on account of the local remedies rule). There are also more cases that, for some reason, do not appear in the website. The following are the ones that the author traced from the Annual Activity Reports of the Commission, but with no details: *Andargachew Tsege and and Yemsrach Hailemariam (Represented by Reprieve and REDRESS) v Ethiopia,* Communication 507/15; *Eskinder Nega Fenta and Reyoot Alemu v Ethiopia,* Communication 461/13; *Ethiopian Human Rights Project v Ethiopia,* Communication 599/16; *Abubaker Ahmed Mohamed & 28 Others (represented by X and Y) v Ethiopia,* Communication 455/13; *Equality Now and EWLA v Ethiopia,* Communication 341/07; *The Indigenous Peoples of the Lower Omo v Ethiopia,* Communication 419/12; and *Omo Valley and Lake Turkana Communities v Ethiopia,* Communication 397/11. From the Reports on which these communications are featured, it can be seen that many of them are seized and some even went past the admissibility stage. Unfortunately, no information is provided on these communications. Repeated email requests for clarification were unfortunately not responded to by the Secretariat of the Commission.

57 See the ratification status of the Charter at 'Ratification Table: African Charter on Human and Peoples' Rights,' African Commission on Human and Peoples' Rights (2018) <http://www.achpr.org/instruments/achpr/ratification/> accessed 5 May 2018.

Along the way, the Council was supported by other four non-governmental organisations.[58] At the centre of the contention was an alleged violation of various Charter rights by the respondent state through a decision made based on laws that regulate charities and Civil Society Organisations (CSOs) in Ethiopia.

Accordingly, the CSO Agency (the Agency), which is established under the Charities and Societies Proclamation No. 621/2009, froze the assets of the Council without notice and court warrant, including a bank account in the amount of US$ 566,000. The funds had been acquired from both domestic and foreign sources since 2002.[59] The basis of the measure was premised on the allegation that following the enactment of the law in 2009, the Council diverted funds it had acquired from foreign sources to its new status as a domestic human rights organisation. However, this contravenes said law, as the allowable limit that such organisations can acquire from outside sources is put to 10 percent.[60] Following the action, the Council challenged the legality and timeliness of the measure, contending that the laws do not give the Agency the right to freeze accounts and that the decision indiscriminately affected funds acquired from outside sources before the legal effective date, among others.[61] The legal challenge was first taken to a Board (established by the same law) and then to the Federal High Court with no success. On the basis of provisions of the Proclamation and other subsidiary laws (one regulation and one

58 *Human Rights Council and Others v Ethiopia,* Communication 445/13 (Human Rights Council case), para 1.

59 Ibid para 6.

60 See Federal Negarit Gazeta, 'The Charities and Societies Proclamation' Proclamation No. 621/09, art 88(1). In fact, the Agency has allowed the first Complainant to draw an amount equal to 10 percent of the latter's annual budget every year. The Agency intends to allow this until the entire fund is used, even if it claimed that it is empowered to transfer seized assets to another society or charity with similar objectives. (See ibid para 39). Currently, the Council is not using this 10 percent allowance as it has other ways of acquiring this modest amount from other sources and is hoping that the Agency/government would eventually release the fund in its totality, considering the important role that the Council is playing in advancing human rights in Ethiopia. Phone interview with Ato Betseate Tereffe, Executive Director, Human Rights Council, on 26 September 2017. That said, the law is one of the few pieces of legislation that is prioritised for amendment following the reform agenda of the Abiy administration. Accordingly, a draft amendment of the law is prepared by the Justice and Legal Affairs Advisory Council and submitted to the Office of the General Attorney for further consideration. See Bamlak Tadesse, 'Charities, Societies Law Amendment Comes to First Draft' *Afro Afro 105.4 FM* (2 November 2018) <http://www.afro105fm.com/afrofm.com/2018/11/02/charities-societies-law-amendment-comes-to-first-draft/> accessed 5 May 2018.

61 Human Rights Council case (n 58) paras 8–9.

circular) enacted subsequently, the Board and the Federal High Court ruled that the Agency indeed has the power to act as it did under the circumstances described. At last, the Council took the case to the Cassation Division of the Federal Supreme Court, which likewise upheld the decisions rendered hitherto.[62] It was following these procedures that the case was lodged before the Commission, claiming that the right to fair trial (article 7), freedom of expression (article 9), freedom of association (article 10) and the right to property (article 14) were allegedly violated.[63] It must be stressed that at the domestic forums, the Council attempted to challenge the legality of the Agency's decision without invoking a constitutional issue or right, whereas in the communication lodged to the Commission, Charter rights allegedly violated through the decision of the Agency did feature, as was to be expected.[64]

2.2 *Admissibility Issues – the Central Theme of Contention for the Commission*

In line with the relevant laws and jurisprudence of the Commission, the complainants explained how the application complies with the admissibility requirements. Regarding the Exhaustion of Local Remedies Rule, which emerged as the single most important issue of contention, they claimed that the above-outlined steps that were taken comply with the Charter requirements. The respondent state expectedly took issue with this. In this regard, it argued that the rights implicated in the application are guaranteed under the FDRE Constitution directly or through the application of article 9(4) of the same, which makes international treaties ratified by the country become part of its domestic law.[65] The respondent state then went on to explain that in the constitutional arrangement of the country 'courts of law have no power to interpret the Constitution,' and that this power is in the exclusive province of the HoF, as assisted by the Council of Constitutional Inquiry (CCI).[66] Besides, to prove the effectiveness and sufficiency of the remedy the respondent state claims should

62 Ibid paras 9–11.

63 Ibid para 16.

64 This is clear from the decision of the Cassation Division. See *Human Rights Council v Charities and Societies Agency*, File No. 74039, Volume 14 (decided 13 September 2012) 299–305. This is also visible in the communication, see particularly para 53. As stated above, one of the admissibility requirements under the Charter is the compatibility of applications with the Charter, which is understood, among others, as requiring the establishment of a prima facie violation of provision(s) of the African Charter. See for instance *Kenneth Good v Republic of Botswana*, Communication 313/05, para 86.

65 Human Rights Council case (n 58) para 32.

66 Ibid para 33.

have been exhausted, the state presented the case of Mr. Melaku Fenta.[67] In that case, the HoF indeed found a provision that provided for a first instance jurisdiction of the Federal Supreme Court for higher federal officials to be unconstitutional, based on the right to appeal and equality rights of the accused.[68] Thus, the argument of the state appears to be that since the rights alleged as violated by the complainants are to be found in the FDRE Constitution, the relevant CSO laws and their interpretation by the Board and courts should have been challenged for their unconstitutionality. A failing of this would imply non-compliance with the Exhaustion of Local Remedies Rule.

To this, the complainants offered three-tiered alternate replies. First, they argued that a constitutional review was not necessary as the grievance did not necessitate constitutional interpretation and that it was neither requested, nor deemed necessary by the relevant courts.[69] Second, the HoF and CCI are not courts of judicial nature in the context of article 56(5) of the Charter and thus are not to be exhausted.[70] Their composition is relied upon as a primary reason for this. The complainants also mentioned *Alfred B Cudjoe v Ghana*, where the Commission stated that 'the internal remedy' to which article 56(5) refers entails a remedy sought from courts of a judicial nature[71] in support of their argument. Third, the constitutional review would still be ineffective and insufficient, they contended. To this end, the complainants alleged that the HoF would not operate impartially and has no obligation to decide requests according to legal principles.[72] Accordingly, the Commission framed three issues along the lines of these arguments.

67 Ibid para 35–40.

68 See House of Federation (2017) 2 Constitutional Decisions Journal, 7–30.

69 Human Rights Council case (n 58) para 41. The complainants are presumably referring to the fact that a court seizing a case needs to defer it for constitutional interpretation to the CCI 'when it believes that the interpretation of the constitution is necessary to decide the case.' See Federal Negarit Gazeta, 'Proclamation to Re-enact for the Strengthening and Specifying the Powers and the Duties of the CCI,' Proclamation No. 798/2013, art 4(3). For details of deferral, see Takele Soboka Bulto, 'Judicial Referral of Constitutional Disputes in Ethiopia: From Practice to Theory' (2011) 19 African Journal for International and Comparative Law 99.

70 Human Rights Council case (no 58) para 42.

71 *Alfred B Cudjoe v Ghana* (1999) Communication 221/98, para 9.

72 Human Rights Council case (n 58) para 43. Despite attempts, the actual application sent to the Commission was not accessible either from the Commission or the Council itself. The author hopes that the document might have expounded these and others arguments better.

2.3 *The Commission's Analysis and Decision*

In relation to whether a constitutional review was necessary, the Commission noted some variance between the points of the claim in the domestic procedures and the ones presented to it. Thus, it has correctly noted that the challenge at the domestic forums was about the interpretation of the relevant laws as allowing the Agency to freeze assets and the timelines of the measure taken, as well as about the fact that it was made to affect funds acquired prior to the effective date. At the same time, however, the complaint before the Commission challenges aspects of the laws as being against Charter rights. In the words of the Commission, the complainants 'neither pleaded the case that the measures complained of violated any of the fundamental rights guaranteed under the Respondent State's Constitution, nor the case that certain provisions of the CSO Proclamation are inconsistent with the fundamental rights' at home.[73] It has further criticised the complainants' argument as follows:

> The Complainants are content to have the complaint examined under the lenses of fundamental rights guaranteed under the Charter as a proper means of redressing the grievance. Inexplicably, they deemed a similar procedure irrelevant at domestic level.[74]

This means, argues the Commission, that it would

> undertake the same exercise as the one that would have been undertaken by the relevant domestic body: interpreting the rights guaranteed under the Charter alleged to have been violated and assessing whether the impugned provisions of domestic law and the measures taken under them are consistent with the rights so interpreted.[75]

The conclusion was premised on the assumption that the competence of constitutional review in Ethiopia 'is exclusively vested in the House of Federation assisted by the Council of Constitutional Inquiry.'[76] That said, the failure is also said to have denied the respondent state 'the very opportunity Art. 56(5) is designed to afford.'[77] Accordingly, the Commission overruled the defence. On the argument that the courts did not refer the case for constitutional

---

73 Ibid para 54.
74 Ibid para 57.
75 Ibid para 54.
76 Ibid paras 51 and 52.
77 Ibid para 58.

interpretation, the Commission ruled that it was the duty of the complainants to lodge the application for constitutional review.[78]

On the issue of whether the HoF/CCI are judicial organs, the Commission stated that the ruling in the *Cudjoe case* has been restated, as it did not supply reasons for limiting local remedies to 'courts of judicial nature.'[79] What matters is not the nomenclature by which the national organ is called, the Commission reasoned, but 'its demonstrable effectiveness in redressing a particular violation.'[80] It added that the remedy, for the sake of article 56(5) should 'operate in strict observance of the procedural guarantees of a fair hearing by a competent, independent and impartial organ' and that it should be based on enforceable law, as opposed to being merely discretionary.[81] In light of these standards, the Commission noted the following as bases to draw a conclusion: that the HoF settles constitutional disputes (FDRE Constitution article 84(2)) and that this is part of a justiciable matter, as envisaged under article 37 of the same; that the HoF is assisted by an expert body, the CCI; and that both the CCI and the HoF have an obligation to follow certain procedures in carrying out their mandates.[82] Accordingly, it observed that the HoF is a sui generis body on constitutional matters and concluded that '[t]he fact that the House of Federation is not a court of law does not obviate its suitability to handle constitutional review as a remedy.'[83]

On the third point, by accepting the respondent state's submission that the *Melaku Fenta case* demonstrates that the HoF delivers effective remedies, the Commission found the case to be comparable to the present case in that a law is being challenged as violating certain fundamental rights[84] and thus, the constitutional review system should have been undertaken. Further, the contention of impartiality was addressed in light of the fact that the HoF '...does not take part in the law-making process' and thus, 'to the extent that the House of Federation does not participate in law-making, it could not be in a position of conflict of interest when it sits to review the constitutionality of laws passed by the House of Peoples' Representatives.'[85] Thus, it ruled the communication inadmissible for lack of the Exhaustion of Local Remedies Rule.

---

78 Ibid para 57.
79 Ibid para 59.
80 Ibid paras 59 and 60.
81 Ibid para 59.
82 Ibid para 64–67.
83 Ibid para 68.
84 Ibid para 71 and 73.
85 Ibid para 68 and Udomban (no 54).

3 Assessment of the Decision

In the subsequent sections, the reasoning and final decision of the Commission in the case are analysed. The section mainly focuses on two main issues. First, the writer will examine whether the constitutional interpretation by the HoF was needed as a requirement for admissibility. Then, the extent to which the HoF and the CCI would provide effective remedy of a judicial nature will be scrutinised. The parameters utilised in the assessment include the jurisprudence of the Commission, as well as legal and factual realities surrounding the HoF/CCI. To this end, as also partly introduced above, relevant case law of the Commission is used. At this juncture, it is noteworthy that the Commission has a demonstrable history of fidelity to its jurisprudence, as one can notice from almost all of its case decisions. Indeed, consistency is a virtue to be had. The analysis will encompass relevant laws regulating the HoF/CCI, decisions passed by these organs, as well as expert opinions regarding the HoF/CCI and attendant issues. This approach is also in line with the approach taken by the Commission, as it takes into consideration 'the circumstances of each case, including the general context in which the formal remedies operate in its decisions.'[86]

3.1 *Is Constitutional Review (by the HoF) a Remedy to Be Exhausted?*

Article 56(5) only mentions available (if any) local remedies. One of the issues that needs consideration is whether what is required under the provision is intended for complainants to exhaust all available remedies, or whether there is a different way of doing it. In this regard, the majority of decisions from the Commission tend to address the issue in the affirmative. In this regard, a domestic remedy has been defined as 'any domestic legal action that may lead to the resolution of the complaint at the local or national level.'[87] Frequently, the Commission has demanded all remedies, if effective and sufficient, to be exhausted. For instance, in Communication 308/05, the Commission noted that article 56(5) is satisfied only after all local remedies have been exhausted.[88] The same conclusion is reached in the *Anuak case*.[89] In a different case that also involved Ethiopia, the government claimed that article 56(5) refers to 'all

86 Anuak case (n 20) para 49.

87 Viljoen (n 2) 83–84.

88 Majuru case (n 45) para 76. On this point, it is pointed out that the 'interpretation of the local remedies criteria can ... not be understood without some knowledge of that general context.' Udomban (n 16) 15.

89 Anuak case (n 20) para 50.

local remedies,' with which the Commission seems to agree.[90] Of more relevance to our discussion is a decision in the *Purohit case*,[91] where the Commission impliedly accepted that local remedy includes challenging the constitutionality of a law in dispute. The Commission's Communication Procedure also affirms this.[92] The stance of the Commission was even clearer in *Njoku v Egypt*, where it underscored that 'all local remedies provided by Egyptian law, including the possibility of having the case reviewed' had been exhausted by the complainant.[93]

In other cases, the Commission has been more considerate. For instance, in one case, the Commission opined as follows:

> The exhaustion of local remedies requirement under Article 56.5 of the African Charter should *be interpreted liberally* so as not to close the door on those who have made at least a *modest attempt* to exhaust local remedies. Under this Article, all the African Commission wishes to hear from the Complainant is that it has approached either local or national judicial bodies.[94]

This position is specifically pronounced in cases where there are multiple procedures that can deliver comparable remedies. To this end, the Commission asserted that 'when a remedy has been attempted, use of another remedy which has essentially the same objective is not required.'[95] Most importantly, in situations where a non-judicial body can provide a remedy comparable to that of courts, the Commission has clearly preferred courts to other mechanisms.[96] In a final analysis, so far as the nature of the remedy is such that it is capable of redressing a violation alleged, the trend has been to demand that all such remedies be attempted, regardless of the name of the organ. This is so, as Brownlie highlights, 'since remedies may be available whatever the constitutional status of the agency taking the measure concerned. The test remains

---

90 See GTK *Interight (on Behalf of Gizaw Kebede and Kebede Tadesse) v Ethiopia*, Communication 372/09 (Gizaw case), para 44.

91 *Purohit and Moore v The Gambia*, Communication 241/01.

92 African Commission on Human and People's Rights, 'Information Sheet No. 3 – Communications Procedure' (undated) 6.

93 *Njoku v Egypt* Communication 40/90, para 57.

94 *Bakweri Land Claims Committee v Cameroon*, Communication 260/02, para 55 (emphasis added).

95 *Kenneth Good / Republic of Botswana*, Communication 313/05, para 55.

96 Gizaw case (n 90) para 71.

that of the reasonable possibility of an effective remedy.'[97] In light of this, therefore, the insistence of the Commission that a constitutional review, as such, be sought in the case at hand seems to be in line with the dominant approach.

Yet, it is a questionable characterisation that any legal issue that might somehow implicate a constitutional provision is a constitutional dispute and thus involves the HoF. To begin with, it can be argued that almost any transgression of a law somehow results in the violation of some human right. Thus, the fact that the petitioner's legal challenge could have been framed as a rights issue does not necessarily mean that there was a need for constitutional interpretation. The approach of the Commission in this regard is arguably dangerous, as it gives the impression that any legal issue would necessitate constitutional interpretation and should thus be lodged up until the HoF as a condition for Ethiopians to access the Commission. Thus, there seems an agreement that in Ethiopia, constitutional interpretation is only warranted when 'there is a real and important disagreement between two or more constructions of a constitutional rule…each of which is forcefully persuasive.'[98] This is not demonstrated in the decision.

Besides, even if a constitutional construction was needed in the case, the conclusion that the HoF is exclusively mandated to entertain constitutional disputes is a rather rushed one. In this regard, it needs to be stated that the respective role of the HoF and ordinary courts regarding the interpretation of the Constitution is one of the most divisive areas in the Ethiopian constitutional discourse. Accordingly, three sets of arguments can be discerned. On the one extreme, some argue that constitutional interpretation is part of a judicial power, which is constitutionally and inherently vested in the courts,[99] and thus courts can go to the extent of invalidating laws as unconstitutional as part of their inherent power.[100] On the other extreme, some, including Getachew Assefa, argue that based on the intention of the makers of the Constitution, any scenario that invites the interpretation of the Constitution needs to be

97 Udomban (n 16) 27 citing Ian Brownlie, *Principles of Public International Law* (5th edn, Oxford University Press 1998) 500.

98 Getachew Assefa, 'All about Words: Discovering the Intention of the Makers of the Ethiopian Constitution on the Scope and Meaning of Constitutional Interpretation' (2011) 24(2) Journal of Ethiopian Law, 156.

99 Federal Negarit Gazeta, 'The Constitution of the Federal Democratic Republic of Ethiopia' Proclamation No. 1/1995, art 79(1).

100 Tsegaye Regassa, 'Courts and Human Rights Norm in Ethiopia' in Proceedings of the Symposium on the Role of Courts in the Enforcement of the Constitutions (Addis Ababa, 19–20 May 2000) 114–120.

referred to the CCI and maybe then to the HoF.[101] In between these extreme positions are a range of positions which, one way or another, advance arguments that Ethiopian courts are not devoid of the mandate to interpret the Constitution. Among them, Assefa extensively argues that courts, as a result of their constitutional duty to respect and enforce the Constitution, among others, can review the constitutionality of laws enacted by the executive branch.[102] For Yonatan, the interpretational remit of courts is rather limited to applying constitutional provisions that are clear and plain.[103] For others, empowering the HoF/CCI to interpret the Constitution does not mean an automatic exclusion of ordinary courts to also engage in the business of interpretation.[104] The following stand likely sums up those positions that consider the role as being distributed between the courts and the HoF:

> Where the House of Federation finds the law or conduct to be inconsistent with the Bill of Rights, it will declare the law or conduct constitutionally invalid. Such kind of constitutional remedy is only available in the case of direct application of the Bill of Rights and not in the case of indirect application. However, whenever the Bill of Rights merely applies indirectly to a dispute, ordinary courts and not the House of Federation is primarily responsible for the application and interpretation of the Bill of Rights (of the Constitution).[105]

What is more, a look at the experience of the CCI/HoF and that of courts mirror such diversity. For instance, in one of the earliest cases presented to the CCI,[106] the latter rejected the case as not requiring constitutional interpretation as the law contended did not hail from the legislative bodies and also as it

101 Assefa (n 98) 165; Bulto (n 69) 112 presents a strong argument against constitutional referral being mandatory. Incidentally, the Commission's observation that it is the duty of complainants to exhaust remedies sounds logical. Indeed, courts in Ethiopia do not seem to have an obligation to refer a case to the CCI.

102 See for instance Assefa Fiseha, 'Constitutional Adjudication in Ethiopia: Exploring the Experience of the House of Federation (HOF)' (2007) 1 Mizan Law Rev 32.

103 Yonatan Tesfaye Fessha, 'Whose Power is it Anyway: The Courts and Constitutional Interpretation in Ethiopia' (2008) 22(1) Journal of Ethiopian Laws, 138–139.

104 Leonard FM Besselink, 'The Protection of Human Rights in Federal Systems – The Case of Ethiopia' as cited in Assefa (n 98).

105 Rakeb Meselle, 'Enforcement of Human Rights in Ethiopia' (APAP, 2002) 21. See Assefa (n 98) 141–152 for a review of more authors on the issue.

106 *Ethiopian Blind Persons Association v Oromia Education Bureau and Jimma College of Teachers Education*, HoF File No. 4/94 (November 2003, unpublished) Unpublished decisions of the HoF that are referred to in this work are all on file with the author.

is left for the courts to decide the legality or constitutionality of subsidiary laws. In a recent case, on the other hand, the HoF entertained a constitutional protest against a decision of a school head and found it unconstitutional based on the right to access to justice.[107]

In more recent cases, the HoF has further echoed conflicting messages. For instance, in a case that involved a (disguised) sale of rural land in the form of mortgage acquisition, the HoF provided that the relevant courts should have set aside these transactions in line with their obligation to respect and enforce the Constitution under articles 9(2) and 13(1) of the Constitution.[108] Further, in another case the HoF went to say that courts should have rendered a contract, which would ultimately deprive farmers of their land under various disguises, as unlawful and unconstitutional on their own initiative.[109] On the other hand, it has rejected to entertain cases that arguably need authoritative interpretation. For instance, in a paternity-related case,[110] the courts ordered a DNA test to ascertain the paternity of the applicant against the objection of the defendant, based on right to bodily integrity. The CCI and the HoF considered it as not warranting constitutional interpretation even if competing rights that directly flow from the Constitution were engaged. In other cases, the HoF went to great length to weigh evidentiary matters on issues of common property in marriage, issues that could arguably be settled with the relevant ordinary laws.[111]

Some decisions of the Cassation Division of the Federal Supreme Court also reveal that it is expounding constitutional provisions in settling cases. For instance, the way the Division uses the constitutional right to property in file number 69291[112] is strikingly similar to the decision of the HoF in comparable cases.[113] Both the Court and HoF first analysed the relevant constitutional provision and then proceeded to other legislation to invalidate a contract.

In relation to the issue at hand, the Commission further commented that by not taking the case to the HoF before it was lodged to it, the country was not given a notice of the alleged violation. As many cases entertained by the

107 See *Tariku Mekonnen v Education Bureau of Addis Ababa, Yeka Sub-Sity*, HoF File No. 018/15 (September 2016, unpublished).

108 *Hasay v Tensa'A Kutale and others*, HoF (March 2016, unpublished).

109 See *Kelebie Tesfu v Ayelign Derbew*, HoF (June 2015, unpublished).

110 *Tsegaye Abebe v Biruk Asfaw*, HoF (August 2017, unpublished).

111 See for instance *Azeb Tufa v Alemayehu Menghistu*, HoF File No. 015/15 (September, 2017, unpublished) and *Werku Nikedimos v Seblewengel Werku and Mamite Werare*, HoF File No. 022/15 (September 2017, unpublished).

112 *Jemal Aman v Tewabech Ferede*, Federal Supreme Court, Cassation Division, File No. 6929, Volume 13 (1 November 2011) 423–442.

113 See for instance *Alemitu Gebre v Chane Desalegn*, HoF (February 2016, unpublished).

Commission show, it takes prevailing situations of countries into account in its analysis and adjudication of cases.[114] In light of this, the piece of legislation that triggered the legal action is one of the most publicised and harshly criticised laws in the country.[115] Actually, the Commission has in its Concluding Observations both in 2010[116] and 2015[117] identified the Charities and Societies Proclamation as an area of concern. It is submitted, thus, that the Commission should have taken judicial notice of this fact, as is common in its other decisions.

Therefore, in light of the foregoing, the decision of the Commission that runs on the assumption that only the HoF can entertain constitutional disputes – a very contested issue in itself – and without due notice of the controversies

114 Ibid (n 18 and 19).

115 See for instance the following documents attesting to the magnitude of the publicity: Amnesty International, 'Ethiopia: The 2009 Charities and Societies Proclamation as a serious obstacle to the promotion and protection of human rights in Ethiopia' (written statement to the 20th Session of the UN Human Rights Council, 18 June – 6 July 2012) <https://www.amnesty.org/download/Documents/16000/afr250072012en.pdf> accessed 5 May 2018; Human Rights Watch, 'Ethiopia: New Law Ratchets up Repression' (2009) <https://www.hrw.org/news/2009/01/08/ethiopia-new-law-ratchets-repression> accessed 5 May 2018; Meskerem Geset, 'The New Charities and Societies Proclamation and its Impact on the Operation of Save the Children Sweden – Ethiopia' (Save the Children Sweden, December 2009) <https://resourcecentre.savethechildren.net/sites/default/files/documents/1605.pdf> accessed 5 May 2018; The International Center For Not-for-Profit Law, 'Civil Freedom Monitor: Ethiopia' <http://www.icnl.org/research/monitor/ethiopia.html> accessed 5 May 2018; Council of the European Union, 'Declaration by the Presidency on behalf of the EU on the adoption of the Charities and Societies Proclamation by the House of Peoples' Representatives of the Federal Democratic Republic of Ethiopia' (30 January 2009, Brussels) <http://europa.eu/rapid/press-release_PESC-09-7_en.htm> accessed 5 May 2018; Sisay Alemayehu, 'CSO Law in Ethiopia: Considering its Constraints and Consequences' (2012) 8(4) Journal of Civil Society, 369–384.

116 See the African Commission on Human and Peoples' Rights, 'Concluding Observations and Recommendations on the Initial, 1st, 2nd, 3rd and 4th Periodic Report of the Federal Democratic Republic of Ethiopia' (12–26 May 2010, Banjul, The Gambia) <http://www.achpr.org/files/sessions/47th/conc-obs/1st-to-4th-1998-2007/achpr47_conc_staterep1234_ethiopia_2010_eng.pdf> accessed 5 May 2018. The Commission was particularly wary of the 10 percent limit and its potentially negative repercussion on the works of civil societies and recommended that the state reviews it. See paras 45 and 72.

117 See the African Commission on Human and Peoples' Rights, 'Concluding Observations and Recommendations on the 5th and 6th Periodic Report of the Federal Democratic Republic of Ethiopia' (21 April to 7 May 2015, Banjul, The Gambia), paras 26 and 30 <http://www.achpr.org/files/sessions/18th-eo/conc-obs/5-2009-2013/concluding_observations_ethiopia_eng.pdf> accessed 5 May 2018. The Commission criticised that the State did not respond to the recommendation made in the previous round of its Observation.

surrounding the piece of legislation at the centre of the case, is weak, to say the least.

3.2 *Remedies of Judicial Nature – Effective Remedy – How Do the HoF/CCI Fare?*

To the extent that the Commission did not necessarily go by the nomenclature in determining whether a certain organ can or cannot deliver a remedy of judicial nature is well received.[118] It is also in line with its established jurisprudence of the Commission on the subject matter. Accordingly, the key features that the Commission developed as determining factors for an organ and its remedies, which should be of judicial nature and thus should be exhausted, are: that it works in strict observance of procedural guarantees of fair hearing; that it is independent and impartial; and that the remedy it provides is non-discretionary.[119] It is thus clear that the naming as such is less important in this regard. Related to this, the Commission in one of its decisions clearly stipulated that '[a]dministrative or quasi-judicial remedies which do not operate impartially are considered as inadequate and ineffective.'[120]

Applying these standards against the CCI and HoF, the Commission was drawn to several facts, among others: the HoF is assisted by an expert body (the CCI); both organs have an obligation to adhere to certain procedures to ensure a fair hearing; and the HoF does not have a law-making role and is thus impartial. Based on these observations, it qualified the HoF as being capable of delivering effective remedies of judicial nature. Let us now turn to briefly examine the accuracy of the observations and conclusion in light of the nature and context within which the HoF/CCI works, as is warranted by the works of the Commission.

The CCI, as stipulated under article 82 of the Constitution and article 15 of Proclamation No. 798/2013, is composed of the President and Vice President of the Federal Supreme Court, six legal experts and three individuals to be designated by the HoF. It investigates constitutional disputes and forwards its recommendations to the HoF if it finds it necessary to interpret the Constitution. According to this mandate, the CCI has, as of the end of October 2018, disposed

118 See Musila (n 15) 450 ff on why it is not only the judiciary that can provide an effective remedy.

119 See ibid (n 80 and 81).

120 *Zimbabwe Lawyers for Human Rights and Institute for Human Rights and Development in Africa (on behalf of Andrew Barclay Meldrum) v Zimbabwe*, Communication 294/04, para 51.

more than 2040 cases.[121] 70 of these have been adjudged as needing constitutional interpretation and are accordingly forwarded to the HoF for final decision. Around 355 cases have been brought to the HoF in a form of appeal, challenging the recommendation of the CCI.[122]

Indeed, the CCI and the HoF have an obligation to entertain cases that directly come from complainants or courts.[123] The decisions of the HoF also reveal that it considers itself as an enforcer of the rights enshrined in the Constitution. A clear indication of such an understanding is readable from the few decisions it has rendered.[124] Yet, the fact that in a great number of cases the CCI would simply and without reasoned justification reject a case as not warranting constitutional interpretation, compromises the sense of duty to entertain a case. The writer has seen many few-liner 'decisions' from the CCI, where no explanation is given as to why the application does not warrant a constitutional interpretation. This is against a legal stipulation that '[t]he decision or recommendation of the Council shall clearly show the detailed description of the case, the reason it believes there is a need or no need for constitutional interpretation and its conclusion.'[125] Accordingly, the observation of the Commission is also questionable that the House follows certain procedures to satisfy the fair hearing guarantees that it has set and that it is impartial.

Related to this, the Constitution mandates both the HoF and the CCI to adopt their respective rules of procedures[126] and enforce to them. However, there are no procedures that can help them ensure a fair hearing in the process of constitutional interpretation yet. Indeed, the HoF recently adopted a

121 According to a news briefing resealed on 14 November 2018 via the official Facebook account of the Supreme Court, the CCI has thus far entertained 3724 cases of which 2040 cases are decided. In only 65 of the cases decided the CCI found unconstitutionality.

122 Phone conversation with the Registrar of the House of Federation, 15 November 2018.

123 See for instance FDRE Constitution (no 99) arts 83(1) and 84(2–3); See also Federal Negarit Gazeta, 'Consolidation of the House of the Federation and the Definition of its Powers and Responsibilities Proclamation' Proclamation No. 251/2001, arts 4(1) and 13; and Federal Negarit Gazeta, 'Council of Constitutional Inquiry Proclamation' Proclamation No. 798/13, art 3. The officers at both the CCI and the HoF also work with such an understanding. Interview with Desalegn Weyosa, General Secretary of the CCI Office (28 September 2017, Addis Ababa) and Ato Muluye Welaley, Director, Directorate of the Constitutional Interpretation and Self Determination Affairs under the HoF (25 September 2017, Addis Ababa).

124 A brief look at the decisions of the HoF (11 cases published in two volumes of the Journal of Constitutional Decisions and other 16 unpublished decisions), the great majority of them are individual cases and are related to the human rights part of the Constitution.

125 Proclamation No. 798/13 (n 123) art 12(2).

126 See FDRE Constitution (n 99) arts 62(11) and 84(4).

Directive on rules of procedure,[127] while the CCI does not have such rules in place. Yet, the document mainly focuses on facilitating the daily functioning of the HoF and the different committees thereunder and has very little to contribute in terms of ensuring a fair hearing for complainants. To begin with, the objectives of the Directive are to make the process of receiving and handling cases more efficient and speedier, and the HoF more accessible.[128] It does not consider impartiality or fairness of the process. The reading of article 31 of the Directive also suggests that the CCI is only expected to provide a reasoning in cases where it concludes that there is a need for constitutional interpretation, against the stipulation in the Proclamation mentioned above. In other words, it only undertakes an interpretation when it is of the opinion that the law, decision or conduct complained about is unconstitutional.

Thus far, complaints are only allowed when in elaborated writing.[129] Therefore, other than the initial written submission, there is no mechanism that allows for complainants to be heard or to defend a counter argument from the other side, usually the state.[130] This falls short of the right to be heard, including the right to defence.[131] Besides, the CCI and HoF handle complaints behind closed doors, despite an indication that '[t]he Council may hear cases in a public transparent manner according to Article 12(1) of the Constitution, the details of which is to be regulated by a directive that the Council may adopt.'[132] At this juncture, it should be mentioned that the Council can 'call upon pertinent institutions or professionals, to appear before it and give opinions' and 'may require the presentation of any evidence or professional and examine same' if it deems necessary.[133] According to an official at the CCI, the CCI does indeed carry out investigations, including by visiting relevant places and meeting parties concerned. Similarly, before the HoF passes a final decision it may 'call upon pertinent institutions, professionals and contending parties to give their

127 House of Federation (HoF), 'Directive for the Reception and Handling of Constitutional Interpretation and Self Determination (Identity) Related Complaints' Directive No. 2/2018 (January 2018, on file with the author).

128 Ibid art 3 and art 17, the latter also provides time ceiling within which various types of cases shall be decided.

129 Also hinted in Proclamation No. 798/13 (no 123) art 3(1) and HoF Directive No. 2/2018 (no 127) art 11.

130 Ato Desalegn (n 123) argues that this is only logical since the CCI is not and cannot serve as another level of appeal.

131 African Charter (n 6) art 7(1(c)). The Commission has articulated the rights, among others, in *Avocats Sans Frontières (on behalf of Gaëtan Bwampamye) v Burundi*, Communication 231/99.

132 Proclamation No. 798/13 (n 123) art 10(4).

133 Ibid art 9(1–2).

opinion.'[134] The Director of the Constitutional Interpretation and Identity Matters at the HoF also expressed that they conduct investigations on the field and gather information when necessary. This practice, however, does not alleviate the challenge with regard to the right to be heard. Admittedly, with a view to making the HoF more accessible, the Directive enables petitioners to post their complaints by mail or fax numbers and for free, and it allows complaints to be lodged through representation.[135]

What transpires from the relevant legal provisions and interviews conducted with the relevant officers is that complainants cannot, as of right, demand to present their cases in person. Neither can they examine the evidence presented by a contending party, usually a governmental office. As an 'adequate opportunity to prepare a case, present arguments and evidence and to challenge or respond to opposing arguments or evidence' is one of the core elements of fair hearing,[136] it is clear that the HoF does not have this in place. To borrow Takele's expression, 'the House does not have an in-built system to ensure the right to be heard for a private party contesting the law's or decision's constitutionality.'[137] In the absence of this crucial element of fair hearing, the Commission's ruling in this regard is not tenable. One might also add that the CCI and HoF tend to take clarification letters that they seek from governmental entities for granted, without giving complainants the chance to access and refute such letters.[138] Representatives of governmental entities have better access to explain their cases and thereby influence the opinion and decisions of the different organs in the CCI and HoF. This consequently puts complainants in a disadvantaged position, which goes against the essence of fair hearing.

When it comes to the issue of impartiality, the Commission in its assessment of the HoF mainly focused on the understanding that the latter does not have a law-making role, and thus concluded that it is impartial. To begin with, the factual assumption is questionable. Among others, the HoF is mandated to determine all civil matters necessary to establish and sustain one economic community on which the House of Peoples' Representatives can act.[139] This

134 Proclamation No. 251/2001 (n 123) art 10.

135 HoF Directive No. 2/2018 (n 127) arts 8, 9, and 12. As of mid-November 2018, no complaint has been lodged to the House through fax or postal service, according to the registrar of the House.

136 ACHPR Guidelines (n 14) part A(2(e)).

137 Bulto (n 69) 121.

138 See for example *Ato Andenet Kebede v Justice Bureau of Regional State of Afar*, HoF/Office of the House Speaker/5/266 (decided on Meskerem 30, 2010 E.C (October 10, 2017 G.C), unpublished); *Regasa Seyoum and others v Mustofa Keder and others*, HoF/Office of the House Speaker/5/267 (30 September 2010 E.C., unpublished).

139 FDRE Constitution (n 99) arts 62(8) and 55(6).

goes to the extent of preparing and submitting draft bills to the House of Peoples' Representatives.[140] This is technically part of law-making. Further and most importantly, this might put the HoF in a difficult situation, as there is every possibility that the constitutionality of a law that it has initiated in accordance with this mandate can be challenged. For instance, one can imagine a situation where in the future, constituent states challenge such laws as encroaching the federal-state power-sharing arrangement, and the issue ending up at the very same HoF that initiated the law for a final determination.

Most importantly, the fact that the HoF does not have a visible role in the law-making process does not necessarily make it impartial. Impartiality has much to do with independence and the ability to withstand influence. Among others, the members of an impartial institution need to serve independently without any improper influence.[141] As a result, therefore, the composition and how they conduct their adjudicative mandate matters, both in actual terms and in the public eye. In one of the earliest cases decided by the Commission, it stated the following:

> Jurisdiction has thus been transferred from the normal courts to a tribunal chiefly composed of persons belonging to the executive branch of government … whose members do not necessarily possess any legal expertise. Article 7.1.d of the African Charters requires the court or tribunal to be impartial. Regardless of the character of the individual members of such tribunals, its composition alone creates the appearance, if not actual lack, of impartiality. It thus violates Article 7.1.d.[142]

The HoF greatly resembles the situation discussed in the case partly quoted. The HoF is composed of representatives of nations, nationalities and peoples of Ethiopia.[143] As such, the composition gives the HoF 'the profile of a political organ than a judicial one.'[144] As Yonatan would bluntly put it 'The House is obviously a political body.'[145] Moreover, many of the members work either in the executive or legislative branches of the regional governments and some

140 Proclamation No. 251/2001 (n 123) art 34(3).

141 Yonatan Tesfaye Fessha, 'Judicial Review and Democracy: A Normative Discourse on the (Novel) Ethiopian Approach to Constitutional Review' (2006) 53 African Journal for International and Comparative Law 77.

142 *Constitutional Rights Project v Nigeria,* Communication 60/91, para 14.

143 FDRE Constitution (n 99) art 61; Proclamation No. 251/2001 (n 123) art 47.

144 Assefa (n 101) 31.

145 Fessha (n 141) 73.

even hold a higher office at the federal level.[146] As a matter of fact, for a considerable time the office of the Speaker of the House was held by a minister.[147] Further, the regional governors and the speakers of the regional councils are also de facto members of the HoF.[148] That said, '…there is nothing in the rules of procedure of the House or other relevant laws that require a member to abstain from participating in a discussion that concerns the constitutionality of a law which he or she enacted as a minister or member of the federal or state government's executive branch.'[149] A recent interview with the HoF Speaker in relation to an identity-related controversy[150] clearly reveals how political the organ is. Clarifying how a committee meant to investigate and identify related controversies in relation to the Welqait and Raya areas was established, the Speaker mentioned that even if the complaints that led to its establishment were not lodged following the laws, its establishment was politically decided in a meeting, in which the speakers of both houses, the Minister of Peace, the Prime Minister, and his deputy convened. It is curious how these various organs got involved in a case that as per the laws and procedures the HoF should have dealt with.

Besides, the composition of the CCI in which the Commission relied heavily on characterising the HoF as being capable of rendering remedies of judicial nature, raises some issues in light of the foregoing considerations. For once, the fact that the President and Vice-President of the Federal Supreme Court are respectively the chairperson and deputy chairperson of the CCI[151] might trigger unwarranted conflict of interest in the sense that they may consider a case twice or even more often.[152] There does not seem to exist any bar against such incidents. In one of the cases that the HoF decided in its September 2017

146 Ibid 78.

147 The appointment on 30 April 2018 of H.E. W/ro Keriya Ibrahim, one of Tigray People's Liberation Front's (TPLF) nine Executive Bureau members, who stands at the apex of the party line as a speaker of the HoF, also strengthens the observation. Moreover, the way she was elected to the HoF by the regional council (of Tigray) reveals even more. During the Council deliberations, the candidate's long-time service in and understanding of the executive body in the region was advanced as a major reason that won her a unanimous vote.

148 Assefa Fiseha, 'Constitutional Adjudication through Second Chamber in Ethiopia' (2017) 16 Ethnopolitics 295, 297.

149 Fessha (n 141) 78.

150 Keriya Ibrahim, House Speaker of the HoF (Interview with Tigray TV, November 2018).

151 FDRE Constitution (n 99) art 82(a–b); Proclamation No. 798/13 (n 123) art 15 (a–b).

152 Tsegaye Beru, 'An Outline for the Study of Ethiopian Constitutional Law' (2015) 43 International Journal of Legal Information 234, 312, 246–247; See also Fiseha (n 148) 306.

meeting,[153] a former Shari'a court judge tried to challenge the constitutionality of a disciplinary action taken against him, complaining that the President of the Federal Supreme Court had the chance to decide/sit on his case three times, namely: (1) on a complaint that he lodged against a decision of a court administrator in his capacity as an administer of the Supreme Court to which judges of the sharia courts belong;[154] (2) as a chairperson of the Federal Judicial Administration Council[155] to which an appeal was lodged;[156] and finally (3) as a chairperson of the CCI.[157] Deciding the case, the HoF simply stated that the Constitution has mandated this, citing article 82(2) of the same.[158]

Therefore, it is maintained that without a bar on such a practice, at least in the eyes of the public this seems to compromise the impartiality of the CCI, and it does not fulfil the test of the Commission's own jurisprudence on the impartiality of tribunals. According to the Fair Trial Guidelines adopted by the Commission, impartiality of a tribunal is compromised if 'a judicial official sits as member of an appeal tribunal in a case which he or she decided or participated in a lower judicial body.'[159] However, the Commission in the case at hand opted to remain completely ignorant of these facts.

Moreover, the fact that the members of the CCI can be removed with simplicity weakens the stature of the CCI to stand the test of independence of tribunals, including tenure, as developed by the Commission.[160] Accordingly, with the exception of the chairperson and the deputy, the other nine members of the CCI can be removed by various bodies. The relevant rule reads that these members 'may be removed from membership by the designating or appointing organ before the end of his term' and provides commission of disciplinary

153 *Adem Abdela v Federal Judicial Administration Council*, HoF File No. 120/2015 (Abdela case).

154 This seems to be pursuant to Federal Negarit Gazeta, 'Federal Courts of Sharia Consolidation Proclamation' Proclamation No. 188/99, art 20(2).

155 See Federal Negarit Gazeta, 'Amended Federal Judicial Administration Council Establishment Proclamation' Proclamation No. 684/2010, art 5(1(a)).

156 For a comprehensive appraisal of the Sharia Courts Administration, see Mohammed Abdo, 'Legal Pluralism, Sharia Courts, and Constitutional Issues in Ethiopia' (2011) 5 Mizan Law Review.

157 Personal Interview with the Shiek Adem Abdela, 27 September 2018, Addis Ababa. He is not knowledgeable if the President sat in the case before the CCI, as the decision does not contain information regarding the members that voted in the decision. The decision is actually a three liner, where it is only stated that the CCI did not find the complaint as warranting constitutional interpretation with no justification for it.

158 Abdela case (n 153).

159 ACHPR Guidelines (n 14) part A.5(D.iv).

160 See for instance ibid part A (4).

offences or incompetence as grounds for dismissal.[161] This would mean that the six experts might be removed by the House of Peoples' Representatives or the President of the State.[162] For the remaining three members that hail from the HoF, they can be removed either by the HoF or their respective regional councils, as it is these very councils that merely appoint individuals to represent the state in the HoF, even though the Constitution provides a possibility of having them elected by the people.[163]

Finally, the admissibility ruling of the Commission on the case can also be evaluated in light of a different case brought against Ethiopia before the Commission, which also discussed the standing of the CCI. The case[164] revolves around a revocation of a license for the production of river-washed sand by a regional governmental body, based on a directive issued by a federal Ministry. The complainants challenged the decision in the *Wereda* and High Courts of the regional state; in both courts the decision was in favour of the complainant. However, the decision could not be enforced. Accordingly, the complainants took the case to other governmental organs including the CCI, where it was considered as not warranting a constitutional interpretation.[165] Following the attempts, the case ended up with the Commission. One of the defences that the respondent state (Ethiopia) put forward as a defence against admissibility is particularly relevant. The state argued that the issue at stake, the right to conduct a mining operation, is accorded by a Proclamation and not the Charter, and thus the communication should be rejected for want of article 56(2).[166] The Commission rejected this line of argument and stated that the invocation of such rights as the rights to property (article 14) and fair trial (article 7) would satisfy the condition under article 56 (2). Comparing such a decision to the one in the *Human Rights Council* (HRC) *case* under review, two problems can be pinpointed. In the earlier case, the Commission did not take issue with the fact that at domestic courts the complaint was not articulated as an issue of right (even if that was possible); contrastingly, in the Human Rights

161 Proclamation No. 798/13 (n 123) art 19.

162 Ibid art 15(c).

163 FDRE Constitution (n 99) art 61(3); There has not been any election thus far. See Fessha (n 141) 72; Temesgen Sisay Beyene, 'The Question of Independent and Impartial Constitutional Adjudicator in Ethiopia: A Comparative Study with Germany and South Africa' (2012) 3 Bahir Dar University Journal of Law 67, 109.

164 Gizaw case (n 90).

165 Ibid para 36. It is also noted that the complainants took the case to other institutions, including some Federal ministries, the Human Rights Commission, Office of the Ombudsman, and the Ethics and Anti-Corruption Commission. See ibid para 71.

166 Human Rights Council case (n 58) para 62.

Council case it went in the diametrically opposite direction without a convincing reason, by insisting that constitutional issues must have been framed and taken to the HoF. From the perspective of the respondent state, while it considered a revocation of work license as not triggering a Constitution/Charter issue, it somehow did staunchly argue in the recent case before the Commission (Human Rights Council) that the freezing of assets indeed triggers a constitutional issue. It is submitted that in handling the HRC case, the Commission should have taken the defendant state at its word from an earlier case, or at least should have attempted to exhibit some consistency.

In the same case, the Commission, sticking to a narrower understanding of local remedies as 'the ordinary remedies of common law that exist in jurisdictions and normally accessible to people seeking justice,' noted that

> the time the Applicants took to seek their grievances through non judicial remedies such as lodging a petition with the Ethiopian Federal Government, the Parliament, the Ethiopian Human Rights Commission, the Public Ombudsman, the *Council of Constitutional Inquiry* and the Ethical and Anti-Corruption Commission, they could have used that time attempting to exhaust the ordinary remedies of a judicial nature in Ethiopia.[167]

At this stage, the Commission clearly characterised remedies of the CCI as non-judicial. Given the emphasis that the Commission placed on the CCI while assessing the HoF in the *Human Rights Council case*,[168] it clearly shows that it took quite different positions in the two cases without an explanation.

It should also be noted that the CCI only assists and does not replace the HoF. The CCI is merely an advisory body to the HoF and cannot pass binding decisions.[169] Accordingly, the HoF has disregarded the CCI's recommendations on some cases.[170] Thus, even if the CCI was in as good of a position as portrayed

167 Ibid para 71 (emphasis added).

168 Human Rights Council case (n 58) para 70.

169 Assefa (n 101) 14.

170 These include the *Banishangul-Gumuz Case* (decided in March 2003) 1 Journal of Constitutional Decisions, (July 2008) 1–34. In a recent case that involved the issue of access to justice the course of re-acquiring an urban house that was illegally taken, the HoF clearly took a different position and set aside the recommendation of the CCI. See *The Wife and Successors of Wassihun (10 people) v Housing Agency*, HoF (decided in May 2012), 2 Journal of Constitutional Decisions (March 2017) 35. The same reversal also took place in a recent case that dwells with complex issues of employment and access to justice. See *HezkeAl Mara v SNNP Roads Authority*, HoF/Office of Speaker of the House/5/262 (decided on September 30, 2010 E.C., unpublished).

by the Commission in terms of helping the HoF deliver an effective remedy of judicial nature, it would be a far-fetched interpretation to take that virtue for the benefit of the HoF.

Finally, the author would like to offer a brief reflection on how the ongoing reform initiatives in Ethiopia and its promises may help in addressing the limitations identified is in order. As things stand, there has not been specific discussion pertaining to the HoF. Moreover, since the reform initiatives and plans of the new administration are not documented, there is nothing concrete to be said with regard to the HoF. However, the general impression developed from the various statements the authorities gave suggest that there might be attempts to de-politicise public institutions. If this is to be followed through, the HoF is likely to benefit in the case that its critical offices are staffed by competent professionals and its overall functioning is grounded on detailed laws. Other than this, the composition of the HoF is likely to stay as it is, as it is entrenched in the Constitution and any change in this regard necessitates constitutional amendment, an issue that is not being publicly discussed.

4 Conclusions and Recommendations

It appears that the African Commission on Human and Peoples' Rights is slowly garnering the reverence it seeks to establish and that states are progressively taking it more seriously. This is visible, for instance, in the rising attention that member states are lending to complaints before the Commission. That said, the number of communications/cases against Ethiopia before the Commission is growing. In light of this, the Commission's characterisation of the House of Federation in the case reviewed will arguably remain relevant for some time, given the Commission's trend of cross-referencing to its earlier factual and legal analyses – even if unfortunately, this was not done in the case under review. Therefore, it is imperative to reflect on issues regarding institutions of paramount importance such as the HoF, so as to inform the Commission and potential complainants, among others. It is also hoped that pointing out some of the limitations of the African Commission/CCI in light of the standards developed under the African Charter on Human and Peoples' Rights can help in their improvement.

This chapter demonstrates some issues on which the Commission's analysis and subsequent decisions can be questioned. Among others, it is shown that the Commission did not go through with testing the standards that it has identified against the factual realities of the HoF/CCI. For instance, independence, impartiality and observance of procedures to ensure a fair hearing were identified as the major criteria for remedies to qualify as being of judicial nature and thus effective. However, the Commission did not properly apply them on the HoF and the CCI. It rather considered only a few and rather superficial aspects as important factors in its decisions, including the fact that there are certain procedures and that the HoF is not involved in law-making. It is argued that had the Commission gone deeper into the actual composition and functioning of the HoF/CCI, it would have been likely that it reached a different conclusion. If not, it would have certainly raised far more interesting issues around the HoF/CCI. It is, of course, submitted that the complainants might not have raised many of the issues in their application and replies that might have compelled the Commission to go further.

That said, as the Commission sometimes invites for the re-submission of complaints after local remedies have been properly exhausted,[171] doing the same in this case might have encouraged the complainants to follow through. At any rate, there was a possibility for the complainant to bring the case to the HoF and in case of an unsatisfactory result to lodge it back to the Commission. However, it appears that the law that cuts the funding source of civil organisations in Ethiopia has achieved exactly what the complaint was all about. In this regard, the Executive Director of the Council explained that their shrinking finances and mundane daily tasks prevented them from pursuing the case through following the Commission's 2015 decision.[172]

In general, the HoF and the CCI are found to not give effective remedies when assessed against the admissibility requirements under the African Charter. The major shortcomings in this regard stand out as being the fact that the composition of the HoF vitiates semblance of impartiality of judicial or semi-judicial organs and that there is no mechanism for the HoF to guarantee procedural fairness.

In light of this and in order for the HoF to qualify as an organ that can provide an effective remedy worthy of exhausting before one proceeds to the Commission for remedy, the following interventions would be necessary.

Firstly, the way 'constitutional interpretation' is currently understood in the works of the CCI and HoF must be re-examined. So far, constitutional interpretation is taken as synonymous with a finding of unconstitutionality. As such, an issue that strongly bears a constitutional right and requires due deliberation

171 Viljoen (n 2) 92. Accordingly, the Commission has reconsidered some communications that were initially ruled inadmissible. For instance, see *Dr Curtis Francis Doebbler v Sudan*, Communication 235/2000 (a case involving Ethiopian refugees residing in the Sudan), where the inadmissibility rule was reversed.

172 Interview with Ato Terefer (n 60).

and analysis without necessarily leading to a finding of unconstitutionality does not stand a chance for expounding. If the CCI somehow reaches a conclusion that a law, practice or decision contested does not violate the Constitution, it does not explain how such a decision is reached and simply concludes that there is no need for constitutional interpretation. This might have emanated from the fact that no principles or clear guidance of how and when constitutional interpretation is warranted are developed. Constitutional interpretation in the sense of explaining and expounding a constitutional right or principles shall therefore be undertaken when the issue at hand raises a clear dispute with a strong constitutional importance, regardless of the final outcome.

Second, putting in place mechanisms that ensure procedural fairness in the proceedings of the HoF will be necessary. Admittedly, undertaking the formal procedures of ordinary courts is not tenable. However, there needs to be some way of balancing when it comes to accessing the CCI and HoF or their respective committees. As things stand, while complainants have almost no possibility of explaining their cases in person, government agencies whose laws or decisions are being contested have a better access. Closely related to fairness and quality of decisions, it is recommended that unless a matter warrants a closed session for a strong reason, meetings and discussions of the HoF should also be open to the public. In that way, the quality of decisions and fairness of considerations can be improved.

Third and most importantly, the CCI needs to provide reasoned justifications for its positions, including when it holds that there are no constitutional violations. Given the fact that this is a hallmark of organs with adjudicatory role, the CCI must work on this. Even on those cases where a violation is established, utilising such tools as constitutional principles, relevant human rights jurisprudence and conventional interpretation principles and considerations are rare and need to be improved.

Fourth, when it comes to the composition of the CCI and HoF, so far as no amendment is introduced there are interventions that can improve their standing as organs of a judicial nature within the framework of the Constitution. Among others, it is imperative to ensure that no member of the CCI and HoF sits or votes on an issue s/he has previously participated in deciding. This limitation needs to be enshrined in the relevant laws. With regard to the HoF, avoiding high-ranking executive members from serving in the HoF would be a way that deserves serious consideration if political influence is to be minimised.

Index

Printed in the United States
By Bookmasters